Accents as Well as Broad Effects

William A. Coffin, *Mrs. Schuyler Van Rensselaer* (1890). Museum of the City of New York.

Accents as Well as Broad Effects

Writings on Architecture, Landscape, and the Environment, 1876–1925

⸺ɷ ᘐ⸺

Mariana Griswold Van Rensselaer

Selected and edited by
David Gebhard

UNIVERSITY OF CALIFORNIA PRESS
Berkeley · *Los Angeles* · *London*

University of California Press
Berkeley and Los Angeles, California

University of California Press, Ltd.
London, England

© 1996 by the Regents of the University of California

Library of Congress Cataloging-in-Publication Data

Van Rensselaer, Schuyler, Mrs., 1851–1934.
    Accents as well as broad effects : writings on architecture,
landscape, and the environment, 1876–1925, Mariana Griswold Van
Rensselaer / selected and edited by David Gebhard.
        p.   cm.
    Includes bibliographical references and index.
    ISBN 0-520-20126-4
    1. Van Rensselaer, Schuyler, Mrs., 1851–1934—Aesthetics.
2. Architecture, Modern—19th century—United States.
3. Architectural criticism—United States. 4. Landscape
architecture—United States—History—19th century. I. Gebhard,
David. II. Title.
NA2599.8.V36A5 1996
720'.92—dc20   95-19614
                                                            CIP

9 8 7 6 5 4 3 2 1

Contents

Illustrations

Introduction

BY DAVID GEBHARD

I

In the spring of 1893, the New York publishing house of Charles Scribner's Sons published a small volume entitled *Art Out-of-Doors: Hints on Good Taste in Gardening*. On the title page, the author, Mariana Griswold Van Rensselaer, cited a brief quotation from the writings of Francis Bacon: "A Man shall ever see, that, when ages grow to civility and elegancy, men come to build stately sooner than to garden finely; as if gardening were the greater perfection."[1] She dedicated the book "To my friends in Brooklyn who taught me to care for the art which stands nearest to nature." Her "friends in Brooklyn" referred, of course, to the landscape architect Frederick Law Olmsted and the architect Henry Hobson Richardson.

What must have struck the reader then, as it does now, is the unusual nature of this volume. It was not, like so many of the published writings of the 1870s through the 1890s on architecture and landscape, a guide to the layout and design of private and public grounds. There were no illustrations and no garden plans. Instead, Van Rensselaer wrote about a series of broad issues concerned with how one should approach design and reordering of the landscape.

---

1. Francis Bacon, "Of Gardens," in *Essays by Francis Bacon* (Chicago and New York: Belford, Clarke and Company, 1888), 164.

The subtitle of the book, *Hints on Good Taste in Gardening*, indicates her intent. She borrowed the substance of this subtitle from an earlier, much-admired volume, *Hints on Household Taste*, written by the English architect Charles Eastlake.[2] Eastlake's goal had been twofold: to encourage his upper-middle-class audience to take interior design and the design of furniture seriously and to provide them with a basis for judgment, that is, of taste. Van Rensselaer followed suit in the realm of landscape architecture. Her aim was to convince her public that the design of the landscape was art and that it was of great importance. Then, she set down principles of judgment which she felt should be applied to the design of the landscape. The qualities she felt to be most essential (for architecture as well as for landscape architecture) were "breadth, repose, simplicity, and fitness."[3] She went on to indicate how these abstract concepts could be realized by "harmony between part and part and between detail and detail, concentration of interest, variety in unity, stimulus for the imagination."[4]

Art Out-of-Doors was reviewed in a number of the serious literary magazines of the time, as well as mentioned in the *New York Times*.[5] On the whole, the reaction was favorable, although one has a feeling that many of those who wrote these reviews either did not understand her intent or had not in fact really read the book at all. By the time that *Art Out-of-Doors* was published, Van Rensselaer was already a well-known literary figure in New York. Her first published writings had appeared in *Harper's Monthly Magazine* and in *American Architect and Building News* in 1876.[6] From this date until her death in 1934, she authored a wide variety of articles on travel, art and exhibitions of art, architecture, and landscape architecture.[7] Matching the diversity of subject matter in her articles was the assortment of magazines in which she

---

2. Charles Eastlake, *Hints on Household Taste*, 2d ed. (London: Longmans, Green, & Co., 1872).

3. Mariana Griswold Van Rensselaer, *Art Out-of-Doors* (1893), 35.

4. Ibid., 35.

5. Reviews were published in *The Atheneum* 102 (September 2, 1893): 321; *The Critic* 22 (June 24, 1893): 413; *The Dial* 15 (October 1, 1893): 193–194; *Garden and Forest* 6 (May 24, 1893): 229–230; *The Literary Digest* 7 (October 7, 1893): 15; *Review of Reviews* 7 (June 1893): 619; and the *New York Times*, May 21, 1893: 3.

6. Mariana Griswold Van Rensselaer, "Prayers" (a poem), *Harper's Monthly Magazine* 52 (April 1876): 690; "Optical Illusions," (1876), 174–175.

7. For two well-researched lists of Van Rensselaer's writings, see Cynthia D. Kinnard, "Life and Works" (1977), 305–328; and Lois Dinnerstein, "Opulence and Ocular Delight" (1979), 368–396.

published.[8] These ranged from such literary magazines as *The Century Magazine, Harper's Weekly, North American Review,* and *Lippincott's* to America's first professional architectural journal, *American Architect and Building News,* and then to the country's first magazine devoted to the environment and the landscape, *Garden and Forest.* In addition, by 1893, she had written two often-cited books. These were her much admired monograph from 1888, *Henry Hobson Richardson and His Works* (another first; in this instance the first monograph on an American architect) and her popular tour volume of 1892, *English Cathedrals,* which was often reprinted over the years.[9]

2

Mariana Griswold Van Rensselaer was born in New York City on February 25, 1851. Her parents, Lydia Alley and George Catlin Griswold, personified the wealthy establishment of New York City.[10] Mariana was one of seven children; she had three sisters and three brothers. Her father, a native New Yorker, was involved in a number of business activities, many of which he had inherited from his father. Her grandfather on her mother's side of the family, Saul Alley, was also a successful and respected businessman, with interests in shipping, railroads, and real estate.

As was generally the case with daughters of the well-to-do, Mariana received her early education at home from private tutors. The family resided at several residences on Fifth Avenue; their last residence before

8. For a broad picture of magazines published from the 1870s through 1900, see Frank Luther Mott, *A History of American Magazines 1865–1885* (Cambridge: Harvard University Press, 1938); Frank Luther Mott, *A History of American Magazines, 1885–1905* (Cambridge: The Belknap Press of Harvard University Press, 1957). Regrettably the author did not provide us with a reasonable picture of the audience of these magazines, what classes read them, or the extent of their distribution.

9. Van Rensselaer, *Henry Hobson* (1888) and *English Cathedrals* (1892).

10. "Mariana Griswold Van Rensselaer," *Appleton's Cyclopedia of American Biography* (New York: D. Appleton, 1889), 6: 253; Hamlin, "Mariana Griswold Van Rensselaer" (1943), 207–208; Early, "Mariana Alley Griswold Van Rensselaer" (1971), 511–512; "Mrs. Van Rensselaer, Art Authority Dies," *New York Times,* January 21, 1934: 29; "Mrs. Van Rensselaer Dies; Descendant of Pioneer New York Family," *New York Herald Tribune,* January 21, 1934: 18. Mariana Griswold Van Rensselaer's life is presented in detail in Kinnard, "Life and Works" (1977), 1–52; and Dinnerstein, "Opulence and Ocular Delight" (1979), 11–44. See also Kinnard, "Mariana Griswold Van Rensselaer" (1981), 181–205; Warshaver, "Psycho-Geographic Tradition" (1979); and Koenigsberg, "'Lifewritings'" (1990), 41–58.

they went abroad was 91 Fifth Ave.[11] During the summer months the family often went to the Connecticut and Rhode Island coasts. When she was fourteen years old, she and her parents visited her uncle's (J. N. A. Griswold) house at Newport, a house that had been designed by Richard Morris Hunt.[12] Her interest in suburban architecture and landscape architecture, as Lois Dinnerstein has pointed out, most likely developed during these teenage years.[13] Characteristic of what was expected of girls of the upper middle class and wealthy at this period, she must have begun to acquire a knowledge of horticulture. This knowledge served her well when in later life she began to write on landscape architecture.

In the late 1860s, her father closed the family shipping firm, and in 1868, he and the family moved to Dresden, Germany. There was at the time a sizable colony of English and Americans in Dresden, and it would appear that the Griswolds fitted into it with ease. Mariana, who was seventeen years old when her family left for Europe, remained abroad for five years. She continued her studies (perfecting her command of German and French) and traveled extensively throughout Europe with her family, visiting museums and many of the principal monuments of architecture and landscape architecture. By the time she left Europe, she had read many of the new and old books in German and French on art and architecture. It is likely that during these years she developed her deep interest in landscape architecture, both through visits to actual gardens as well as by reading a number of the late-eighteenth- and early-nineteenth-century classical writings on the subject.[14]

Mariana may have first met her future husband, Schuyler Van Rensselaer, either in New York or in Newport (Schuyler's parents' home was only a few doors away from Mariana's childhood home). Schuyler was educated at Harvard University and spent a year studying mining engineering at Columbia University.[15] Between 1868 and 1871, he continued advanced studies of mining engineering at the Mining Academy at Freiburg, Germany. During this period in Europe, he undoubtedly renewed his friendship with Mariana. In 1871, he returned to the United

11. For a description of the family's home see Frank Gray Griswold, *Afterthoughts: Recollections of Frank Gray Griswold* (New York: Harper, 1936), 3. Mariana Griswold Van Rensselaer, "Fifth Avenue" (1893), 5–18.

12. Dinnerstein, "Opulence and Ocular Delight" (1979), 13.

13. Ibid., 14.

14. Ibid., 20–27.

15. Kinnard, "Life and Works" (1977), 13–14.

States and formed a partnership with George W. Mayhard as consulting mining and metallurgical engineers.[16] Schuyler returned to Europe in 1873, where he and Mariana were married in Dresden on April 14. They returned to the United States after only a brief stay in Europe and settled in the small community of New Brunswick, New Jersey, where Schuyler's parents lived. Their only child, George Griswold, was born there on February 11, 1875. The Van Rensselaers temporarily lived in Europe (once again in Dresden) from April 1876 through May 1877, during which time Schuyler studied recent developments in chemical patents relating to metallurgy.

From 1877 through 1882, Schuyler worked for the Chicago, Burlington and Quincy Railroad Company. He then returned to his own mining business, traveling across the continent to California and into Canada. His health became increasingly fragile, and in March 1884, he died of lung disease. A few months later Mariana's father died in Dresden, so she and her son went to Europe to be with her mother. She returned to the United States in 1885, and she and her mother, together with her sister Louisa, purchased a house at 9 West Ninth Street in New York City. In 1894, after a lengthy battle with tuberculosis, her son died in Colorado Springs, where she had taken him in hopes that he could regain his health.

Mariana was unquestionably close to both her husband and son. As one would expect, their early deaths had a decided effect not only on her life but also on her writings.[17] Schuyler's death after some eleven years of marriage spurred her to concentrate even more of her energies on her writing. In contrast, her son's death seems to mark a moment when she slowly began to reduce her writing activities and began to engage in more social and political activities. One might suspect that segments of her 1896 short story *One Man Who Was Content* are at least indirectly autobiographical.[18] In the story, Schuyler's death was transformed into the wife's illness and early death, and then the way in which the "man" plunged himself into politics correlates with Mariana's involvement with new causes after the death of her son in 1894.

---

16. Ibid, 14.
17. Ibid., 15–19.
18. Mariana Griswold Van Rensselaer, "One Man Who Was Content," *Century Magazine* 31 (December 1896): 287–293. This short story plus several others were published the following year as a book: *One Man Who Was Content and Other Stories* (New York: The Century Company, 1897).

Van Rensselaer did not completely abandon writing after her son's death. During the mid- to late 1890s, she continued to write for a number of magazines, especially for *The Century Magazine* and for *Garden and Forest*. In the late 1890s and early 1900s, she obviously spent a considerable amount of time researching and writing her *History of the City of New York in the Seventeenth Century*.[19] She also began to write and publish an increased number of her poems in magazines: in 1910 Macmillan Company brought forth a volume of them, and in 1921 the Atlantic Monthly Press published a collection of her children's poems.[20] At this time, she also translated from German such works as Wilhelm Reinhold Valentiner's *The Art of the Low Countries*.[21]

By the mid-1890s she had already become an established and well-recognized writer. Articles she had written earlier were republished in other magazines and books. For both the World Columbian Exposition of 1893 in Chicago and for the Pan-American Exposition of 1901 in Buffalo, she was asked to write sections of the catalogues. In the case of the Chicago fair, she wrote on "The Fair Grounds." [22] For the Buffalo Exposition she contributed two pieces, the first of which, "From an Art Critic's Point of View," provided a broad assessment of the fair's site-planning, landscape architecture, and buildings.[23] The second piece dealt with the paintings exhibited at the fair.[24]

With her New York–New England lineage and her modest wealth, she tended to look askance at many aspects of the "Gilded Age," especially at the activities of the newly emerging individuals of capitalist wealth. Reflecting the traditional feeling of genteel obligation, she obviously had a deep concern over the exploitation of the working classes. In one of her many articles in the *New York World,* she commented, "[W]e cannot say that the rich of New York are really generous."[25] She went on to chide the wealthy for ignoring "the Christian demand for

19. Mariana Griswold Van Rensselaer, *History of the City of New York in the Seventeenth Century* (New York: Macmillan Company, 1909).

20. Mariana Griswold Van Rensselaer, *Poems* (New York: Macmillan Co., 1910); *Many Children* (Boston: Atlantic Monthly Press, 1921).

21. Wilhelm Reinhold Valentiner, *The Art of the Low Countries*, trans. by Mariana Griswold Van Rensselaer (Garden City, New York: Doubleday, Page and Company, 1914).

22. Van Rensselaer, "The Fair Grounds" (1893).

23. Van Rensselaer, "From an Art Critic's Point of View" (1901), 25–28. Van Rensselaer also produced a picturebook on the fair: *Photography of the Pan-American Exposition at Buffalo* (New York: 1901).

24. Van Rensselaer, "How to Look at Pictures" (1901), 83–85.

25. Mariana Griswold Van Rensselaer, *New York World,* December 24, 1884: 4.

that brotherly love which can only spring from brotherly acquaintance." [26] In "People in New York" (1895), she observed that "the extremes of riches and poverty is bitterly expressed by the contrast between what have been called Upper and Nether New York. Indeed, nowhere else except London is this meaning so bitterly expressed upon so large a scale. . . . But would our slums exist if we all knew about them and their fatal work—streets and acres of tenements in which decent living is impossible, which are poisonous to the souls as to the bodies of their inmates? Would our present methods of manufacture and trade be permitted if we all grasped their deadly effect upon individuals, their deadly menace to the well-being of the community as a whole?" [27]

It was in the mid- to late 1890s that she turned her attention to issues of public education (she was president of the Public Education Association from 1898 to 1906). She, like many other professional women of the time, became embroiled in the issue of women's suffrage in the late 1890s. Although she had registered and voted when she was in Colorado with her son, she was opposed to women's suffrage and wrote an anti-suffrage article, "Should We Ask for the Suffrage?" which was widely quoted and reprinted.[28]

Like those of many others, Van Rensselaer's attitude toward her gender and its relationship with men produced two very opposite responses in her thinking. On the one hand, she seemed willing to accept the traditional secondary role of women within Western European society, while on the other, she was resentful of the secondary place of women. This ambiguity in how she viewed herself as a woman and a wife is apparent in the manner in which she signed her writings. In many of her articles she did not openly comment on her gender, signing them simply as "M. G. Van Rensselaer," but in all of her books she signed herself "Mrs. Schuyler Van Rensselaer." It could, perhaps, be argued that the conventional use of her married name was more an index of her desire to acknowledge her strong upper-class position than a remark on her gender. But still, the use of this convention as opposed to the use of initials must be considered a comment on how she viewed herself as a woman.

26. Ibid.
27. Van Rensselaer, "People in New York" (1895), 546–547.
28. Mariana Griswold Van Rensselaer, *Should We Ask for the Suffrage?* (New York: J. J. O'Brien and Son, 1894). Her position on suffrage had been expressed in a series of six articles published in the *New York World* on May 12, 14, 19, 20, 27, and June 3, 1894. All on p. 4. For a discussion of her position on women's suffrage, see Kinnard, "Life and Works" (1977), 34–35, 281–285.

Some of her letters, a few of her poems, and certainly her short story *One Man Who Was Content* illustrate her adherence to the traditional role that a woman sacrifice herself for family and husband.[29] One suspects that her general characterization of the upper-class woman in New York is close to a self-description: "All will agree that the New York woman, individually and collectively, leads in the combination of the results of money, good taste, unaggressive self-content, and the highly finished physical bearing which, in the vernacular, is called 'style.'"[30] Earlier, in 1892, she had written a piece, entitled "The Waste of Women's Intellectual Force," in which she had said that "in the women of America, it seems to me, lies the nation's best hope of intellectual advance."[31]

There can be little doubt that her husband did not approve of her activities as a professional writer. In a letter written on September 2, 1881, to S. R. Koehler, she remarked of her husband's attitude toward her writing: "While I have a husband to work for me I cannot bind myself to any regular employment, nor would he for a moment consent that I should do so. It was to a great degree against my husband's first wishes that I took the position I hold on the 'World.' . . . People say that the fact of being a woman need not limit one's activities, but I do not find it so."[32]

Though Schuyler did not approve, Mariana was obviously determined to continue writing. The list of articles she wrote between 1876 and mid-1884 is impressive. These comprise several of her major pieces on architecture and art including the many articles she wrote on art and architecture for the *New York World*.[33] Though she had a modest private income, she looked upon her writing activities as an important supplementary source. As Cynthia D. Kinnard has carefully documented, Van Rensselaer often felt it necessary to write to editors asking them to make their payments promptly.[34] The slowness of editors to pay for ar-

29. Van Rensselaer, *One Man Who Was Content* (1897).
30. Van Rensselaer, "People in New York" (1895), 540.
31. Mariana Griswold Van Rensselaer, "The Waste of Women's Intellectual Force," *The Forum* 13 (July 1892): 620. This piece by Van Rensselaer is discussed in Kinnard, "Life and Works" (1977), 280–281.
32. Mariana Griswold Van Rensselaer to S. R. Koehler, September 2, 1892, Koehler Collection, Archives of American Art. Quoted in full in Dinnerstein, "Opulence and Ocular Delight" (1979), 35–36.
33. Kinnard, "Life and Works" (1977), 305–310; Dinnerstein, "Opulence and Ocular Delight" (1979), 368–374.
34. Kinnard, "Life and Works" (1977), 24–28, 37.

ticles may have had something to do with her gender and also perhaps with a perception that she did not really need the money. (But it should be noted that complaints about payments for writings seem to occur frequently. One suspects that such slowness of payment was [and is] characteristic of the profession. Even major literary figures such as Mark Twain were continually complaining about slowness of payments.) Perhaps, as even happens to the well-to-do, her occasional financial problems had more to do with "cash flow" at a particular moment than a long-term need for income from her writings.[35] One suspects that her concern about being paid promptly was, at least in part, a reflection of her view of herself as a professional writer.

During the final twenty-five years of her life, she wrote a small number of important articles, published many of her poems, and in 1925 republished her 1893 volume, *Art Out-of-Doors,* to which she added three new chapters plus an updated list of books on landscape architecture.[36] Although in no sense as active and visible as she had been in the 1880s and 1890s, she was still looked upon as a prominent figure in the New York literary scene after the nineties. In 1910, she received an honorary Litt.D. degree from Columbia University, and in 1923, at the formal opening of the new permanent home of the American Academy of Arts and Letters, she was awarded the society's gold medal. She was the second person in the history of this society to receive this award.[37]

In January 1933, the architect-critic-historian Talbot F. Hamlin was asked by Dumas Malone to write a biographical entry of Van Rensselaer for the *Dictionary of American Bibliography.* He replied that he would be "very pleased to do" one.[38] A month or so later he wrote to Malone, that "I would love to do a biography of Mrs. Van Rensselaer, but aren't we rushing things?—after all, it would be bad to be premature . . . I discovered that the lady is alive even today, and listed in the

35. When Van Rensselaer died in 1934, in the midst of the Great Depression, she left an estate of $215,958, a sizable sum for those years. See Kinnard, ibid., 27, 51 n. 91.

36. Two volumes of her poetry were published. These were *Poems* (1910) and a volume of poetry for children, *Many Children* (1921). (See n. 20 above.) Over the years, but especially after 1900, her poems were published in such magazines as *Atlantic Monthly, Harper's Weekly, Century Magazine, North American Review,* and others. See the listing in Kinnard, "Life and Works" (1977), 305–327.

37. *Proceedings at the Formal Opening of the Permanent Home of the American Academy of Arts and Letters* (New York: American Academy of Arts and Letters, 1923), 38–39.

38. Talbot F. Hamlin to Dumas Malone, January 14, 1933, Talbot F. Hamlin Collection, Avery Library, Columbia University.

telephone book." [39] With her death the following year, he did write the entry for the *Dictionary*. Though there are condescending passages in Hamlin's entry, he was on the whole appreciative. He wrote that "her work is important as the almost perfect expression of cultural breadth, a cultivated tolerance, and an artistic sensitivity which, united, were characteristic of the finest flowering of nineteenth-century American life." [40]

In his 1924 volume, *Sticks and Stones*, and again in *The Brown Decades* (1931), Lewis Mumford had cited Van Rensselaer's monograph on H. H. Richardson. [41] But it was Henry-Russell Hitchcock, Jr. in his *The Architecture of H. H. Richardson and His Times* who provided the first appraisal of Van Rensselaer as a historian-critic. [42] He wrote, "This book [referring to his own 1936 volume] is not a biography of Richardson. An excellent biography by Mrs. Schuyler Van Rensselaer exists. . . . This [Hitchcock's own new volume] is a study of Richardson's architecture in the light of the setting in which he worked. This setting could be taken for granted by Mrs. Van Rensselaer when she wrote in 1888. But the setting and Richardson's architecture itself were denigrated and forgotten by the next generation. . . . Mrs. Van Rensselaer was an admirable architectural critic, intelligent, sensitive, and discriminating. Her comments on Richardson's buildings are almost always extremely sound. But, as a biographer should be, she was somewhat carried away by the personality of her subject." [43]

In the years after World War II, *Art Out-of-Doors* and her anthology of short stories, *One Man Who Was Content and Other Stories*, were republished. [44] In addition, several of her critical writings on architecture were published in anthologies. [45] In 1952 Lewis Mumford included her essay "Client and Architect" in his collection of essays, *Roots of*

39. Talbot F. Hamlin to Dumas Malone, February 20, 1933, Talbot F. Hamlin Collection, Avery Library, Columbia University.

40. Hamlin, "Mariana Griswold Van Rensselaer" (1936), 208.

41. Lewis Mumford, *Sticks and Stones* (New York: Boni and Liveright, 1924), 243; *Brown Decades* (New York: Harcourt, Brace and Company, 1931), 255.

42. Henry-Russell Hitchcock, Jr., *The Architecture of H. H. Richardson and His Times* (New York: Museum of Modern Art, 1936), vii–viii.

43. Ibid.

44. Mariana Griswold Van Rensselaer, *Art Out-of-Doors* (1925 ; reprint, Philadelphia: National Council Books, Inc., 1959); *One Man Who Was Content and Other Stories* (1897; reprint, Freeport, New York: Books for Libraries Press, 1969).

45. Lewis Mumford, ed., *Roots of Contemporary American Architecture* (New York: Reinhold Publishing Corp., 1952); Thomas C. Jones, comp., *Shaping of America* (Chicago: J. G. Ferguson, 1964).

Contemporary American Architecture.[46] In a brief biographical note, Mumford describes Van Rensselaer as "an advanced woman of her day, she appreciated the work of Richardson, and her treatment of him is not merely the first full-fledged monograph on the work of an architect to be written in America, but an outstandingly good critical biography in its own right." [47] Like Hitchcock, Mumford felt that she was too contemporaneous with Richardson to give "sufficient attention to his departures." What Mumford meant at this point is that Rensselaer was not out to advance, as he was, certain causes of twentieth-century modernism.

Her reputation as an architectural historian-critic began to emerge more fully in the 1960s with, first, excerpts and then with two separate reprintings of her 1888 volume on H. H. Richardson.[48] The first of these, published by Chicago's Prairie School Press, contained an introduction by James D. Van Trump.[49] In it he praised Van Rensselaer both as a writer and as a critic: "She knew well the 'language' of architecture and she discussed the art and its practice lucidly in its own terms. On this score she could put some modern architectural critics to shame. . . . [S]he was . . . amazingly astute in her evaluation of his [Richardson's] buildings. Her opinions would agree, for the most part, with modern critical estimations." [50]

With the continued response to Richardson's work, Van Rensselaer was, of course, always mentioned, either in introductions or in footnotes. In the 1969 reprint of the Richardson book by Dover Publications, Inc., William Morgan commented on Van Rensselaer as a historian and as a critic.[51] While he asserted that she was a "distinguished woman critic," he also characterized her as an "amateur" architectural historian. As was true for the reviewers of the earlier Prairie School Press edition, Morgan seemed, as well, to be uncomfortable with her gender.

James F. O'Gorman in his 1974 volume, *Selected Drawings: H. H. Richardson,* comments on Van Rensselaer's biography of the architect

    46. Mumford, *Roots* (1952), 260–268.
    47. Ibid., 429.
    48. Gifford, *Literature of Architecture* (1966); Van Trump, introduction to *Henry Hobson Richardson* (1967); Placzek, introduction to *Henry Hobson Richardson* (1969).
    49. Van Trump, introduction to *Henry Hobson Richardson* (1967), i–vi.
    50. Ibid., v–vi.
    51. Morgan, introduction to *Henry Hobson Richardson* (1969).

that it was "highly readable and on the whole still valuable as criticism." [52] In his "Notes" for *H. H. Richardson: Complete Architectural Works,* Jeffrey Karl Ochsner said that "Mrs. Van Rensselaer was a unique Victorian as well as an art and architectural critic." [53]

James D. Van Trump, in his 1967 introduction to her Richardson volume, commented that "as one writes, it is possible that some graduate student is even now at 'work on' a Ph.D. dissertation on the career of this not unimportant critic." [54] A decade or so later such dissertations indeed began to appear, accompanied by several articles, including an excellent biography on Van Rensselaer by Cynthia D. Kinnard.[55]

A word should be injected about Van Rensselaer's personality and her relationships with a good number of America's major artists, architects, and landscape architects. While she was in many ways a traditional upper-class woman of the time, she still decidedly rejected many of the normal protocols of her class. Her article "The Plague of Formal Calls" indicates her rejection of what she considered to be a waste of time devoted to senseless social conventions.[56] Two works of art depicting her, an 1888 bronze relief by August Saint-Gaudens and an 1890 painting by William A. Coffin, hint at her reserved, but not unfriendly, character. Kinnard includes a remark by the illustrator Joseph Pennell that "he was deadly afraid of her" when he met her in 1884, which is probably more of a comment on him than on any formidable quality in Van Rensselaer's personality.[57]One suspects that her confidence in her social position together with the quiet day-to-day life with-

52. James O'Gorman, *Selected Drawings: Henry Hobson Richardson and His Office* (Cambridge: Harvard University, 1974), 31.

53. Jeffrey Karl Ochsner, *H. H. Richardson: Complete Architectural Works* (Cambridge: MIT Press, 1982), 14.

54. Van Trump, introduction to *Henry Hobson Richardson* (1967), iii.

55. Kinnard, "Life and Works" (1977); Dinnerstein, "Opulence and Ocular Delight" (1979); Warshaver, "Psycho-Geographic Traditions" (1979); Lois Dinnerstein, "Thomas Eakins' 'Crucifixion' as Perceived by Mariana Griswold Van Rensselaer," *Arts* 53 (May 1979): 140–145; Kinnard, "Mariana Griswold Van Rensselaer" (1981), 181–205. Koenigsberg, "'Lifewritings'" (1990), 41–58. Cynthia Zaitzevsky, in her article "The Olmsted Firm and the Structures of the Boston Park System," established Van Rensselaer's authorship of the unsigned editorial "Architectural Fitness," which appeared in the August 1891 issue of *Garden and Forest.* Zaitzevsky reproduces that entire article in hers.

56. Mariana Griswold Van Rensselaer, "The Plague of Formal Calls," *Scribner's Monthly* 19 (March 1880): 787–788.

57. Joseph Pennell, *The Adventures of an Illustrator, Mostly in Following His Authors in America and Europe* (Boston: Little, Brown and Company, 1925), 158, as quoted in Kinnard, "Life and Works" (1977), 25.

out family and her activities as a writer markedly separated her from much of what would have been considered the normal social life of the wealthy.

Van Rensselaer met and knew almost all of the major late-nineteenth-century figures in the arts, architecture, and landscape architecture. In some cases, such as with Augustus Saint-Gaudens, Frederick Law Olmsted, and Charles Sprague Sargent, one can speak of friendship, though even in these instances, the friendship seems to have been more professional than intimate. In the case of Henry Hobson Richardson, it would be an error to think of their acquaintanceship as that of close friends. We cannot even be sure as to when Van Rensselaer first meet Richardson; it probably was not until after the architect had moved to Brookline, Massachusetts, in 1874.[58] Of her various professional colleagues, it was only Richard Watson Gilder, the editor of *The Century Magazine,* who could be considered a very close friend.[59]

Throughout her life, Van Rensselaer was an ardent reader. Her ability to read French and German with ease meant that she was exposed to much of the major late-nineteenth-century literature relating to the arts. Her knowledge of the literature is illustrated by the extensive reading list she supplied for just the field of landscape architecture alone in the recommended readings on the subject that she added to the 1925 edition of *Art Out-of-Doors.* This list shows how well she kept up with the subject even after 1900. Her life from the time of her son's death in 1894 was a full one, with writing, research, readings, and almost annual trips to Europe.

3

In her roles as a writer, historian, and critic, Van Rensselaer sought to project herself as knowledgeable, objective, and rational. The first need, as she continually reminded her readers, was to have a reasonable command of factual information (past background, as well as present information) and with that as a basis to proceed with analysis and then final judgments. While the fact or illusion of the rational and objective was one of the characteristics of criticism in the mid- to late nineteenth cen-

58. Kinnard, "Life and Works" (1977), 135–137.
59. Gilder was editor of *The Century Magazine* from 1881 until 1909. See Rosamond Gilder, ed., *Letters of Richard Watson Gilder* (New York: Houghton Mifflin, 1916).

tury, it certainly was not the predominant pose in writings of the time on the arts including architecture and landscape architecture.

In his 1893 review of her *English Cathedrals,* Charles Moore (strongly reflecting his own preconceived views on medieval art and architecture) took her to task for her efforts to remain objective. "Mrs. Van Rensselaer is not always sufficiently discriminating. With a laudable desire to see good wherever it may exist, she is apt to fancy that she finds architectural merit where there is comparatively little of it; and what she apparently means for catholicity sometimes betrays, we think, a lack of sound judgment." [60]

A reviewer of her *Art Out-of-Doors* in *Garden and Forest* remarked on her general desire to minimize her subjective response to her subject. "There is an interesting chapter on formal gardening, and some charming ones upon the beauty of trees, in which the writer permits herself some play of fancy concerning the repose of trees as contrasted with the unrest of others, and shows a tender sense of their individual characteristics, as well as artistic perception of their value in composition. In these we get a more personal note than is generally admitted, the whole tone of the book being rather abstract and authoritative as becomes what is really a treatise." [61]

While she certainly wished to have her judgments appear as objective as possible, she did not avoid forceful expression of her own taste. Her two models of a critic-historian were the French restorer and theoretician, Eugene Viollet-le-Duc, a person she often admiringly mentioned in her writings, and the American landscape architect A. J. Downing. What she wished to avoid was the appearance of judgments derived from solely emotional reactions, as she felt John Ruskin did in so many of his writings. Don Gifford, in reprinting sections of her text on Richardson in his 1966 *The Literature of Architecture,* perceptively summed up her approach: "Her art criticism is not so abrupt and polemic as that of many of her contemporaries; on the contrary, it is balanced and considerate; this is not to say that she was unsure of her evaluations, but she delivered her evaluations with a cultured pose that was contemplative rather than activistic." [62]

60. Charles Moore, review of *English Cathedrals,* by Mariana Griswold Van Rensselaer, *Atlantic Monthly* 71 (February 1892): 271.

61. Review of *Art Out-of-Doors, Or Hints on Good Taste in Gardening,* by Mariana Griswold Van Rensselaer, *Garden and Forest* 6 (May 24, 1893): 229–230.

62. Gifford, *Literature of Architecture* (1966), 436.

If we look around the American scene at other writers of the time who wrote on architecture, landscape architecture, and planning, we find that her sense of detached objectivity separates her from most of them. In the writings of Russell Sturgis, Montgomery Schuyler, and Peter B. Wight in architecture, or Charles Eliot in landscape architecture, their strongly asserted judgments are dominant. Compared to these writers, Van Rensselaer is far more subtle in the way in which she injects her judgments into her writings. According to Van Rensselaer, architectural taste based upon objectivity is arrived at when one first has all of the pertinent facts of the project in hand and one has a reasonable acquaintanceship with the history of architecture (by implication, the critic has developed an urbane taste). An excellent illustration of what she meant by assembling the pertinent facts can be gleaned from her long and detailed examination of the then new Metropolitan Opera-House in New York.[63] Early in this article she sets down the principle upon which this design is based: "[T]he aim in all opera-houses is that the spectators shall see and hear as well as possible, but never before had this been insisted upon with so entire a disregard of the requirements of architectural effect." [64] The article then progresses to discuss the building in detail in order to examine how it responded to the functional and aesthetic requirements of an opera house. After presenting the facts of the building's design, she then compares it with other contemporary European opera houses—La Scala in Milan, the opera house at Bordeaux, the Grand Opera House in Paris, and Wagner's opera house at Bayreuth. With the contemporary and historic facts in place, she then proceeds to make a rational architectural judgment. She concludes, "But architecturally it is a fine creation, imposing not alone by its size but by its dignity, simplicity, and intelligent adaption to its ends." [65]

In the mid-1880s she published an article in *The Art Review* entitled "Wanted—A History of Architecture." In it she complained about what was then available in published histories of architecture.[66] She posed the question: "What is the best book to put in the hands of an advanced class in school desirous of taking up the history of the world's architecture in general? ... There is none what-ever, for the one or two which

63. Van Rensselaer, "The Metropolitan" (1884).
64. Ibid., 76.
65. Ibid., 88.
66. Van Rensselaer, "Wanted—A History of Architecture" (1886), 15–19.

nominally exist are useless." [67] She concluded her piece with the observation that "if I were quite young, and a man, and rich—strong and resolute enough to make poverty serve the turn of riches,—it seems to me that there are few things which would tempt me more than a project of this sort" (i.e., the writing of an objective history of world architecture).[68]

There were two themes which dominated all of her writings on architecture and the landscape. She felt that when designing a building or a segment of the landscape, the architect or landscape architect must respond first to fitness of purpose, but this response must be of an aesthetic nature. "Americans are gradually learning," she wrote in an editorial in *Garden and Forest* in August 1891, "that fitness, appropriateness, is the foundation of all artistic excellence." [69] The term "fitness" can, of course, be equated with function and certainly the argument for functionalism was a recurring theme in both European and American writings on architecture and landscape architecture in the mid- and late nineteenth century. In an article highly critical of the 1893 Chicago Exposition, the landscape architect Charles Eliot entitled his piece, "What Would be Fair Must First be Fit"; and Daniel Denison Shade in his 1895 volume, *The Evolution of Horticulture in New England*, wrote, "yet there are certain general principles to be recognized, if success [in landscape architecture] is to be obtained. Among these should be congruity or fitness." [70]

As with Eliot, Slade, and earlier, A. J. Downing, Van Rensselaer felt that solving the problem of fitness was an essential first step. For her,

67. Ibid., 17. Van Rensselaer does not mention any specific authors in her text. One could assume that she was not happy with James Fergusson's three-volume *A History of Architecture in All Countries From the Earliest Times to the Present Day* (London: John Murray, 1862–67), or A. Rosengarten's *Handbook of Architectural Styles* (New York: D. Appleton & Co., 1876). She probably considered Eugene Viollet-le-Duc's *The Habitations of Man in All Ages* (Boston: James R. Osgood, 1876) more of a theoretical exposé rather than a history of architecture. One suspects that she would have been a little more satisfied with the offerings in the 1890s with the publication of H. Heathcoate Statham's *Architecture for the General Reader* (London: Chapman and Hall, 1895), or above all, with Banister Fletcher's classic *A History of Architecture on the Comparative Method* (London: B. T. Batsford, 1896).

68. Van Rensselaer, "Wanted—A History of Architecture" (1886), 19.

69. Van Rensselaer, "Architectural Fitness" (1891), 385–386; This piece was subsequently published as a chapter, "A Word for Architecture," in her 1893 volume, *Art Out-of-Doors* (pp. 191–201 in the 1893 edition; pp. 189–201 in the 1925 edition). See Zaitzevsky, "The Olmsted Firm" (1973), 167–174.

70. Charles Eliot, "'What Must be Fair Must be Fit," *Garden and Forest* 9 (April 1, 1896): 132–133; Daniel Denison Slade, *The Evolution of Horticulture in New England* (New York and London: G. P. Putnam's Sons, 1895), 146.

fitness entailed not only the solution to utilitarian problems, it also encompassed a symbolic expression of its function. She thought that fitness in landscape architecture or in the siting of a building must also be appropriate, that is, the solution should be in rapport with nature. As she explained, the response which then follows must transform the design into an art object, and this could only come about in the hands of an artist. Without the artist, there can be no landscape architecture or architecture. In her series of articles on "Landscape Gardening," she wrote, "Intelligent amateur work is certainly better than unintelligent, and the more intelligent the amateur worker becomes, the more certain he is to realize that only the artist can truly succeed in art." [71] In describing the relationship between client and architect she wrote, "The first commandment is that an artist is needed for an 'unimportant' as well as for an 'important' building; and the second commandment is that when we set an artist to work we should let him work as freely as possible." [72]

At the conclusion of the First World War there was a widespread enthusiasm in America for building war memorials. Van Rensselaer commented on this enthusiasm in an article "Appropriateness in War Memorials." [73] In this piece she returned to the theme that art must be produced by artists: "An artist should not only execute the work, but advise in advance as to its character and its placing." [74]

Two other attitudes important in her writings must be mentioned. She, like several other nineteenth-century architectural critics, was not enamored with the idea of strident originality. "It is as utterly foolish to talk of throwing away our legacy of art, and of beginning afresh with the intent to develop 'something American,' as it would be to hold the same language with regard to science, industry, morals, manners, feelings, tastes." [75]

She did indeed believe that changes of necessity would take place, and she also felt that the peculiarities of the peoples and geography of America would produce a landscape and buildings different from those of the past and quite distinct from those of Europe.

71. Van Rensselaer, "Landscape Gardening, I" (1887), 157.
72. Van Rensselaer, "Client and Architect" (1890), 320.
73. Van Rensselaer, "Appropriateness in War Memorials" (1919), 274–275.
74. Ibid., 274.
75. Van Rensselaer, "American Country Dwellings, I" (1886), 11.

4

Of the visual arts, or as she labeled them the "Arts of Design," it was landscape architecture more than painting or architecture with which she felt the closest kinship. Her definition was broadly environmental: "This is the art," she wrote, "whose purpose it is to create beautiful compositions upon the surface of the ground."[76] Her own intense feeling about the practice of landscape architecture was pointedly revealed in her remarks about the profession: "There is no profession whatsoever—unless it be the landscape painter's—which suggests to the imagination so delightful an existence. It offers the chance of a life spent largely out of doors, in which the love of nature may be indulged, not as a casual refreshment, but as the very basis and inspiration of one's day's work."[77] Turning to landscape architecture, or as she labeled it "landscape gardening," she posed for the potential practitioner the same series of needs which one finds for an architect: a knowledge of the functional requirements of a project, a thorough understanding of the site, and a knowledge of the history, in this case, of landscape design. To these two considerations she added another, namely, an acquaintanceship with horticultural material.

In her three-part article "Landscape Gardening," published in the *American Architect and Building News,* she carefully set forth the great importance of landscape design in America.[78] She began by asking the American middle- and upper-middle-class public to realize that the need to design the landscape is an art and that they should engage an "artist" in landscape design to carry out a project. She then proceeded to suggest how the lay public can obtain the needed historical background so that they will be in a position to form reasonable judgments relating to landscape design.

There can be no doubt that her own commitment in landscape design was toward the "naturalistic," as espoused early in the century by A. J. Downing and by her two friends Frederick Law Olmsted and Charles Sprague Sargent. It was Sargent who provided her with an outlet for her many writings on landscape architecture in the pages of his magazine *Garden and Forest.*[79] In *Art Out-of-Doors* she wrote, "I

76. Van Rensselaer, "Landscape Gardening—A Definition" (1888), 2.
77. Van Rensselaer, "Landscape Gardening, I" (1887), 158.
78. Van Rensselaer, "Landscape Gardening" (1887–88).
79. *Garden and Forest* was published in New York City between the years 1888 and 1898 under the editorship of William A. Stiles. It was financed and sponsored by Charles

have assumed that the naturalistic methods of gardening are the most interesting and important to Americans . . . " for "nature speaks to us more variously and naturally in America than in Europe.[80] But, as with Downing and Olmsted, she did not dismiss the tradition of formal garden design. One surmises that she felt that she was obligated to be objective in looking into the tradition of the formal garden, but it was not her predilection. She observed that the naturalistic garden stems directly from nature and if successful, is in full rapport with it. The formal garden does not delicately humor nature, rather it "boldly compelled [the garden] in a direction opposite to any of those which she ever chooses."[81] She pointed out that a formal garden is in essence a piece of architecture: "It is as artificial, almost, as a building."[82] While the formal and the naturalistic gardens are quite opposite to one another, she indicated that it is often impossible at times to draw too complete a division between the two. Informal effects will of necessity enter into the most formal of gardens, and even an informal garden for, say, a suburban residence more likely than not will exhibit some formal passages.

Her ideal, though, remained the naturalistic garden. She continually made reference to "Nature's work," and she argued that each environment should cultivate its own character. She wrote, "The true artist . . . would accept Nature's frame, outline and materials, and paint his pictures according to her local specifications."[83] Van Rensselaer's open acceptance of an environment and its native plant materials is a far cry from those who advocated the formal garden. Louise Shelton, in her 1915 and 1924 *Beautiful Gardens in America,* lamented the fact that the climates of much of North America made it impossible to fully adhere to the classic formal garden tradition of Europe.[84] In contrast to the turn-

---

S. Sargent, Director of the Arnold Arboretum of Harvard University. See S. B. Sutton, *Charles Sprague Sargent and the Arnold Arboretum* (Cambridge: Harvard University Press, 1970), 131–133, 178–179.

80. Van Rensselaer, *Art Out-of-Doors* (1915): 157; "Landscape Gardening, II" (1887): 264.

81. Van Rensselaer, *Art Out-of-Doors* (1925): 163.

82. Ibid., 163.

83. Ibid., 41.

84. Louise Shelton, *Beautiful Gardens in America* (New York: Charles Scribner's Sons, 1924), 41. As with many of America's turn-of-the-century advocates of the formal garden, Shelton suggested numerous substitute trees and plants, but it is quite obvious that she would have been most happy if all of the horticultural material of Europe could comfortably grow in the varied climates of North America.

of-the-century formal gardens advocated by Charles Platt, Edith Wharton, and Louis Shelton, Van Rensselaer summed up her strong love of the "naturalistic" style. "In what is called the 'naturalistic' style of gardening it uses them [the materials of nature] to produce many effects which, under favoring conditions, Nature might have produced without man's aid. Then, the better the results, the less likely it is to be recognized as an artificial, and artistic, result; the more perfectly the artist attains his end, the more likely we are to forget that he has been at work." [85]

5

In addition to her volume on Richardson and her popular *English Cathedrals,* Van Rensselaer wrote a wide array of articles on architecture and the decorative arts. A number of these writings were not concerned with objects per se, that is, with an individual building or specific interiors but with broader issues. In the case of the decorative arts she took Ruskin and Eastlake to task for their insistence on certain "dogmas": "sincere construction" imposed limitations on the use of color, and the designs within "all decorative arts must be conventional." [86] Again, as in her other writings, Van Rensselaer was too urbane to "buy" any unflinching connection between ethicality and art. Her stance on the issue of structural honesty sums up her reactions to these dogmas: "The laws of art require that structure be indicated sufficiently to *satisfy the eye*." [87] Thus, the viewer's general aesthetic reaction is what really counted for her, not necessarily all of the facts of construction, of joinery, of the nature of materials, etc.

Other of her articles on architecture have to do with the more general issues: the ideal training of an architect, the ins and outs of architectural competitions, and the relationship between architect and client. When she did turn her attention to specific buildings or groups of buildings, her initial and oftentimes her major focus was an environmental one: the way a structure was sited, how its design did or did not reflect nature in a rural or suburban situation, or what contribution, if any, the new structure made to an urban situation. Her article on Grant's Tomb in New York's Riverside Park, essentially ignores the building (and the

---

85. Van Rensselaer, *Art Out-of-Doors* (1925), 4.
86. Van Rensselaer, "Decorative Art and Its Dogmas" (1880), 213–220, 342–351.
87. Ibid., 216.

well-publicized competition held for it) and essentially concerns itself with the proposed siting of the memorial.[88] The architect's response to the urban situation of Madison Square Garden or the Boston Public Library was her principal concern. In discussing McKim, Mead and White's Madison Square Garden, she devoted the first pages to a history of the site in New York City and what it looked like at the time she wrote. Then, she analyzed the contribution to the city of the new building. With the Boston Public Library, she again discussed the site, Copley Square, Richardson's Trinity Church, and how the new building fitted into what was already there.

Writing in 1952, Lewis Mumford felt that Van Rensselaer had by the early 1890s "succumbed to a general drift toward eclecticism with an emphasis on McKim, Mead and White's Renaissance." [89] A reading of her writings on McKim, Mead and White's Madison Square Garden and the Boston Public Library, or on the 1893 Chicago "White City" and the 1901 Pan-American Exposition in Buffalo, certainly do not indicate that she had "succumbed" to the new Beaux Arts tradition of classicism. Rather, it could be suggested that her critical position in regard to the new classicism, whether in architecture or city planning, was closely akin to her tolerance and reaction to the formal garden in landscape architecture. She was perfectly comfortable with the classical order of the new Renaissance, but she never became a passionate advocate of it.

In her first visit to the Chicago fair in 1892, she commented, as one would expect of her, first on the nature of Olmsted's planning of the site. Then, turning her attention to its architecture, she wrote, "It will be the first real object lesson America has had in the art of building well on a grand scale; and it will show us how . . . our permanent streets and squares ought to be designed." [90] Van Rensselaer accepted Beaux Arts classicism so long as it was carried out with appropriate reticence. Speaking of the newly developed interest in the Renaissance ideal, she noted that we should look "to those earlier, purer types of Renaissance work which best deserve the name."[91] As an image, she thought it worked

88. Van Rensselaer, "The Grant Monument for Riverside Park" (1891), 27–28.
89. Mumford, *Roots* (1952), 429.
90. Van Rensselaer, "The Artistic Triumph of the Fair-Builders" (1892), 531.
91. Mariana Griswold Van Rensselaer, "The Development of American Homes," in *Household Arts*, ed. Candice Thurber Wheeler (New York: Harper and Brothers Publishers, 1893), 50.

fine for public and private buildings within an urban context. She was not, though, comfortable with it for suburban and country houses. Her ideal of a dwelling in the country was to let nature dominate and the building assume a secondary, nonassertive posture. In her 1893 chapter for Candice Thurber Wheeler's *Household Art,* she wrote, "Nor is the irregularity of our plans [for suburban and country houses] really a defect. We ought not to be content with the simpler, more formalized planning of French houses."[92]

Just as she felt more at ease with the simplicity and informality of the naturalistic garden, she also responded more deeply to the informality of the wood and stone-clad dwellings of the late Queen Anne–Colonial revival (the Shingle style). In her article on the Eastlake style (Stick style) Fairman Rogers house at Newport, Rhode Island (1874, designed by the Philadelphia architect Frank Furness), she wrote, "In Newport, where the architecture is so varied, it is easy to see how great the latitude is and how quickly this sympathy between the house and its environment, or lack of it is felt. An instance of this sympathy is in the house of Mr. Fairman Rogers at Ochre Point. There is nothing striking in its appearance, but it makes an integral part of the landscape, and only on close inspection does it appear with what art this effect is secured."[93]

Though Van Rensselaer admired the composite version of the late Queen Anne and Colonial style country houses, still she obviously felt more at home with the more reserved and refined examples of this domestic architecture. In some cases, she argued against the shingle cladding of country houses, as she felt that this mode of sheathing was too vernacular, too primitive. Nor did she feel comfortable with every instance of H. H. Richardson's cultivated primitivism, such as one finds in the great rough stones used to clothe his Ames Gate Lodge at North Easton, Massachusetts. "Richardson on occasion," she wrote, " . . . reproduces the almost barbaric strength and exuberance of the Romanesque days without due remembrance that those days were unlike our own, and that the unlikeness springs from our greater intellectual refinement."[94]

92. Ibid., 40.

93. Van Rensselaer, "Newport Villas: Mr. Fairman Rogers's" (1881), 3. The Rogers house, "Fairholm," was a large Eastlake residence which was built in 1874. It was known and written about because of its extensive gardens. See George Mason, *Newport and Its Villas* (Newport, 1875), 82–84.

94. Van Rensselaer, "American Country Dwellings, III" (1896), 429–430.

Although Van Rensselaer was, as we have already noted, highly complimentary of the design of McKim, Mead and White's Madison Square Garden, she still had several reservations. A building for entertainment should, as she pointed out, be festive, but still she felt a good design called for some degree of reserve: "But if we examine more particularly into the designs of the ornamental motives themselves, we feel that the proper degree of sumptuousness has been achieved at some cost of refinement . . . in short, the ornament of the Garden looks best from a distance. Then the eye cannot analyze all its detail." [95]

6

Van Rensselaer's writings on landscape architecture and architecture are most understandable if we put them in the context of her many pieces devoted to the country-scape or the cityscape. Her first extensive excursion into studies of the environment was her small 1895 volume, *Allegheny Mountains,* based upon her observations in western Pennsylvania, where she had briefly lived with her husband in 1878.[96] Her approach in this piece and others was to let her description of nature, the terrain, and the climate and its vegetation dominate. She also provided a history of the region and a comment on man's "improvements" to the place. The contrasting play between that which is native to the place and man's new order is beautifully captured in her poetic mode of writing. "The drives are very beautiful throughout all of this region. It is hard to say which are more lovely, the open highways, where the eye sweeps the far-receding hill-tops, or the narrow dark, and odorous tunnels through the forest primeval." [97]

In striking contrast, she observed of the newly developed railroads and steel industry of this region of the Alleghenies, "A solitary locomotive, symmetrical, polished, docile, glides slowly over our heads. Surely it is alive in this magic midnight,—a living, magnificent child of steam and iron and man's intelligence. Gigantic level rays from the Bessemer building far behind us fall upon it. . . . Is there no poetry in our nineteenth century and its work? Is there no majesty, no impressiveness, no food for the imagination, in its iron, and steam, and flame, and speed

95. Van Rensselaer, "The Madison Square Garden" (1894), 743.
96. Van Rensselaer, *Allegheny Mountains* (Philadelphia: Allen, Lane and Scott, 1885). Sections of this book had been published earlier in *Lippincott's Magazine.*
97. Ibid., 11.

and power?" [98] Such an ode to the machine seems to go back to the 1850s with Horatio Greenough's arguments for functionalism, while the poetic imagery of her description anticipates the passionate worship of the machine upon the part of the twentieth-century Italian Futurists.

It was in Van Rensselaer's writings for *The Century Magazine,* in such pieces as "Fifth Avenue" and "Picturesque New York," that she asked her readers to experience a part of the urban environment rather than concentrate their attention on individuals buildings.[99] Her approach in all of these environmental writings was to go back in time and then proceed to the present moment. Always, it was not just the man-made physical aspects which demanded her attention, rather it was the inner relationship between these artifacts, people, and nature.

In "People in New York," her supposed subjects were those who inhabited the place, but in fact she ends up by bringing in a wide variety of environmental issues ranging from a wonderful description of the elevated railroad to penetrating criticism of laissez-faire capitalism which had produced such bitter poverty. In Van Rensselaer's hand the city of New York City emerged as a revealing example of Uvedale Price's eighteenth-century "picturesque." In speaking of the picturesque and New York she wrote, "If I must attempt a bit of defining myself—it is made up of harmonious and alien elements. It must have some elements which speak to the aesthetic sense and also some which speak to that love of sharp and telling contrast, to that delight in the fortuitous and surprising, which is equally innate in our souls." [100] Her approach to the picturesque included not only the physical urban landscape but also people and, above all, the passing of time. "But the deliberate hand of man has, during this period [the years from the mid-1860s through the early 1890s], done for New York almost as flame did for Chicago. Old New York has been torn down, and another city has arisen on its site." [101]

The breadth of Van Rensselaer's writings on the nonurban environment, especially within the pages of *Garden and Forest,* is remarkable. Some of these and others of her writings provided her readers with a poetic as well as analytical look at individual places ranging from the al-

98. Ibid., 40.

99. Van Rensselaer, "Fifth Avenue" (1893), 5–18; "Picturesque New York" (1892), 164–175.

100. Van Rensselaer, "Picturesque New York" (1892), 164.

101. Ibid., 175.

ready mentioned small book *Allegheny Mountains* to intimate yet critical looks at Newport and Nantucket. Other pieces explored parts of the New England countryside: "July on the Shores of Buzzard Bay" or "Early Autumn near Cape Cod." All of these writings ask us to experience the present with a strong awareness of the past. All indicate an extraordinary understanding of horticulture and the physical environment. Her approach in each of these writings was to first capture the place in its smallest details and then to conclude with a sensitive, broad view. She concluded her piece on Nantucket in this fashion: "But, nowhere else on our coast is there so broad an expanse of uncultivated land, so simple as regards large features, so varied as regards those of minor size, so impressive in a general view, so interesting to the eye of minute examination." [102]

In several other articles she turned her attention to "roadside improvements." Using examples which she was familiar with on or near the Cape, she argued for letting the individuality of nature dominate the sides of our roads. She thought that we should not attempt to inject a single regional or national uniformity to our roadsides. The pressing needs for privately sponsored organizations to watch over and "improve" local environments formed the subject of "The Good Work of an Improvement Association at Narragansett Pier." "But the main thing," she wrote, "to be noted in the change that has been quickly worked in this summer resort is not individual beauty of this plant or of that, or of these grounds or those, but the general improvement in the aspect of the village as a whole." [103]

One of the most remarkable examples of her environmental sensitivity is the chapter "Changes," which she added to the 1925 edition of her *Art Out-of-Doors*. One of her subjects in this chapter was the relationship between the expanding suburbias, the countryside, and the automobile. "I have implied that the automobile, born only twenty-five years ago, has largely helped to alter for us the conditions of country life." [104] While she recognized the good that the automobile had accomplished, she also had a number of reservations. She gently chided planners and landscape architects to design roads and highways which were in sympathy with the landscape. Taking on even broader issues,

102. Van Rensselaer, "A Glimpse of Nantucket" (1888), 448.
103. Van Rensselaer, "The Good Work of an Improvement Association" (1895), 309.
104. Van Rensselaer, *Art Out-of-Doors* (1925), 409.

she took Mumford to task for asserting that the 1893 Chicago exposition had "checked natural development" by advocating Beaux Arts Classicism.[105] She reiterated the point which she had made in her writings at the time of the fair that what counted in both the Chicago and Buffalo expositions was that they "implanted among us a belief in the beauty of concord, of harmony, in the need for organization, for cooperation in the arts."[106]

7

A final comment should be made relating to Van Rensselaer's literary style. Her ideal in writing perfectly matched her views on architecture, landscape architecture, and the environment; namely, it employed a simple, direct, and unpretentious use of language. It conveyed a cultivated ease which by implication mirrored her social position in New York society. While the vocabulary she used was rich and varied, she employed it to help, not hinder, our understanding of what she was writing about. Though a number of her writings were accompanied by illustrations, it is obvious that she did not feel that these were absolutely essential for her presentation. In such major works as *Art Out-of-Doors* or in her series of articles in *Garden and Forest* on the history of landscape architecture, no illustrations were provided, nor were they really needed. As a writer she took on the task of rendering word-pictures which she hoped would portray the building, garden, or landscape she was discussing.

It might be argued that her contemporary readers had, in many instances, the advantage of being able to draw on their own firsthand remembrances of the subject she was discussing. But while such personal acquaintanceship would perhaps have enriched the reader's response to her writings, they are not in fact essential. We, today, can easily read them without having any personal firsthand experience. Her careful craftsmanship in the art of writing was such that the word did not rely on accompanying visual images. The only cautionary note for the reader (both then and now) is that many of her writings are rich in ideas being expressed, and one must read them with great care. Her central themes are always apparent, but she often leads her reader off in various directions which either enrich or even in some instances counter her major thesis.

105. Ibid., 416.
106. Ibid., 417.

Van Rensselaer's writings on the landscape, on landscape architecture, and on architecture reveal how perceptive was her understanding of what her age was about (for bad, as well as good). Yet, there is a classical quality present in her writings which makes them extremely applicable to the present. Perhaps the main reason for the relevance of her writings for us today is her broad environmental approach coupled with her knowledge of the specific (whether it be the species of plants or the nature of a color to be used for details within a building). Finally, she had a sense of tolerance and willingness to entertain varying points of view in her writings, which was needed when she wrote and certainly is even more so today.

Though most of her writings convey a sense of the rational, of objectivity, and of calmness, she was not ambivalent in expressing her critical judgments. She did not mince words when she wrote of the late 1870s restoration of the German Romanesque palace of Henry IV at Goslar that those responsible for its restoration had produced a "lie." [107] Speaking of the architects involved with this restoration she observed that, "men have been found to maim and desecrate and sheathe with falsehood the great Romanesque palace of the Hartz." [108] And in contrast to most of her contemporaries, she was not at all enamored with John Ruskin and his writings and his work as an artist. When she encountered an exhibition of his drawings in New York, she wrote, "There is little that is original or peculiar in the work. . . . The catalogue is the most important part of the exhibition,— of more worth without the drawings than they with its comments." [109] She went on to note that we shall "be struck by the fact that there is not a *picture* among them." [110]

Van Rensselaer's evolution as a critic represents a fascinating personal comment as well as a comment on her time. Her first writings tended to the specific and often were conditioned by her purely aesthetic response. Thus a good number of her pieces written in the decade of the 1870s are concerned with art as art. These were followed in the 1880s by a general shift towards architecture and then landscape architecture. By the time that she published *Art Out-of-Doors*, it was the broad environment which commanded her attention. Then in the late

107. Van Rensselaer, "The Restorations at Goslar" (1878), 120–121.
108. Ibid., 121.
109. Mariana Griswold Van Rensselaer, "Mr. Ruskin's Drawings" (1880), 72.
110. Ibid., 72.

1890s and early 1900s she seemed to have turned inward, writing history and publishing her poems. But even in the decades after 1900 she sallied forth again and again with perceptive pieces which addressed broad issues, such as the formation of public taste or the impact of the automobile on suburbia.

In a 1923 article, "American Art and the Public," she commented not only on the needs of public art, but on her own requirements as a critic, "But expression is naught unless it is also communication. To be articulate is naught if one cannot also be audible."[111] Her voice indeed was strong, perceptive, and audible. Through her writings it is possible for us today to critically appraise many aspects of the late-nineteenth-century American scene.

111.   Van Rensselaer, "American Art and the Public" (1923), 637.

PART I

Architecture and the Decorative Arts

Architecture as a Profession

The practice of architecture stands upon a different footing from the practice of the other arts. We enjoy the products of these, but it can hardly be said we *use* them, and we can do without them if we will. But buildings we use, and buildings we must have. Choice only comes in play to decide whether those who construct them for us shall be artisans or artists, "builders" or "architects." Therefore, however truly the latter name may be deserved, architectural artists cannot be artists only. Theirs is not a pure art, but a craft in which esthetic and practical elements meet and work together—in which not beauty merely but beauty *and* serviceableness must be considered. And they are never independent creators but always executives of the wishes of others, intrusted with a succession of tasks of very definite kinds. In short, when architecture is recognized as an art for which there is a wide spread need, it takes its place among the liberal professions—side by side with theology, medicine, and law.

Thus, fortunately, it has come to stand in America today. Had one been asked twenty years ago which of our arts showed least signs of vitality, which gave the least promise of development into a stage marked by general seriousness of effort and by results at once good in quality and national in feeling, the answer would doubtless have been, Architecture.

The Chautauquan 7 (May 1887): 451–454.

And had one then been asked in which of the arts our public took the smallest interest, the reply would assuredly have been the same. Yet to-day the average American architect (at least of the younger generation) is, I think, more intelligently in earnest with his work and better endowed for its execution than the average American painter, sculptor, poet, or musician. In no other art have we so many men who rise above the average with work that is exceptionally good and, in the true sense of the word, original. And in no other has yet appeared a man who is so emphatically to be called a man of genius as the late H. H. Richardson.

Popular interest is growing with the growth of things to feed upon. It has not quite kept pace with their development; the public does not yet appreciate at their veritable value the best among our recent buildings. But the most important sentiment is rapidly widening and deepening. Year by year we recognize more clearly the difference between true architecture and mere construction, and the infinitely greater value of the former. Year by year those clients grow in number who desire that even the most simply utilitarian of structures shall be made a work of art—even a factory, a railroad station, a warehouse, or a barn. We want more architects than our fathers wanted, and we require of them much more accomplished service. The builder's trade is as flourishing as ever, but above it there now stands a well established, highly honored, lucrative architectural profession.

One more path is thus opened to those young Americans who desire to put their brains as well as their hands to use. But it is not a path which should heedlessly be entered or which can easily be trodden to genuine success. Architecture has always covered a wide field—from engineering on the one hand to decoration on the other; and even he who means to devote himself to some particular part of this field must begin by learning something of its whole extent. Moreover, wide though it has always been, it is far wider to-day than in earlier centuries, and presents a greater variety of problems, and allows a greater diversity of materials and consequently of constructive processes. The use we make of iron, for instance, has vastly enlarged the sum of the knowledge that the conscientious student should acquire.

Let us see what would be the ideal education for such a student in our day and land:—

In the first place he should have a good school education followed by a full academic college course. Without this he will not be able either to study his art or to carry on his subsequent practice to the best advantage.

To study his art to the best advantage means, for instance, that he must acquaint himself with all the forms bequeathed by earlier ages, and must learn, not only what they are, but how they came to be and wherefore they were used. If he does not do this, he will be unable to use the elements of his art intelligently and easily when his own time comes to build; and to do it requires such a thorough understanding of the outer and inner history of nations as can only rest upon a basis of wide general culture. Again, an acquaintance with French, at least, among the modern languages is essential. And still again, the broadest, deepest cultivation is demanded for the fostering of that precious quality called *taste*.

Then, to practice his art to the best advantage, an architect must be able to meet any possible client upon equal intellectual terms. No other artist comes into such direct personal contact with his patrons. No other has such a need to understand what *they* want, as well as what he wants himself. No other is so dependent for a chance to do his best, upon his power to influence their judgment, to control their wishes, to fall in with and yet guide and elevate their tastes. *Tact*—which means a keen insight into other minds and a perfect control of one's own mind and tongue—is desirable in every relationship of life, but absolutely essential if one would succeed in architecture. And tact grows best and quickest through such commerce with cultivated men of various aims and ages as college life supplies.

The next necessity would be a course of special training in one of our architectural schools; the best being those connected with Columbia College in New York City and with the Technological Institute in Boston. Two or three years are required for such a course which includes instruction in the history of the art, in mathematics and mechanics, in draughting and designing, and in various other necessary matters. This foundation gained, at least a year or two should be passed in the office of some practicing architect where theoretic knowledge is put to practical tests and where a thousand things are learned that no school can teach. Then and then only, a foreign journey should be made. Another year or two should be passed in some European school (preferably by far in the *École des Beaux Arts,* in Paris), and as many months as possible should be devoted to travel. And travel should mean serious study too. No superficial sight-seeing will serve the would-be artist's turn. Not the mere attractiveness of the things before him must fix his attention, but their usefulness with regard to the work he himself will have to do. He must examine new buildings as well as old ones, humble buildings as well as monumental, details as well as major features, and, it need hardly be added, methods no less than results. And he must familiarize himself with all those accessory arts and handicrafts which will be called upon to complete his future works, must learn what is meant by good decorative painting and sculpture, good glass and iron, wood carving, furniture and stuffs.

I dwell at length upon these necessities because they make it clear why courses of technical training, of historical study and of practical work at home should precede a European trip. To see before one has learned how to see is not to see at all. To learn before one knows what to learn is a waste of time and effort. "If you send a boy to Paris when he is fresh from college or even from an architectural school," I heard an architect say not long ago, "he will lose the best part of his opportunity. Every day he spends in an office before he goes abroad will show him *what he wants most to know*—will give him a new peg upon which to hang, ready for future use, some valuable fact or illuminative idea." Once I asked a young man who had been for several years with a prominent New York firm, why he had never been to Europe. He replied, "I can only count upon going once, and I am waiting till I know enough"; and yet he already knew so much that he had been entrusted by his firm with the design and construction of more than one important building.

This, I repeat, is the ideal education for an American architect to-day. It costs much money as well as labor, and consumes so much time that an independent start in life must be deferred till the thirtieth birthday is approaching. But it is the education which not a few of our best architects have thought essential. And though the proportioning of its years between home and foreign study may be varied, no great deduction from the total sum of those years can be made if the best is to be done for that inborn talent which, of course, I presuppose. In Mr. Richardson's day, for example, the facilities for thorough study at home were by no means what they are now. But he had had a four years' course at Harvard College before he went to Paris. In Paris he studied diligently for almost seven years. And, as during much of that time he was obliged to support himself by working in architects' offices, he gained practical as well as theoretic knowledge before he came home to make his start in life.

But ideals are not always possible of attainment even in education. Here, therefore, are some sensible words to show the simplest and shortest rational way of getting an architectural training. They are quoted from a letter, not meant for publication, recently written by an architect to a would-be student.

"You are unwise to spend time or money in preparation for a business for which you may be entirely unfitted. Doubtless your architectural tastes are good. Then go to some library and look through the cuts in the architectural journals for the last two or three years and note the names of those architects whose work you admire. Write to some of these men and find who will receive you. It is customary in the larger towns for new pupils to pay for the privilege of office instruction (which they may or may not receive); but doubtless some one will be willing to receive you if you say, 'I wish to work for a few months until I can tell whether it is feasible for me to study architecture.' At least that was my good fortune (I stayed five years). There is great diversity in the management of offices. In some you will be able to see and hear all sides of the matter, and in others the work is subdivided and specialized so that it will take many months to gain a fair idea of an architect's many duties and perplexities; and these are what you must see for yourself to appreciate.

"During this probation you will learn to 'trace' and 'fill in' and will do well to stipulate for late morning hours (say 10 or 10:30) so that you may daily have some time to sketch and examine the work under way. This division of time is best because you will be less observed in the morning and will be on hand during busy office hours to see, hear, and learn. If you decide to enter the profession, take advice from different architects with regard to course of study and place of pursuing it. But do not bind yourself to anything that will debar you from office practice which you should pursue for some hours daily through your entire course. This will accustom you to that balance of work and study which every architect must maintain through life."

The advice contained in these last words is too narrow to be taken unless necessity compels. In the majority of cases a student would hardly have sufficient strength of mind or body to combine office work with *thorough* participation in the work of a school, supplemented as this certainly should be by much private reading and practice with the pencil. But one thing is certain: both practical knowledge and theoretical knowledge must be gained somehow and at some time. The more of each, the better; and the more strictly the one is made to fit into and supplement and illustrate the other, the better once again. If circumstances are such that no school can possibly be attended, a large amount of theoretic knowledge may yet be gained from books and photographs. Many architectural books are very costly, but some of the costlier are to be found in most public libraries; and a good workman in any branch

knows that he can never spend his money half so well as upon the tools
of his trade. And here I would insist again upon the absolute necessity
of a knowledge of French. If it were a means of reading nothing more
than Viollet-le-Duc's great "Dictionary", it would still be very needful.
But in fact the larger part of the best extant literature of the art—technical, descriptive, historical, or simply suggestive of general aims and
ideas—is closed and sealed to those who read English only. Moreover, if
a man knows French, a brief stay—and the briefest is of priceless
value—can be made at very small expense in that land which contains
the best architectural school and the finest examples of both medieval
and modern work. Travel on foot is the best as well as the cheapest sort
for the student, but a difficult sort if he does not understand the local
tongue.

The prizes now offered by the architectural profession are very great
in the way of honor. And in the way of minted gold they are considerable, though not nearly so rich as those proffered, for example, by the
law. But it is already a crowded profession; and at least in the large eastern cities it seems to be over-crowded. Experiences are seen to differ, of
course, if one looks into them. I know of some firms in New York and
Boston which have more business than they can well manage. And I
hear of others, quite as long established, which at times are almost idle.
I know of certain young men, newly out of famous offices or newly
home from foreign study, who have started without delay upon careers
that promise to be brilliantly successful; yet of others, equally well
trained and able, who do not dare to "set up for themselves", but prefer the safe obscurity of subordinate service. The farther west one looks,
the less crowded the profession seems. But then, the farther one goes
west, the less, generally speaking, will be found the demand for architectural *art*. And as our new gospel of art was first preached on the Atlantic sea-board, it will also be found, quite naturally perhaps, that
when important architectural service *is* required in the far west, an eastern firm is often preferred above all local aspirants. The very best
chance for a young architect to day, I think, is to connect himself for a
considerable time with some well-known eastern firm and then to "go
west" with the prestige of its name behind him.

Social as well as geographical position also counts for something in
the chances of success. So intimate is the temporary relationship between client and architect that we cannot wonder or condemn if the former sometimes chooses his executive chiefly for the reason that he is a
friend or relative or that, although a stranger, he belongs to the same so-

cial stratum as himself. A single act of choice made for no other reason than this, may start a young architect on a prosperous career simply by giving him an opportunity to show the very best that he can do; while another, equally able to do well, may wait years for similar permission. For if he respects himself and his art, he will not be willing to engage in those unbusiness-like and undignified contests called "unpaid" or "open" competitions; and "limited," "paid" competitions, into which certain architects are asked to enter, are largely controlled by the same influences which affect definite private commissions. But it must of course be added that the best of chances will profit none but the capable. A man is lucky if he is promptly started in life with an order to build a big house for his first-cousin. But if he builds it big and bad, he can hardly reckon upon a continuance of even family patronage.

Personal bearing and address count for infinitely more in the long run, than the most "valuable connection." And this brings me back to the point I made with regard to general culture. Wherever the student's lot may be cast, however narrow may be his opportunities for technical training, let him try his very best to train his mind, his taste, his perceptions, and his manners. "Manners Makyth Man" was the device of William of Wykeham; and it was a singularly appropriate device for one who was not only a great prelate, courtier, and patron of education but also one of the very greatest architects England has ever borne.

When I speak of the necessity resting upon an architect to meet his clients, whoever they may be, on equal intellectual terms, and to influence, direct, and in a certain sense control them, I do not mean that he must have a mere glib tongue, still less that his attitude should be marked by the quality our boys call "cheek." I mean that his address should be of the same sort and his influence of the same kind as those which distinguish the legal or the medical adviser to whom, within his special province, all other men naturally and gladly defer. Intrinsic force of mind and character, real knowledge, well based self-reliance, genuine cultivation, are the only grounds upon which such true power can rest. Any one who knew Mr. Richardson knows this. His personal force and charm were quite as remarkable as his artistic talent, and to their influence was very largely due the extraordinarily good opportunity which he secured for the exercise of this talent. Had his general education been less thorough he would have had a far less firm, comprehensive, and pliant grasp upon his artistic ideas. And had he been less the cultivated, silver-tongued, strong-willed yet genial gentleman, he would never have persuaded men to allow him to express those ideas so fully.

"How can a man build a house to suit a gentleman if he does not himself know how a gentleman likes to live?" These words, spoken the other day by an intending client, may seem both superficial and narrow in their bearing. But a deep meaning and one of widest application may be read into them. How can a man do intelligent, refined, and beautiful work in this complicated art unless he is himself intelligent and refined, and broad as well as keen in his perception of what beauty means? And why should he be allowed to try, in an art where the result is so permanent and so costly, unless he can clearly convince a client of his fitness?

As regards those inborn qualifications which must be considered before this or any profession is chosen, there is something important to be said.

Perhaps no one should paint or carve who cannot be reasonably sure of producing examples of the best work of which the chisel or the brush is capable. Perhaps a third rate painter or sculptor leads neither a worthy nor a charitable life. But architecture is a necessary trade as well as an art. Its work *must* be done, and as nature is not likely ever to give us geniuses in sufficient number to do the whole of it, the second or third rate architect is a very necessary and valuable citizen. All our architectural work cannot be great, but all of it ought to be good; and fair intelligence, earnest study, and conscientious effort may make it good, though only a high artistic gift can make it great. Moreover, there is a business side as well as a practical and an esthetic side to architectural practice. The architect's relations with his clients upon the one hand and with his artisans upon the other, are very complicated and far-reaching and often involve the expenditure of enormous sums of money. To quote from the letter already once cited: "The architectural artist is frequently worried into an early grave by business details unless he is so fortunate as to meet and harmoniously combine with the other half of his professional being, the capable man of affairs." A student may resign himself to holding the place of business partner in a firm if he finds his talents unequal to a more conspicuous place, and may still feel that he is doing his art good service. Again, the management of those details of interior construction which involve the use of iron may be assumed as a specialty, or combined with business management if mathematical and mechanical, prove greater than purely esthetic, ability.

In conclusion I would say that an inborn "gift for drawing" is not so sure a sign of architectural ability as is popularly thought. Such a gift, if combined with others, is of course a valuable possession. But given good perceptive powers—and without these let us hope that no one will think of architecture as his profession—the hand can be cultivated to a degree of skill which will answer all fundamental needs. To sketch an old building charmingly is by no means synonymous with studying it intelligently or even with making a helpful drawing of its forms. A pretty original drawing does not necessarily mean a design for a good building, nor does the lack of ability to make such a drawing imply the want of constructive imagination. Half a dozen young men who have passed through his office can draw more beautifully than Mr. Richardson could; and during all the busiest years of his life he rarely took a pencil in his hand except to make a rough little first sketch or to hint at alterations in the drawings of his subordinates.

Client and Architect

Fancy a painter unable to make pictures except when some one says to him: Paint now, paint this or that, and paint it thus and so; or a poet or musician forced to wait for similar behests, and getting them, very often, in the shape of uncongenial themes and narrow limitations. Imagine this and you will realize the architect's actual position, and the contrast between his life and that of other artists. Of course, the difference is neither accidental nor designed, but inevitable. It is the natural result of the fact that architecture is not an art pure and simple. It has a practical side. Its products are not mere objects of beauty. They are useful objects made beautiful, and they cannot be spun out of the artist's brain, but must cost a great deal of money. When useful, costly things which take up a great deal of space are in question, demand must precede supply. The poet or the painter caters to the public's taste; the architect serves the public's express wishes.

These facts mean two things. They mean that the architect must be something more than an artist, and that the client has a part to play which is only less important—which from one point of view is even more important—than the architect's own. As neither perfectly fulfills his duty in America to-day, it may be worth while to define in brief what that duty is. Let us begin with the client.

North American Review 151 (September 1890): 319–328.

I

The client—whether a unit or that multiple of units called a commit-tee—should remember that architecture is not practical only, but that its æsthetic side is as inevitable and important as the utilitarian, should re-alize that he who meddles with artistic things owes a duty to others as well as to himself, and know that this is especially the case when the re-sult is to stand conspicuously before the public eye. It is false to say that there are structures which need not be "architectural" at all; that men may build at times, yet put all thoughts of art aside. Everything that ever was built is a good work of architecture or a bad one. If it plainly shows that its builders did not even try to make it good, it is only the more inexcusably bad. We are not naïve savages. We know that if a man is hungry for food or for beauty our obligation is the same, and we must give him the best that opportunity allows. When we insist that our neighbors shall daily look upon barrenness or deformity, when we fill what before was placid, empty space with crying shapes of ugliness, we are bad citizens, brutal neighbors. Some one has said that to build a hideous house is to indulge in the worst form of selfishness, and I am not sure that he exaggerated much.

Thus the client, whatever he means to build, should look about him for an architect, in the sense of a man who values at its highest the artis-tic side of every problem, great or small, elaborate or simple, and has thoroughly prepared himself to treat it. This is the first and the great commandment: an artist is needed for an "unimportant" as well as for an "important" building. Indeed, these words should not be used as they commonly are; for architectural things are most important in their aggregate, and in making up this aggregate it is the smaller units which play the larger part. If every twenty-five-foot house in New York could be made truly excellent, inside and out, would we not gladly give in ex-change our few large and sumptuous buildings?

The second commandment is that when we set an artist to work we should let him work as freely as possible. "Undoubtedly," you may say; "but who is to decide just what is meant by these words?" In a letter I received not long ago from an American architect I find the following answer; it may sound startling, but, believe me, none could be more true and wise:

"The public must first learn to trust us as it does lawyers or doctors, before architecture can develop into a great art. Only when a public has learned to put its interests in building into the hands of trustees who are architects, can the latter do their best work. Any examples otherwise produced are accidental and not healthful developments."

That is to say, the architect's client should reason with himself somewhat in this fashion: Here is a problem to be solved which is very difficult, as demanding both a practical and an artistic solution. Here is a man whose profession it is to deal with such problems. The respect I feel for professional skill in other directions, artistic or practical, as the case may be, I should now feel with double strength. Of course, I must tell him exactly what I want, as I must describe my state of body to my doctor or my business tangle to my man-of-law. But, this done, I should feel sure that he will know best how my wants can be supplied. Of course, he is working for me, but so is my doctor, so is my lawyer. I am not more interested in the outcome of his efforts than of theirs; it is not a sign of folly, a confession of disgraceful ignorance, to defer to professional skill when they are concerned: the folly would be, and the ignorance and disgrace, did I try to doctor myself or to plead my own cause, or, after engaging some one more competent to do it for me, did I dictate to him, cavil at him, and hamper his hand at every turn. And by just so much as art is more subtile and, so to say, more professional than anything else, by just so much ought I to be most modest, most scrupulous, most trusting, when her ministrants are at work for me.

But this, American Public, is exactly what you do not say to yourself, except of very recent years, and in the very rarest instances. You do not see that it is just as foolish to refuse professional help in building as in law or medicine, and a great deal more selfish; nor, when you ask an architect's help, do you follow and help him with half enough docility and trust. You must have your own say about his work, and your own share of credit if it succeeds. Truly, you own the result. But it belongs also to the artist and to the world at large, and their interests are quite as important as your own. The architect, it cannot be said too often, works only when you give him the chance, and only as you permit. Just now our art is in a transition stage. This is a crucial time, when every effort is of such importance that you would be glad to escape from all responsibility, eager to shift it all upon the architect, if you were only a little less ignorant with regard to the depth of your own ignorance. What you ought to know is that in any profession, and especially in so complicated a one as this, the weakest professional is likely to do better than the cleverest amateur.

Whatever you want, then, go to an architect for it; not to a carpenter, or a mason, or your own still more profound incompetence. Tell him all your practical, material desires, and insist that they shall be respected. That is to say, if you are quite sure what they are, and quite certain that it is possible to respect them. This is by no means always the case. To be unsettled, vague, self contradictory, unpractical, impossible, is one of your most common faults, and one for the inevitable results of which you are only too apt to blame your architect. Settle your practical desires and state them clearly; and, if you will, pour out your vague æsthetic wishes; try to explain those crude artistic preferences, those misty, formless visions which you are pleased to call "my own ideas." But then go home, and leave him who is a trained artist, an experienced planner and constructor, to work out your problem in his own way. If what you get is exactly what you want, be very thankful; say that you are; and give the credit where credit is due. And if what you get is not quite all you want, or exactly what you think it ought to be, why, be thankful still; for the chances are (nay, the certainty is) that, had you interfered, the result would have been more unsatisfactory still.

This, then, American Public, is, as I conceive it, your duty in matters architectural. Or—for I must now confess that I have been playing the part of special pleader—this would be your duty, everywhere and always, and without possibility of doubt, if the architectural profession also recognized its duty clearly and was unanimously bent on its fulfillment.

II

In turning now to you, The Profession, can it be said that you have no shortcomings? Are there not many things in your attitude towards your client and towards your art which must be reformed, if you, if he, and if that art are to profit and to prosper as they should? Of course, you will agree that the public should trust you as it trusts the legal or the medical profession. But are you sure that you deserve to be trusted to quite the same extent? We are pretty certain that any lawyer or physician "in good standing" will do his very best for us. He may be stupid, but he is not likely to be uneducated, careless, or unfaithful. Theory would teach us to have the same confidence in you; but does experience prove that we always can? When we ask you and pay you to do a certain definite thing, can we feel confident that you will know how best to do it, and will do it as exactly as you can? that you will not slight it in favor of more interesting work, and will not causelessly alter it into something more like your own idea of what we ought to want? Can we feel confident that, if the task is small and cheap, you will approach it as carefully as though it were large and costly, or that, when we name the sum we want to pay, you will scrupulously respect the limitation, and scrupulously give us the most and the best you can within it? Many men in other professions sin by making things cost more in the end than they said they would in the beginning; but do they sin as frequently, frankly, and light-heartedly, or with as many specious maxims in excuse, as you? Do not say that the conditions differ. Of course they do, and of course in your case they are singularly complex and difficult. But your responsibility is increased, not lessened, by the fact. If it is peculiarly hard for you to make your clients understand the difference between a desirable or necessary increase in cost and an increase which comes merely from wilfulness, carelessness, selfish ambition, or stupidity on your part, then it is peculiarly needful that you should never be careless or selfish or more stupid than poor mortality is sometimes allowed to be. If it is essential that your client should have more confidence in you than in his lawyer or physician, then you should be still more conscientious. You should work unusually hard to inspire that trust which to you, and to the general progress of your art, is so absolutely indispensable. And this I do not think that, as a profession viewed in the mass, you yet have done.

I know that as a whole—as an Architectural Profession really worthy of the name, as something different from a mere body of building creatures—you are very young in America. Every one who cares for our art must recognize this fact, must see in your youth lusty strength, right ambition, and healthful promise; must have followed your progress thus far with admiration, and must believe in your future. If you could hear all that is said about you by serious and critical observers, I am afraid you would grow conceited. You are by no means conceited now. Indeed, you hardly realize as yet what surprisingly good work you have done as compared, not with your fathers only, but with your rivals over sea. Yet with all the respect, gratitude, and admiration that they feel for you, I think such observers see that you have faults, and that they are faults of character rather than of artistic endowment. Now, faults of character do not greatly matter with artists who paint or carve or even write, but with you they matter in the most vital way. An architect cannot shut himself up in his closet. He must come in contact with the public both as artist and as man; the public must trust him, while it need only weigh the poet and the painter after the act; and their product it may take or leave, while it is obliged to keep whatever you bestow. Therefore it is that, as men and artists, you must set yourselves a lofty standard. You must respect yourselves, respect each other, respect your client, and respect your art (each for its own sake and always all together), if you have any hope that the public will do the same.

Let me hasten to say that there are some among you who fulfill this ideal. There are American architects who come pretty near to being models of all an architect should be. That is,—for I want to explain myself quite clearly,—they have prepared themselves in a thorough, all-round way to deserve the professional title; they think in the first place of their art and what it demands of them, in the second place of their client and his inalienable rights, and only in the third place of themselves; and in thinking of themselves it is still for art they care more than for pecuniary profit. To do all this means much labor and constant self-abnegation. But they know that they are artists, and if they did not mean to do it all, ought they to pretend to the artist's name or standing or reward?

Does this look like a fancy picture in your eyes, American Public? It is a faithful portrait, drawn from more than one original. As a picture of the whole profession it would, indeed, be flattered; yet it ought to be such a picture; and until it is, or, at least, until some distinct approach is made to the qualities it exhibits, the profession as a whole will never win the position it should, the public as a whole will never take the attitude it ought, and our art as a whole will never have the best chance of development. I may quote again, as a summing-up, from the letter already cited. It was written hastily for private reading, not as a formal confession of faith, but is, therefore, all the more significant.

"I have never spoken to you on the subject of the responsibility of my profession in this new country, where we have to create its status, but I feel its importance most keenly. The public must first learn to trust us as it does doctors or lawyers, before architecture can develop into a great art. . . . Therefore, every architect, no matter what his genius, who shows any lack of conscience or devotion to the responsibility his client has laid upon him, does more to ruin the cause of true architectural advance than any design of his creation can counterbalance. . . . I am proud of the men in my office. Thus far they have been but average fellows, but all seem quickly to feel the responsibility and dignity of their profession, and learn to accept the self-restraint and sacrifice it entails. . . . Of myself I may say that I have never yet had a chance to do anything great, but I have been patiently fitting myself for that opportunity (should it ever come) by trying my best and uttermost on everything, no

matter how unimportant it may be; and I do not really think that anything has ever passed through the hands of our firm that greater care
could at the time have improved."

Is not this, in truth, the heart of the matter—loyal trust on the client's
part, loyal service on the architect's? When we say that the architect
should think first of his art, do we not mean that he should prove that
some kind of art may result from the faithful solution of the given problem, instead of trying to produce a higher kind, or a kind easier of production, by wilfully altering the problem? If he reveres his art, and wishes
to make the public revere it, he should never doubt of its capacity. And if
he is sure that in the given problem his capacity cannot keep touch with
the capacity of art, then, as an artist, he has no right to meddle with it—
whatever he might decide to do as a mere money-making man.

III

Which, now, will be more in fault, public or profession, if there does not
soon grow up that happy accord upon which the future of our art depends? If loyal trust is not the rule, and does not always meet with loyal
service, where chiefly rests the responsibility of developing a better state
of things? Chiefly, I think, upon the public; and for several reasons.

In the first place, it is the public which in each given case must take the
initiative. The architect cannot choose his client; the client must choose
his architect, and it is his own fault if today he does not choose a good
one. Then, in the second place, the profession, with all its faults, has certainly gone further than the public on the road to ideal excellence. The
great advance it has made in recent years towards loyal service—which
means, be it remembered, both competent and conscientious service—
has been due to its own right instincts. The public has never asked that
its architects should fit themselves better for their work than they did in
former years; nor when they have thus fitted themselves is it properly
conscious of the fact or properly grateful for it. Do we clearly see the
kind and degree of difference which marks off our good buildings from
our bad ones? Do we so intelligently, so persistently, encourage trained
ability that untrained incompetence need feel greatly discouraged?

Nor are we more careful to foster professional honor and frankness
than to foster true art. That system of competitions which has been supposed the best aid to art and the best protection for the client is an-
swerable for much that we deplore. Open, unpaid competitions are an

abomination. It is folly, and something worse, to ask the members of a respectable profession to show us their ideas for nothing, and to expect to get their best ideas or the ideas of the best among them. Limited, paid competitions, where certain chosen artists are asked to submit schemes for comparison, and are promised a fair reward for their trouble, should stand on a different footing. But they are often managed with so total a lack of respect on the client's part, not only for art, but for mere labor, and so total a disregard for the precepts of business good-faith and common honesty, that they, too, have become a by-word and re-proach. I cannot dwell upon this thorny subject here; those who care to pursue it may take a file of the *American Architect and Building News* and look up the references under the index heading "Competition." Let me only beg of my reader that, whether he be architect or client, he will never countenance in any way an unpaid competition; that, if as a client he shares in the management of a paid one, he will keep the Eighth and Ninth Commandments—will mean what he says and say what he means and stand honestly by his meanings and sayings, and will not try to get something for nothing, or more than he asked for the price he agreed to pay; and that, if as an architect he takes part in such an en-terprise, he will try not to break the Tenth Commandment in deed, or word, or thought.

But a competition is a make-shift thing at best. In the majority of cases an architect should be chosen in the same way as any other pro-fessional adviser. It is easy to discover his standing among members of his own profession, easy to estimate his past results, and easy to draw conclusions from the effect he produces upon you as a man. Or, if all this is not always easy, it is not as hard or as risky as to judge from those architectural drawings which are so misleading to the untrained eye. Of course, it is more difficult to make sure in advance of conscientiousness than of capacity. But, as a general rule (which is not, perhaps, without exceptions), capacity implies at least artistic conscientiousness, for it means thorough preparatory training; and such training means right ambitions, since no strong external pressure has enforced it.

The subject of architectural drawings is too important to be passed over with a word. Much of our trouble in the past has come because the public does not understand that it takes an architect's eye, or, at least, an experienced eye, to read an architectural drawing rightly. At its best it is a conventionalized thing; at its worst it is about as mendacious a thing as one could find. The effects a novice admires most on paper are often the very ones he will not notice or will not admire in the building. The points which on paper seem least important are often those which will tell most strongly in brick or stone. Even that picture which is called a perspective cannot easily be understood; and a plan, a section, an elevation, are not pictures at all, but signs and symbols, which the novice often misconceives most entirely just when he thinks he has un-ravelled every knot. It should be a maxim, therefore, that never in com-petitions of any kind should judgment be pronounced without the tak-ing of expert testimony. The interests of the client and those of the architect both demand that some competent artist, not himself con-cerned in the matter, should be asked—and paid—to explain the sub-mitted designs.

Even apart from competitions, the public's conduct is not what it should be to encourage loyal service. Often enough in all his dealings the client shows a disregard for truth, honesty, and business methods which he would find very shocking were the architect the sinner and he the sufferer. And when the work is complete, he constantly takes credit for good ideas which do not belong to him, blames his architect for de-fects that his own ignorant demands have brought about, and, above all, cries out against an excess in cost that has been necessitated by changes from the original scheme which he himself has suggested.

Finally, our building customs are not yet arranged on a genuine busi-ness basis, and this is chiefly the fault of the public. With the best will in the world, a client rarely knows what he has a right to expect from his architect in the way of executive service, and almost always expects too much. "Superintendence" is a bone of contention between them, and will so remain until the public realizes all that is meant by architectural work, as a combination of art and science, and is willing to pay a fairer price than at present for its proper execution.

In short, the American architect has less reason to trust the American public implicitly than the public has to put confidence in him. Therefore upon the client even more than upon the architect—and yet upon him, too, in no inconsiderable measure—lies at this moment the responsibil-ity of improving our condition in matters architectural. If we are to have that reciprocal loyalty in trust and service from which alone can grow a healthy, prolific, and truly national art, the public must learn to bear itself as intelligently and honorably as the profession does to-day, and thus encourage the profession to still greater conscientiousness.

3

Architectural Fitness

Americans are gradually learning that fitness, appropriateness, is the foundation of all artistic excellence, and, though the lesson is not yet fully acquired, we are making visible progress toward the realization of this quality in our various classes of buildings. The improvement is perhaps most manifest in our country houses, which we design with a more intelligent regard for the requirements of site and environment than we did even ten years ago, and a truer sense of the fact that in such houses simplicity is a cardinal virtue. There has been a reaction against conventionality on the one hand, and against ostentation on the other, and it has been inspired by a new-born feeling for architectural fitness.

But in a reaction men are almost certain to go too far, and so it is not surprising to find that in trying for simplicity we sometimes fall into rudeness. This shows, of course, that we have not fully understood the meaning of fitness as an architectural term; we have remembered that a structure should harmonize with its surroundings, but have forgotten that it should also harmonize with the ideas of cultivated men and women who are the heirs of all the ages, living in a state of superior enlightenment, and inheriting the practical processes as well as the tastes of countless generations of skillful builders. Moreover, in thus trying to express part of the significance of the word fitness, we may miss true

Garden and Forest 5 (August 19, 1891): 385–386.

simplicity; for civilized, intelligent men can produce rude-looking structures only by an effort so deliberate and self-conscious that it lays them open to the charge of affectation.

We cannot object to an Adirondack camp or a fishing-lodge or a hillside studio, be it ever so rough and rude. It is designed as a shelter in a semi-savage sort of existence, and may be as appropriate to the temporary needs and pursuits of its inhabitants as to the wild scenes amid which it stands. But when costly buildings in civilized neighborhoods are built for permanent use in imitation of the materials and methods naturally adopted for temporary homes in the wilderness, it may be questioned whether the interests of true simplicity, or of true appropriateness, are subserved.

The tendency to which we have referred finds many illustrations in the use of boulders, or roughly cut stones, in constructions which should wear a refined and dignified aspect, as well as a simple one. Undoubtedly, this practice has been largely inspired by the example of Richardson. An architect so original, strong and skillful as he could not fail to influence profoundly the general course of his art; and, as with every great master, this influence has been partly for good, partly for evil. Few other buildings in this country, and certainly no other small building, have excited so much attention, been so often described, pictured and discussed as the gardener's lodge which he built, of huge rough boulders, in the village of North Easton, near Boston. It is, indeed, a picturesque and interesting piece of work, but it has certainly been imitated in ways which Richardson never anticipated, and he would have been distressed by a sight of some of the progeny it has engendered.

In certain places and for certain purposes the use of boulders, whether large or small, is not only allowable, but praiseworthy. It is both sensible and appropriate to use them, for example, in the foundations or the basement of a country house on land where they abound and can be had at little cost and trouble. But even in such spots as this it is seldom desirable that whole houses should be built of them, for we do not want an American country home to wear the aspect at once rude, unrefined and ponderous, which their sole employment gives.

In other parts of New England one may wisely use, instead of boulders and for a similar purpose, stones roughly split from neighboring granite-ledges; but, again, and for the same reasons, it is seldom wise thus to construct a whole house. We want simplicity and we want solidity, but we do not want coarseness or the affectation of simplicity. A house with an interior such as every American demands, made comfortable by a hundred ingenious devices and beautiful by the skilled work of a score of different artisans, should have an exterior of consonant expression; and rough-hewn stones or roughly cemented boulders cannot give this expression.

But it is not only in private country homes that our methods of using stone are frequently erroneous. Country churches and public buildings, and even the most ambitious city structures, are often open to criticism in this respect. Even in urban parks the effort to adapt the architectural work to rural surroundings may be a departure from genuine simplicity. A park is one of the most complicated and refined of the artistic creations of mankind; and its beauty and unity may be impaired if any feature of man's creating does not show the same kind and degree of skill and refinement as the others that surround it. A park must depend for the most part upon nature for its charm, but it must also conspicuously depend upon art; and it is trite to say that when art is set to work its activity should be frankly and clearly confessed. No matter how rural in character a park may be, or how pure and undisturbed the sylvan charm of some of its remoter parts, there is no place where the work of man ought to be done with greater skill, more perfect finish, or (using the term in its best sense) a franker artificiality. Almost all such work is done in this manner in all our parks. Their driveways are not constructed like country roads of even the better sort; their lawns are not left like fields to a growth of untended grass; nor are their shrubberies allowed to grow in the wild luxuriance so beautiful beside a rural highway. When the engineer and the horticulturist are thus showing the highest level to which modern science and art have attained, the architect should work in a spirit similar to theirs. Structures which look rough, casual, almost barbaric and affectedly simple are not appropriate in a carefully tended pleasure-ground, planted with exotic trees and flowers and bisected by scientifically built and neatly curbed roads, even though we may know that as much thought and as much pains, of a certain kind, have been expended on their construction as though the outcome were more clearly artistic and refined.

The Central Park was laid out before the modern taste for boulders and rough-hewn stones had developed, and in it one may well study the method of treating architectural features in such a place. Here and there, in quiet corners and shady nooks, we find rough little flights of steps and rustic summer-houses of unhewn wood; but in all conspicuous places, and for all important constructions, work of a more polished and elegant sort is employed. But in the new Franklin Park at Boston, for example, there are structures in the most conspicuous situations which would seem more appropriate in a woody glen a hundred miles from any town. A drinking-fountain, carefully built of jagged stones so that it looks as if carelessly thrown together for a temporary purpose, may have a beauty of its own, but whether it is fitly placed beside the principal building, and near the principal driveway of an urban park, is open to question. Steps of rude slabs, scarcely revealing the use of the chisel, hardly seem appropriate in contact with the accurately shaped and smoothed curbing of this drive. In building the gateways at the principal entrance to this beautiful pleasure-ground it seems to have been the artist's purpose to make them inconspicuous, and thus disturb as little as possible the rural effect of the outlook over the distant country. But the existence of gateways, and their eminently artificial character, cannot really be disguised; and to build them wholly of small boulders sacrifices beauty and appropriateness to an unattainable end. A comparison of these gateways with those recently erected at one of the southern entrances to Prospect Park, in Brooklyn, would prove, we think, that the more confessedly artistic a work of art is made the better is its effect in such a situation. And at Prospect Park the low marble seats, small classic-looking shelters and graceful piers, interfere no more with the prospect than the rugged-looking seats and shelters at Franklin Park.

Of still more doubtful propriety is the use of unhewn stones in the construction of bridges. It seems contrary to the primary canons of art that an arch should have voussoirs of irregular shape and different lengths, so that, instead of seeming strong and homogeneous, they appear to be sliding past one another. Yet many rustic bridges have been erected in this fashion. How Richardson thought a bridge in a park ought to be built is shown by the one over which Boylston Street crosses the Fens in Boston. It is entirely devoid of ornament, perfectly simple; but with its wide, graceful, yet vigorous sweep, its beautifully modeled buttresses and coping, and the carefully finished surface of its stones, it is as true and refined and as noteworthy a work of art as any of the more elaborate things he ever built. Not far away now stands another bridge of three arches, built in the prevalent "natural" manner. In general design it is very good, and were its fabric as architectural and its finish as perfect as those of Richardson's bridge, the two would form a most happy contrast. But it looks weak despite its actual solidity, and careless despite the careful study unquestionably bestowed upon it, while its curtain of vines is not, we think, a fortunate substitute for an architectural balustrade in a work of art designed for a place which will soon be in the heart of a great city. In structures such as these we seem to be trying to go back to the infancy of art, but such efforts can hardly result in true simplicity or true appropriateness to modern tastes, conditions and abilities.

4

The Restorations at Goslar

Since the restoration of the Wartburg no more important architectural work has been undertaken in Germany than the rehabilitation of the imperial palace at Goslar. Perhaps, indeed, when we consider the nature of the building, it will not seem necessary to limit my statement to Germany. The restorer's aid has in all countries been principally afforded to ecclesiastical structures. Here, owing to the number of more or less perfect contemporary models, his work, however locally important, is less difficult, and even the most successful result must be less instructive than if he had been employed on the restoration of a great civil building. Such buildings of the eleventh and twelfth centuries do not exist except in a state of ruin. Little remains to give the art-student a picture of the interior of a Romanesque building; nothing to give the German people in general as true an idea of the surroundings amid which their ancestors lived, as they can easily gain of these amid which they worshipped. So when the question as to how the ruinous Wartburg should be treated was first started, it is easy to see why the method ultimately chosen was the most desirable. The choice lay, as ever, between the two rival methods of conservation and restoration. The former contents itself with clearing away every probable accretion of more recent times, and taking every possible precaution for the preservation of what may

American Architect and Building News 3 (April 6, 1878): 120–121.

remain of primitive work. The other method,—to restore the relics under our hands according to the testimony of historical record, of literary illustration, and of æsthetic analogy to as nearly as may be the appearance they wore when fresh from the fingers of architect and decorator,—was the method applied to the Wartburg. It may be a question, whether the complete restoration of a Romanesque church that had fallen into such decay as had overtaken the Wartburg, would have been a laudable, much less a necessary, work. Enough remains of ecclesiastical architecture of that period to give the most careless student a fair idea of its character and æsthetic value. What might remain of old work in such a ruinous example would be more valuable than the pseudoperfection of a restoration. But, as I have said, no building remains sufficiently perfect to give a fair idea of the civil architecture of the time, or to characterize the mode of life and thought of Romanesque builders. Difficult as it was by a minutely careful scrutiny of existing monuments to gather sufficient data for the work of restoration, yet the most intemperate advocate of simple conservation can hardly fail to find the result satisfactory, and must at all events approve of the scrupulous archæological judgment with which the work was done. All students who have seen the Wartburg are far better able, even if some of the details are presumably rather than demonstrably correct, to conceive in their perfection and appreciate in their ruin the numberless remains of Romanesque dwellings scattered throughout Europe, than they would be if its restoration had been confined to conservation. Whatever original work may be covered by or lost amid modern work is amply atoned for by the increased legibility and value of every contemporary ground-plan and chisel-stroke in Europe.

When it came to be a question of restoring the great imperial palace at Goslar, things stood differently. The Wartburg was ready to serve as interpreter,—should not Goslar be purified and preserved, but left untouched by the restorer? A decision either way, had such decision been conscientiously carried out, would have met with approval from all impartial observers. But it must be universally deplored that neither of the two courses indicated above was chosen, but a course that has made out of the once superb residence, noble even in its ruin, a monster neither old nor new, a lie, as has been said in Germany, against which every tourist, every art-student, every German ought to be strenuously warned. The Wartburg was the stronghold of romantic and legendary Germany. Goslar, one of the most important centres of historical and heroic Germany. Against the beautiful and reverent treatment of the

one, we have to set the desecration and transformation of the other. The
Franconian emperors were nearer to us in the half-ruined corn-maga-
zine of twenty years ago than they can ever be in the travestied and
modernized palace of to-day.

The old "burg" of Goslar needed enlargement, we find, as early as
the year 925, but the celebrated royal residence and chapel were not
founded till 1056, becoming the favorite residence of their builder,
Henry III, and his son, Henry IV. The city was sacked and the buildings
much damaged by Henry, the Lion, in 1180, and it was very probably
then that the palace fell from an imperial residence proper to become
the residence of imperial delegates. Later it was ceded to the city, and
has been used in succession as courthouse, arsenal and armory, Jesuit
college, prison, hospital, theatre, and grain depot; and in parts for still
other purposes. It will be imagined that the work of restoration was
likely to be both necessary and difficult. First determined upon by the
last king of Hanover, to whom the city ceded the palace, the project was
furthered by the Prussian rulers, when in 1866 the city fell to them, and
with it the ownership of the palace. It was a long and tedious work before an architect who had devoted years to the study of the buildings
could clear away the accretions of centuries, discover the original plan
of the structure, and throw into a model his ideas as to its original appearance. So carefully and so cleverly was this done at length, that there
seems to have been no exception taken to his translation of present di-
lapidation into past perfection. Unfortunately, however, no sooner had
he accomplished this much than the Prussian government took the proposed work out of his hands and put it into those of the government architect of the district,—a man who, capable enough in his own field,
had until this time been chiefly occupied with railway buildings. Associated with him was a practising architect of Goslar, superintendent of
the works, and two others as advisers, so that four brains were set to
work on the same problem, with the hope that a successful unity might
result from their efforts. It can hardly be a matter of surprise that no
measure of success has in fact been attained, but that the restoration
must be adjudged something worse than a failure. That some parts of
the original structure have been preserved from further decay is all that
can be said, and this by no means compensates for the damage that has
been inflicted on the buildings as a whole, nor for the alteration and fal-
sifying of the parts in detail.

The imperial residence consisted of four parts,—the large hall, a
wing on either side of it and the chapel of St. Ulrici. The great hall was

a two-story building, 189 (German) feet in length, 60 in width, and 42 in height to the eaves of the high-pitched roof. In the middle was a sort of transept, which projected little from the building but made a great gable in the front of the roof. The low ground-floor was occupied by one large room,—the gathering-place for the emperor's attendants, the flat wooden ceiling of which was supported by a row of piers and arches running through the middle of the apartment. The upper and principal story was likewise of one room, forming the hall proper, its front consisting of an immense open arcade of seven windows, the centre and largest one being 36 feet high and 24 wide; each window was divided into three by two free columns. Stately exterior staircases gave access to this story. This, the main portion of the palace, had been preserved to the present day in great perfection, considering the age and the vicissitudes it had seen. There is no arcade of the kind at the north that compared with this even in its decay.

Of the original structure of the north wing nothing remained; but the foundations of stone built into the rear wall of the existing building bore the date 1576, so that it was comparatively very recent. The south wing showed of the primitive structure only part of the front wall, and the foundations, including those of the inner partitions. This wing connected the hall with the chapel,— one of the famous double churches of Germany,—a circular building of eminently beautiful proportions, much injured, it is true, in parts, but showing many clear traces of original work.

Passing to the recital of the mistakes—to use the mildest term—that have been made in the so called work of restoration, be it premised that all the new work that has been superadded to this early Romanesque building has been put up in well-developed fourteenth century Gothic. Further, the original design of the building must undoubtedly have been that of a great hall with two mighty stories flanked on either hand by a wing less lofty and of less stately proportions. This is evident to those who have studied the ruins, and evident no less from the æsthetic necessities of the case when we consider that the wings must have contained the dwelling-rooms, inferior in size as in importance to the great hall. The restorers, however, have seen fit to build the north wing up to the height of the main building and to give it *three* stories. It need hardly be said that a three-story dwelling of the eleventh century, especially where space was available to any extent, would have been a very anomalous structure. Not only is such work a complete lie when it pretends to "restore" the original state of the wing, but it dwarfs and ruins the fine central structure which had so fortunately been preserved to us. Does not the excuse have an old and familiar sound when we read that this was done to provide a suitable residence for future official visitors to Goslar? Further, after much money had been spent on this modern erection, lack of funds was pleaded as an excuse for a shabby profanation of the main building. The pitch of the roof was lowered, among other things, and the high gable fronts, so distinctively German, cut off and hidden under an unbroken roof.

Thus far the restorations have now progressed, but still other desecrations are proposed for speedy execution. It was ascertained by careful scrutiny that the great arcade was originally provided with a defense against the weather in the shape of perforated inner shutters of wood, with small glazed panes inserted, and by heavy curtains. It is now proposed to render the hall more fit for use by nineteenth century officials by glazing the entire extent of the apertures, thus producing, as has been said, the effect of a badly planned greenhouse. Even the chapel itself is not free from the threats of the restorer. The principal interior decoration of the hall is to be an immense fresco representing the "Proclamation of Versailles" in 1871. Thus the aim is avowedly not to guard this fortunately preserved structure of the eleventh century against further decay, nor to restore it to the condition in which it was left by its founders,—the greatest, perhaps, of German sovereigns,—but to transform it into a building fit for modern purposes, repaired and decorated not to the glory of Henry IV but of William I. When we think of the pride the German people take in the pious and clever rehabilitation of the Wartburg it is hard to realize who in Germany has permitted such desecration, or who has been found to execute it. When we look to the cathedral of Speyer,—perhaps the finest of Romanesque cathedrals,—which was built at the southern extremity of their empire by the same dynasty who erected the "Pfalz" at Goslar in their northern mountains and which is sanctified by the tombs of all four Franconian emperors,—when we look at the careful and reverent and faithful way in which it has of late years been repaired and decorated, it seems almost incredible that in the same country, at the same epoch,—not, it is true, without many indignant protests,—men have been found to maim and desecrate and sheathe with falsehood the great Romanesque palace of the Hartz.

5

Color in Rural Buildings

The use of color on the exterior of buildings is a subject to which in recent years American architects have given much attention. Foreign examples of strongly colored or polychrome work, both ancient and modern, have been seriously studied; the particular characteristics of our climate and atmosphere have been considered; and it has been recognized that in America, where the air is clearer and the light more intense than in northern Europe, very marked effects of exterior color can be used with good results.

The pale gray stone almost universally employed in Paris is admirably suited to local atmospheric conditions. Every painter knows that the atmosphere of northern France contains moisture enough to make a soft grayish envelope for all terrestrial objects, and to give the sky a soft and rather pale tone; and the so-called Caen stone of Paris is neither too white nor too dark to fit well into the scheme which the great colorist, Nature, has laid out. In Holland and England, where the air is still more moist, the deep red so commonly used for roofs is equally appropriate, coming out well against the heavy skies and harmonizing with the strong dark greens which much dampness produces in foliage and grass. But go to the south of France and to Spain and Italy, where the air is clearer, the light more forcible, and the sky bluer,

Garden and Forest 5 (March 30, 1892): 146–147.

and you will find that the best colors, and those most generally employed, are vivid yet light—chiefly whites and yellows, which, as a painter would say, have the same "value" as the clear bright greens of the vegetation, the yellows and whites of the soil, and the blues and whites of the heaven. And in the roofs a clear, not heavy, shade of brown has generally replaced the deep red of northern countries—a tone which is not too pronounced to mate with the lighter ones, but is welcome among them as giving an accent of contrast and relief. If a bright red roof is wanted in a southern climate, it ought to be a bright light red—not the bright deep red of Holland, where a pale red would seem too weak for Nature's tones, and a clear brown would hardly tell in the landscape at all.

Our summers in the latitude of New York are as warm as those of southern France, and, indeed, New York actually lies in the latitude of Madrid and Rome. Our winters, of course, are very much colder; but atmospheric conditions do not change to correspond with isothermic lines; and all the year round, even in northern New England, we have vivid skies, a pellucid thin atmosphere and a clear bright scheme of natural color. Therefore, as our architects now know, the teaching of the south, not of the north, of Europe should be followed in the external coloring of our buildings.

Much has been done to improve and vary this coloring during the past ten or fifteen years. The streets of New York, for instance, are no longer given over to the dark brown sandstone and the strong red brick which used to rule supreme. Sandstones and limestones of paler colors, pale reddish, yellow and light brown bricks, and even bricks which are almost orange-colored, have been largely adopted, vastly to the increase of beauty of effect. In Boston a quite bright red sandstone is common, light brick is also much used, and Richardson's example has been often followed in the matter of polychromatic treatment. Of course, every result is not good; but we can note gradual growth toward true excellence in the color treatment of our city buildings; and, we are glad to say, white is again coming into favor for buildings in the country.

Once upon a time, of course, white was almost universally used in such buildings. They were almost always of wood, and whether they were simple box-like cottages, pillared Jeffersonian homes, or pseudo-classic or pseudo-Gothic churches, they were almost always given a coat of pure white paint. Then came a reaction, for which, we imagine, Downing was largely responsible. His admiration for English rural architecture was rightly very great, and his perception of the crudeness of such architecture in America was naturally keen. But in trying to reform the ways of his fellow-countrymen he did not realize that under different natural conditions different expedients are to be advised. Many chapters in his *Horticulturist,* and many pages in his books on rural building, are devoted to decrying the use of white paint. After his day we had a long reign of dismal hues—dark grays and sombre browns and dusky yellows—which, if they did not always painfully afflict the eye, did not give it pleasure or harmonize well with the surrounding colors of nature. Later there came a reaction, and in the days when villas were built in fantastic forms and profusely adorned by the jig-saw, bright hues of a wrong kind were applied, two or three, or even more, together, to add in tint to variety in form.

But it was soon felt that decidedly too much variety had been achieved, and another reaction came about. Painting was largely dispensed with; staining was substituted in a way which sometimes gave a pleasing and naturally mellow look, but sometimes revealed a mistaken desire to imitate the effects of age; or these effects were left to produce themselves: the shingles which were generally employed instead of the long-universal clapboards were left to "weather" into various tones of gray, and merely the trimmings and shutters of the house were painted.

These last-named practices are still pursued, but paint has come back again into greater favor, largely as a result of the liking for "Colonial" fashions of building in which clapboards are more appropriately used than shingles; and, owing to the same cause, as well as to a better understanding of the requirements of our atmosphere, clear light tones are generally preferred. We have come to see that our great-great-grandfathers were wiser than we once thought when they painted their stately Colonial houses a pure white or a pale yellow, and relieved them with trimmings and shutters of a darker color; and also that the farmer who had liked his cottage white, probably merely because it looked cleaner thus, was unwittingly more artistic than his descendant, who thought it more dignified and refined to live in a dark gray house with a deep red roof.

The natural tone which weathering gives to shingles of good quality is rarely inharmonious except where the air is strongly impregnated with salt, and portions of the house therefore get an almost absolutely black color that is certainly not desirable. But, as has been said, we realize now that shingling is not appropriate with every style of house, and is usually best on those of relatively modest size and aspect. There are many cases when painted clapboards are much better.

Of course, a white house, standing by itself in a glare of sunlight, is unpleasant to look upon close at hand, and makes an inharmonious spot in the landscape when seen from a greater distance. But this is a trying situation for any house to occupy; when it must be borne with, stone or brick, of not too deep a color, is a better material than wood; and if wood must be used and staining is not desirable, then the best thing is to choose some tint which is nearly, but not quite white,—a pale yellow or a delicate, not slaty, shade of gray. But even a very large house can be white if it is surrounded by trees, for their shadow will temper its glare. Indeed, a white house thus shadowed makes, we think, as a rule, a more beautiful effect in our landscapes than any other. There were recently exhibited in this city a number of pictures by Mr. Leonard Ochtman, painted in Connecticut, and representing pastoral scenes. In many of them the main feature was a white house, or group of houses, accompanied by umbrageous Elms. The artist had not in any degree toned down the color-scheme of New England summer nature, or tried to mitigate the whiteness of his buildings; yet the effect of his canvases was eminently harmonious, and one felt that the color-scheme would have lacked a most desirable note had the houses been anything but a true white. The pictures of many other artists have, in recent years, shown us similar things, and we can discover them for ourselves if we know how to use our eyes when we are actually looking at American landscapes. Notice, for instance, if you ascend the Hudson River, which of the houses on the hill-sides look best, and you will decide that it is almost always the white ones. None looks better than the old Catskill Mountain House, perched up on its steep bluff with a line of forest behind it. Compare its effect with that of the dull-colored Kaaterskill House not far away, and you will be glad that its original color has not been changed.

Indeed, there may be cases where a house can stand apart from trees and yet look well if painted white. This, I think, is when it stands on the edge of the sea, with strong blue color below it, and probably stretches of brilliant white beach to support its own whiteness. Certainly we should not want the color of our whitewashed lighthouses changed. It is this color, quite as much as their conspicuous simple forms, which makes them such welcome additions in any sea-shore view. A further proof of the appropriateness of white in our climate is the beautiful effect that sails make when seen against the shore. We have been foolish enough to imitate the architectural coloring of Holland under our very different skies; but at least we have never felt that our fishing-craft, yachts and sail-boats would fit better into the landscape if their sails were stained with those brownish and deep yellowish tones which harmonize so well with Dutch shores and skies and waters.

Of course, to cover a house with painted clapboards is not the only way of having it white. We might well make a more frequent use than we do of plaster and stucco in their various forms, and a half-timbered house with stuccoed panels of white would often look admirably where one all of white would be too glaring. And then there are limestones and marbles among more costly materials.

Even if absolute white is not chosen, and naturally I do not recommend that it should be used to the exclusion of all other colors, care should be taken to get a tone that is neither too deep nor too strong. Very pale yellow is often the best possible color, while, in the same situation, a deeper yellow would look crude, a neutral tint would be ineffective, a harsh brown or gray would conflict with Nature's scale of color, and a deep red roof would only make matters worse. Gray, if it is light and pure enough, is a very good color, too, especially when relieved by white trimmings and very dark green blinds, and is, indeed, perhaps the best color for houses which stand in exposed situations. It may be so chosen as to give practically the same effect that the weathering of shingles produces under the best climatic conditions.

Brick, in very pale yellow tones, is an excellent material for country houses; and, of course, any color that can be applied to wood can be given to bricks as well, and many of them are better than the strong red which once seemed their only natural hue. Very successful in color is a large old brick mansion in the neighborhood of Boston which for generations has been painted a clear and distinctly lavender gray, the painter never being allowed to mix the tint without one of the family standing by to see that he does not get it too dull and impure.

6

The Grant Monument for Riverside Park

The competitive designs for the monument to contain General Grant's tomb which were exhibited a few months ago have lately been shown again with the annual exhibition of the Architectural League in this city. It has recently been decreed by Congress that the hero's remains shall not be transported to Washington, so it is probable that, if sufficient money is subscribed, the memorial will be erected on Riverside Drive by Mr. John H. Duncan, whose design was selected, last autumn, from among those just referred to. Some of the architect's drawings (of course, on a greatly reduced scale) will be found on this and the following page. These drawings also included a large plan, a section and an elevation of the monument proper; but from the three offered a general idea with regard to the effect of the monument can be gathered. To do justice to the design the interior of the building should be shown, for here—in an arrangement which recalls, but by no means imitates, the tomb of Napoleon in the Invalides at Paris still a bare hill-side to which no artist had given his attention, and the future estate of which was still in doubt, the architect ought to consider its possibilities in his design, and, in conjunction with a landscape-gardener, ought to prescribe some extensive scheme of treatment. But an artist has already here been at work; and has laid out the noblest driveway in the world, and to ignore

Garden and Forest 4 (January 21, 1891): 27–28.

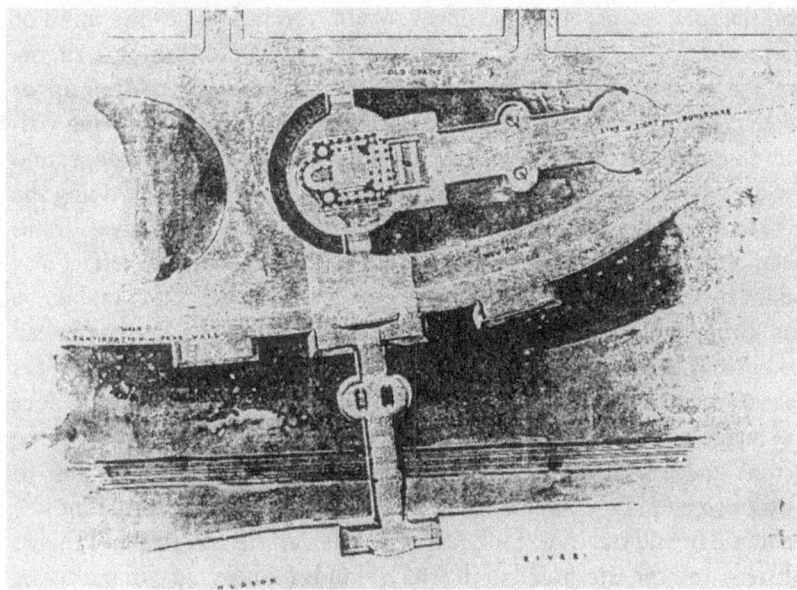

Fig. 1.   Ground Plan of the Proposed Grant Monument, Riverside Drive.
[John W. Duncan, 1890–97.]

these preparatory labors would be doubly unintelligent. Yet, so far as
could be seen from their designs, no adequate thought was given to the
surroundings of the monument by any of Mr. Duncan's competitors. Of
course, all of them had borne in mind the elevated character of the site,
the free approaches to it, and the fact that it will be well seen from a
great distance to those who shall come by land or water. But none of
them seems to have felt the necessity for uniting the building to its environment in an integral way, or the desire to improve so rare an opportunity for extended and varied architectural effort. Mr. Duncan, however, has done this; and despite the superiority of his monument (in its
interior at least) to that of any of his rivals, it is not improbable that his
sketches for its surroundings largely influenced the committee in their
choice.

It will be seen that he has not placed the tomb quite parallel with the
river-bank, but somewhat diagonally, in order to make it face the line of
the Eighth Avenue Boulevard. The way in which this driveway forks, so
as to afford a direct approach to the tomb and an encircling road as
well, seems very intelligent, and the great flights of steps, crowned by an
equestrian statue, would rise with excellent effect from the terrace. Access to the outer terrace is afforded to persons on foot by the short lat-

eral flights of steps, while carriages would turn in front of the tomb or
drive around it. But the most ingenious and interesting part of the
scheme is that which shows the way in which access from the upper
level to the river is supplied, meeting the practical end of allowing visitors to approach directly from the landing-stage at the river's edge, and
the artistic end of bringing the river itself into the scheme and doing the
best that could be done to conceal the intrusiveness of the railway. It has
been objected, that the great stairway will have a ladder-like effect and
ought to be very much wider. Possibly it might, to good advantage, be
somewhat wider; yet, on the whole, the objection hardly seems well
taken, and is apparently inspired by the inability of unaccustomed eyes
to read an architectural elevation rightly. The lateral view certainly does
not suggest a ladder-like effect, nor is it probable that a full view of the
actual structure would do so, whatever the drawing might suggest to
untrained eyes. Of course the effect is bridge-like, but the structure will
be a bridge and ought to look like one. The various terraces and flights
of steps and the triumphal arch which stands midway up can hardly be
judged in reproductions so small as those given here. But a general idea
of the scheme is all that it is proposed to give, especially as it is probable that only its general idea is as yet fixed in the architect's own mind.
It may be explained, however, that the retaining wall will be masked at
its base by plantations of trees; that the spaces on either side of the
tracks will be laid out in a harmonizing way, and that broad zigzag
driveways, which are not suggested in these hasty sketches, will ascend
from the river level to the high ground on either side of the stair, supporting it to the eye and greatly increasing its dignity and the coherence
of the whole design.

Of course much more money will be needed for a comprehensive design of this sort than for an isolated monument. But Americans are slow
in giving money only when not convinced that they will receive its value
in return, and whatever the sum they may here spend, they will get its
value only if the surroundings of the monument are well considered.
Mr. Duncan's design for the tomb itself shows how a portion of it may,
with good effect, be built in the beginning to contain the sarcophagus,
while the remainder is left for future execution. But the ultimate success
of the enterprise is more important than the immediate enshrinement of
the sarcophagus; and, therefore, it would seem the better plan to spend
the first installment of money upon the approaches, retaining walls and
terraces. Build these, and before long the tomb will surely be built. But
build the tomb first, and who knows how long we may have to wait for

the approaches, since the public so faintly appreciates the necessity for placing a building well even when it takes real interest in the building itself? Unless this building is fittingly placed, it will discredit us as a people incapable of valuing a magnificent opportunity; and to be fittingly placed means that it must be united with some such wide architectural and landscape-gardening scheme as Mr. Duncan's drawings suggest. It is fortunate that an architect has been selected who has shown himself capable of realizing the true nature of the problem.

7

The Artistic Triumph of the Fair-Builders

The unanimous voice of the thousands of people from all parts of the country who have visited Chicago during the past year and seen the great Fair being built declares that it will be—nay, that it already is—a wonderful success from the artistic point of view. Their testimony has, I think, shown all intelligent Americans that Chicago will triumph just where they may have thought her most likely to fail, and has convinced them that the Exhibition, taken as a whole, will be a very beautiful sight. Nevertheless, most persons who have merely heard what others could tell them do not yet realize the true quality and meaning of the beauty of the Fair, or appreciate what an insistent demand it will make upon their attention. They know that there are always many beautiful sights to be enjoyed during the months of summer, and they think that they may choose this one or another, without much consideration, as whim, habit, convenience, or the state of their pocket-books may suggest.

Therefore one who realizes what the interest of the Fair will actually be feels that no duty is clearer than the duty of making it manifest. It will be a misfortune and disgrace if the committees and artists who are working so devotedly and well fail of their due meed of comprehension and applause, and a still greater misfortune and disgrace if the Ameri-

The Forum 14 (December 1892): 527–540.

can people fail to profit fully by their efforts. Of course no one can hope really to explain just what this great Exhibition will be, for there are no adequate terms of comparison and illustration to use. But it is possible at least to record the impression which, even in their incomplete state, the Fair grounds have made upon one's own eye and mind, and to give a few reasons why no intelligent American, and none who wishes to become intelligent, should fail to visit them next summer.

This Fair of ours, in its general aspect and judged from the artistic point of view, is not only much more successful than, two years ago, we believed it could be; it is much more successful than any that has ever been created in this or another land. It is not only comparable to the beautiful Paris Exhibition of 1889, and not only equal to it; it is greatly superior. And its excellence is not an imitation or even an adaptation of any precedent, but has been achieved upon entirely new and original lines. It is perfectly certain that every one who goes to Chicago next summer will be astonished, no matter how much he may have heard and believed in advance; and it is just as certain that he will be charmed, no matter how good or how captious his taste may be. Indeed, the more intelligent he is, and the more intimate is his acquaintance with general questions of art and with the character of previous international exhibitions, the more he will be amazed and delighted. Only those who know how hard it is to produce a high degree of beauty on a vast scale and in complicated ways will fully appreciate what they see at Chicago, realizing that the difficulties which always exist were in this case increased by the necessity of absolutely creating an appropriate site for the buildings. They, and only they, will fully understand that they are beholding one of the most beautiful of sights and, considering its genesis, distinctly the most wonderful sight, in the world—a sight the character of which, I am unafraid to say, has not been paralleled since the Rome of the Emperors stood intact with marble palace, statue, terrace, bridge, and temple, under an Italian sky no bluer than our own.

Of course, big as it is, our Fair is a small place compared to imperial Rome; and fine though its structures are, some of them show conspicuous faults. But taken as a whole, considered as a great complex yet single work of art, viewed as a vast panorama of stately architectural and natural features, I believe that no place of its extent in the modern world has been so impressive, so magnificent, so imperial in its beauty. It seems an astounding fact that it can really exist. It seems a miracle that it can have come to life within the space of two years. It is impossible to think that a spectacle of equal beauty will again be created in our lifetime; for in no other city will the designers of an exhibition have at command the shores and waters of a veritable ocean, and from the admirable use made of these shores and waters a large part of the beauty as well as the originality of the Chicago Exhibition has sprung. Man had here to conquer Nature in one of her most recalcitrant moods. But having conquered her, the result is more admirable as well as more individual than could have been any result won by a less desperate struggle.

This, then, is the first answer to the query whether it will be "worth while" to visit Chicago next summer even if it does not seem convenient: It will be if you care to see one of the most nobly beautiful and distinctly the most interesting of the existing creations of the hand of man. But there is another answer which should reinforce this one: It will be worth your while to take a great deal of trouble and make many sacrifices to visit the Fair if you care to learn, in a very short time, more about certain very important matters than months of home study or foreign travel could teach you—to gain much valuable knowledge and many fruitful impressions which there has never before been such an opportunity of gaining, and probably never will be in the future while you live.

It is well, I think, to make as clear as possible this distinction between the mere pleasure and the instruction which a sight of the Fair will afford. We can imagine a very pretty, charming, and amusing exhibition which, except as its art-collections might exert a nobler influence, would not teach us much about art. We can imagine a site made picturesque by the hand of Nature which would tell us nothing more than that a naturally picturesque is better than a naturally ugly site. And we can fancy it covered with buildings, gayly attractive to the untutored and possibly even to the tutored eye, which would not show what true architectural excellence is, or, much less, that harmony in variety is the highest result attainable in a complicated artistic undertaking. But the aspect of the Columbian Fair will be very different from this, and I wish especially to emphasize the fact because I think the American public likes even better to inform and cultivate than to amuse itself; because I think that to lay stress upon the educational value of the Fair is to use the best means of persuading all Americans that they ought to visit it.

In the first place, it will show that very unpromising natural materials can be mastered by men, if they are true artists, and turned to the account of noble beauty. From any elevated point on the Fair grounds you will see a limitless expanse of water to the eastward and a limitless expanse of flat prairie to the westward. You will already know that much of the ground immediately beneath you was not even solid, ugly prairie, but treacherous marsh. And looking over this ground now— here with its straight, stately, wide canals and architectonic terraces, and there with its irregularly-shaped lagoons and islands—you will understand how a great artist like Mr. Olmsted can absolutely create in a way which almost equals Nature's own. To-day it seems a simple enough idea—this bringing in the lake to solidify the land, this digging channels for the water and using the earth that was taken out to give the building sites consistency. But it was one of those very simple ideas which only a great man conceives, and one of those very practical ideas which only an artist conceives. That is, while a practical man might have seen the feasibility of the scheme, only an artist could have seen its desirability; and only a great artist could have been impelled to insist upon executing it by foreseeing how diversified beauty—variety in harmony—could thus be secured even better than upon a more naturally advantageous site. Mr. Olmsted is the only man in this country or in any country, I believe, who could have foretold how, by making use of that lake-overflow which seemed to others a fatally negative fact, he might prepare for formal, architectonic beauty of effect in one portion of the grounds, and for irregular, picturesque beauty in another portion, and yet might so associate and harmonize the two that the transition from his straight quays and canals to the varied outlines of his islands and lagoons would become the finest feature of the magnificent whole. Furthermore, while thus actually creating a great part of the site, Mr. Olmsted, assisted by Mr. Henry Codman, has created a great part of the vegetation which clothes its more picturesque tracts, covering lagoon-shores and islands, in the space of two seasons, with green growing things that look as though Nature herself had planted them a long while ago.

When the character of the Fair site is thus studied a great lesson in art will have been learned as it could not be elsewhere in the world to-day. The visitor will see that, despite the intensely practical character of the enterprise, artists were needed at the very outset; he will see that when architectural works are in question the ground-plan is of primary importance; and also that in preparing it the architect should ask the aid of the landscape-architect. As this is the first, so it will be one of the most valuable of all the lessons that the Fair will teach. I think no indi-

vidual success achieved on these vast and varied grounds will be so
fruitfully instructive as Mr. Olmsted's; for of all the arts, the art of landscape-gardening is the one that Americans least appreciate—the one
whose importance they always underestimate even when, by a rare
chance, they recognize its existence. The example set by the organizers
of the Fair in employing Mr. Olmsted before they employed any one else
ought to bear immediate fruit all over the country, among private owners of domains wide or narrow, as well as among architects and public
officials. One has only to fancy what a Fair at Chicago must have been
without Mr. Olmsted's help to understand how, in a corresponding degree, lesser enterprises may profit from similar help.

The next lesson will be with regard to the need for concordant effort
in complicated architectural undertakings. Perhaps, had each of the
great Fair buildings been built in independence of all the others, each
would have been in itself as majestic, as scholarly, as beautiful as most
of them are to-day. But they would not have been by any means the
same buildings that we see to-day; and their general effect would have
been the effect of the typical American street or square where good
buildings chance to stand, only greatly magnified and therefore with all
faults of awkward contrast and inharmonious association greatly emphasized. Any one of us can point to good and beautiful buildings in
American towns; but can any one think of a single satisfactory large
group or long perspective? Beautiful groups, beautiful perspectives, a
stupendously beautiful architectural panorama is what the Fair will
show us. It will be the first real object-lesson America has had in the art
of building well on a great scale; and it will show us how, on a smaller
but still sometimes a very large scale, our permanent streets and squares
ought to be designed. The most careless eye will understand why this
vast architectural panorama looks so well. Every one will see that it is
because, although many architects were at work, they worked together
in brotherly accord—by no means crushing out their artistic personali-
ties, but basing the expression of individual tastes upon a broad fundamental agreement with regard to the placing, the general style, and the
dimensions of the structures, and the scale of their major features. Every
one will understand that this was the only way in which harmonious variety of effect could have been secured, and that no kind of inharmonious diversity could have been so agreeable or impressive, however admirable the individual structures might have been. And he will see that
while the panorama as a whole is so magnificent because of its unity, the

beauty of each structure is enhanced because the beauty of its neighbors agrees with it.

I think also that intelligent observers will feel that for the chief group of buildings the best possible architectural scheme was chosen. No other styles could have served so well as these allied yet not identical Renaissance styles in giving the architects a chance to build in agreement with each other and yet to meet special practical needs and express individual tastes. The essential dignity, the truly modern spirit, and the practical as well as æsthetic plasticity of Renaissance architecture will be convincingly displayed; and, despite the fact that these buildings are not just like the ones we need to shelter our daily lives and works, their aspect ought to prove that Renaissance forms of art are the best for current use. If this be proved, then one great step will have been taken toward the achievement in our towns of that harmony in variety which alone can make them beautiful. Modern English architecture has been hampered by a strong leaning, sentimental rather than reasonable, toward Gothic fashions, inappropriate alike to the intellectual temper and to the practical needs of our time. American architecture has been hampered by an unbridled wilfulness of effort, a perpetual seeking for novelties in the shape of crude inventions or of revivals of unfamiliar ancient architectural types. The sooner our profession agrees upon some broad general basis for the exercise of its exceptionally strong powers of invention, the sooner we are likely to achieve a well-developed coherent national form of art. The establishment of such a basis would, of course, be greatly hastened by a general inclination of popular taste toward some one broad and plastic form of art. And I think the Fair, by bringing Renaissance art into popular favor, will thus do the country a very valuable service.

Moreover, when the Fair buildings are seen in a complete condition, the public will feel the importance of the landscape-architect, not only as an anticipatory planner but as a finishing decorator, and will realize that in completing a great architectural creation he and the architect and the sculptor must work hand in hand. The beauty of the site and the main buildings will make itself fully apparent only when the quays with their stately balustrades and flights of steps, the esplanades and terraces with their stretches of turf and flower-bed, the minor buildings, kiosks, and seats, the columns, colonnades, bridges, fountains, and statues, and the lights, flags, and awnings are all in place; and then it will be so varied yet homogeneous, so splendid in total effect yet so finished in detail,

that we shall hardly be able to give special credit to any one artist or
kind of artist. We shall feel simply that Art has been at work as she used
to work in the great old days when a common æsthetic impulse united
all her ministrants, and a generous enthusiasm for the general result led
each to think as much about his brother's success as about his own.

This impression was made by the Paris Exhibition of 1889, but not
with the same degree of force. All the more important features of the
Paris grounds were, indeed, carefully and consistently designed and
arranged. But a certain license was granted in smaller matters to individual exhibitors, and there were many little constructions and details
which did not harmonize with their environment, and plainly bore a
commercial, advertising stamp. At Chicago all large structures which
would be out of keeping with the desired general effect of the grounds
(except those erected by foreign governments and by our individual
States and Territories, which have been massed together at the northern
end of the inclosure) have been relegated to a great street called the
Midway Plaisance that runs westward from the boundary-line formed
by the railroad tracks; within the main portion of the grounds no ex-
hibitor or vender will be allowed to build the smallest object without official sanction of its design; and all semi-useful or wholly ornamental
details will be superintended by Mr. Millet, the Chief of Decoration,
from the great awnings on colonnade or bridge to the little ones on the
passenger-boats, and from seats, drinking-fountains, and sign-posts to
the myriad flags which will enliven the cornices of the buildings. The art
of monumental decoration will be as well exemplified as the art of monumental construction.

It is well worth noting, too, that while commercialism will be kept
within due bounds, no conspicuous appeal will be made to the mere
sense of surprise and wonder. That taste for the new and marvellous as
such which foreigners are so apt to call a distinctively American trait
will not be pandered to at this American exhibition, although it seems
to be thought essential that it should be pandered to in European exhibitions. We have not felt that we needed a phenomenally tall tower such
as Paris built in 1889, or a phenomenally large telescope such as she
proposes to build in 1900, or anything resembling that huge "Egg of
Columbus," fitted up as a restaurant, which figured at the recent Columbian festival in Genoa. We have felt that the pure beauty we could create would suffice to make the Fair a marvelous sight, and that our people would be attracted by it without the help of special marvels of a
useless and inartistic kind. Special marvels of a scientific sort will indeed

be shown, like the roof of the Liberal Arts Building, the largest by far which has ever been constructed. But, like this, they will all exist in answer to definite practical needs; and such ornamental marvels as Mr. French's sixty-feet-high statue of the Republic were demanded by the general scale of the buildings and will be much less remarkable for size than for beauty. We have turned the tables on the Old World in this respect: It is now for us to say "How transatlantic!" when works of constructional art appeal first of all to the sense of amazement.

On the other hand, the Fair presents one special object-lesson of a very different kind— one demonstration of the art how not to build— which every American ought to see. This is the United States Building. By far the most serious blot on the beauty and unity of the great architectural panorama, every citizen ought to study it in order that he may understand, through its contrast with its neighbors, how rapid has been our architectural advance since the days of that Philadelphia Exhibition where it would not have looked incongruous, and thus may realize how sadly the Great Father at Washington lags behind his children. This Government building is bad because it was built by a government architect. I mean that, as our Government now practises architecture, no good architect will take employment under it; and that if one did, he would have a hundred times more work to manage than he could manage properly. It will be worth while to have this conspicuous failure stand on our Fair grounds if it teaches the people and their executives the absolute need for reform in the building methods of the National Government. I cannot now speak of the multiform lessons in special matters of architectural art which even a cursory study of the other Fair buildings will teach. They will be observed, of course, more attentively than have been any other buildings in our land; and their occasional faults, as well as their frequent and surpassing excellences, will surely bear valuable fruit in the development of popular taste.

The most admirable of them all is the Fine Arts Building; and within its walls wonderful lessons will be taught by the collections to which all the world will contribute. No one except the directors of this part of the Exhibition can yet fully realize what the richness and, to American eyes, the freshness of these collections will be. Mr. Atwood's splendid courts and galleries will be filled by no heterogeneous crowds of native and foreign works, bewildering in their mass but only moderately instructive upon examination. The choice of American pictures, for instance, will be carefully regulated—more carefully, I think, than has ever been the case in any of our largest annual or occasional exhibitions; yet the space allotted to them is very extensive, and there will be good works enough to fill it adequately. For the first time the American public will have a real chance to see what the American painter has accomplished, for his best works will be shown from the earliest days (represented in a retrospective or historical collection) down to the present moment; and the witness of the pictures hung in the Art Building will be supplemented, moreover, by the conspicuous mural decorations of this and the other buildings. From all foreign nations which practise painting representative collections will be sent, chief among them, of course, the one which will come from France, to be selected by the chief government officials and foremost artists of Paris, and to be housed by itself in one of those spacious annexes each of which contains one-fourth as much wall-space as the big Art Building itself.

But, I need hardly say, pictures will form only a part of the art collections. The whole of the immense cruciform central area of Mr. Atwood's building will be given up to works of sculpture and to casts from these and from architectural carvings. The famous Trocadéro Collection in Paris—the finest array of architectural casts in the world—is being reproduced for the first time especially for our Fair; and, especially for our Fair, the Greek Government has established a factory where all the important antiquities it owns will be duplicated, to be sent as the Greek nation's chief exhibit. I do not yet know how much, in the way of modern sculpture, will come from Paris; but I have no doubt that enough will come to make our public acquainted, for the first time, with that great living school which rivals the Renaissance schools of sculpture and surpasses, perhaps, even the modern French school of painting. These are but a few examples of the things that will stand in the sculpture gallery; and I can give no idea at all of the general effect of this vast gallery—five hundred feet in length and fifty in breadth, crossed, under the sumptuous central dome, by another arm of equal width and not greatly inferior length. It will show the most splendid array of sculptured works that the modern world has ever collected together; and, of course, its teaching, even more than that of the picture-galleries, will be supplemented by the adornments of the other buildings, and also by the monumental decorations of the grounds. If we merely walk about among the Fair buildings, without entering any of them, we shall see independent sculpture and what I may call applied sculpture on a scale and in a variety hitherto unknown to us.

Chief among the monumental decorations will be Mr. McMonnies' elaborate fountain and Mr. French's huge simple figure of the Republic, facing each other from opposite ends of the Great Basin. Both of these are triumphs of technical skill, of imposing beauty, and of fresh inspiration—more individual in character, while not less excellent in workmanship, than anything of the same sort that was to be seen in Paris four years ago. Among the less conspicuous works of a similar kind many will be remarkably good, although, of course, there is still a doubt with regard to others, and we cannot expect so numerous a collection of monuments and portrait-statues to be universally satisfying in view of the very recent development of anything that deserves the name of an American school of sculpture.

As a whole I think its strictly architectural sculpture will be the Fair's weakest feature. Yet some of this too is admirable, and the rest will teach the much-needed lesson that architectural as well as independent sculpture demands the hand of a skillful artist. Artisans' work, or the work of unskillful artists, which we should pass without a protesting glance in our streets, will here seem so distressing that a new standard will be set up in the public's mind, to react eventually upon the aspect of our streets themselves.

If I can thus merely hint at the Fair's richness in works of architecture, sculpture, and painting, I cannot do even as much with regard to its promised treasures in the way of those minor works of art which, of course, will convey lessons of priceless value to artists and artisans in many branches. Some of them will be housed in the Art Building, others in the building for Manufactures and Liberal Arts, and others again in the structures erected by foreign governments and in those along that Midway Plaisance where the characteristic abodes of almost all the world will be reproduced and its manifold industries practically illustrated.

I do not record all this chiefly for the benefit of those who are already interested in matters of art. They will profit much, but there are others who will profit even more, by visiting the Fair. Incomparably attractive and useful as explaining what is meant by beauty, it will be still more beneficial as proving how highly beauty ought to be esteemed. This is the great lesson which our public at large still needs to be taught; and no other experience could teach it as will a sight of Jackson Park next summer. Even if it were as easy to travel through Europe as to go to Chicago, European travel, however prolonged and extensive, would not make upon the average American the same distinct and deep impression, fertile in promises of future personal and national development.

The average American travels in Europe to enjoy himself, not to instruct himself in matters of aim and conduct; to cultivate his mind, perhaps, but not to enlarge the bounds of what I may call his intellectual conscience; to learn what has been done in other lands, but not to discover what ought to be done in ours. He and his country, he thinks, are laws unto themselves. That a thing once was done elsewhere is small reason why it should again be done here. That certain ideas and aspirations prevail in France is no proof that they ought to prevail in America. As a nation, he believes, we must think for ourselves, act as we see best, aspire in ways of our own—work out our intellectual as we have worked out our political problems. When as a nation we find that art is essential we shall make strenuous efforts to cultivate it; but the fact must be proved on our own soil and in ways which seem accordant with the general temper and trend of American existence. A hundred years ago we would not have a king, although all the outer world declared we should and must; and to-day we will not give ourselves to art, though all the world maintains we ought, unless, under American hands, art can prove its own desirability, its own necessity.

Could anything prove this so instantly, so impressively, as a sight of our vast, beautiful, and very costly Fair— our city of palaces of art which has been built to typify and explain America's prosperity and promise, and has been built by men who are as wide-awake, practical, and modern-minded as they are cultivated and generous? Could any men testify, in the ears of the average American, with regard to the relative value of any mundane thing so convincingly as these "representative business men" of the "representative city" of the West? The men who have organized this Fair, determined its aspect, and spent many millions upon it for the sake of pure beauty are themselves average, typical Americans—embodiments of common sense, active, shrewd, practical, and very successful according to the most strictly utilitarian standards. They are men who know better than any other kind of men what life means and might mean to the average American; and they will be believed in this their showing of what American conditions permit, need, and ought to include. They have said, in a voice which has already gone around the world: "The most desirable of all mundane things is beauty; the thing most precious to a nation is art; what we must show our fellow-countrymen is not a simply practical or a cheaply showy exhibition, but the most truly and magnificently artistic one that can possibly be created; and it does not matter what it costs." They have said: "For this we are willing to spend ourselves and our money—not merely for the safe and comfortable housing of practically serviceable things, the display of man's ingenuity, the exhibition of scientific progress, the exaltation of money-making, the tickling of uncritical eyes; but first of all and above all else for the glorification of true art, for the explanation of the highest kinds of beauty, for the preaching of the gospel of that noble pleasure of the eye through which the mind is cultivated, the heart purified, and the life of a nation enlightened and sweetened."

Not a man or woman will go to Chicago next summer—not a farmer, artisan, or mechanic, shop-keeper or factory-girl, practical inventor, scientific student, or millionaire Philistine—without recognizing that the Fair has been based and built upon these ideas. And to each it will carry a conviction with regard to the worth of such ideas far stronger than could be carried by the voice of every cathedral and picture, palace and statue and garden that the Old World contains. Through the voice of the big, busy, practical, money-making city of Chicago America herself has said: *Lo, it is not Mammon you should worship, but the light-bringing, health-giving gods of intelligence, refinement, and beauty.* And all America's children will listen, believe, learn, and practise as they would in obedience to no voice save her own. When as a nation we are convinced that art is indeed a thing of first importance and priceless value, then American art, which has done so marvelously well under hampering conditions, will have an unhampered path before it and will lead us whither, to-day, no man dare predict. As a nation we shall be thus convinced, I am sure, if individually we determine that nothing except the sternest necessity shall keep us from visiting the Columbian Fair. And when art eventually profits, the whole nation of course will profit with it, and in ways practical and material as well as intellectual, spiritual, and moral. The ephemeral character of the Fair, I may add, will simply increase the impressiveness of its testimony. If it has been worth while to spend so much labor and money for beauty which will last during six months only, what ought we not to be willing to expend for beauty which will endure through the lifetime of many generations?

But even this is not the whole and, perhaps, not the very best of the matter. While the Fair will cultivate the nation it will stimulate personal virtue by the force of striking examples of admirable personal conduct, and will give us fresh trust and confidence in the American people and its institutions. The unselfish, public-spirited devotion of the organizers and artists of the Fair—their willingness to sink individual claims upon public notice for the sake of producing a magnificently harmonious general result—will point the moral that to succeed in a great enterprise the best way is not to think chiefly of one's self. And a lesson in true patriotism as well as in right personal behavior will be writ very large upon the splendid panorama. The longer we look at it the more impressed we shall be by the fact that we have done it—we ourselves, the American people, without foreign help or counsel; and thus we shall learn not only to appreciate American artists and firmly and fruitfully to believe in American art, but to think with new faith and reverence of the institutions which have developed the American citizen of to-day. We ought never again to be tempted to commit the unpardonable sin— to "despair of the Republic"—having seen that the Republic is capable of supremely successful effort in intellectual as well as in political paths. And the lesson impressed upon ourselves will be impressed upon foreigners also, to the future profit of the freedom of the nations.

Foreigners as well as we will understand that the American People has done this work, of and by and for itself; and they will see that it is the best work of its kind which has ever been done. "This is less an exhibition of things than an exhibition of ideas," said President Carnot when he opened the Paris Fair in 1889. The same words will be true of our Fair, while the chief idea it will express will be even more significant than the chief one expressed in France. There it was shown, in the face of royalist Europe, that a republican government could succeed intellectually as well as politically. Here it will be shown that a republican people can thus succeed in an even higher degree than a republican government.

If among my readers there is any American who despairs or even doubts of our Republic as fertile soil for intellectual and spiritual progress, let him go to Chicago next summer and come back with a new heart in his bosom. And if there is any who thinks he could not be more full of hope and faith than he is to-day, let him also go for the sanctioning and exalting of his present confidence. Above all, it is the children who should be taken—that young generation upon which the future of the Republic rests, and the sons of which, if it develops as we have a right to expect, will, I firmly believe, head the world's advance in those intellectual paths where progress in art should run parallel with progress in general knowledge, in science, in literature, in the betterment of social conditions, and in morality. A lesson like the one Chicago will teach, received in impressionable years, will be the best gift that any American parent can bestow upon a daughter or a son. A trip to Chicago will be a pleasure-trip truly. But it will also be a voyage of discovery, opening routes which will lead the nation to the fountains of intellectual power, to those green meadows and pleasant waters which encompass lives open to the enlightening, sanctifying inspirations of beauty and the attractions of unselfish intellectual endeavor. And it will likewise be a journey fruitful in the influences which go to make good citizens, true patriots, wise and public-spirited Americans.

As a pleasuring-place Jackson Park next summer will have attractions never before approached in our land; but as a place for self-instruction, self-cultivation, it will surpass any other spot in the world. He who enjoys it in the right spirit (and I think this spirit will be forced upon almost every one by the aspect and atmosphere of the place) will enjoy it as the Greeks enjoyed their dramas, not as modern men usually enjoy theirs. It will be a national play-ground on an enormous scale; but in its aspect and its influence as the amphitheatres of Greece deserved this name, not as the ball-fields and race-courses of our time deserve it.

And yet this is the place which those self-styled Christians who do not believe Christ's distinct assertion that the Sabbath was made for man, not man for the Sabbath, desire to have closed on the one day of the week when our mind-hungry, beauty-starved, ignorant but eagerly ambitious masses could best make use of its civilizing and uplifting ministrations.

The Madison Square Garden

If I should try to name the most beautiful building in New York, plausible contradictions would immediately follow; for there is no critical balance in which architectural works of widely different sorts may rightly be weighed against one another. But it is neither rash nor invidious to name the building which most conspicuously increases the beauty of New York. Size, type, station, environment now limit the field for comparisons; and when intrinsic beauty is appraised within this narrowed field, the Madison Square Garden asserts itself without a rival. Nothing else in all New York has done so much to dignify, adorn, and enliven its neighborhood; nothing else would be so sorely missed by all New-Yorkers were ruin to overtake their dearest architectural possessions.

I

Ages ago, as precipitate New York counts time,—that is, about fifty years ago,—Madison Square still recalled the name of Tieman's Farm; a House of Refuge for sinful boys stood in its center; and on the corner now held by the Fifth Avenue Hotel stood Corporal Thompson's Madison Cottage, where, at the Sign of the Buck-horn, explained by a huge pair of veritable antlers, the trotting men of the period found frequent

---

The Century Magazine (45) 25 (March 1894): 732–747.

Fig. 2.   Madison Avenue Façade, from the Roof of the Reform Club. Drawn by A. F. Jaccaci. [McKim, Mead and White, 1887–91.]

refreshment for themselves if not for their beasts. Close at hand beasts of several kinds were housed and fed in Franconi's hippodrome until about the year 1856, and boys not sinful enough to be incarcerated played ball where the Worth Monument now stands. This shaft was erected in 1857, and to-day almost every one thinks that it is a memorial only. But it covers a grave: the hero of the Mexican war must sleep as he can between the rush of Fifth Avenue and the rush of Broadway.

The Fifth Avenue Hotel was built in 1859, and the enterprise was thought extravagantly rash. Yet by this time Flora McFlimsey was living on the square, and many other houses as fine as hers must have been were already fronting upon it; the brown church on its eastern side had been erected in 1854, and not long after the war the Union League Club, growing luxurious, took possession of the Leonard Jerome mansion, which, growing still more luxurious, it has since abandoned to the University Club.

The last few lusters have worked changes here, as everywhere in New York, but less radically here than on Union Square. Shop-windows always existed beneath the hotels which line part of the western side of Madison Square. Spreading farther to the north, where Fifth Avenue succeeds Broadway as the boundary, they have not involved much alteration in the house-fronts above them; Delmonico's, on the northerly corner, wears a quietly domestic look; dwellings still compose much of the eastern and the whole of the northern side, except where they are overtopped by the Hotel Brunswick; and although we find shop-fronts again on the southern side, again they have not brought about wholesale reconstruction. The most conspicuous innovations, however, are the very newest—Madison Square Garden itself, and the huge white insurance building which now dwarfs the old brown church.

Gazing at this, as at the Holland House crushing the white church at Fifth Avenue and Twenty-ninth street, an interesting query suggests itself. Of all the architectural types invented by our far-off ancestors, ecclesiastical types are those which have best served modern needs. Until within very recent years the architect, when asked to build a city church, merely needed to reflect how he should design it—not, in a fundamental sense, what he should design. The proper scheme was ready to his hand, with a choice between stately tower and slender spire as its crowning feature; and even with very modest dimensions sufficient dignity was assured to his result. The case is grievously changed to-day; and what is the architect to do about it? How can he make the house of God outrank, as it should, the houses of men, when they build the bodies of their houses taller than he is often able to build his towers? What is to replace the significance of the spire now that it has become a finger which points, not toward heaven, but toward the chimney-pots of adjacent hotels? The poetic ecclesiastical schemes which once were full of stateliness and vigor now look puerile and mean beside the prosaic commercial schemes which have been rendered needful by the costliness of our soil, and possible by the development of iron construction and the invention of the elevator. The old church scheme can rarely enlarge itself enough to reconquer its old supremacy—and what shall we invent in its stead? Look at the new white building on Madison Square, and mark the childish ineffectuality of the church beside it; or look even at the cathedral on Fifth Avenue, and see if it has the right air of prelatical domination. What you will feel is either that our churches must give up the struggle for altitude, and rely for eminence upon richness of minor feature and decoration, or else that we must care enough about them to build them as majestically as we have built our great amusement-hall. The Madison Square Garden may be hurt, but it is not likely to be crushed by any neighbor.

II

When Madison Square was young, the block which touches its north-eastern angle was covered by a railroad station; and this was not a solid and impressive structure, such as we should try to build on a similar site to-day, but a mere low, sordid shed. It was called the Harlem Railroad Station, but it played the same double rôle that the Grand Central Station does to-day: from one side the cars started for Albany, from the other side for Boston. The cars, not the trains; horses were the motive power at first as far as Thirty-second street, where the engines were attached in the unprotected street, and, a little later, through the new tunnel as far as Forty-second street, where the real journey still began beneath the open sky.

When the Grand Central Station was built at this latter place, the site of the old station was left as a vacant lot. Barnum's tent was annually pitched upon it; and after a while, to protect this and other shows, brick walls were built around it, and united by a makeshift sort of roof—composing what hardly deserved the name of a building, and therefore was given the still more inappropriate name of a garden. At times, however, the interior was transformed into some semblance of a covered garden, and the place was very pleasant of an evening while Thomas's orchestra played amid the plants and tables. And so the name which it bequeathed to the present structure might, were accuracy more precious than anything else, be read as the Madison Square Beer-garden. Dog-shows and chicken-shows, horse-shows and industrial exhibitions, also claimed shelter in the queer, casually developed barrack, finding accommodation nowhere else, but finding it more and more uncomfortable here as their importance steadily increased.

Thus at last it became very clear, on the one hand, that New York needed a more seemly structure for such purposes, and, on the other hand, that the old site should be retained. We see, therefore, that the genesis of our beautiful new Garden was natural, unforced, spontaneous. It appeared in answer to a genuine need, an oft-repeated popular demand; and now we hardly understand how we lived so long without it. But this is true only of its general character, not of its peculiar stateliness and beauty. New York would have been content had any decent-looking, well-planned, fireproof building replaced the patched-up, grimy, drafty, combustible old shed; and it should be forever grateful to the few good and wealthy citizens who gave it so much more than it asked. For once common sense and business acuteness did not entirely control a great business enterprise. Forerunners of the builders of the Fair in Chicago, the builders of the amusement-palace in New York thought as much of beauty as of practical efficiency, and took unwonted financial risks; and thus far they have been fain to accept the thanks of the public in lieu of part of their anticipated gain. But their case must be sweetened to them by the thought that they have succeeded so well in securing beauty which will delight the eyes of many generations. They are in happier case than the builders of the Fair: they have not built for a season only.

When they determined to make the new Garden as satisfying to the eye as site and purpose would permit, the choice of architects cannot have given them much trouble. At least, it seemed to the public to fall naturally upon the men who, in recent days, had been the most widely active among the improvers of New York—Messrs. McKim, Mead & White.

If you want to realize what these men have done for our city, consider, to begin with, the Madison Square Garden, and then the yellow and white church on one side of Washington Square and the white Washington Arch on the other side, the Judge Building at Fifth Avenue and Sixteenth street, the Columbia Bank at Fifth Avenue and Forty-second street, the Bank of America, the Yosemite apartment-house, the Hotel Imperial, the Herald Building, and the power-house at Broadway and Houston street; the Century Club, the Players' Club, the Metropolitan Club, and the club-houses for the Deutscher Verein and the Freundschaft Society; the Villard houses on Madison Avenue behind the cathedral, and the big Tiffany house on the same avenue at Seventy-second street; the business building on the southeastern corner of Broadway and Twentieth street, and the one diagonally opposite: these will be enough to convince you that they have done more than any other single architect or firm for the improvement of our city. Yet these are not all the structures of a public or semi-public kind which they have built for us, while our best up-town streets are sprinkled with dwelling-houses of their designing.

Every one who understands how modern architects work knows that when two or three are associated together, it is unjudicial and often very unjust, to lay the blame or credit for any result elsewhere than upon the firm as a whole. Yet the public is very prone to do just this thing. Naturally, no one can help believing that some division of labor is practiced in an office which is so crowded with important tasks, and which produces works so diverse in character; and probably, where the public insists upon seeing the creation of one hand only, that hand has, in fact, directed the enterprise. Nevertheless, it should always be remembered that no artists can work side by side and in partnership for years without deeply influencing one another, even if they do not always work hand in hand; that when there is a partner whose name the public seldom speaks because he is more concerned with questions of construction than of design, he deserves a particularly large share of recognition in these days of constructional complexity and experiment; and again, that the many unnamed subordinates who compose "the office" (there are sixty in the office of which I write) are often active and responsible in undertakings which redound only to the honor of their chiefs. Thus professional etiquette merely echoes the demands of justice and common sense when it says that the work of any firm, of any large office, should always be publicly credited to that firm, to that office.

III

The Madison Square Garden covers the whole block which is bounded by Fourth and Madison Avenues and by Twenty-sixth and Twenty-seventh streets. Although the main desire of its founders was to supply New York with a large covered amphitheater, our soil, in any central situation, is so precious that no foot of the site could be left unused. Therefore, while the middle of the block gives room for the amphitheater, 300 by 200 feet in diameter, all the rest of it is filled, out to the street-lines, with other apartments, space being found not only for many needful offices and accessory rooms, but also for a restaurant, kitchens, a theater, and a concert-hall with which a large foyer, or supper-room, is connected.

Fig. 3.   The Roof Garden. Drawn by A. F. Jaccaci.

The chief fault which has been pointed out in the design of the Garden as a whole is excused by this forced utilization of every foot of the site, this close welding together of what may be called several distinct buildings. It is a fundamental precept in architecture—some people say that it should be considered an inviolable law—that the exterior of a building must translate its interior, not of course, as regards every constructional feature, but in so far that truthfulness of expression will be secured. This precept has been very frankly transgressed in the design of the Garden. Its exterior—a great straight-walled rectangle, everywhere roofed at the same level except where a tower springs high from the southern side—tells us little about its interior, and what it does tell us is not always veracious: for example, the big window in the middle of the Madison Avenue façade does not light a big apartment, but merely a lobby.

I believe, however, that any one who is not a formalist or a purist will acknowledge that few human laws, in the domain of architecture or any other, are so broadly based upon eternal necessities that they cannot once in a while righteously be broken. And if, as I think, there may sometimes be excuses for transgressing the architectural law of interior and exterior correspondence, certainly the problem here proposed to Messrs. McKim, Mead & White plentifully supplied them. Perhaps it might have been possible to fit, in some more truthfully expressive fashion, as much interior variety and compactness as they have secured with as much exterior unity, repose, and dignity: this is not for me, or for any layman, to decide. But to laymen's imagination it does not seem quite possible; and no matter how heartily we may indorse the general claim of the law of expressional truth, we are for once content with such measure of expressiveness as has actually been secured in the Garden. I mean that while no one can tell from its outward aspect how its interior is divided, or to what special purposes any parts of it are put, any one can tell that it is a building for popular uses, and for popular uses of festal sorts. Theater, amphitheater, concert-room do not reveal or even suggest themselves outside; but we plainly perceive that we are in presence of a great amusement-palace. For once, I repeat, this suffices; and with such a problem even this could not have been achieved except by skilful and imaginative artists.

Practically the amphitheater, with its annexes (which include an exhibition-hall and accommodations for hundreds of animals below the level of the street), is entirely successful. Architecturally it is impressive mainly by reason of its size and its agreeable proportions. Unless decorated for some special occasion, it looks thin and bare, and particularly in the day-time, for at night its garlands of electric lights add a certain amount of what may almost be called architectural accentuation. But of course such a place is not meant to be seen unfilled by crowds of people; even the founders of the Garden had bottoms to their purses; and it would have cost an immense sum to make the amphitheater as delightful to the eye as the adjacent theater and concert-hall—even if this could have been accomplished without lowering its seating-capacity.

The theater (it is called the Garden Theater) occupies a space of about 120 × 90 feet at the northwesterly angle of the block, and is separated from the rest of the building by unbroken walls, running from cellar to roof, and also by an air-space for more complete isolation and protection. It is a playhouse of the usual type, seating twelve hundred people, but prettier, I think, and more truly architectural in its charm, than any other in New York. I remember only two theater interiors in this country which I should care to visit in cold blood by daylight for the mere sake of their architectural interest. One is Mr. Atwood's Music Hall on the lake-front at the World's Fair (alas! already destroyed), and the other is the Garden Theater, with the graceful swing of its curved lines, its stately colonnades, its delicately modeled decorations, and its unusual air of joyousness combined with refinement.

Doubtless faults could be found with this, as with every theater interior that has ever been designed, but the concert-hall on the Twenty-sixth street side of the building must satisfy the most careful observer. Here all the constructional lines are horizontal, and the floor is level throughout—facts, of course, which render an architect's problem much easier than it can ever be in a true theater. But a mere rectangular room may lack points for criticism to lay hold upon, and yet be far from beautiful. This room is very beautiful. What strikes one first is the singular harmony of its proportions. But it also wins vigor, individuality, and charm from the treatment of its walls as series of deep, arched recesses which transform the galleries into the semblance of large *loges,* five on each side of the room. The molded decoration is fittingly sumptuous, yet not too heavy or profuse; and charming figures, modeled by Mr. Martiny, admirably suit and enhance the attractive character of the architectural motives. As yet this interior lacks desirable accentuation with gold, and, perhaps, with touches of color stronger than the creamy tint which will always predominate; but it is already very striking and very satisfying— at once ornate and delicate, reposeful and gay. And when one remembers that here, as well as in the theater, the architects were confined to strictly fireproof materials, one begins to understand why their success in interior decoration has done much to establish their high repute.

It is an old joke in New York to speak of them as Messrs. McKim, White-and-gold; but it is a very friendly joke, for we know that they have done us good service in popularizing the types of decoration which it indicates. In truth, they have done us almost as good service in this way as by popularizing the use of light, clear, and cheerful colors in exterior work.

To those who are wise in such matters, the Madison Square Garden may well be as interesting in the constructional as in the artistic sense. But I hope that no one will expect me to sketch it from that point of view. An untrained observer cannot understand modern methods of iron construction as he may the simple lithic methods of the Egyptians and the Greeks, or even half-understand it, as he may the very complicated lithic methods of Gothic centuries. He can do no more than humbly mourn his ignorance of a very important subject, rejoicing if it is so entire that he is not tempted into speech even when speech is clearly required of him. I am willing, for instance, to say that the great roof of our amphitheater is supported by twenty-eight columns, that the span of the roof-trusses is 170 feet, and that there are six main trusses and sixteen half or radial trusses. But I know that even these few facts might be more significantly expressed; and farther than this into the juggleries of men who make iron cat's-cradles and spider-webs do the work of old-fashioned brick and stone, I should be very loth to pry.

IV

Pale yellow brick and white terra-cotta form the exterior of the Madison Square Garden; and I think that New Yorkers are almost more grateful for the beauty of this exterior than for the comfort and pleasure which they find within it. I have confessed that we are not to judge it by the strict architectural canon of definite expressiveness. But judging it more simply, as a great building for festal public uses, we find few points to criticize. These architects long ago departed from the Romanesque path of Richardson, with whom two of them studied in their youth. They work consistently in the spirit of Renaissance art, although they vary somewhat in choosing its severer or more ornate modes, according to the differing demands of different kinds of structures, and often very freely in adapting the chosen mode to modern needs and tastes. It would have been impossible for them to conceive the Madison Square Garden with the bold, simple solidity suited to such a work as the Judge Building, or the classic repose and purity so satisfying in the Boston Public Library; and the general scheme they devised for their amusement-palace could hardly be bettered. It is bold and vigorous enough to be very dignified; light enough to be very graceful; lively, and yet stately enough, to be rightly expressive. And these words apply as truly to the amount, distribution, and massing of the ornament as to the proportioning of the walls and the placing of the windows, to the con-

Fig. 4.   Gallery of the Concert Hall. Drawn by A. F. Jaccaci.

trasting characters of the Madison Avenue and the Fourth Avenue
façades, and to the station, scale, and treatment of the colonnades
above and below, of the eight picturesquely varied belvederes, and of
the tall and buoyant tower.

Thus far we can find no fault except, perhaps, with the way in which
two of the belvederes are crowded against the base of the tower. But if
we examine more particularly into the design of the ornamental motives
themselves, we feel that the proper degree of sumptuousness has been
achieved at some cost in refinement. Even the central motive of the
Madison Avenue façade, with its window cut through a great slab of
purplish marble, and its luxuriant borderings, is not, in idea, too rich;
but it looks a little too heavy, because its details lack something of the
sobriety, distinction, and purity which Messrs. McKim, Mead & White
secure when they are at their very best in ornamental design, even of a
highly elaborate sort. We recognize a flavor of the over-blown, the
baroque, which we are not accustomed to associate with their names,
and which we cannot think essential to the richness rightly desired for

the exterior of the Garden when we consider how fully, without any over-emphasis, this quality has been obtained in its interior. In short, the ornamentation of the Garden looks best from a little distance. Then the eye cannot analyze all its details, and it proves itself as successful and charming as, from any point of view, do the proportions and architectural features of the building, and its warm and soft, yet clear and brilliant, color.

The finest of all its features is the tower. One cannot but think first and chiefly of this whenever the Madison Square Garden is named; and indeed, we prize it so highly that we sometimes forget that the Garden was not built for the sole purpose of springing this tall pedestal for the golden Diana.

Like the rest of the Garden, the tower has not escaped the fate which dogs all conspicuous people and things in this criticizing world. But I think no one denies its beauty: what some people deny is merely that its builders deserve much credit for its beauty. It is not an "original" piece of work, they lament; it is a copy. And must not an architectural copy be ranked as low as a copied picture? At the best, can it have any more value than a cast from an interesting statue?

Such words exasperate those who know how difficult it is to build, in any way, after any pattern, a tower as beautiful as Diana's; and still more those who have really compared Diana's tower with its prototype. In the first place, an architectural copy is not a thing which can be executed mechanically, without artistic skill; in the second place, this tower is not a copy—it is an adaptation; and again, while even a very free adaptation, like a very close imitation, may be good or bad, this one is extremely clever and extremely good.

Its prototype, as need hardly be said for the thousandth time, was the famous tower in Seville called the Giralda, from the turning figure of Faith upon its summit. The Giralda is in two distinct parts, separated from each other by nearly four centuries of time, and just as widely by disparities in style. The lower part, which rises to the height of 185 feet, and is about 45 feet in diameter throughout, is of Moslem workmanship and in the Saracenic style, and was built in the latter half of the twelfth century. What may then have been its termination no one now can say: the present belfry, which, with its several stages, adds 90 feet of height, was built in 1568 by Ferdinand Riaz in a heavy, florid, late-Renaissance style, palpably discordant with the graceful Saracenic below.

Our tower is not in two parts, but from base to crown is a consistent, harmonious piece of work; and in style it resembles neither portion of

the Giralda. Its general scheme—its outline, and the nature and proportioning of its main parts and features—is borrowed boldly from the Giralda. But below it is only 35 feet in diameter; it is 350 feet in height to
the points of Diana's crescent, as against the 275 feet credited to the Giralda; and in every detail of treatment and decoration it is a fresh design. The lower part is much more simple and severe than in the Moor-
ish tower, recessed horse-shoe windows and rich sunken paneling being
replaced by plain, narrow lights quite differently disposed, and by inconspicuous patterns due to a slight diversity in the color of the bricks.
And above, the successive belfry stages have been treated in an earlier,
lighter, more graceful and refined Renaissance manner, with, again,
some changes in the arrangement and proportioning of the minor features. Add to these differences in height, style, and treatment a wholly
new method of construction, and a wholly new scheme of color, and
how can one rightly speak of direct reproduction, of imitation, of copying? Our architects borrowed what was best in the Giralda,—its general
scheme,—and then did not strive to reproduce either the difficult beauty
of its lower portion, or the rather clumsy details of its top, but recast the
whole conception as in a new mold, producing a tower which is not
only fair to look upon, but appropriate to its purpose and its station in
our modern town. In truth, the individuality which they have worked
into their adaptation of two old architects' ideas is so distinct and interesting that they would do themselves excellent service should they
hang a photograph of the Giralda where every one entering Diana's
tower might study it for comparison.

Furthermore, the Giralda springs in isolation from the ground; our
tower from a long façade sixty feet in height. This fact again has caused
critics to criticize. I can only say that to me it has never seemed a mistake: our tower has never seemed anything less than an integral and
well-supported part of the complex structure to which it belongs, auda-
ciously asserting its own personality, yet gracefully harmonizing with
the aspect of the structure beneath it. And its greatest merit always
seems the lordly seriousness of its lower walls, relieving the elaboration
of the long façades below and the lightness of the open belvederes, and
justifying the jubilant charm of its own belfry stages.

V

The moment the Madison Square Garden was finished, it became the
center for the popular amusements, and, to a great extent, for the fash-

ionable amusements, of New York. And during its short life its rôle has steadily grown more active, more conspicuous.

Naturally, its most peculiar usefulness resides in the amphitheater, which, even when its floor is wholly occupied by performers, has fixed seats for six thousand spectators, and, when chairs are placed on the floor, can accommodate ten thousand comfortably, or twelve thousand if they do not mind being crowded.

Of course, good as its acoustic properties are, no speaker can be heard from end to end of so great a space. For certain kinds of music also the amphitheater is too large; yet there are other kinds which have often sounded admirably under its enormous roof. Big flower-shows have been held in it, sometimes with delightful effect; and public balls have been given for which all other apartments seemed too small. But neither flower-show nor ball looks its best here, for each leaves empty the mounting rows of gallery-seats. For certain other kinds of shows, however, which do not demand general beauty of effect, no place could surpass our amphitheater. Go to a big poultry-exhibition, for instance, or to the bench-show which is held every spring, and you will think only of the marvelous number of fowls or dogs that can be well displayed and well tended. Then wait until Barnum's circus comes—every seat up to the roof will be crowded, and three rings, by giving you three times your money's worth, will spoil your pleasure unless you have the philosophic mind which contents itself with enough. There could hardly be a better place for a big circus than this, or for a moving spectacle of any sort. Have you forgotten when Kiralfy came, a couple of years ago? His Columbus pageant followed a circus performance and I noticed that few of the people who call themselves artistic in New York cared to wait for it after the trained dogs and the clowns had been admired. But those who did wait saw, I think, the most fairy-like and artistic spectacle which has ever been shown in New York; the people at large appreciated it, and once more they felt that there never was such a satisfactory place for seeing such fine things.

But they feel this most strongly, and the Garden's unique serviceableness is most plainly proved, when the horse-show opens in November. With this amphitheater and its basements at command, we are able to have such horse-shows as, under cover, no other city in the world can organize. They are becoming of national service, of international interest; every class of our population delights in them; and, as Fashion has made them peculiarly her own, the hundreds of gallant steeds often seem but half the spectacle—so diligently and so gorgeously, day by day

for a week, and especially night by night, does all "society" dress itself
in its best and go on parade in the boxes to see the parades in the ring.
No other city ever presents a complex spectacle just like this; and it
would be impossible here without a building just like our Garden.

Music which is not suited to the amphitheater can be heard, and to
the best advantage, in the concert-hall, which measures 110 by 75 feet,
and seats sixteen hundred people. Traditions of famous masters and famous performers are quickly gathering within its walls, and for lecture
purposes it is also often in request. Masculine New Yorkers take peculiar delight in public dinners, especially when their admiring women-
folk will consent to come in late—to look down from a gallery upon the
remains of the feast and listen to the eloquence it has unloosed; and
there is no other apartment in New York so good as this one, for the
diners themselves, or for their gentle audience. Again, as "society" has
discovered, no other apartments are so good for subscription-balls as
this and the adjacent supper-room; and smaller dinners, or lectures or
concerts to audiences of six hundred, may be given in the supper-room
itself.

With the gay record which amphitheater and concert-hall are thus
making for themselves, with the Garden Theater equally popular and
successful, and with the much-discussed frivolities of the roof-garden
open to summer pleasure-seekers, who can deny our great building's
protean usefulness? Is it any wonder that we do not understand how we
lived so long, even half-content, without it?

VI

But the utility and beauty of the Garden itself are not the only benefits
that its founders have conferred upon New York. We may believe that
it will preserve the whole of Madison Square from all degrading, and
even from all baldly commercial, innovations. The Garden was erected
at a critical time, when no one could foresee whether or not the square
would remain the center for New York in its pleasure-seeking moods;
had the character of the square changed, it must have changed for the
worse; and moreover, where could another amusement center have been
found so spacious, so attractive, or so accessible to the dwellers in all
parts of the city and in all its sister cities and suburbs? Madison Square,
in fact, is the one and only natural up-town center for New York to-day;
every one lamented when its prestige seemed upon the wane, and every
one rejoiced when the very valuable block to the northeastward of it

was reserved for its accustomed service, and the new Garden was built so big and so beautiful that it will never be removed. "I am here to stay," it very plainly says; "and so other places of amusement must stay, and other fine buildings must come; and at all events for many years, New Yorkers, in their idle hours, will be tempted to gather nowhere else."

From the moment of her unveiling, and as long as she was allowed to live with us, the golden Diana which Mr. St. Gaudens set on top of our yellow tower was the most popular personage in all New York. But the architects of the tower, and other good judges, thought her too large for her place, and the sculptor was not satisfied with her pose or her draperies; and so, last spring, she was sent to Chicago, and for many months there was no Diana on Diana's tower. But while its quondam occupant was swinging over the low dome of the Agricultural Building, pointing out the beauties of the Court of Honor to crowds of her quondam fellow-citizens, those who remained at home were discovering, not only how much they had cared about her, but how insistently the tower itself required a finishing figure. Where she will live in future I do not know; but she can never come back to her original place: it is filled already by a newer and smaller namesake. Diana the Second is, I think, a more thoroughly successful figure than Diana the First; she is more buoyantly poised on her supporting foot, while the other, raised less high, appears more graceful to far-distant observers; and the sweep of her light draperies is more free and supple. But every New Yorker may claim the right of private judgment as regards the question whether she proves that Diana the First was too large. And whatever the general decision upon this point may be, and whatever the general indorsement of her superior personal charms, I am sure a long time will pass before she outlives the reproach of being a usurper. How could we love any Diana the Second quite without reserve until we have time to forget that she *is* the second?

Seven stories of bachelor apartments, and then a cafe, are contained in the tower, above the level of the Garden roofs: but as its inner diameter is only thirty feet, and part is filled by staircase and elevator, they are not very commodious. The most important service performed by the tower is apparent only when the elevator stops as near heaven as it can go, and we climb nearer still, and enjoy the wonderful prospect to which we have come—the long, narrow panorama of the mighty city, very broken as to outline and, for the most part, red in color, but sprinkled with the green of foliage and blotched with the yellow and white of our newest tall buildings; then the streams of silver water encircling it, and then the low line of the Long Island shore, and the higher, greener line of the New Jersey hills.

Truly, it is not a panorama of high artistic beauty such as Diana the First saw this summer at Chicago; but it is so beautiful in another fashion, and so varied, that it seems only natural that Diana the Second should whisk about, facing north and south, east and west, ever pointing her arrow at some newly interesting sight. May it be long before she gets so tired of her post as to cease turning about to contemplate New York; for when she ceases, it will mean that her feet have rusted to her pedestal, that the tower and the Garden have fallen into decay, that the life and the laughter of New York have departed.

9

The New Public Library in Boston:
Its Artistic Aspects

Is that the new building for Trinity parish?" a Boston lady asked when Richardson's now famous church was about half complete; and then she added, "It is very queer!"

"Yes," replied her companion, slowly, in a reverent tone—"yes; art *is* queer."

Richardson himself happened to overhear these words, and thought them very funny. But they have also their serious and instructive side. They have often recurred to me, with a sort of typical significance, as formulating, in a brief and handy way, what may almost be considered a national attitude of mind. Vaguely silly on the surface, they may be interpreted, if we ponder them a little, as a confession of ignorance combined with a profession of willingness—nay, of eagerness—to admire. And this, considering our people broadly, and not alone in the art-pursuing circles of our largest towns,—this seems to be the present temper of the average American with regard to architectural art, if not, in some degree, with regard to art of every kind.

On the whole, it is not a temper to deplore. It marks a distinct step forward from the time when ignorance was cherished with supreme indifference, and we may hope that it prophesies a time when interest will have engendered veritable knowledge, true because reasoning appreciation.

The Century Magazine (49) 28 (June 1895): 260–264.

Fig. 5. The Boston Public Library. (McKim, Mead and White, architects.) From a photograph by A. H. Folsom. [1887–95.]

Nevertheless, it is a temper which may easily lead the mind away from the right—the reasoning—path of development. Sensibly as well as modestly one can say, "These things seem strange or odd to me, yet I am ready to believe that they may be very fine." But if one says, "Many things which must be fine seem odd to me, and so I may consider oddity and excellence the same," then his modesty o'erleaps itself, and turns to a rashness which will lead him far astray; and this is precisely what has happened with multitudes of Americans in our time. Their interest in art has been awakened, and therefore they are no longer content with monotonous ugliness, common-place uniformity. But because their judgment has not developed, they allow mere novelty as such to impress them, and are most surely over-awed by it when it is most eccentrically emphatic. For proof, you need only think of the aspect of Fifth Avenue or of Beacon street thirty years ago, and contrast it with the upper West Side streets of New York, with the Back Bay streets of Boston, or with Michigan Avenue in Chicago.

If, now, you will look at our pictures of the new Public Library in Boston, you will understand why Boston as a whole did not appreciate it fully at first; and you will also understand why, from the very first, good judges of art, well content with its degree of beauty, were doubly glad because of that beauty's kind and character. It is not an eccentric building; it is not a picturesque building; it is not conspicuously original in design. It has no diversities of mass or outline, no strong contrasts of color, no striking individual features, no showy decorations. Therefore the public, not finding it "queer," needed time to learn that it was very good. It was called cold, uninteresting, severe, unsympathetic, monotonous, and conventional. The tower of Trinity, beautiful, but in a very different way; the showy taller tower of the "new Old South Church"; and the gaudy front of the Art Museum, not beautiful at all, but only gaudy—these also faced on Copley Square, and in the eyes of ignorant observers they seemed to reproach the library for its cold neglect of the rich resources of architectural form and color, and for its reticent refusal to declaim about the millions of money it had cost.

But from the very first a good many other people fitted its qualities with truer names. They praised its dignified simplicity, its symmetrical serenity, its classic calmness and repose, the harmony of its features and proportions, the excellence of its materials and their treatment, the charm of its very pale gray tone relieved by the strong yet not aggressive red tone of the roof, the delicate vigor and good taste of its decorative details, and the noble result of all of these—the stately yet reserved and quiet expression of the building as a whole, admirably appropriate to its name and purpose. They did not expect such qualities instantly to please a public which for a generation had been dazzled by architectural pyrotechnics, deluded by showy eccentricities, bewildered by things which were partly sensible and partly "queer," and charmed by the exuberant, romantic spirit of Richardson's really admirable art. But they did expect them eventually to prevail. Their belief has been justified, and this fact means that the architects of the library have won a victory, not only for their own building, but for the general cause of architectural sobriety, dignity, simplicity, and refinement.

Moreover, while a great artist may achieve these qualities, no matter in what architectural style he works, it was well that a Renaissance style should be chosen for a building of such great importance— one of the offshoots of classic rather than one of those of medieval art. Mr. Richardson's vigorous, original, impressive, and often very sensible and beautiful use of Romanesque motives almost convinced America for a time that her true architectural path had thus been pointed out. But the results of recent years have proved once more the old truth taught by the prowess of Ulysses—it is the power of the man that makes a big weapon useful. We are gradually learning now that modern weapons, modern ideas and expedients, are the best for the men of to-day. We are steadily gaining belief that the art which, in modernized versions, was

reborn with the birth of modern civilization, and which is the living art
of Europe still, is the one to be adopted by America and adapted to her
multiform, thrice-modern needs. An effective exposition of this truth
was made on the Chicago Fair grounds, and we may be very glad that
Messrs. McKim, Mead & White perceived it some years before the Fair
was built.

Despite its simplicity and reticence, the exterior of their library is
conceived and adorned in such a way that it can never be mistaken for
a building of purely utilitarian purpose. Clearly it is a civic monument,
although as clearly it is one devoted to serious intellectual ends. And its
builders rightly felt that a greater degree of sumptuousness would be
appropriate within its walls, as expressing its erection by a populous
and prosperous city, with a past enriched by intellectual achievement,
and with fine ambitions for a still broader and more fertile future. In realizing this idea, the architects have worked, inside their building, in
ways which recall Italian Renaissance art rather than the French development which is shown by their exterior. But no lack of concord results:
we merely feel that different yet harmonizing needs have been met by
the use of different yet harmonizing artistic expedients.

A low platform, approached by wide, encircling steps, lifts the library effectively above the level of Copley Square. The three arches of
the main portal admit us to a vestibule from which three great doorways open into the entrance-hall. Beyond rises a monumental staircase,
branching from its wide landing halfway up into two stately flights that
end upon a columned gallery; and from this we enter Bates Hall, the
general reading-room, which stretches across the whole front of the
building, and is lighted by its main range of windows. The vast extent
of this hall, 217 feet in length, 42 feet in breadth, and 50 feet to the
crown of its barrel-vaulted ceiling, justifies the magnificent proportions
of the staircase, showing what a multitude of readers and borrowers the
library must serve, and suggesting how manifold and how spacious its
other apartments must be.

This is but a hasty survey. It grants me no time to take you through
so large and complex a structure, or even to note the arrangement of its
parts, distributed through the four wings which inclose its central court.
But we may at least look down into this courtyard from the balcony beyond the door on the staircase landing, or actually enter it through the
Boylston street portal. It is encircled on three sides by graceful columnar arcades of marble, above which rise walls of yellowish brick, delightfully warm and rich in tone; and with its spacious air of dignified

retirement, it is admirably expressive as a feature in a place which will be frequented by the public for other than practical business purposes, yet not for purposes of trivial pleasure. Coming immediately upon it from a raw, prosaic American street, our surprise makes but the more impressive and seductively poetic the pure and simple beauty of its shadowy arcades, the solid nobility of its upper walls, the peacefulness of its sunny central area of turf, and its pervading atmosphere of carefully considered art and cloistered quietude. Seats will be provided beneath its arcades and, under protecting awnings, also upon their roofs; and during the long warm months of the year it will be a place without a parallel as yet on American soil—a place owned by the public of a great city, where hours or even moments of repose or study will be doubly fruitful, feeding the most careless or unconscious eye with the food of high artistic loveliness.

And thus I am brought to speak of the fact which, more than any other, has already made this building famous. The most interesting thing about it is that each and every portion of it has been planned with the wish to secure the highest possible degree of beauty, in as many and as varied ways as are consistent with its artistic unity, and with respect for its fundamental character and purpose.

Its projectors knew (another thing that some of us were first convinced of by Chicago's Fair) that architectural beauty cannot be completed without the help of the sister arts, that a worthy house for Boston's books could not be built unless painter and sculptor should give the architect their aid. But they also knew that the building's mission was to spread and encourage knowledge; they felt that an intimate acquaintance with beauty is one of the most precious and fructifying kinds of knowledge; and, realizing that this, in most of its branches, cannot be acquired from books, they determined to reinforce the voice of books with the voice of art itself.

Very magnificent are the materials employed by the architects in their interior work, from the delicate mosaics of the entrance-hall, and the yellow Siena marble of the great staircase, to the carved and colored woodwork, brought from an old French château, which adorns the trustees' room. But these material splendors will be accompanied, enhanced, and refined by painted and sculptured work as exceptional in its way. Puvis de Chavannes, the greatest modern master of decorative design, is already painting pictures which will fill the panels and line the gallery of the staircase hall. Otherwise commissions have been given to American artists only. But need we regret this fact, knowing that St.

Gaudens is to model symbolical groups for the great pedestals which, outside the building, flank the main portal, while he has already ornamented the escutcheon above it; that Abbey's "Search for the Holy Grail" (already shown in part in Chicago and New York) is the frieze for the large delivery-room; and that Sargent (whose work is likewise partly complete to-day) will depict the "Religions of the World" in the staircase hall of the second floor? Then the apse-like end of Bates Hall is to receive a painting from Whistler's hand; French is to model a figure of Emerson for the same room, and the bronze doors between the entrance-hall and the vestibule; the lions on the staircase, memorials to the members of two Massachusetts regiments, were made by Louis St. Gaudens; and while McMonnies's statue of Sir Harry Vane already stands in the Shakspere room, his beautiful Bacchante, bought by the French Government for the Luxembourg, is to stand in duplicate on the courtyard fountain.

Of course there is space for many more artists than these in Boston's Library, and of course it will be long before the work of decorating it is complete; but no such beginning has ever been made before in a civic structure on American soil. We realize how full a measure of praise this library deserves when we remember that here for the first time the highest possible ideal has been conceived for us, and as regards not only architectural magnificence but artistic completeness in the broadest sense. Nor should we forget that this exceptional monument, destined, we may believe, to raise the standard for public buildings all through our fatherland, has been paid for in the noblest possible way. Individual generosities have bestowed neither the house itself nor its adornments, nor has State or national aid been asked for it. It has been constructed and it will be adorned by the city of Boston for the city of Boston—by those burghers as a whole who, as individuals, down to the humblest and meanest among them, will be equally entitled to enjoy its beauty and to profit by its precious stores.

10

Eleventh Annual Exhibition
of the Architectural League of New York

Posters and book-covers, jugs, curtain-poles, hat-racks and burnt wood table-tops are not things of the highest intrinsic importance, and they have but the slightest connection with architectural art; yet, in this architectural exhibition, scores of things of these and similar kinds, and of designs for such things, have good places on the well-lighted walls of the galleries, while a series of very interesting park and garden designs, including some of the most important of Mr. Olmsted's recent works, are consigned to the walls of the entrance corridor, where they cannot be seen at all until the approach of evening commands artificial illumination. Moreover, while all the hat-racks and the poker-work and the American designs for Chinese rugs are carefully paraded in the catalogue, it makes no mention whatever of these valuable designs in the corridor. The Architectural League's Hanging Committee and Catalogue Committee seem to have united to declare what has often been said by outsiders—that almost every one in America knows the value of landscape and garden art better than the architects, who ought to be the foremost celebrators of its importance. Certainly the League cannot complain if the practitioners of this art refuse to contribute again to its exhibitions.

The most interesting thing in the whole exhibition, to the general public, and the most instructive, were it properly displayed, would be

Garden and Forest 9 (February 26, 1896): 88–89.

Mr. Olmsted's scheme for the permanent disposition of the quondam Fair Grounds at Jackson Park, in Chicago. It is a masterly piece of work in conception and in execution. The good sense, the imaginative force and the artistic skill shown in remodeling the features of land and water and the architectural elements bequeathed by the Fair, and forming them into a coherent, varied and beautiful lake-side pleasure-ground, are as great as those that were shown by the original transformation of a desert swamp into a sumptuous place of palaces. This design will soon be reproduced in the pages of *Garden and Forest.*

Among the other designs by Mr. Olmsted and his associates which have been relegated to the corridor's outer darkness are those for the grounds of Biltmore, Mr. Vanderbilt's place in North Carolina; for Auldwood, Mr. Hoagland's place at Seabright, on the sandy New Jersey coast; for Bleak House, Mr. Winans' place on the rocky shores of Newport; for Mr. D. Willis James' inland place in New Jersey; for the grounds surrounding the mansion which Mr. Hunt built for Mr. Ogden Goelet in the heart of Newport; for the grounds of Washington University, at St. Louis; for Seneca Park, in Rochester, and for South Park, in Buffalo. These form a remarkable series of varied works, showing many types of garden and park design from the almost strictly formal treatment appropriate on a small Newport place, where the house is an adaptation of a stately French château, to the markedly naturalistic treatment befitting a site like that of the Rochester Park, where water plays almost as prominent a part as land in the general effect. Had they been displayed as they should have been, conspicuously, in some position of especial honor, the League would have shown that it understood the meaning of art in the noble sense of the word, and realized the intimate relationship between gardening art and architectural art, and the public would have been interested and instructed as we cannot hope will now prove to be the case.

When the architectural designs in the galleries are studied the action of the two committees seems all the more inexplicable; for they reveal among our architects a growing sense of the need for gardening art in connection with all buildings which do not stand upon crowded city streets. Chief in importance, perhaps, is the elaborate design of Messrs. Carrère and Hastings for a large country house set at the end of a long narrow, rocky point projecting into Long Island Sound, and approached through a natural forest with which it has been united by formal gardening arrangements, conceived on a larger scale than has often been seen in this western world. This scheme, I hope, may soon be reproduced in these pages; and likewise an interesting suggestion of Messrs. Bell & Langton's for the rearrangement of Madison Square in this city.

Many pictures of country houses, whether good or bad in themselves, gain interest by the incorporation of their environment in the architect's design. I do not mean that this environment is always better imagined than the house itself, or even as well imagined; merely that any proof that our architects are coming to realize the interdependence of the two arts is very welcome. One common fault is still the undue prominence of stretches of gravel in the vicinity of the main front of a house. Of course, it is often involved in the mistake of incorporating the carriage-entrance with this front. But there are instances where the carriage-drive runs to an entrance in another side of the house, yet, nevertheless, a gravel path cuts off the main façade from the lawn, not only offending the eye by its own barren line, but preventing any proper system of planting about the house to connect it integrally with the soil and give it an air of harmony, unity and repose. Summer days are few in our climate when a lawn is unfit to tread upon; and, to preserve its beauty and that of the house itself, other entrances than the one which should lead immediately to the grass might well be used upon these days. Messrs. Rossiter & Wright have grasped this idea in several excellent designs. A striking instance of too much gravel, necessitated in part by a faulty placing of entrances, is Messrs. Parfitt Brothers' "Three Houses at Hill Crest," No. 112. In their "House at Cedarhurst," No. 127, Messrs. Romeyn & Storer have drawn no gravel line between the main front and its lawn; but they have based the semicircular porch upon a wide rectangular stretch of flagstones, not even raised to form a terrace, which makes an ugly blot upon the lawn, and has not as much excuse in the way of possible convenience as a path.

No carriage-drive reaches the door in the long façade of Messrs. Renwick, Aspinwall & Owen's "House at Baltimore," No. 148; but the straight path which approaches it, between two stretches of grass surrounded by low hedges, is absurdly broad—almost one-third the width of the façade. Apparently to relieve the barren effect thus produced, the centre of this path has been filled with a group of flower-beds, which, of course, as they are evidently out of place, merely add to its ugliness, and also interfere with the convenience of pedestrians. Equally bad, in another way, is Mr. A. P. Valentine, Jr.'s, "Plan of a House and Home Grounds," No. 179, where there is no grass at all, but a meaningless arrangement of multiplied straight-lined paths intersecting monotonous shrubberies; and still worse is Messrs. Jardine, Kent & Jardine's "First Study for a Country House near New York," No. 226. Here the large house stands upon a high terrace, and below this the foreground is filled with wide, contorted paths and large flower-beds of graceless and inharmonious shapes, encircling an oval basin of water which is not brought into any relation with the architectural lines beyond it. More ambitious and more interesting is Messrs. Snelling & Potter's "Sketch for a House at Tuxedo," where the disposition of the paths and drives is both sensible and pleasingly symmetrical.

In pleasing contrast with garden arrangements appropriate to our climate is the entrance path to a cottage at Burlingame, California, shown in a water-color drawing by Mr. A. Page Brown, No. 330. Among the distinctively rural structures which seem particularly good I may note Messrs. Wainright & Munoz's "Golf Club House at Seabright," No. 76, and Mr. Atterbury's "Model for a House on an Adirondack Lake," No. 373. This is an interesting example of a large house kept low, as is appropriate in the indicated situation, and built of stone and unhewn logs. It may be thought, however, that in the Adirondack woods a shingled roof would have more of the virtue of fitness than the tiled roof which the house now bears.

Several well-designed tombstones of a simple kind prove that we are gradually learning that it is not only large and costly memorials to our dead which demand an artist's care. Among them are Mr. Robert Brown's "Memorial Cross," No. 175, and the "John Hancock Memorial," No. 167, by Mr. Schweinfurth, the designer of the excellent simple tombstones, a series of which were published in *Garden and Forest,* vol. ii., p. 198. Very beautiful in a more elaborate way is the late Mr. Hunt's design for the Belmont tomb at Newport.

A dignified and wholly appropriate design is Messrs. Cady, Berg & See's "Memorial Gateway for Yale University," No. 339, with simple brick piers and delicate elaborate wrought-iron work. In a series of beautifully executed water-color drawings, Messrs. Howard & Cauldwell suggest a number of gateways for the new parks in the northern part of New York city. Their conceptions are excellent, in so far as the modest size and open, unobstructive air which should characterize the entrances to naturalistic parks are concerned. But the particular architectural style chosen for their piers and pillars seems less well imagined. Something more simply classical would be more pleasing to a cultivated taste and more in keeping with the general character which American architecture bids fair to develop, than these rather heavy, baroque,

seventeenth-century motives. And a singular carelessness of the requirements of scale is seen in the same artists' "Birds'-eye Perspective of Proposed Park and Approach to Grant's Tomb," No. 181. It is a good idea
that Morningside Park and the Riverside Drive should be connected at
this point, and that in this way a dignified vista should lead the eye toward the tomb when approached from the east. The idea is well carried
out by making a wide, straight avenue form each end of the approach,
while halfway between the two parks it broadens out into an open
space covering the area of four city blocks. But this area is designed by
Messrs. Howard & Cauldwell in a way that would be appropriate to a
small courtyard. The features they have selected are so few and of such
a character that only after long study does the observer realize how
wide the included area really is. Quite a different scheme, and one of
many more parts, would be needed to give the space of four city blocks
a suitable effect. And, by the way, our general ignorance in regard even
to the nomenclature of gardening art is shown by the fact that this bald
and strictly formal arrangement is called a "park."

In conclusion, it may be said that, while the drawings in this exhibition show a commendable growth in the desire to utilize the resources
of gardening art, they prove that our architects have still a great deal to
learn, not merely with respect to its right management, but also with respect to its ideals and the difference between its various branches. They
prove how very wise it was, even in such a case as that of the Goelet
place at Newport, where only strictly formal gardening elements were
desirable, to combine the work of a landscape-architect like Mr. Olmsted with that of an architect like Mr. Hunt.

Decorative Art and Its Dogmas

It would be a pleasant task to retrace the history of twenty years and show how rapid and how creditable has been our recent progress in the cultivation of beauty. Whatever our actual rank may be as workers in art or judges of the artwork of others, our comparative rank as against our predecessors of the last generation is certainly high. We can confidently say that art is far better loved by us than it was by our fathers, far more accurately known, far more wisely criticised. In its actual practice, too, we have improved, and there are sure signs, I think, of a swifter and broader improvement in a future very near us.

Our most noteworthy advance in actual achievement has perhaps been made along the line of decorative art—that art which has been explained as "ornamenting a useful thing," in contrast with the art which "represents a beautiful thing." But though this is the department where past results have been greatest, it is, on the other hand, the department where the outlook seems least full of promise to the careful prophet— to him whose data are drawn from underlying principles as well as from results already wrought. It has been contended that this is so because decorative art is a lower, simpler thing than strictly creative art of any kind—a thing easier to fathom, master and exercise at the outset, less rich in capabilities of development and progress. But such an argument

Lippincott's Magazine 25 (February 1880): 213–220.

goes very wide of the mark. If we were true connoisseurs in our appreciation of ornament, if we were true artists in its application to every detail of our surroundings, it would become not only a pleasant atmosphere about us, but a potent educator as well. We should pass from each attained level to a higher one of subtler enjoyment and skilfuller design. The time would never come when we should necessarily stagnate, as we now show signs of doing amid the rather incongruous débris that marks where we have theorized and experimented for some fifteen years.

It is, therefore, not to the pleasant labor of praising our pretty interiors that we may most profitably address ourselves just now. It is not to the task of contrasting those interiors in a self-satisfied way with the ones where our fathers and mothers dwelt some thirty or forty years ago—abodes of grim provincial ugliness or gilt and gaudy copies of Parisian elegance, in itself a none too worthy model. It will not be quite so pleasant, but it may be more wholesome, to seek out such mistakes as mar the very good work we have most certainly done, and see how it is they threaten to limit or to maim our further possible achievements. Some of them have been inevitable, the result of inexperience or experiment. These will be outgrown or eliminated, and leave no progeny of vital error behind them. But others are the logical outcome of defective thinking, of one-sided judgments, or of provisional theories that bid fair to crystallize into narrow and absolute dogmas.

It was natural that when our interest in artistic things increased it should first be practically shown in the department of decoration. When we began to realize the very low grade of our art-instincts and perceive the very inferior character of our performance, it was natural that we should be most forcibly distressed by the things that lay nearest to us. Works of art in the strict sense we could, at the worst, do without entirely. Useful things we were obliged to have always with us—if not in beautiful shapes and colors, then in shapes and colors that were an incessant and unabatable annoyance. In our first enlightenment, then—an enlightenment that was merely the realization of our great ignorance—we were forced to attempt the actual exercise of decoration. It was a widespread popular wish and need that caused the almost simultaneous appearance of so many books on "household art" in this country and in England; as is proved, indeed, by the rapidity with which their teachings were assimilated and put in practice. To how many who were vaguely dissatisfied with their surroundings, acutely conscious of their stumbling inability to better them very materially, did Mr. Eastlake's *Hints,* for example, come as a deliverance! What was their joy at finding "beauty made easy," to all appearance, in his straightforward, confident pages! It is unnecessary to remind ourselves through how wide a circle his and kindred lessons have spread, nor how much good they have wrought. Yet they have not, as their students are apt to imagine, given us the broadest and truest possible ideas on the whole subject, much less caused our practice to be actually, as well as comparatively, admirable. The ostensible aim of the first apostles, at least, of the new cult was to pave the way for the entrance of originality into the fittings of our homes. Their lessons and the queerly exaggerated inferences of their devotees have in fact, however, only furnished us with a conventionality of a more desirable pattern than we knew before. It is not even conventionality of the most perfect possible type: still less is it apt to give place to the expression of original, characteristic taste. These shortcomings would not of necessity prophesy stagnation in the future: they might be merely temporary halting-places on our upward path. The threatening fact is that we do not see them as shortcomings, do not tolerate them as halting-places, but praise and admire them as ultimate goals. Our mistake has come about very naturally. It has arisen from the fact that our defective practice has not always grown out of theoretical fallacies or utter blunders, but out of half truths that were useful in the beginning of our reform. We see the good they have wrought—we see that they were once indispensable to us. We do not see that they must now be cast aside or broadened if we would continue to improve. The purest truth would have been wasted on us at first: we could not have attempted to put its precepts into action. For, as I have said, decorative art was preached to us as the very first chapter of our education, and the preachers could not say in the beginning, "Leave your worship of ugliness and pursue true beauty in its highest shapes, each man as it seems good to him." They dared not say, "Shun conventionality: let each man express his own taste in his own way." It was necessary first to demolish—to remove out of our sight things which would for ever contaminate our eyes, to remove out of our minds ideas that would for ever vitiate our judgments; and, secondly, to replace both the things and the ideas with the best substitutes that could be immediately comprehended by our blunt perceptions and executed by our clumsy hands. The first preaching was of necessity negative. It began by forbidding styles of work that had run into absurd exaggerations or been degraded into caricatures of their true selves. The mistake we have made lay in accepting such negative precepts as positive laws, and in looking upon the provisional reform which followed as perfection absolutely attained. Our "working hypotheses," by a very usual process, have been set up as unassailable axioms. In consequence, we have come to condemn as alike wrong the perfectly artistic and admirable use of the interdicted styles and that misuse of them which rightly led to their interdiction. The only possible remedy for defective or mistaken theories is a reference to the best practice of the past. Let us see, therefore, what are the dogmas in which we believe just now, and whether they are in conformity with or in opposition to the principles acted upon by the greatest artists and endorsed by the most universally and spontaneously æsthetic peoples.

Let us ask our neighbor who is fashionably artistic what are the laws by which he guides his taste, what are the rules to which he defers when beautifying his home; for be sure that such a one will be apt to think and work by law and rule. The main points of his answer will be somewhat as follows: All articles must be "sincerely" made; bright colors as a rule should be avoided; a strict line must be drawn between representative and decorative art, and all decoration, properly so called, must be "conventional." If we think back ten or fifteen years, we shall agree that these principles were wise and useful for the reform of then flagrant abuses, for the abolition of the detestable modes of work then universally followed. Those who remember most acutely our homes at that period—still more those who knew the typical interior of the British middle class—will realize that the conscientious application of such rules must in all cases have resulted in a marvelous improvement. But if we think back farther still, or if we look abroad beyond the borders of the Anglo-Saxon race, we shall find that they are not laws of ultimate and universal necessity—that they have, in truth, been nowhere followed where the very highest results have been achieved. In a word, as negative, provisional, preparatory teaching they were valuable: as positive precepts for all future conduct they must prove most hurtful. Let us take them in detail, and note the abuses by which they were called forth, as well as the prejudicial way in which they now seem likely to exert their influence.

First, as to the necessity of "sincere" construction. Construction is indubitably the first and most important element in articles of furniture or use as distinguished from articles that exist primarily because of their beauty. There is no doubt, also, that at the time when the recent reform began construction was terribly degraded. It was not only lost sight of as a priceless means of producing beauty, but the highest beauty was thought to consist in its deliberate concealment or falsification. It is unnecessary to dilate on the special articles in use, with their bent and con-torted outlines, their unmeaning angles and flourishes, their clumsy, su-perfluous legs, their pendants and urns and heads, and machine-turned ornaments of shapes impossible to describe. Be it noted—for this is the main point of my argument—that these perfunctory elaborations of structure were not beautiful in any sense. They were "false" and de-testable, not by being unnecessary only, but by being hideous and inap-propriate and mechanical. They were perfunctory, as I have just said, not spontaneous. They were not produced by that inextinguishable de-sire for beauty which among artistic peoples prompts the workman's hand to elaborate everything it touches, and shows him at the same time how to make elaboration in all cases truly decorative. They were pro-duced simply by a resolve at all events to avoid plainness. We were in-capable of producing or appreciating good simplicity, and fondly fan-cied that any article not plain was of necessity "decorated." Now, if we wished to bring about a better state of thinking and working, it was necessary to abolish together the notion of which I speak and the ugly products resulting from it. It was necessary to cut away, root and branch, the idea that elaboration and ornament were essential to beauty. It would have been folly to have said at the beginning, "Elabo-rate more skillfully—construct, design, carve like true artists, not like clumsy machines." How *could* we have done so when we were not able at first even to see the difference between good and bad? The virtues of simplicity of all kinds were preached through the gospel of "sincerity," for so bad had been our habits that elaboration and insincerity were in-deed synonymous terms. Its preaching was valuable—nay, indispens-able—at the time, but it should have been regarded as preparatory only. Unfortunately, it came to be preached as a final and complete religion, and to be exaggerated, moreover, in plausibly dangerous ways. The doctrine that structure should not be falsified, nor the appearance of it feared, was cast into the dogma that it should always be visibly ex-pressed. We are still told—though there has been, perhaps, very lately, a slight falling off in the vehemence of the telling—that nail-heads and rivets and hinges and supports and all similar means employed by the constructor to attain his ends *must* appear prominently to the eye. Truly, they *may*, and it is often wise to use them as the keynote of the or-namentation. But there is no artistic law—and, spite of Mr. Ruskin and Mr. Eastlake to the contrary, artistic laws are the only ones to be con-sidered in art—why they should of necessity show, any more than all the stitches in our coatseams or all the dowels in a Greek column. The

mediæval workman, so much quoted as authority, often, it is true, ornamented his constructive devices, because he was one of those who,
wishing to elaborate everything they make, know by instinct just how
to do it. But on occasions where he did not so wish he did his necessary
devices with all complacency, and we may most assuredly do likewise.
We are told that we must not have extension-tables, because they are
"insincere." A better reason might be that they are certainly unbeautiful when extended. But as they are to be draped, this does not hold, and
there is no possible artistic (or moral) reason why they should not pull
out if convenient. There is no greater "insincerity" and affectation than
to sacrifice a real convenience for the sake of something that does not
do its work so well. Nor does this advocate the toleration of ugliness,
for if we were true artists we should be able so to shape *anything* that it
would not be unpleasant to the eye or jar with neighboring objects capable of still higher beauty.

Furniture upholstered throughout is another thing that has been forbidden. Here the complaint is that it looks as if it had no structure at all,
because none is palpable. This is absurd, for the outlines and the mode
of covering show the construction as distinctly as plump human flesh
shows the bones of humanity beneath it. There is no more artistic necessity for the tangible exhibition of constructive devices in the one case
than in the other. And there is, I reiterate, and can be, no question of
morality and "sincerity" in the matter. The laws of art require that
structure be indicated sufficiently to *satisfy the eye*. Surely, more is not
a necessity on the small scale of interior fittings when more has never
been demanded in architecture, the most constructive of the arts. The
Gothic workman was quite content if his spire *looked* firm: no tender
conscience impelled him to exhibit the true causes of its firmness. And
no tender conscience, moreover, forbade his creating false ones to reas-
sure the doubting eye—false ones which simulated the strength that was
really obtained in quite other ways. And the Venetian calmly plastered
out the structural lines of his palace-front, and was satisfied when Gior-
gione laid his fresco without regard for them. This very work of stucco-
ing, by the way, is another thing that has been most utterly condemned,
especially in England, where it is far more usual than with us. But the
true fact is forgotten. Stucco is not intrinsically immoral. English stucco
is bad because utterly hideous, while Venetian stucco was admirable because more beautiful than stone or marble. Surely it was as artistic as a
wall where every brick may be counted in unmitigated sincerity of
shape and color.

As we have seen it to be with form, so has it also been with material. It was necessary at first to strongly advocate simplicity. We had no eye for intrinsic beauty, and we fondly thought to buy it with many ducats. Is not this belief, that costly things as such are more beautiful than cheap things can be, merely the love of elaboration in another shape, merely another form of the terror of simplicity? When we could not afford expensive things we sought to imitate them in cheaper wares. When this was manifestly impossible, the cheap things were abandoned to their inherent ugliness. It was wise to disregard them, for they could not be improved. Wall-papers heavy with gilding, lace curtains whose patterns we did not notice, stiff silks crude in color and ugly of fold,— these were of necessity beautiful because costly. Where these could not be had our walls went white and our windows bare. Effects of rare building materials might be imitated after a fashion. So we grained our woodwork and marbled our papers, and painted our oilcloths in parody of mosaic flooring. And up stairs, where this was not attempted, we gave up our woodwork, like our walls, to the despair of unvaried whiteness. Here, again, it will be seen, simplicity needed to be taught, and was well taught through the gospel of "sincerity." It was necessary to do away with the painted wood's pretence of natural grain, with the ghastly veining of glazed-paper marble, with the coarse machine-work that aped hand-carving, with the bas-reliefs and mouldings that were only glued on, with the marble mantels whose figure- and flower-sculpture and the frescoed walls whose figure- and flower-painting were alike the hideous record of untrained hands and unsensitive eyes. And it was necessary, besides abolishing all this, to show that beauty might be won from cheap materials as from simple shapes. We soon learned to paper our walls with twenty-five cent hangings of soft and gracious tints, to paint our pine doors in unison, to curtain our windows with cheesecloth or burlapping, to stain our floors and then soften them with rag rugs, to build our chairs and tables perfectly straight and plain; and, so doing, to make our rooms more satisfactory, more artistic, more beautiful in every way, than were the gaudy parlors of the aristocracy or the white walls and hair-cloth of the middle classes. But when we went on to say that cheap materials had some inherent moral value unshared by their costlier sisters, when we began to pride ourselves on having drawn beauty from simplicity to such an extent that we scorned the aid of richer fabrics, we almost made the new movement ridiculous. We have already begun to see the folly of such a mood, and the "æstheticoeconomical school," as it has been called, no longer dares to arrogate all virtue to itself. Better pretty chintz than ugly satin, but better still, a thousand times, a beautiful brocade, an Oriental embroidery, an embossed velvet. And better a thousand times marble, rare woods, gold and bronze than their cheaper substitutes, if only, I repeat, style and workmanship be as good.

With color—to pass to our second dogma—the case has been similar. It is not too much to say that a few years ago we were absolutely destitute of the sense of color—apathetically cold to its vivid or its delicate charms, and protected by our apathy against its most violent offences. The middle-class parlor was white and black, with a raw and glaring Brussels carpet; and in more wealthy neighborhoods the dark-green dining-room, the bright-yellow drawing-room and crimson library of one house were varied in the next by the mere substitution of blue or crimson for the drawing-room, green for the library, and tan-color, perhaps, for the dining-room. It was necessary to begin our reform by preaching the folly of such absurd narrowness, by showing that there were a thousand available tints and combinations besides these five orthodox solid colors—by demonstrating that it was not well to furnish a whole room in one unvaried shade, or imperative that a color be glaring in order to be lovely. More than this. It was necessary to do away entirely with most of the colors in use, since they *were* glaring rather than simply bright, and since our eyes could not appreciate the difference. So the virtues of dead colors and half-tints and manifold slight contrasts and combinations of nearly allied shades were preached, and preached to our infinite benefit. It would have been hopeless to say, "Keep your bright colors, but purify and grade and combine and contrast them, and relieve or soften or intensify them with duller tints." We could not have done it. The trumpet-tones of red and yellow, the still more unmanageable force of vivid blue, the startling intensity of white, the strong voices of light green and deep purple were utterly beyond our control. They stunned and confused us, and we were wise to study the laws of harmony and educate our perceptive powers by means of the lower, softer, more easily managed harmonies of brown and gray and olive, russet, sage, cream, maroon and all dusky tints. Successful results were more easily achieved with them, and partial failures were not so shocking. Great, indeed, is the delight they have afforded to eyes accustomed to a glaring color in monotonous extension or in painful relief against gilded furniture and dead-white walls. But when we go on to claim for our *feuille-morte* coloring the monopoly of all artistic and decorative value—yes, even when we accord it the lion's share of such value—we go very far wrong. The most highly developed color-sense has *always* sought the brightest colors, but knew how to get them of just the right kind. It has been well said that no color can be too intense if of the proper quality. What we fail to realize is, that between one bright tint and another bright tint of the same color there may be all the difference there is between richest beauty and distressing ugliness. Half-tints, on the contrary, are almost always good, and are more or less easy of combination. They never can sin as flagrantly as the pronounced colors, which so far surpass them in possibilities of radiant excellence. In color, as in other things, mediocrity is the safest, but not the most glorious, path. And in art, as in all things, the degradation of the very best results in the very worst.

Let us look back for confirmation of these words to the best work of the past. Under the turquoise sky of Egypt and its bewildering sunsets, beside its glittering river, amid its yellow sands and salmon-tinted rocks and fields of literal emerald, the artist relieved his architecture and painted his frescoes with bold primary colors in strongest contrast. And the Assyrians worked in a different way toward a similar end. The Greeks, too, delighted in the whiteness of marble and the glitter and shine of all polished things, and, so far as we can judge, in simple contrasts of decided color, as simple, but also as decided and self-confident, as the lines of the architecture they accompanied. There was no hesitation or mystery or reserve about either. How could there be, when Greek eyes had been trained on Greek landscape— on the solid sapphire of its seas, the broad purple of its hills, the yellow and crimson of its evening skies, the perfect clearness of its atmosphere? Let us now come nearer home and restore in fancy the North Gothic interiors, which we too often conceive as monochrome merely because they have been denuded of their best beauty. We cannot say with exactness, perhaps, how the walls were covered in the Romanesque period, but we have still much of the glass which came later, when the walls contracted and the windows spread and absorbed into themselves the office of decoration, fulfilling that office by means of the most vivid color the world has ever seen. Should we so lose ourselves in the refulgence of a rose-window at Notre Dame or Cologne if it had been wrought in even the subtlest harmony of half or neutral tints? And in Southern Gothic, where we have wall-color left in fresco or mosaic, it is vivid enough, and surely properly "decorative" also. In the pictures of the greatest schools, whether cabinet paintings of huge canvases for the permanent covering of wall and ceiling, we find the same thing—not reticence, but most daring mastery. Rubens in the foggy North, Titian and Veronese in the glow of Venice, are the most renowned of colorists, and also the most brilliant. Even in their pictures to-day we see this—in the passionate depth of Titian, in the bright, clear contrasts of Veronese, in the carnival of audacity we call the work of Rubens. And they have certainly all lost more or less of their original vividness during the centuries' passage. In these pictures the draperies and flesh-tints may, it is true, not be so bright as it is possible for actual draperies and the colors of actual flesh and hair to be. But this is not because the artist preferred the more subdued scale. It was imposed upon him partly by the fact that no pigment can literally render the brilliance of many actual things, and still more by the fact that he must render the whole chromatic scale, from the darkness of shadowed black to the dazzle of sunshine on a white ground, by one poor octave of opaque tints. The scale of actual color must always be adapted and condensed, and there is no one thing the artist may dare to paint with the whole force of his palette, for everything else would of necessity be falsified in the sequence. Mr. Ruskin has explained this most elaborately, and it is a truism in the mouth of every teacher of art, theoretical or practical. But the untrained are apt to forget it, nevertheless, and apt neither to mark the originality of every master in arranging for himself his artificial scale, nor to appreciate the skill of the greatest colorists in expressing by its perfunctory means as much as possible of vividness and light as of shadow and depth and darkness. There is a *Marriage of Cana* by Paul Veronese in Dresden, with a superb figure all in orange that dominates the picture, and dominates, indeed, the whole company in the room where it stands, magnificent progeny though they be of Veronese and Titian and Tintoret. The color is not as bright, to be sure, as the color of a real orange stuff might very well be. But we may feel sure that a man who could delight in its comparative intensity, judged by the forced reticence of all painting, would delight in the most resplendent hues that sun and Nature or costly dyes on silken surfaces could work.

Of Japanese and other modern Oriental art I need not speak in detail: it pleads my cause too forcibly, in too evident a manner. Year by year we appreciate it more thoroughly, and enjoy its real beauty, I believe, more sincerely. Its vivid color, which at first startled, then amused us, we are gradually learning to reverence as we ought. To its influence is due whatever of reaction there has been against the dull coloring we have so over-prized. Perhaps before long we may dare to imitate its boldness and apply its teachings to our own very different ends.

The love of intense color must go hand in hand, by the way, with the appreciation of rich stuffs to which I have already referred. It is impossible in any but the noblest materials—I speak now of woven tissues, not of ceramic wares—to realize pure and brilliant colors. A gorgeous crimson chintz is impossible. The lustre of satin or the depth of velvet is necessary to bring out the tint, and the shadows and lights of heavy folds to give its full gradations. Of the necessity of rich stuffs to perfect color, and the power of the two in combination to hide even defects of form, we shall be convinced if we think a moment on the costume of Venice and Spain in their classic days. If we criticise its picturesque effects, we shall see how often beauty depends entirely on material and color—how often it is wanting if we look for it in form alone. The tightly-drawn, long, flat bodices display the shimmer of satin, the glow of velvet, to the best advantage, but the form of the woman within is utterly hidden—nay, travestied. The tight or puffed sleeves, the heavy perpendicular folds of the full skirt gathered on the hips, show most magnificently the rarest gradations of color the material can exhibit, and bring out most perfectly its heavy richness. But they tell us nothing of the limbs they cover. It makes no difference what was below many of the robes Velasquez painted. The woman, apart from the superb life of face and hands, was but a frame upon which to display the utmost beauty of the loom. This is not the way in which the Greek chiton and chlamys covered and decorated and explained the body beneath, following its shape with suggestive undulations, yielding to its every motion and interpreting both shape and motion with a beauty almost higher than the undraped form could show. Softness was all that was needed for such a dress. White flannel would have been an excellent material where form was the first thought, but fancy a dress of white flannel made like that of Titian's *Lavinia* or of Pharaoh's daughter in Veronese's *Finding of Moses* at Dresden! Color such as the Venetians loved is impossible without richness of surface and fold to render it. And richness of surface and fold would not make us admire some of the forms the Renaissance tolerated without color to dazzle and enthrall us. The black satin Fortuny painted so marvellously in a portrait seen at one of the New York Loan Exhibitions could not redeem an unpleasing form as do the cream satin and green velvet of Titian, the yellow damask of Veronese and the rich brocades Velasquez knew.

Two of our three self-imposed dogmas have now been noticed—the dogma that preaches a so-called "sincerity" in form, and the one that preaches the reticence of a low key in color. There still remains for con-

sideration the third dogma, which demands that a line be drawn between decorative and representative art, and that the former be restricted to "conventional" design. All three dogmas are, of course, more
or less connected with each other, but this last is held with the greatest
tenacity and viewed as the most important. So it threatens to outlive the
others, and have a more deadening effect upon our artistic future.

PART 2

"Recent Architecture in America"

12

Public Buildings (1)

There is a point of difference which marks off architecture from the
other arts, and is commonly held to be distinctly in its favor. Emerson
says it is "a mixed art whose end is sometimes use and sometimes
beauty." More exactly, it is a mixed art whose ends are use and beauty
interwoven. And this blending of the utilitarian with the strictly æsthetic insures to architecture a peculiarly unbroken life—insures that
men will always build, though they may cease to carve or paint or sing.
Perhaps this fact is not, however, so advantageous as is usually thought.
Looking at the works produced when artistic instinct has been lost and
dull gropings or mistaken aspirations have tried to play its part, and re-
membering that the world cannot so easily, with the advent of a better
taste, rid itself of the architect's as of the painter's or the sculptor's
legacy of failure, we may feel, perhaps, that it would be better if the art
at times could cease entirely—could die to effort as it does die to success. But as no theoretical decision as to what might be for the best can
alter the fact that building must go on, and as we know, I repeat, that its
results are among the most permanent of man's creations, it is evident
that in no art whatever have we so vital an interest as in this. With no
art is it so essential that the people at large should be sufficiently enlightened to know good work from bad, and to encourage the good by

The Century Magazine (27) 6 (May 1884): 48–67.

public as well as by private effort. Doubly is this the case, moreover, since no art, be it noted, is dependent upon patronage in the same way as is the architect's. The result of ignorance in regard to architecture does not, as with the other arts, mean apathy alone and the mere loss of possible delight. It means the multiplication of wretched works that must remain for an unlimited period of time, to disgrace the memory of their generation and to corrupt the taste of later comers.

There is much good building going on at the present moment in this country, as it is hoped will be shown in these papers. If it were quite clearly perceived by the public to be such,—that is, if it were more evidently distinguished from the bad work flourishing beside it,—there would be less excuse for their preparation. That this bad work does so rankly flourish is by itself sufficient proof of a widespread deficiency in knowledge, since, as I have said, architecture always comes in answer to a distinct call of patronage.

It is instructive to note in this connection the character of our recent architectural work done under government supervision. As stated in the Treasury report laid before the present Congress, no fewer than twenty-seven government buildings, many of them vast in size and costliness, have been in process of erection during the year just closed, in almost as many different cities of our land. It is safe to guess from the examples with which we are most familiar that very few of them are sensible structures, not one a really admirable work of art—safe to say that scarce a single building put up under Treasury direction since the days of Mr. Potter's service could by any stretch of courtesy be included in a list of our true successes. The various local governments of state and city have a little better record to exhibit; but it will be found that most of the works coming under the general head of "public buildings," which will here be named for praise, while intended, it is true, for public or semi-public use, yet owe their existence to the fortunate instinct of individuals or of private corporations.

There was, as Mr. White has lately shown my readers, a distant time when building as a fine art was in our country the rule and not merely the exception. While our fathers were colonists or very young republicans they built very well—sometimes beautifully, and almost always honestly, intelligently, appropriately, and with a simplicity of aim and manner that was the very reverse of affectation or vulgarity. But the years which lie between their time and ours were dead indeed to art— were characterized at first by a helpless sort of ignorance, and later on by crass vulgarity and barbarous display. It is not necessary to describe these phases in a detailed way, since I am by no means essaying to write a history of American architecture. Every reader who has used his eyes will find in his own memory types of the various sorts of failure we achieved—types which are only interesting now as standards by means of which to gauge the undeniable advance of very recent years. I may say one word, however, with regard to the kind of work that came in fashion soon after that early kind which Mr. White has praised. The remains of the "classic style" that flourished for so many years—in stone in our large cities, in pine boards and paint and stucco in our smaller towns—have long been pointed out for ridicule even by those who hold no other architectural tenet with distinctness save this as to the ludicrous folly of attempting to fit Greek temple forms to our modern uses and our often cheap materials. Such attempts are no doubt mistaken, and their results are often ludicrous enough. Yet after all the fashion has, I think, been rather unduly berated, for it had a certain amount of at least comparative excellence. It proved that its generation admired, if but in a stupid sort of way, the finest architectural style the world has ever seen. Later on, admiration was transferred to far inferior models, while current methods of adaptation and execution remained quite as stupid and grew still more inartistic. And a poor work following a fine example though at an immeasurable distance, is better at all events than another work in which execution and ideals are alike despicable and ugly. And be the work poor as it may, there is a dignity and a simplicity about Greek forms which prevent utter barbarism or hideousness of result—which prevent, for one thing, any accent of vulgarity. There are many far worse public buildings in New York than the Custom-House on Wall street. We might easily count up those which are much better, at least from an artistic point of view. And the pillared wooden temple which does duty for church or courthouse in the village street is usually a far better thing in itself, and far more agreeable in its testimony to the taste if not to the practical wisdom of its builders, than is its later neighbor—a bastard structure with vulgarized reminiscences of many styles and no styles, and much riotous ornamentation in sanded zinc and jigsaw carving.

The ties of this our new world with the old are of such complex sorts that it would be impossible to guess, without inquiring into facts, whence may have come our impulse in any artistic path. Such inquiry will show that in our architecture we have largely followed England, though her example has not been consulted by our painters or our sculptors. England, as is well known, has been through a varied and perplexing architectural experience since the beginning of the century. First, there dawned the Greek revival, instigated chiefly by the publication of Stuart and Revett's "Athens." Then came the Gothic revival, bringing about the famous "battle of the styles" between classicism in general and mediævalism in general, and the faction fights (almost as bitter) of the mediævalists among themselves. Every phase of English Gothic had its exclusive advocates, and there were others, almost as exclusive, who enforced in stone as well as in speech and print the claims of French or Tuscan or Venetian builders as the best models for the modern architect to follow. Then, just when the main battle seemed to have decided itself in favor of mediævalism, and when the partisans of the triumphant movement seemed to have settled into some sort of agreement among themselves,— or at least into such mutual toleration as would let them all live and work in their several ways and insure the advance of the Gothic movement as a whole,—just when its teachers and preachers began to draw breath and consider their cause gained for all time to come, began an unexpected reaction among the younger men into a love for late Renaissance work. "Queen Anne" is the term popularly used of this newest style, and may do as well as any other meaningless ticket to label its results when they must be mentioned. But no term could be historically more inexact. The builders of Queen Anne's day—whose influence we see in our own colonial work—discreet, sober, and dignified, even when nothing more, would be the last to accept the paternity of the motley new fashion, which is in truth less English than Dutch, and less "Queen Anne" than a mixture of Jacobean and Georgian manners, and which most rarely counts among its qualities those of discretion, sobriety, and dignity.

All these successive phases in English work were imitated here in more or less faithful and more or less successful ways. Of the Grecian fashion I have already spoken. It reigned for a time as wholly as it did in England, though with variations due to our lesser wealth and our different materials. The Gothic movement, however, was not quite so cordially indorsed on this side of the water as upon the other. English Gothic forms found little favor except for ecclesiastical and collegiate work. It was only the Venetian Gothic which at one time bade fair to be really popular with us. Many important buildings were erected in this style, like Mr. Wight's Academy of Design in New York, and the large structure on the corner of Boylston and Tremont streets in Boston. In it Mr. Eidlitz designed some of his best work, as, for example, the piano warehouse on the west side of Union Square. Messrs. Potter and Robinson, again, who at one time were the most prominent of our younger architects, have usually preferred this style, and with it have done some excellent work, notably on the Princeton College campus. But none of these buildings especially concern us here. I cannot try to praise everything good that has been done in the past—even in a past which lies close behind us. I can only endeavor to show what is being done *to-day* in ways that bid fair permanently to influence the development of our art. And Venetian Gothic with us is already, I think, a thing of the past. Isolated examples will continue, very likely, to be built; but it will hardly count any steady adherents among the younger men in whom lie the promise of our future.

The recent "Queen Anne" fashion has been taken up here with much enthusiasm. I cannot speak, except through an acquaintance with the prints in English journals, of its very latest essays on the parent soil; but it seems to me as if, with all the wildness and folly that have sometimes marked its presence here, we have still been somewhat more sober, if somewhat less ambitious, than our brethren. Both here and there good work, too, has of course been done when the style has been discreetly dealt with. But what our share in them amounts to I can only show in later portions of my commentary.

Just now I would add that, strong as has been the influence of England on our work, it has not been so exclusive as is commonly thought— at least by Englishmen. Much of our best architecture claims a very different parentage. Italian Renaissance examples have directly inspired some of our most important essays, and modern French fashions have evidently dictated the forms of very many others. Domestic work in New York, again, is chiefly founded on the "high stoop" model, which is not English but Dutch; and though this manner of building has scarcely touched either Boston or Philadelphia, it has become largely characteristic of Washington and of our newer Western cities. And the so-called decoration adopted for it when it deviated from the simplicity of the original Dutch model and evolved the typical "brown-stone front" of New York, is not English, whatever else it may be called. The statement often made by writers in English architectural journals that there is nothing good or bad in America which has not its exact prototype with them, is very wide indeed of the truth. We have been and still are not only far more continental, but far more original in our architecture than we even realize ourselves. To ask how often this originality has been a thing to boast of, is to open up quite another question—a question which would need first of all for its decision the settlement of the time-honored problem as to whether mistaken originality or the servile copying of good examples is the more promising mood in art. Two things are, however, certain. One is that our real epoch of productivity is but just beginning; and the other is that, whatever its course may be, whether peaceful or distracted, whether resulting in failure or success, it will work itself out on lines of its own—not upon those suggested by the contest still raging on the soil of England.

Perhaps the first thing that will be expected from a writer who proposes to discuss recent efforts and future probabilities, will be a definite programme as regards this matter of style—a statement of personal preferences, with the reasons why they seem justified by the needs of our day and clime. But such a programme I by no means intend to give. My aim, I repeat, is chiefly to show what is actually being built in various departments of the art; and though no commentator, perhaps, can be quite without theories as to what *ought* to be built, yet all ideals of future success must, to be of any value, base themselves on what seems probable, or at least possible, in the given case. Present essays are of very different sorts, even within the limits of true excellence; and through them many things are day by day working themselves a little clearer to our sight. Whatever considerations of a theoretical or prophetical sort I may have to advance,—they will not be many nor dogmatic—may better, therefore, be postponed till we shall have gained some acquaintance with our current art and shall be able to use its results as terms of illustration.

Since our recent works are of many different kinds, is there any standard by which they may all be tested and their excellence, when it exists, shown to be something more than mere accordance with that personal prepossession commonly known as the "taste" of a writer, which is often either vague or prejudiced and to which I, at least, shall not appeal? Certainly there must be. All art is judged—when really *judged* at all—far more in deference to reason and to tangible, demonstrable qualities, and far less in deference to blind instinct or "feeling," than is popularly thought. It is only a very ignorant observer who can give no logical reason for the faith that is in him before even the most ethereal, most spiritual results of art. How much more must this be true of architectural work, whose ends are those of use as well as beauty.

Old Sir Thomas Wotton, first of English writers on the subject, tells us that the architect's task is to provide us in his structure with "commoditie, firmness, and delight." It is popularly believed, I fear, that the last-named quality is the most important. So it might be, if we wished to regard the purely æsthetic side of the art alone. But we never *should* so wish; and, in fact, we cannot so regard it even if we would, since architectural beauty is not, as is too often thought and written, an extrinsic, superficial thing, depending altogether on ornamental features, but is inevitably bound up with the very attainment of "firmness" and "commoditie." The really vital beauty of an architectural work consists in its clear expression of these two qualities, and of the material way in which its parts are framed; for architecture is, like every other art, *first of all a means of expression.*

What every true work of art aims at is to express through the representation of something external to himself a meaning or an emotion which the artist feels. The external motive which is the painter's or the sculptor's medium he finds in some form or effect of nature. But the architect finds his in the character of his proposed building, the functions of its several necessary parts, and the qualities and demands of its material. This is to say, that the aim of his work is to show with clearness his idea of how a given structure should be built, considering its site, its size, its purpose, and also the kind of material and quantity of ornament permitted him. Thus we see that as in the other arts, so in architecture, conception is the most important thing. If the conception is adequate and is thoroughly well expressed to the eye, the result will be a good, though possibly not a beautiful, work of architecture. But if the architect is an *artist,* he will use his structural elements in ways that will not only be sensible and expressive, but æsthetically pleasing. He will secure by them those effects of composition, of color, and of light and shade, which (and not mere decoration) are his main helps toward the production of "delight." An architect cannot, even for the mere beauty of his work, treat his structure as a painter treats his canvas—cover it entirely, leave it to play no part in his visible result. He must, whether he will or no, treat it as the sculptor treats his clay,—must work with and not upon it. He must model it, and its modeling will tell that story of success or failure which can never be merely painted or sculptured or inlaid on its surface. If his materials are not plastic beneath his hand, if he does not shape them so as clearly and beautifully to express his intentions and his feelings, if, in a word, he does not *build* a beautiful thing, he will miss his mark in spite of all possible decorative effort. Decoration may, indeed, vastly increase the distinct expression and the beautiful effect of his building, but decoration can never *make* a good work of architecture,—can rarely, even in its noblest forms and its greatest profusion, redeem one which is weak in other ways. We see, therefore, that decoration cannot even be considered apart from constructive forms. It must grow from them, depend upon them, follow their lead and enforce their speech, if it is to be architectural in fact as well as name. The building itself should provide from the outset for the adornment it is to receive, should dictate its character, give it the lines it is to emphasize, the spaces it is to fill,—should prescribe, in a word, the voice with which it needs must speak. For not abstract beauty (to repeat) but beautiful expression is the architect's concern, in the final ornamentation as in the first planning of his work. Constructive and decorative features must strive together toward this same end, and the latter always be dependent on the former.

If these things be true,—and I think they cannot be questioned,—we feel at once the falsity of the belief to which I have referred above—the belief that building and architecture are two different things, that delight alone is the object of the latter, and (consequently upon the first decision) is to be attained through superficial decoration—through the addition of what Mr. Ruskin, who champions this belief, actually calls "unnecessary features." From this mistaken theory, consciously or unconsciously held, have come not only most of the stupidity and vacillation of modern criticism, but much of the poverty and falseness of modern work itself. No; building and architecture are not to be divorced. The chief elements in architectural beauty, as in architectural strength and fitness, are *structural* elements. With these the builder must not only secure his "firmness," but must make its character apparent to the eye. With these he must not only provide, but reveal, the special sort of "commoditie" which has been the object of his effort. And with these he must achieve the greater part of that "delight" which he can vastly enhance, of course, by the consonant elaboration of ornamental motives, and the appropriate employment of the painter's and the sculptor's skill. A building that is structurally beautiful will please the eye,— the educated eye, I mean,—though no "unnecessary feature" be superadded. There is nothing more beautiful on earth to-day than the naked skeleton of a Greek temple after every atom of its decorative sculpture has been stripped and shattered from its place. There is nothing more admirable than a perfectly plain Gothic interior of good design. The castles of Edward I are as fine in their soberer way as are his churches, and Albert Dürer's towers and the warehouses of Nuremberg are as fine in theirs as are her ornate house fronts. Elaboration may add a charm that their simplicity does not possess; but it needs no elaboration to make them works of architectural art. It is not because the towers of the Brooklyn bridge are plain that *they* are not works of art. It is because beauty was not considered in planning their masses, and because their constructive features do not properly explain their purpose. If an architect had fashioned them, he would very likely have left them as simple as they are to-day; but he would have built them beautiful in outline, and would not have fallen so far short of expressional design as to make the openings for the cables—the very why and wherefore of the towers' existence—mere casual holes cutting the cornice through. And there is no reason, save our apathy or artistic weakness, why every factory or grain elevator in the land might not be made, in its simple and humble way, a work of architecture too.

But in dwelling on the really vital law of architectural expression some critics go much too far. They demand that a building should not only be truthfully expressive, but should be this in a precise, particular, and complete way, even to the possible detriment of beauty of result. But this art, like all others, is a "system of compromises," in which certain desirable things must often be partially suppressed in order that others may get proper recognition. And just here is one of the few points in which architecture—most human and non-natural of the arts—may take a lesson from nature's work. In building her organisms nature rarely quite conceals, and never misrepresents, her structure and her purpose by her appearances; but she does not reveal them crudely, bluntly or minutely. Her expression is often abstract, veiled, condensed,—so to say, *typical* rather than explanatory. And so may be the architect's. So must it often be, indeed, especially in these days of complex modern life when the purposes and uses of buildings differ in so many really immaterial ways. Not all structures can definitely, very few perhaps can quite explicitly, tell the observer of all the secrets of their fabric or of all the needs to meet which they were built. But all—and here is the true reading of the law—should be so far and so truthfully expressive that their fabric will not be actually misrepresented to the eye, and that when their needs are known, their architectural outcome will seem completely inspired thereby and entirely in harmony therewith. And he is the best architect who selects with the truest instinct what things he will express—who sees most unerringly which are fundamental and must be shown, and which are accessory and may be unexpressed.

Still another lesson that nature teaches—and a most important one—is that a structure, to be sensible, expressive or delightful, must be an organism, a whole, with parts many or few as the case may be, but with such unity and harmony and interdependence between them all that a single coherent impression is the result. No portions of a work should seem casual, perfunctory, or immaterial. Each should seem right and proper in its own place, put there for some good and evident reason, which in the very best work will be at the same time constructional, expressive, and æsthetic.

This, then, is what we ask our architects to show us in their work,— not first of all, I am very sure, strict adherence to the precedents of some style of former days, but *rational art*. They must build sensibly, meeting as fully as possible the practical requirements of their task. They must build appropriately with regard to the nature of their site. They must build honestly, showing their material, whether noble or humble, for what it is, and making the best of it. They must build truthfully, concealing as little as possible their interior by their exterior, or the nature of their structural forms by the fashion of their surface and their decoration. And they must build beautifully, too, giving us pleasure through their composition, and, when it is allowed them, through wise ornament as well. These different aims involve, as I have said, occasional compromises and concessions; for beauty and truth and common sense are not always to be attained together. We are therefore sometimes called upon to decide in how far an architect has been justified in neglecting beauty for the sake of the sterner qualities of his art, or in securing it by some sacrifice of these. But it will always be the best kind of beauty that will come through no subordination or concealment.

One general rule, moreover, may be laid down to guide our criticism. This is the rule that as a work of architecture is both very conspicuous and very long-lived, its aim should be "to satisfy and not to startle." The fact that a building is "striking" is often held to prove it fine. But the best buildings are those which, whether striking or not,— oftener not, perhaps, at least in modern work,—will seem better and better as the days go by: will not grow oppressive or aggressive or impertinent, or tame, flat, and uninteresting, in proportion as they grow familiar.

Another thing which it is well to bear in mind is, that while a building must be judged by its intrinsic and evident qualities, a wider charity should restrain our judgment of its builder. A painter or a sculptor may usually do the kind of work he pleases and in the way he pleases, hampered only by limitations in himself. But an architect is always bound— and often hopelessly thwarted and coerced—by the practical requirements of his problem, and by the tastes, the fancies or the follies of his patron. Not often does he really get a chance to show all the strength that may be in him.

Let us look now at some of our recent public structures and see what excellent types we can find among them.

I think I cannot do better than begin the list with the new Medical School building that Messrs. Van Brunt and Howe have just put up in Boston, since in it we have good architecture reduced to its simplest, barest form. I have said that a building to be good must be an organism, a whole, composed of related and interdependent parts. *Composition* is, in fact, the architect's greatest task, and success in it the highest triumph he can gain. If the composition of his masses is scattered, ineffective, a thing of shreds and patches, and not a unity, he fails. But if the opportunity for this composition with masses is denied him altogether,—if he is obliged, as so often in our cities, to build a mere rectangular box without even a visible roof,—how shall he give his work that look of life and growth, and intelligent adaptation and expressiveness, which will mark it as an architectural conception, as an organism, and not a mere pile of brute material? But one resource is left him. He can still compose with what are called in technical parlance his *voids and solids*—with his windows and his wall spaces. Some of the most beautiful architectural composition in the world has, indeed, been done with no other constructive factors—as in the house fronts of Venice and the palaces of the Italian Renaissance time. Here, however, ornament comes largely into play, and beautiful materials do their part as well. But it was a much humbler and more difficult problem that was set in the Boston Medical School. The task was to build a great square box, wholly of brick, with no ornamentation, and with the necessity for floods of light in the interior. Yet there is beauty in the result—architectural beauty of the strictest kind, though no atom of that "picturesqueness" which popular criticism falsely considers its equivalent. If the Boston reader will look at this building, especially at the side which faces Trinity Church, he will see what I mean by good and effective and expressive composition, achieved solely by the sensible and artistic disposal of windows and wall spaces and very flat pilasters. And if he will look—I venture to say, though such pointing of comparisons is no pleasant part of my task—at the new building for the Technological Institute, which stands near by, and in which the conditions of the architect's task were almost precisely similar, he will see what I mean by inartistic, mechanical design. Of course, had ornament been added to

Mr. Van Brunt's structure (the only traces of it now present, the little gable over the front and the vases above the cornice, are distinctly detrimental to the whole), it would have gained vastly in beauty. The eye would then have been interested and delighted as we approach the building, not merely satisfied and impressed as we view it from a distance. Take the same design, build it of fine materials, and decorate it with good ornament, and we should have a very beautiful building. But, naked as it stands it is a good piece of architectural composition and so a good work of art—far more satisfactory than many buildings whose profuse and charming details have been applied to an unintelligent design.

I wish I could speak from personal inspection of the new library for the Michigan University which Mr. Van Brunt has also built. It offered problems of a similar sort as to the necessity for considering practical needs alone, but it gave full scope for composition with its masses. From the drawings it seems to be a work of peculiar architectural excellence, almost wholly devoid of ornament, but admirably adapted to its purpose, and boldly, clearly and agreeably expressing its interior by its exterior. No features, large or small, exist save such as were dictated by absolute necessity; but these are so conceived and so arranged that they result in great strength and originality and dignity. The same intelligence in composition, the same good management of masses and obligatory features, often distinguishes Mr. Van Brunt's work, even when the details are not of the most satisfactory kind. Surface beauty he may miss, but the body and bones of architectural beauty he very often shows us.

Look, now, for another instructive contrast, at the New York Post-office, where the architect had as fine a chance as heart could wish: a splendid site; practical requirements which, on such a site, need not have hampered him to any great extent; and money enough to give him noble materials and all the ornament he wanted. But what is the result? Modeling with the masses has been, indeed, attempted, but so imperfectly carried out that we do not get a single effective mass, a single powerful shadow, a single decisive line. Of composition with the voids and solids there is no trace at all; we see no wall spaces that can so be called, and the windows are distributed with monotonous, mechanical regularity. We miss, accordingly, all such impression of solidity and dignity as the eye demands in so large a building; we miss all expression of interior through exterior forms; we miss all proof of an artistic conception in the builder's brain; and we miss, in spite of the fact that there is no plain surface where the eye can rest, all evidence that he understood the aim of decoration. It is a big, costly, conspicuous structure; but no one calls it a work of art. And it is, I am sorry to repeat, only a type of our governmental erections. But if we would have a proof that municipalities may do even less well than the general government we may look at the new City Buildings in Philadelphia, which are worse than our Post-office because equally unintelligent, and much more showy, elaborate, and pretentious.

Take, now, an example very different from any thus far noted; take the little Crane Memorial Library which Mr. Richardson has built at Quincy. Our engraving does not show all its charm; neither its beautiful materials (light yet warm Quincy stone in the walls and dark red Longmeadow sand-stone in the trimmings) nor the details of its ornamentation. Yet I think every reader will call it an attractive work, for it is, in fact, *picturesque*. Vastly as the value of picturesqueness is overestimated in the popular mouth, it is still often a desirable and a worthy quality when great dignity or grandeur is not demanded in a building; but only, be it noted, if it is achieved naturally and truthfully, not in forced fashions or too evidently for its own sole sake,—when it is the happy and easy result of a sensible arrangement of features really necessary or desirable in themselves. Such is the case with this little library. It is architecturally sensible, straightforward, expressive, and unaffected; and so we rejoice in the artistic instinct that could also make it picturesque and lovely. Its picturesqueness will be found to result, if we examine, from the irregular disposition of its structural parts— of the gable, the turret, the doorway, and the windows. Each of these features has come in strict and simple accordance with the demands of interior convenience. The large window lights the reading-room; the smaller, high-placed openings light the rank of alcoves; the door is made so large, from expressive if not from practical necessity, since here is a building which should distinctly invite the foot of every passer-by; the turret holds the staircase, which leads to the storage-room above, and this is lighted by the gable windows and the "winkers" in the roof. Thus much for the features themselves; but their irregular disposition is also motived by practical and not by willful reasons. Since the stairway must debouch upon the platform afforded by the gable, it must break the line of this; since the doorway must be so wide, its moldings must be boldly stopped against the tower—for to have shifted it further to the right would have brought it into too close contact with the great window, or have displaced this. A more timid builder would have made his doorway smaller, and so have lost his chance for forcible expression; and

Fig. 6.   Interior of the Crane Memorial Library, Quincy, Mass. [Henry H. Richardson, 1880–83.]

a less artistic one would not have known so well how to bring harmony and grace and true—not forced— originality and picturesqueness out of the irregularities which offered the best solution of his practical problem. Another point to be noted is the way in which the decorative value of color is made *architecturally* valuable—the bands of darker stone binding the various parts of the composition together, and accenting its important lines and features. The carved ornament, too, is concentrated, not dispersed, and so helps the general expression. With regard, finally, to this general expression, I will add that, though we may not at once perceive that the building is exactly what it is,—a library for free public use,—yet we know it is something of the sort; and when its purpose is told its appearance is found most appropriate—and rather more minutely expressive, indeed, than we can often hope to see. To the delicately wrought interior of this library I shall refer when we come to speak of decoration and of "style" in general.

This is one of the most perfect of Mr. Richardson's buildings; but the same romantic, artistic, picturesque instinct is almost always shown in his art, though sometimes not held so well in hand by strict architectural feeling. It was only after several less completely satisfactory essays in a similar direction, indeed, that he arrived at such simplicity and truth of design as here. A larger library at Woburn was, I think, his first attempt in the Romanesque, round-arched style to which he has since faithfully adhered. So it is not wonderful that the richly picturesque and florid possibilities of this style led him into exuberance of rather too pronounced a sort. But as over exuberance of a really strong and attractive kind is not a common failing in modern architecture, and as it is never, I think, combined in Mr. Richardson's work with affectation, forced animation, or mere display, we do not much complain of it.

At North Easton, near Boston, Mr. Richardson was given a peculiarly fortunate opportunity in the commission to build, on an elevated rocky site overlooking the village, two important structures—the Ames Memorial Library and a Town-Hall, also a memorial offered by the same family. He was fortunate, also, in having the assistance of Mr. Frederick Law Olmstead in the arrangement of the connecting grounds and terraces, and the result is one of the most delightful groups of harmonious yet contrasting works of which we yet can boast—but a group, unfortunately, which lies off the highway of travel, and can only be seen at the end of a special pilgrimage.

The library is less imposing and less picturesque than the one at Woburn,—which is, indeed, rather too imposing and too picturesque,—while it is not so simply graceful and charming as the one at Quincy. It shows a less marked originality, more conventionalism in its design; and it sins a little in expression, I think, by the prominence of its tower. This, which at Quincy was given only its due importance as a staircase turret, is here carried well above the roof, and asserts itself in a manner rather out of harmony with the purpose of the building. Towers, like all other architectural features, have a meaning of their own—though the meaning of none is more commonly ignored or misconceived. A tower is first of all, in one shape or another, an ecclesiastical feature. Or it is, as in ancient castles or the palaces of Italian towns, an actual necessity for aggression or defense. Or in open forms it is a belvedere for outlook, and thus appropriate to many modern structures. Or, finally, it is a symbol of dominion and authority. This last was its function, for example, in the municipal buildings of the Netherlands, and such was its significance in the middle ages, when in more countries than one a royal per-

Fig. 7.   The Ames Memorial Town-Hall, North Easton, Mass. [Henry H. Richardson, 1879–81.]

mit was needed before it might be built. This, too, seems to be its proper service at the present day. As the town halls of Belgium lifted their great towers to give the hour with clock and bell and to proclaim the might of the civic arm, so ours should serve a similar practical or symbolic purpose. Thus, while we object a little (on expressional grounds) to the tower that Mr. Richardson has given his North Easton library,—which, be it observed, is, on the whole, an excellent work that we should hardly stop to criticise were it another's and not Mr. Richardson's,—we approve the one he has added to the town-hall close at hand. The *loggia* of this building, with its massive arcade and broad open space within, is not only most effective in itself, but as expressive as is the Quincy door—marking the building as the chief gathering-place of the villagers; and the row of uniform large windows in the front well explains the presence of the great hall within. The library is built of the same materials as the one at Quincy, and the hall of dark stone below and brick above, the tower rising in admirably picturesque fashion from its rocky foundation.

Let us turn now to one of Mr. Richardson's works which is very different in site and purpose, and so, very properly, is different also in effect—to Sever Hall at Cambridge. Here a few large recitation-rooms of simple plan were required of him; and as the building stands in the college yard, dignity and not picturesqueness was well conceived to be its proper character, together with a certain simplicity and symmetry that would keep it harmonious with the older buildings close about it.

Sever Hall is, I am very sure, one of the most perfect of our recent works; and considering the nature of its excellence, it is one of the most instructive. First of all, it is instructive as showing that an architect who can be more romantic, exuberant, lavish, and ornate than any other of our builders, can also upon occasion be as quiet, as simple, as reticent, and discreet as the most conventional among them. But since he is an artist, he does not become conventional in becoming simple. There is, in truth, much more originality in the quiet success of Sever Hall than in many more striking works, whether by his hand or by another. It is not necessary to describe the building in detail, since the engraving is before us. I would only note that it is built of brick, with the decoration carved also out of brick, and with but a slight use of stone about the openings; and that the fortunate introduction of the great round arched doorway (an introduction from which many builders would have shrunk, in view of the square-headed openings which otherwise prevail throughout) is what gives a grateful touch of piquancy to the whole. I wish I could also show the reader the grouping of the windows at one end of this building to prove how simply and easily (*if* we presuppose an artist) variety may be secured, and the most perfect quietude and harmony yet prevail.

In the second place, Sever Hall is especially instructive, because though it is excellent, admirable, and beautiful, it is *not* picturesque. I have already referred to the specious attractions of picturesqueness in architecture, but must dwell upon them still a little further; for no more pernicious fault afflicts our popular criticism—and, by inevitable reaction, our current practice—than the ceaseless, irrational desire for picturesque effects.

Every one who has traveled abroad with the average tourist who professed and often really felt an interest in the architectural work of former days, must remember how entirely that interest was inspired by picturesque effects. Sometimes these effects are, I repeat, a legitimate and immediate outcome of true architectural excellence; but more often they are accidental, posterior, wrought by the hand of time,—softening and

harmonizing shapes, adding or subduing color,—and not by the deliberate purpose of the builder. Such is to a great extent the unsurpassed
picturesqueness of St. Mark's at Venice,—coloristically beautiful, but
architecturally by no means one of the world's finest buildings. Such is
the attraction of many a poorly designed Gothic interior; and from the
touch of decay and dampness comes much of the external picturesqueness of all old buildings in our northern clime. I do not say that this coloristic, accidental, time-wrought charm is an illegitimate object of admiration. It is often one of the greatest aids to beauty an architectural
work can gain. Not always, however,—though there are doubtless persons who would prefer to see even the temples of Egypt furrowed,
lichen-stained, and buried in foliage, and would fain wreath the pure
columns of the Parthenon with tangled veils of ivy. And in no case
should it be forgotten that such accidental picturesqueness is *extrinsic*
to true architectural excellence; that a plain, whitewashed interior,
which would be passed by with disdain by the average artistic traveler,
is often architecturally a far finer thing than another—like the Lorenz-
kirche in Nuremberg, for instance—which is bewilderingly delightful to
a painter's eye. It is to a painter's and not an architect's eye, indeed, that
picturesqueness chiefly speaks. The two senses may, of course, be
brought to bear together, and when they both are gratified delight will
be immeasurably heightened. But with these facts in mind we shall see
the folly of always demanding picturesqueness in a modern structure.
Sometimes, as I have said, it can come naturally and appropriately, and
then it is a thing to be thoroughly admired. But oftener it must be left to
the working of the hand of time, and not be forced by a perversion of
architectural or decorative effort. It is the mistaken desire for its attractiveness which has led to the worst modern use of Gothic forms, and the
worst vagaries of the "Queen Anne" fashion, and which has contorted
so many of our country cottages into the semblance of card-board
boxes put together by a Chinese child. It is this desire which has covered
many buildings that might otherwise have been good with profuse, mistaken, disturbing decoration. It is this which has so corrupted our taste
that we cannot appreciate simplicity, straightforwardness, common
sense, and quiet beauty—those greatest because most rational and lasting charms in architecture. Many people, I imagine, test the beauty of a
building by the effect it would produce upon a painter's canvas. But no
test could be more false. Very likely, some two hundred years from now,
when the color of Sever Hall shall have been deepened, variegated, and
mellowed by time, when accident and decay shall have eaten into its

moldings and softened its lines and surfaces, and when clinging vines shall have added their variety, an artist will gladly transfer it to his sketch-book. To-day he might not care to do so; but it is architecturally just as fine a thing as it will be then. I will not dwell upon it longer, save just to note the reticent dignity of its symmetric roof treatment; for a fantastic, irrational, unquiet treatment of his roof is one of the commonest sins into which the modern builder falls—led, of course, by his straining after picturesque effects.

The new Law School building which Mr. Richardson has built just outside the Cambridge Yard is more in his typical style; richer, more elaborate, more imposing—much more ambitious, if not so simply perfect. In it he has taken a course with regard to color which usually results in failure. It may be given as a general rule that where contrasting colors are used, the lighter should be employed for the main fabric and the darker, which always appears the stronger, for the trimmings and decorations that are the most emphatic parts. But there is no rule without exceptions. We do not quarrel with the color of this building, though dark stone has been used in the walls and a light Ohio stone in the trimmings. The quantities are so well adjusted,—the trimmings being made more prominent than usual,—and the artistic taste shown in their disposition is so true, that the result is charming.

I have thus far not spoken, except by implication, of excellence of plan as affecting excellence in architectural work. But his plan is, of course, the builder's actual point of departure, on the good disposal and proper expression of which much that is fine in his exterior must depend. The excellence they attain in this important point is one of the surest signs of the advance our younger architects are making. I wish I could show in example how admirably Mr. Richardson has planned this Law School and then expressed its parts; but such attempts are useless without diagrams in illustration.

Every one knows the strange instructive history of the new Capitol at Albany. Or if it is not known it may be read in Mr. Schuyler's interesting paper in this magazine for December, 1879. His criticism is my excuse, moreover, for not dwelling upon Mr. Eidlitz's share in the work or upon Mr. Richardson's treatment of the exterior. But Mr. Richardson's interior work was scarce begun when Mr. Schuyler wrote, and so a word must be devoted to it here in spite of the necessity I feel for passing to other things than his.

The great staircase is still incomplete, but the Senate Chamber and court rooms are almost finished. The former is without doubt the most

ambitious, sumptuous, and costly interior we have yet attempted—
except perhaps Mr. Eidlitz's so different Assembly Chamber in the same
building. But it is also one of the most successful. An engraving can give
but a poor idea of the real dignity of the columns and massive arches of
Sienna marble which subdivide the room toward either end, and which
drew from so good a judge as Mr. Edward Freeman the remark that they
were "worthy to stand at Ragusa." The decoration depends throughout
largely upon splendor of material and beauty of color, and so its effect
cannot be well conveyed either by black and white pictures or by words.
The walls below are of Knoxville marble, and above are paneled with
Mexican onyx framed by strips of Sienna marble. The ceiling is paneled
with oak, deeply and richly carved and touched with color in the background. And there is a lavish yet delicate use of the sculptor's chisel on
the stone, especially in accenting and softening the moldings of the great
arcades. Many people question the wisdom of putting so much costly
art into a chamber of this sort. But after all there are worse uses to
which to turn the money of a rich and extravagant people than to make
it aid in the artistic education of our legislators—since from them comes
so much of the patronage which will mold the future of our art. And
there is no education like the habit of living amid beautiful surroundings. If economy were more apt with us to result in simple beauty, we
might not thus decide; while if our extravagance were more apt to produce ornate beauty we might not be so very thankful for what Mr.
Richardson has given us here—a splendid interior, which in spite of its
lavish decoration must yet thank its architecture proper for the impression it produces.

The Albany Capitol stands at the top of the high hill which dominates the town. Halfway down this hill is a broad open square, and here
stands the new city hall which Mr. Richardson has also built, overlooked by the Capitol, but overlooking in its turn the steep streets
which lie beyond. It was only a fortunate accident, I suppose, which dictated the appropriate situations of these two structures, but in after
years their placing may be cited as a proof of our artistic feeling.

The town-hall has no affinity with the Capitol since it is throughout
a creation of Mr. Richardson's own and not an adaptation of the beginnings of other men. It is a bold piece of work—unacademic, I dare say,
and therefore displeasing to many eyes, but undeniably powerful and
imposing. It gives us what I have heard called "a distinct architectural
emotion" (that rare thing with modern work!)—and not a factitious
one either, since we like it better, I think, the more we look at it. Here

we have again a great porch and *loggia* expressing the building's public purpose; and here again the tower is well in place as an expressional feature—in addition to which it performs the practical service of storing in convenient ways the valuable archives of the town. Every observer may hold his own opinion as to the æsthetic success attained by the daring expedient of building the body of the tower of unbroken light stone and the open top of unbroken dark stone; but there is no question as to the skill with which the windows have been placed in its base so as to give ample light within and yet not weaken the solid appearance of the whole. What is perhaps the finest feature of the tower, however, cannot be clearly felt from an engraving: the graceful yet strong and re-assuring line formed as it broadens toward the base.

When we have studied Mr. Richardson's work in other departments, I shall try to say a word with regard to its characteristics as a whole. But now we must turn to other builders, and see what of excellence they offer.

Mr. Haight's new buildings for Columbia College are among the most interesting and successful of our recent works. Two large structures have already been erected, and a third will soon replace the old one that remains. We shall then see an extremely effective and picturesque group resulting from the intelligent and artistic resolution of a difficult problem. It was no easy task to take such a site— only a single city block—and yet secure such ample accommodation and illumination together with so much external variety and charm—so much diversity, and, at the same time so much harmony. The little college yard, too, has been preserved—fortunately, for practical reasons, and also for the sake of expressional interest. The style chosen for the work—a late type of English Gothic—is appropriate here at least, and is used with great intelligence and taste, though with a freedom which is a different thing from mere grammatical precision.

Here, again, I should like to be able to show the excellence of the planning. The class rooms, laboratories, and studies are large, convenient, and well shaped, and are fitted with appliances for ease and comfort that would surprise a student of any former generation. The corridors and staircases are admirably arranged to distribute a hurried crowd with the least confusion: and throughout there is an abundance of light not easily to be attained with such a complicated plan. Little scope was given for purely decorative effects, but such ornament as exists is admirably used to accentuate the most interesting features of the scheme—as, for example, in the staircase arcades, one of which we have here reproduced.

The library is, however, the feature of the greatest individuality. First one enters a rectangular room, thirty-six by fifty feet, filled with stacks for books. This opens into the reading-room— one hundred and twenty feet by fifty—by means of a pointed arch, so wide and lofty that the two form indeed but a single great apartment, the arch coming toward the end of one of the longer sides of the reading-room. This is lighted by large windows above, and small ones, rather widely spaced, below, thus affording the best illumination while avoiding the shut-up feeling that comes when all the openings are above the level of the eye. The ceiling is a barrel vault, supported on either side by a semi-vault of similar section; and there is a huge fire-place at either end of the apartment. The finish here, as in other parts of the building, is of brick, slightly glazed as to surface. The color is pale yellow diversified by bands of dull red— applied in no strictly symmetrical way, but with a skill which at once emphasizes dimensions and gives a desirable accent of freedom and variety. This sort of interior finish, though common I believe in England, is rather a novelty with us, and worthy of remark since it offers a fortunate way of securing color in the fabric itself—color that is absolutely permanent as well as satisfactory. I may add that the bricks are not quite uniform in tint so that an effect of coldness and hardness of tone is avoided. But the great feature of the room is the arch of which I have already spoken, flanked by the circular stairways which give access to the upper shelves. Its beauty of form and great size—thirty-four by thirty-six feet—give dignity and distinction to the whole composition, and turn what might have been a merely excellent into an extremely imposing apartment. Meeting a structural necessity—that of really uniting the two rooms—in the frankest and the simplest way, it gives us a touch of freedom, originality, and grandeur which we should never have got from an architect to whom his craft was a formulated thing of laws and precedents, and not a practical and vital art. It is built of the red brick, square in section, with plainly chamfered angles, and no touch of ornament—no beauty save that which comes from its own bold and graceful shape. I do not know of any recent interior which surpasses this in showing how true and impressive architectural beauty may be produced in the most simply structural way, provided real artistic instinct is set to work upon the problem, unfettered by the chains of conventionality and dogma. It is as *rational* a piece of work as one could well imagine, and as beautiful in its severely simple way.

Mr. Hunt's Lenox Library is a dignified building which teaches a clear lesson as to the value of a large sobriety and reticence in produc-

ing architectural nobility. This lesson was peculiarly pertinent, moreover, at the time when the building was erected, for showy and pur-
poseless elaboration was then even more characteristic of our art than it
is to-day. It was built, I think, at nearly the same time with the Stewart
residence at the corner of Thirty-Fourth street and Fifth Avenue, and the
reader may be left to judge between the two.

Nor should we pass without a word Mr. Withers's Police Courts at the
corner of Tenth street and Sixth Avenue— one of our few recent important
essays in a florid Gothic manner, and one of the first in which coloristic
variety was attempted. It has great merits—notably in the picturesque
composition of its masses resulting from its intelligent adaptation to an
irregular site. But its composition with voids and solids is scattered and
restless, and its decoration, both in color and in sculptured detail, may be
charged with the same fault. It is overdone to begin with, and what is
done is not so well done as it might have been. I have said that mere architectural composition alone may make a fine building, but here we
have a proof that it is easy to spoil a good design by elaborating it in mistaken ways. This same design more simply carried out, both as to color
and to form, would have been a far more valuable work.

In Boston, too, there is another building, which, while it has evident
faults, has yet much merit—the new Christian Association building of
Messrs. Sturgis & Brigham. This building is agreeably and picturesquely
composed; and is sufficiently expressive of its interior arrangements. But
the point I would especially note is the way in which it meets the necessity—so often laid upon our architects— of making a dignified structure
in which the lower story must be given up to shops. The usual course is
to put the doorway level with the street, and then it is difficult to attain
any proper expression of the main character of the work. But here the
doorway is put at the level of the principal floor, and with its broad flight
of steps it not only forms an effective feature, but completely subordinates the basement. In view of such an excellence we may excuse an ill
disposition of ornament. A projecting oriel window, for example, is in itself a decorative feature, and one which comes very prominently before
the eye. It is, therefore, a proper field for ornament. But here it has been
left completely plain, while a band of decoration has been put close beneath the cornice where scarcely any eye will find it.

At Williamstown, Mass., Mr. Cady has built a collegiate building,
which is a good example of quiet work—well composed, expressive,
straightforward, dignified, and yet not devoid of picturesqueness. It follows with discretion an English Renaissance type, and is a valuable ex-

ample to set beside the confused, restless, inorganic structures we more often achieve when working after similar models. At Yale College, too, I am told that Mr. Cady has done some interesting work; but I am unable to speak of it either from personal knowledge or from such as may be gained by the help of illustrations.

Architecture (and not decoration, as apart from this) is here our subject; but when a bit of interior decoration has a really architectural flavor, it may detain us for a moment. This is the case with the alcove which Mr. S. V. Stratton has lately fitted up in the Society Library building. It is a charming piece of work, and all the more valuable since we are so inclined to think that interior fittings need *not* be architectural, and since no idea could be more pernicious.

13

Public Buildings (2)

In this present paper I shall conclude all I have to say about those among our recent architectural works which come under the head of public buildings—excepting only churches, which demand a chapter to themselves. Since my limits are but brief, since our country is geographically unfavorable to even the most energetic observer, and since our new works succeed each other to-day with great rapidity, it must not be supposed that the list I give is at all exhaustive. I can pretend to do no more than mention the most conspicuous structures which lie within a moderate radius from *The Century*'s home. If, indeed, even within that radius it were possible for me to name *everything* that is good,—conspicuously or modestly good,—my task would be far less interesting than it is, and any commentary at all would be far less clearly called for. Certainly I ought to change the broad title I have chosen, unless the good things I note may be taken as types of more. If I could give a full *catalogue raisonné* of all our recent buildings which are distinctly an improvement on those that were typical a score of years ago,—especially as concerns the principles that have guided and the aims that have inspired their authors,—it would be a proof that they themselves would have no right to be called typical to-day. My excuse for writing lies in the fact that to a great extent they *are* thus typical: the fact that an ever-

---

The Century Magazine (28) 6 (July 1884): 323–334.

growing number of our architects are now doing really rational and artistic work, that the profession as a whole is getting into the right path with more or less celerity; that most of our younger architects, and many of their elders too, are striving to attain success of a similar sort to that which has already been conspicuously achieved by some among their number. Especially will this be true when I shall come to speak of those departments in which, naturally, more work is being done than in the one here under notice—of commercial buildings, for example, and of private dwellings in town and country. But even with regard to public buildings, I am glad to say that my little list is *not* all-embracing. Of very many good things, both far away and near at hand, I doubtless have no knowledge; and even among those I *do* know there are many which, good though they be, do not present such striking individual characteristics as fit them for description here. We may, however, gather great encouragement from the mere general statement that they are honest, sensible, expressive, excellently planned, and modestly artistic structures. That is to say, they are in the strongest and most hopeful possible contrast to the majority of our similar works put up in other and not long-distant years. Particularly do many of the unambitious civic structures of the smaller New England towns deserve this praise. Town-halls and libraries and school-houses are rapidly rising in such places which are admirably suited to their purpose, which are skillfully and truthfully built, and often characterized by no small degree of artistic worth. Desperate vagaries still occur among them, it is true—Gothic and "Queen Anne" and nondescript abominations of all sorts. But year by year they are yielding place to better art. Year by year we mark, I think, an ever-growing tendency to make simple common sense the guide toward beauty as well as toward convenience and stability, instead of an adherence to some conventional type of design and decoration, or a straining effort after obvious "originality." I may stop to note in this connection a Memorial Library which Messrs. Rotch & Tilden have built at Bridgewater, Conn., and a town-hall of Mr. Arthur Dodd's at Sharon, Mass. They are not great works of architecture, I allow; nor are they either ambitious, ornate, or "striking." But they are *good* works none the less; they are sensible, rational, and expressive, accomplishing the given task in a most adequate way, and turning necessary features to artistic account. Just by reason of their modesty, and because they are typical of many more or less successful similar essays, they seem to me important. For, as I have already said (perhaps too often for my readers' patience), we are just now laying the foundation of what we hope may grow to be a creditable development of architectural art; and for this foundation the absolutely necessary beginning is that our artists should cultivate their common sense and practical ingenuity; should rely for their main success on structure, not on ornament; should first of all be *rational*, whether in original or in imitative ways. Even in those humbler works in which wood largely takes the place of sterner materials, we may note much improvement of recent years. A little half-timbered cottage-hospital built by Messrs. Ficken & Smith at Plainfield, New Jersey, for example, is interesting as a proof that in the cheapest structure (this one cost less than $4000) something better may be given us than the time-honored shell sheathed in clapboards or in shingles.

It has been a rule with me throughout that no buildings should be mentioned here which exist on paper only. But nothing is of more importance to the future of our architecture than that good art should be introduced into our simpler, cheaper kinds of work. And so I will make an exception in favor of a design which Mr. Janes, of Albany, prepared a year or two ago for a school-house to be erected in a New York village. It was so sensible, and yet so novel and so charming, that the committee could not make up its mind to indorse it, but substituted instead a brick box, to which no Philistine could take exception. Mr. Janes's design showed brick below and half-timbering and plaster above, and had a natural picturesqueness resulting from the wise arrangement of its plan and fashioning of its obligatory features. Nothing could be more simply rational or more attractive in effect than the large, round-arched windows that rose beneath the gables, their framing and mullions composed simply of oaken timbers corresponding to those of the adjoining walls. It seems strange that we, who often follow precedent so blindly and so foolishly in other directions, should be so loth to look to the past for examples when we work in wood. Only very lately have the admirable half-timbered old houses of England, France, and Germany been consulted for hints that might be followed in our practice with the utmost profit; and even yet we see but rare instances where those hints have been cleverly followed up. And so I wish, indeed, that Mr. Janes's design had been given an actual body, for then it might here have been reproduced.

To Boston I must go back again for a moment, and speak of the Art Museum, which was built some ten years ago by Messrs. Sturgis & Brigham. As to plan, it is perhaps the best work of the sort we have yet erected, and its exterior is not inexpressive. But its chief interest lies in the fact that it was one of our first attempts in the use of strong exterior

color, and the very first, I think, upon a large scale, in which terra cotta
was employed for this purpose. A successful attempt we cannot call it.
The color is in itself glaring and inharmonious—color which the hand
of time will never soften or subdue; and the manner of its employment
is rather unfortunate, taken together with the nature of the decorative
forms it accents. Simple forms may be elaborately colored, but elaborate forms need greater chromatic sobriety; else the result, as here, is almost sure to lack unity, repose, breadth, and clearness of expression.
But we should not be hard upon a first attempt. It was a good thing for
us to have the propriety of strong external color insisted upon, a good
thing to have the resources of our architects increased by the addition of
terra cotta to their list. It has since rapidly grown in favor, and is now
used much more discreetly than in this first instance, though we can
hardly claim that its full possibilities are yet revealed, or its limitations
always respected in our work. Too often, for example, we use it to replace in constructional or semi-constructional features some more
costly material of sturdier nature. But we may hope that our growing
feeling for honesty will relegate it before long to its proper functions. If
so, it may do us excellent service, for its coloristic value is great, and
under our brilliant skies and in our usually pure and smokeless atmosphere color decoration is especially well in place. Our teachers here, I
think, should be those southern races who are not our physical forefathers, rather than those northern peoples from whom we trace descent.
Artistic needs are spiritual, not physical, and climate and natural surroundings mold them more, perhaps, than do the instincts we inherit.
And climate, moreover, is certainly a truer *material* guide in architecture
than is the mere fact of kinship. As a people we are in many ways unlike our English or our Dutch forefathers—in many ways more like the
eager, restless, impressionable nations of the south. And certainly our
climate is neither Dutch nor English. For both which reasons, I repeat,
we are more nearly concerned with questions of color than are Englishmen or Dutchmen. But more of this when we shall come to speak of
style and taste and intellectual needs in a future chapter.

Now let us look very briefly at a branch we have not yet approached—at theatrical architecture.

Inclosed theaters are comparative novelties in architectural history.
They date only from late Renaissance days, and since those days the
needs of stage and audience alike have so vastly altered that we can now
get little help from Palladian precedents. Indeed, this is one department
of our art in which we find, to our refreshment, that imitation plays a

comparatively minor role. The public at large is peculiarly interested in a theater—interested, not in a languid, vicarious fashion, or for æsthetic reasons only, but because the comfort and pleasure of thousands are nightly dependent upon its success. Effort, experiment, and self-reliance are positively imposed upon its builder; for even yet our needs and wishes are being modified from year to year, and constant variations in plan and structure are demanded. So, as a sincere respect for utility and an earnest application of rational thought to practical and æsthetic problems are the true nurses of architectural excellence, we are not surprised to find in the theatrical interiors of the century our best evidence that architecture is still a living and progressing art, if not an art as easily and triumphantly artistic as it was in certain epochs of the past. In the interiors of our theaters, I say,—but by no means in their exteriors. Here to a greater degree the imitation of alien works of other days is possible to the architect, and consequently he calls the "orders" most often indolently into play to adorn (in inexpressive and inappropriate and so in inartistic ways) the exterior of buildings where inside he proves himself not incapable of real inventive power. Garnier's new house in Paris, for example, has an interior which is in many ways most admirable; but outside, in spite of sumptuous display and marvelously clever decoration, it is an architectural sham—nothing more than a splendid piece of scene-painting done in the round instead of upon canvas.

With such a house as Garnier's it would be unjust to compare the great new theater which has recently been put up in New York. When Mr. Cady undertook to build the Metropolitan Opera-House he accepted a task of the utmost difficulty—doubly discouraging, too, since his result was certain to be brought into some such unfair comparison. Both his site and the demands of his clients precluded the possibility of his making it a monumental structure such as all buildings of the sort should be. He was given merely brick for his material, and only a single city block to build upon,—a block, too, which has no open space about it. Even upon this block, moreover, he was not allowed to dispose his theater as he would, but was obliged to fill in every foot of ground it left unoccupied with tall, overshadowing wings destined for another use. It would, therefore, manifestly be unjust, I repeat, to ask for monumental grandeur in his house, or even for an adequate degree of external expressiveness. We can only congratulate ourselves that we have got as much as we have—an honest, unaffected, scholarly, dignified pile, as well designed in mass as was possible under the circumstances, expressive, at all events, of its structural fashioning, and happy in the composition of its voids and solids. So simple and scholarly and unaggressive is it,

Fig. 8.   Bracket of Hammered Brass and Scheme of Fireplace, Conversation
Room, Casino, Newport. [McKim, Mead and White, 1879–80].

indeed, that I fear "the public" does not half realize the debt of gratitude it
owes the architect. But would it not be well if in our other theaters the same
sort of excellence prevailed? Is it not a vast improvement on such a hideous
nullity as our old Academy of Music? And, on the other hand, should we
not be happier if the Casino Theater had been less fantastic, and if the Eden
Museum on Twenty-third street had relied on structural beauty and appropriate, subordinated decoration for its effect, instead of upon a showy accumulation of superficial details, mechanical in spirit, and thrice too plenti-
ful for the size of its façade?

But there was one part of his exterior upon which Mr. Cady could
work in a more untrammeled way than upon his principal fronts. It is to
the back of the house on Seventh Avenue that I would especially direct
the reader's attention. It is nothing, he may protest, but an immense and
almost unbroken brick wall, nearly devoid of ornament and quite devoid
of any attempt at decorative effectiveness. I believe there are even persons who claim that it is not different in any way from the breweries
which deform our suburbs. But, believe me, it is very different. Mere
mass may be, of course, an immense element in architectural power, and
the mass of this wall counts for much in its impressiveness. But this is because it has been intelligently handled. We are all at one in feeling that
our biggest malt-houses are not impressive, are not even satisfactory as
proving their real strength and solidity to the eye. But the ponderous

Fig. 9.   Rear of the Metropolitan Opera-House. [J. C. Cady, 1883.]

bulk of Mr. Cady's wall is *designed,* not merely built, and designed so as to prove its strength most clearly; it has parts and features which are organic, and, though simple, are potent and expressive. Below, it is solid and unadorned but agreeable in its proportions and in the lines of the great buttresses which secure and demonstrate its huge solidity; and above, where a lighter treatment is in place, it is ornamented in a quiet but charming way. Taken for what it is, the back of an opera-house which throughout is a utilitarian and not a monumental structure, I think that a jury of architects would call it one of the best pieces of design the city has to show. And I do not despair of a day when the public will feel the distance that divides it from a typical brewery wall—all the distance that stretches between a simple work of art and an unintelligent pile of bricks. Nay, I am of so optimistic a frame of mind while contemplating the fact that one of our architects has done so well when daring to do so honestly and simply, that I can even look forward to a day when a malt-house itself may do us credit, not dishonor.

When we enter Mr. Cady's house we must still remember the difficulties under which he worked. The unmajestic size and simple fashion of the stairways and passages may be laid to the limitations of the site and the necessity for using fireproof materials. With nothing but iron and cement, and with no outlay permitted for sumptuous painted decoration, it would have been hard to make them either festal or elegant. Even in the auditorium itself the same charity must not forsake us. It is the largest in the world; and to say that means that it was the most difficult to build, both practically and artistically. It is not very hard to build a good small theatrical interior, unless, indeed, the site is cramped, as it often is with us. But so immense an auditorium as a lyric theater demands is among the most difficult of problems, and every added foot of space adds to the practical difficulty of providing seats where all may see and hear, and to the artistic difficulty of making the result architecturally right—neither bald in its simplicity nor so elaborate that the effect of size will disappear and the impression of its unity be lost.

Of the practical difficulty we gain some idea when we look at the plans of the greater European houses. We see that no curve has yet been decided upon as giving the best possible sweep for the tiers of boxes. Each house differs from every other; in each the architect has experimented afresh, and all leave something for the future to improve upon. If we look again at sectional views of these same buildings, we see that the artistic problem is equally far from a definite solution. It prescribes an immense rectangular apartment, surrounded on three sides by curved tiers of seats. The question is how, without interference with sight or hearing, to amalgamate these two factors and bring them into architectural accord. The so-called Italian system of building—common in Germany as well—ignores the room as much as possible, and makes the tiers themselves its sole concern. The French system, on the other hand, emphasizes the room first of all by setting great groups of columns at the four corners to give the roof a visible support, and then puts in its tiers as best it can between them. Neither system quite solves the problem. The first sins through want of constructive expression, and the second stumbles upon a rock of offense in failing to bring the horizontal line of the tiers into organic connection with the vertical lines of the roof supports. We need not stop, however, to consider which sort of semi-failure is the better, which offers the more favorable prospect for a perfect solution in the future. We are discussing Mr. Cady's house alone, and the Italian method was positively forced upon him. Only by its means could he answer the demand of his clients that each and every box should be just like its fellows—in its apparent importance, in its size, and in its facilities for sight and hearing.

In answering this demand, moreover, he was obliged to give up those proscenium *loges* with enframing columns, upon which even Italian builders rely for accent and variety in their scheme, though not for structural expression. Mr. Cady had to solve a new question when he was bidden, in a house of this great size, to run his tiers up to the proscenium wall without diversity or break. It would be too much to say that he found its truest architectural solution; that his design produces that impression of organic unity between all adjacent parts which is essential to perfect architectural composition. The ends of his tiers simply abut upon the proscenium pilasters, avoiding impingement upon base or capital, but not producing an effect of true independence and concord. But the result, if not quite satisfactory to critical analysis, is not unpleasant to the eye. And we should remember that Mr. Cady fails no more conspicuously here than do French architects when they piece in their tiers between their columns.

Great simplicity was prescribed throughout the auditorium, again, by the nature of the materials, which are here, as in the corridors, iron and cement alone. Mr. Cady placed his chief reliance for beauty on the lines of his box and gallery tiers, which repeat each other up to the very top of the house—and beautiful lines they are, both in their many sweeps and in the slight dip they take toward the stage. I may note that when the proscenium *loges* were outlawed, a divergence from the customary horseshoe form was necessitated in the tiers. Here the curve is lyre-like instead, bending forward and then backward again a little near the stage.

The chief points in the modeling of the proscenium are that the opening is, fortunately, kept square, and that the great iron girder which supports the stage wall above the roof of the auditorium plays a boldly visible part in the scheme. The ornamental detail throughout is in very low relief, and carefully studied from early Italian Renaissance models. The general effect of the interior, and of its detail as well, would vastly have gained by a more emphatic color-treatment on the part of the decorator—but with his performance we are not here concerned.

Simplicity, repose, and refinement characterize Mr. Cady's portion of the work. Since these are among the best of architectural qualities, since they are the rarest in our work (especially in buildings of this sort), and since they are those which we must first learn to appreciate and master if we would rise to success in more elaborate and ambitious ways, we can hardly be too thankful for their presence.

If the gay world at Newport had built itself a Casino some twenty or even some ten years ago, I wonder what we should have had? Possibly an imitation of the formal, stately, classicized *Kurhaus* of some German

Fig. 10.   Tower of the Casino Court, Newport. [McKim, Mead and White, 1879–80.]

bath. Perhaps a cousin of those fantastically hideous travesties of Oriental pleasure-houses which we find in so many small foreign watering-places. More probably still, a "Queen Anne" structure which would have looked like an agglomerate of English model-almshouses. At all events, it is safe to say we should not have had anything so sensible yet novel, so simple yet picturesque, so useful yet charming, as Messrs. McKim, Mead & White have given us. The problem was a new one in many respects, both as to the practical ends that were proposed and as to the general expression and sentiment that were desirable to bring the building into harmony with the place itself and with the life whose central point it forms. And the architects were fortunately inspired to set their own wits to work and find a new solution based on common sense and a feeling for beauty, and not on precedent or formula. In its general expression the building is, I think, very adequate and characteristic. It is dignified enough without being formal or pretentious; rural, but not rustic; graceful, intimate, cheerful, with just a touch of fantasy not out of place in a structure whose ends are distinctly frivolous—a Casino which is a mere summer-house for "society's" amusement.

An ideal Newport Casino would, of course, have stood free from all other buildings, and have had an entire exterior to exhibit. It would have found its place upon the cliffs, and delighted us with a matchless outward view as well as entertained us with a sight of the butterfly life within its own inclosure. But with their land worth dollars an inch, even the millionaires of Newport may be pardoned for not making such a sacrifice to beauty. As it stands, the Casino shows but a single simple street façade. Only when we pass under the great archway beneath the club-rooms do we see its really distinctive features. It is hard to describe it, and I regret to say that our single view gives no idea of its attractiveness. Its low, two-storied walls, partly of brick and partly shingled, surround two large quadrangles, the first one filled with plants and flowers, and the second longer one giving space for the tennis courts. And it has the most charming sweep of latticed balcony, breaking here and there into window-like openings giving freer outlook. Nothing could be more sensibly arranged for comfort and convenience, and nothing could be prettier or more picturesque than the general effect of its varied features—irregularly disposed, not for picturesqueness only but to meet actual needs and ends. And within, the club-rooms and restaurants are admirably planned, and are decorated with sufficient elegance to suit their occupants, but with a simplicity and airiness that mark them as for use in summer only. The so-called theater, which closes the inner quadrangle, is in reality a large galleried ball-room with a stage at one end for occasional use. Here the color decoration is in ivory and gold, making an excellent background under gaslight. It, too, is simply treated, but the carving and turning of the wood-work are executed with great delicacy and beauty.

With all the variety and picturesqueness of the Casino's exterior (by this I mean its quadrangle fronts), harmony and unity are preserved throughout—except, perhaps, in the great clock-tower which flanks the entrance arch on its inner face. This we can hardly call as local and sensible in feeling as are the other features. It is a distinct reminiscence of earlier days, a bit of imported mediævalism—a dungeon-keep, I have heard it said, and not a Casino clock-tower. Yet, as I have already protested, a bit of fantasy is not out of place in such a work, and we may excuse this bit all the more since it gives a touch of solidity and strength that we should miss, perhaps, had it taken a lighter form.

At Short Hills, New Jersey, the same architects have built another Casino of a more modest sort, but rejoicing in a visible exterior. My readers can judge of it as well as I, however, since I too know it only through our reproductions.

Fig. 11.   The Short Hills Music Hall. [McKim, Mead and White, 1879–80.]

The railway station is a far more recent invention than even the inclosed theater. It is a child of our own century—a child of that century in which the engineer, as opposed to the architect proper, has come to play so large a rôle. It is unfortunate that there is this distinction, even opposition, between the two professions—unfortunate that with the advent of the railway age the architect allowed to pass entirely out of his control those structures in which the engineer had of necessity to do his part. The consequence is that while this part is often performed in the most admirable way, the part which should have been the architect's falls as well to the engineer—to him who *as* an engineer cannot comprehend it, whom an architectural training alone would have fitted for its mastery. Nothing could be finer in its way than the interior of many a great station, especially in Germany or France, with its colossal, powerful, yet light and graceful iron frame-work. But such a frame-work can hardly be called architectural. It is spun, woven, wrought, rather than truly *built;* and the adjacent parts which *are* built commonly fall far below it in excellence and beauty.

I have already spoken of our Brooklyn Bridge, which is beautiful in those features that fell naturally to engineering skill, in the lines of its cables and wires and in the delicate spring of its long roadway,—as vital and graceful as though it were but a single tense strip of steel. But the towers—the really architectural features—are as poor as the iron web is fine. So it is with our great railway stations. Their walls and constructive features usually are bad *per se,* and have no organic relation to those other parts which we must be content to have unarchitectural themselves, but which might be brought into harmony with their architectural environment. A better accord between the two professions, or a wider training which will make certain men at once architects and engineers, may yet, it is to be hoped, produce more fortunate results. Exceptions to the general rule there are indeed already, especially in Germany, where we find certain great railway termini that are built with a dignity, a simplicity, an appropriateness, and an expressiveness that deserve all praise. Unfortunately we have not much to show at home as yet, beyond abortive attempts in the same direction—stations like the one at Worcester, Mass., for example, which means well, but the effect of which is, to say the least, unbeautiful. And even these are comparatively rare. So far as I have been able to judge, we usually vibrate between ambitiously inappropriate and ugly efforts, like the Forty-second street station in New York, or platitudes of an unambitious and factory-like description. A variant we do find, indeed, in the Broad street station at Philadelphia, but not a quite successful one. With its well-planned, comfortable, and even sumptuous interior we have no fault to find. It is a striking proof, by the way, of our growing demand for luxurious surroundings—a proof that would astonish the original creators of the Pennsylvania Railroad or the travelers of a generation ago. The exterior of the building, too, has excellence, if we consider it from an abstract standpoint; and certain among its features, prescribed by necessity, have been so fortunately fashioned as to be amply expressive,—I mean the basement, with its great arches for the admission of vehicles, and the large windows which light the waiting-room above. But the expression of the building as a whole is far from being what it ought to be. A railroad station, above all things on earth, is utilitarian. It may and should be made beautiful, but its beauty should be of a simple, severe, and, so to say, business-like character. But for this Philadelphia station a florid type of Gothic was chosen, and was elaborated in the most ornate fashion. The design is good in many ways, and a great deal of the decoration is quite charming, *intrinsically considered.* But the effect is not in keeping with the structure's purpose. We gladly accept the Messrs. Wilsons' building as distinctly ornamental to a city which is in rather bad need of architectural adornment; but we cannot accept it as a laudable precedent in its own way. It is attractive, but I do not think it is very *rational.*

Our smaller wayside stations offer, of course, very much easier problems. They are merely waiting-rooms flanked, perhaps, by external
sheds to protect the passengers and traffic; and there is, therefore, no
question about bringing them into harmony with huge engineering efforts. Some improvement has been made in them of recent years, but
there is room for more. The best among them are rarely more than
pretty "Queen Anne" cottages, well arranged within, but hardly laying
claim to architectural dignity. But more substantial work is coming into
vogue, as we may see, among other instances, in several small stations
Mr. Richardson has lately been building in New England. The one at
Palmer, Mass., is the finest I have seen—built of stone of two colors,
massively, effectively, yet simply, and in expressional accordance with
its purpose. Unfortunately it is not yet complete, and cannot here be reproduced. In its stead we give a sketch of a still smaller one at North
Easton.

At first sight, perhaps, the great stone arches look too "original" to
be quite sensible. What is their use, we ask, since there is only a roof to
be supported? But they serve good practical purpose in admitting light
to the waiting-rooms in spite of overhanging eaves, and they are expressionally fortunate, too, as it seems to me. Is not the general effect of
the building just what it should be? Do we not see that it is the roof, not
the wall, which is the main thing; that here is not a place to dwell *in,* but
to stop *under;* that it is not a house at all, but a *shed*—a shed made permanent, stable, sturdy, and picturesque besides? And I must enforce the
point that in such work as this Mr. Richardson, who can be so exuberant at times, and at times so refined and elegant (as in Leroy Hall, for
instance), changes his tone entirely, and becomes eminently business-
like, uncompromising, and severe. The Palmer Station is much more
ambitious than this, but it, too, is strictly utilitarian, though by no
means inartistic, depending for its effect entirely upon its structural features and the contrasted color of its materials.

If we have had one class of structures which more than another has
been the very type of sordid, shabby, brutal ugliness, it has comprised
those hideous receptacles for a long-suffering community known as the
ferry-houses of New York harbor. But even these are coming under the
healing touch of art. I may note as the most striking instance a ferry-
house of Messrs. Ficken & Smith's at Hoboken—a modest wooden
structure, nicely built, tastefully decorated, and showing a street front
in "Queen Anne" fashion that is pleasantly picturesque and sensible
withal. Here for once we have been given a sufficiently agreeable rest-

ing-place for decent human creatures; and could there be a stronger proof that the good leaven is at work, and in a really radical way?

One word I want to say—and this, perhaps, is as good a place as any—with regard to the illustrations which accompany these papers. I should be glad indeed if they could be made *illustrative* in the fullest sense of the term, but that is quite impossible. Lovers of architecture will be aware that even drawings or photographs on the largest scale are never truly illustrative of the general effect of an entire building—so much depends upon our perceiving and feeling of its mere brute size as well as its color, location, surroundings, and every detail of its ornament, and of what I may call its *structural finish*. How, then, must it be with pictures so small as those which fit our page? I need hardly say that they have been prepared with the greatest possible care; and yet I should be sorry to have my readers gauge the accuracy of my criticism by their evidence alone. I am not afraid that I should be found too enthusiastic in any instance if my words were considered in presence of the work itself. But I *am* afraid that I may be, if our pictures only are used as tests by eyes unaccustomed to the discrepancy between good architectural works and any flat reproduction of their forms. This much I had to say, not only in justice to myself, but still more in justice to the architects whose results have come under our notice.

14

Commercial Buildings

Our commercial buildings offer just now a peculiarly interesting field of inquiry. In no department are we doing more work. "Down-town" New York, for example, is being so rapidly remodeled that small trace will be left in the year 1900 of the work that stood but ten years ago. In no department, again, do problems of greater difficulty and novelty suggest themselves; and in none, I think, is more strenuous effort being made to secure better artistic as well as better practical results than have hitherto been common. It is well, indeed, that this should be the case, since we are not, like our fathers, building for a short time only. Their structures have proved but temporary, while for ours a life may be predicted as long as the city's own. No one can ever build them bigger, and, however ugly we may leave them, our children are not likely to pull them down for æsthetic reasons only.

We know well the sort of business buildings that were typical some forty or fifty years ago—simple cubes of brick or stone broken by regular rows of unornamented windows. They were not even to be considered from the point of view of art, but from their very humility were not actively distressing or offensive. Offense came quickly, however, with the dawning of the "iron age." The world then thought it had found a new material which would meet its practical needs as they had never

The Century Magazine (28) 6 (August 1884): 511–523.

been met before, and would revolutionize the art on its artistic side as well. At first a new "iron style" was prophesied; but when this failed to appear, every time-honored fashion was drawn upon for help. Many, diverse, and frantic were the efforts made to achieve success. There were no bounds set to ambition; for the cheapness and facility with which iron could be cast into any shape, put within common reach such possibilities of elaboration and display (of *sham* elaboration and display, however) as had hitherto been reserved for occasional use in the most sumptuous and costly work. Nowhere was there more ambition, more experimenting, and more frantic "originality" than with us—as a walk up the central portion of Broadway will prove. But the ultimate result was as far as possible from the hopes we had cherished at the outset. No new iron style was evolved, and no old fashion showed its fitness for truthful, or even for satisfactory superficial treatment in the novel substance. And I think these years of struggle had a definitely pernicious as well as a merely disappointing outcome. I am sure our public would never have grown to misconceive so utterly the true grounds of architectural excellence, had not the cheap and showy lies of iron been paraded for so many years before its eyes. Had we always kept to brick and stone, we could not have been so lavish with our "applied ornament," and could not have come to love it so unwisely. We could not so have forgotten that construction is the basis of architectural excellence; that simplicity and repose are among its finest factors; and that elaborateness and ornament are only justifiable when attempted in materials of appropriate sorts, and executed with artistic feeling and manual, not mechanical, skill. Surely to iron we owe the greater part of our architectural falsehood, restlessness, ostentation, and vulgarity; and surely to it, the greater part of our present incapacity to distinguish between an organism and an aggregate of inconsequential features; between "decorated construction" and "constructed decoration"; between ornamental detail that is wrought by an artist's hand, and ornamental detail that is coarsely cast in ignoble forms.

It is impossible to find any really good iron buildings among our many thousands. All we can say is that the simplest are the best; or, more properly, the least distressing. The plain fronts that abound, for instance, in the so-called "dry-goods district" of New York are not beautiful, and neither their arches nor their lintels are a satisfactory expression of the qualities of iron. But they are infinitely better, at all events, than elaborate vulgarizations of palatial magnificence like the Grand Hotel with its thousand columns, or the Domestic Building on

Union Square with its colossal statuary, or the Venetian or Arabic or flashy nondescript façades farther down Broadway.

But iron no longer greatly interests us except for interior constructional expedients. We no longer make much use of it in our visible exteriors. It has proved intractable from an artistic point of view,—whether of necessity or owing to our want of ingenuity, I do not pretend to say, though it does seem as though thirty years of earnest effort in every land must pretty well have exhausted its possibilities. And practically it has been tried in fiery balances and found conspicuously wanting. Fortunately for our art, we are forced back almost entirely upon brick and stone as our visible materials.

Are we now to do something really good with them,—something that will be neither a mere square box nor a superficial flourish of mendacious forms and mechanically wrought details? Certainly we are making the effort; and as certainly, I think, we are beginning to succeed. Let us consider, first, the humblest sort of problem, and take as an example of its simple but successful solution a warehouse Messrs. Babb, Cook & Willard have recently erected on Duane street, in New York. There was little to work with here: cheap materials, scanty ornament, and not even a corner site; only one of those high narrow façades that go so far to discourage effort. But effort, intelligent effort, has been brought to bear, and the result is fine in the first and chief essential of good architecture—fine in composition. The straight lines of equal windows demanded in a building of the sort are preserved throughout the lower stories; but their uniformity is relieved by the piers and great round arches which, furnishing strength to the wall, also express that strength and introduce the artistic element of design. The fifth-story openings are accommodated to the arches, and their bold variety completes the effect of intelligent composition. Such a building, as truly as the most elaborate, is an architectural growth, an entity, an organism. It proves that its builder had an idea and knew how to express it; that he was neither a mere mechanical piler-up of bricks and window-sashes, nor a mistaken searcher after that effectiveness which, it is supposed, will result from the introduction of "unnecessary" decorative features. Such excellence seems very easy of attainment,—but only now that we see it gained. Let us imagine one of our unpretentious business streets lined with buildings of this sort—I do not mean identical with it, but analogous to it in simplicity, appropriateness, and architectural feeling. We do not conceive it as a street to be merely tolerated, even if our more ambitious thoroughfares were of equal excellence in a richer way;

rather as one in which we should find true pleasure, and of a permanent, because a *rational,* sort. [. . .]

A leather warehouse, which is still more uncompromisingly utilitarian in effect, and which is yet an intelligent work of art, stands near the
New York end of the Brooklyn Bridge and has fronts on Jacob and
Frankfort streets, though the corner between them is occupied by another building. It is extremely sturdy, almost rude, in effect, and without the slightest trace of ornament—with not even so much as we find
in the little moldings which, inconspicuous though they are, yet add a
tangible grace to Mr. Babb's results. But its wall is composed by means
of piers and arches; it has a strong though simple cornice; and its openings are well designed and varied, those of the ground story being powerful round arches. Its solidity and strength are not more evident than
its fitness of expression, or than its testimony to how much a clever architect may do with a problem so humble that it has long been held beneath the dignity of art. It is only recently, I think, that such simple
works have been confided to hands more skillful than those of the ordinary builder; at least, it is only recently that we have had ocular proof
of an architect's interference. And therefore it is that I count them such
valuable signs of progress. The façades which are being built to inclose
the Bridge arcades and fit them for storage purposes give, by the way,
welcome evidence of a similar sort.

Now, for variety and the sake of pointing an instructive contrast, let
us look at a great wholesale store Mr. Richardson has lately built on
Bedford street in Boston—a work of the richest and most elaborate
kind, and, considering its place and purpose, of the greatest possible
novelty. It would be hard to exaggerate the "true architectural emotion"
it produces when we first see it through a vista of narrow streets lined
with commonplace commercial structures. Mr. Richardson worked, it is
true, under favoring conditions. The site is a rounded corner of two di-
verging streets, facing a third which affords a good distant view, and is
extended enough for good proportions to be possible in spite of great
necessary height; and the money appropriated allowed the use of noble
material and profuse decoration. But other builders have had opportunities as good, or better even, in this immediate neighborhood. It is not
the fault of fate or clients that their results are so far inferior. In Mr.
Richardson's building we see composition of an admirable kind. Variety
exists with quietness and harmony, and imposing solidity in spite of
those wide modern windows which are so often an architect's destruc-
tion. Its beauty is *built,* not applied by means of decoration. This last is

profuse, as I have said, but is guided and inspired by the structural forms. It enhances and accentuates, but does not itself *supply* the element of architectural "delight." A detail to be noted is the comparatively small size and unaccented simplicity of the doorways. Their subordination to the windows in a structure of this kind is as appropriate and expressive as is the emphasis we have seen Mr. Richardson lay upon them in buildings of another sort. Boston may well be proud of this splendid pile of dark-red sandstone, which is without question the most beautiful of all our commercial structures.

And yet we may ask ourselves whether, after all, it is as hopeful a sign for the future of our art as is such a work as Mr. Babb's. It would be absurd, of course, to compare, on their intrinsic merits as pure works of art, the sumptuous richness of the one with the frank poverty of the other. But I cannot too often repeat that architectural creations—especially with us in this first beginning of our art—have another aspect from which also they must be judged. When we look at them sensibly, they seem valuable in proportion as they offer the best practical solution of the most frequent and characteristic problems of our day and land. The power which can do well with humble opportunities, and create true art at little cost and under difficult conditions, is the power of which we have most need. A commercial building is primarily a financial investment, and the architect's art should help, not hinder, a financial success. For one architect who will have a chance like Mr. Richardson's, there will be a hundred to have a chance like Mr. Babb's. To the one we shall look to give us now and then a splendid monument; but upon the others we must depend if the generality of our city streets are to be redeemed from their barren ugliness or hideous deformity. And so I think that Mr. Babb's simplicity affords a presage of greater value than Mr. Richardson's magnificence.

Indeed, a further word of criticism may be registered. He would be an ungrateful critic who could wish that in this one case Mr. Richardson had built in any other way. He would be a theoretical purist who could say that since here we have something far too splendid and ornate to be strictly appropriate for commercial uses, it is something, therefore, which should be distinctly condemned as sinning against architectural excellence because sinning against fitness and expression of purpose. Yet, nevertheless, I think it would be unfortunate if our architects, dazzled by the beauty of this work, should come to look upon it as a standard, or as a model fit for imitation. On general grounds such a conclusion would be false; and on special grounds it would be ex-

tremely hurtful. Mr. Richardson's talent is of a very peculiar sort. Its results are, perhaps, a law unto themselves; but they are sometimes the
last results in the world which should be made a law for others, or
which could be safely diluted with the water of imitation. Take away
the exuberant strength and fervor which enable Mr. Richardson at
times to do unlawful things in a magnificently seductive way, and we
should merely have the unlawfulness without the compensating charm.
We have not, I repeat, so many fine monumental structures that we need
quarrel with this because Mr. Richardson produced it when simply bid
to build a warehouse. But it is not every one who would create a monument instead of a pretentious failure in striving for a similar transformation; and no one at all could do it, I am very sure, if attempting the
task upon Mr. Richardson's lines, and imitating the manner which is
natural to him.

Let us return now to New York, and see how admirable a work of art
may be wrought by the perfectly straightforward resolution of a peculiarly utilitarian problem, and without the slightest recourse to ornamental embellishment. There is no building in the city which has greater
beauty of a purely architectural kind than the huge storage warehouse
that Mr. James E. Ware has erected at Lexington Avenue and Forty-
second street. Certain factors in the programme gave him, it is true, fine
opportunities of a sort which the modern architect seldom enough en-
counters. For one thing, he had a most unusual chance to build great
unbroken fields of wall. We know what effects of imposing grandeur
the architects of old realized in such fields. We know the temples of
Egypt, the warehouses of Nuremberg, the various wide walls of Spain.
And we are tempted to believe that the Roman baths, for instance, are
finer in their present denuded state—in their huge simplicity and structural expression—than when they were overlaid with a gorgeous dress
of "applied" unnecessary features. No complaint is more often in the
mouth of the modern architect or his apologist than the complaint that
such possibilities are not within his reach. But when by chance they are,
how often does he use them well? How often does he even try to use
them at all? Is any sight more common in our streets than a wall, of necessity unpierced, which its builder has seen fit to "decorate" with blind
windows over its entire expanse? Mr. Ware has not fallen into such sui-
cidal folly, nor has he left his wall in a naked monotony which would
make it a mere brute pile, and not a *structure*. He has grouped his windows, strongly accentuated his string-courses, formed his angles of
powerful turrets, and crowned the whole by a finely effective cornice.

He has left his fields in simple strength, but has redeemed them from barrenness, emphasized their scale, and turned his building into an imposing work of architectural art. Purpose and interior disposition could not be more truthfully explained. No feature is added for the sake of beauty only, yet each brings its own quota toward general beauty of effect. In detail, as in disposition, there is nothing with which we can find fault, I think, save perhaps the corner doorway, which might have been either more simple or more forcibly accentuated. Everywhere we see evidence of original and happy inspiration. And it *is* original and happy, because entirely based on practical necessities, which are turned (not forced) into artistic opportunities. The building is, by the way, an especially instructive example of the value of light and shade in enhancing architectural forms. Look at it under a bright sun, and you will see how much it owes to the strong markings of its string-courses, to the depth of its reveals, and to the splendid shadows of its cornice and its turret roofs. It is built throughout of red brick, a slight and welcome diversity of color coming through the use of a somewhat darker tint about the openings.

No layman could have said to himself beforehand that thus and so a warehouse in a modern street should be conceived. But every eye must now acknowledge that this is just its proper form—for use, for expressiveness, and for appropriate beauty. It is novel, unexpected, and original; yet our first glance convinces us that it is *right* as well as strikingly effective. And are not these the reflections always suggested by a truly fine work of art, and by none that is not fine and true? No architect of the day deserves more hearty congratulation than does Mr. Ware for the artistic excellence of this building, and still more for the truthful, rational, strictly architectural way in which this has been gained. Its influence ought to be as strong and vital as its birth was unforeseen and welcome. If it could be transported to some ancient town, and tenderly touched with the softening hands of time and of historical association, its beauty would be recognized by all, as it now is by those who can appreciate architectural success apart from all adventitious aids.

Some of the new retail stores in our large cities, while far from being perfect or even very good works of art, are yet a noteworthy improvement on their immediate predecessors. We cannot really approve, for instance, of the tall Gorham building at the north-west corner of Broadway and Nineteenth street, with its trivial "Queen Anne" detail appropriate only to a structure of one-tenth its size. But since it is of brick, and since its detail, though so feeble, is not loud or vulgar, it is in

happy contrast with such a neighbor as Lord & Taylor's iron shop. At
the south-east corner of Twenty-second street is a much better work,
still weak in composition, but quiet, straightforward, unpretentious,
and agreeable. With others of its class it proves, if nothing more, that
rampant ostentation is going out of fashion.

Messrs. Peabody & Stearns have built in Boston a large corner store
which, in spite of some unfortunate detail, shows a fair attempt at composition and a clever treatment of the porch. This is recessed in the corner, the overhanging story being held by powerful columns which
strike, in a rational and unforced way, an effective note of variety.

In our smaller towns, too, we are giving up the shrieking bathos
which characterized our commercial structures of a few years ago—
their cast-iron columns, their top-heavy cornices of sanded zinc, their
extravagantly awkward detail. If in place of these we usually find as yet
only a more or less fantastic "Queen Anne" design, we must still recognize a distinct step in advance. Though not always sensible or appropriate, and sometimes very distressing, yet such designs have now and
then a sufficient grace or picturesqueness to make us partly forgive their
lack of deeper excellence. And occasionally we find something that is
different in character and really good. One such example I have already
noted at Newburgh; and another, quite unlike it, and of a very charming sort, we see in the Farmers' Bank at Albany, built by Mr. Russell
Sturgis. It is especially interesting since, for once, Gothic forms have
been chosen, and have been treated in a very straightforward, sensible,
and yet effective fashion.

Let us glance a moment at the little Industrial School Mr. Stratton
has built on Sixteenth street, in New York [. . .] and then pass to something very different.

Retail shops and warehouses we have had always with us; but of late
years a new member has been born into our commercial family, which
is one of the most unmanageable architectural children that have ever
claimed attention in any day or land. We see quite clearly that architecture is not an abstract, merely "æsthetic" art, but an art rooted in practical requirements, and molded by material conditions, when we remember that the invention of the steam passenger-lift has brought
about the invention of what have not improperly been called our "elevator buildings," and that they offer problems as new as they are characteristic of American soil, and especially of our cramped New York.
Their chief characteristic is their enormous height. This height might
not be hopelessly obstructive if one's other dimensions could be en-

larged in proportion, if several stories could be put into a lofty roof, and
if windows and wall spaces might be regulated quite at will. But with it
goes, most often, a width that is totally inadequate; almost invariably,
the impossibility of adopting a steep roof; and quite invariably, the necessity for a multitude of small rooms within, and so a multitude of
small and monotonously spaced openings without. What is to be done
with such a problem? I have not been surprised to hear some architects
say, "Nothing. It is hopeless. We may as well surrender at once. The
most we can do is to use good materials and discreet ornamentation. We
can attempt no architectural composition, and if we are expressive we
must, of course, be monotonous, since there is nothing but monotony to
render. We must retire in ignominy behind plain walls and uniform lines
of little windows."

And, indeed, it would have been well if this modest hopelessness had
sometimes regulated action. Especially when we look at our most ambitious apartment houses do we feel that nothing could possibly be
worse, and that the barest factory would have been a good deal better.
But with apartment houses we are not here concerned. Only the "office
building" falls within our present chapter, and when we look at its embodiments we may change our tone a little. I do not know why it should
be so, but certainly our down-town "elevator buildings" are far better
than their up-town brethren. Perhaps it is because in the commercial
work our desire has often been simply to build well, while in our residences we have wished to be stylish, elegant, and even "pretty," too.
Unfortunate desire, and thrice unfortunate results!

By this I do not mean to say that all our office buildings are good, or
that any of them approach the condition of perfect works of art. Some
are hideous, and many are simply commonplace. But some are promising, and others, taking into account the difficulties which have hedged
them round, may fairly be called successful. No skill, no talent, no inspiration, can ever make a really beautiful building if its proportions
must remain radically and glaringly wrong, and if no opportunity is
given for masking them by composition with its roofs and masses. And
yet we certainly are proving that something better may be wrung from
even the worst proportions and the most monotonous masses than absolute deformity or barren nakedness.

Moreover, if we look at these office buildings chronologically, we can
trace, I think, a general advance toward comparative excellence. Surely,
most of the latest among them are better, for example, than the Tribune
building or the Western Union. And when we ask how and why they are

better, we find it is because they are simpler, and because their architects have attempted structural composition instead of relying upon superficial adornment.

The Mills building, for instance, is bad in many ways, but good in the bold disposition of its masses, which has been effected by recessing the central portion, and thus putting the courtyard outside, so to say, instead of inside the structure. The Sherman building, at Broadway and Wall street, is hideously bad below, but its upper stories show good structural intentions in their piers and arches. Nor is the Morse building without evidence of effort in the right direction, as we see most clearly when we compare it with "Temple Court" across the street. And the Williamsburgh Insurance building is also comparatively successful in its main mass, in spite of the grotesque ugliness of its porch, with stumpy columns sliding down its balustrade.

But better than any of these is Mr. Post's Post Building—at once simpler, more rational, and more agreeable than any of its rivals. An irregular site, which might well have proved embarrassing, has been cleverly turned to account, to give division and contrast of mass. The walls are composed—and as well, I think, as was possible, considering their proportions—by sturdy piers and arches; and the modest detail is pleasing in itself, and rightly placed best to perform its office. The use of a single tone of pale yellow brick and terra-cotta throughout increases the refinement and reticence which characterize the work.

Far more costly and ambitious, and far less successful, is the Washington building on the Battery. Here stone is used throughout, and is treated with a profusion of delicately carved decoration. Composition is attempted, but can hardly be said to be achieved; for the tall pilasters which run up to the cornice and are crowned with capitals do not compose the wall and unite its features, as do true piers with arches thrown between them. And the elaborate detail is wasted; for it is too delicate and too small in scale, and is distributed too impartially.

One of the most sumptuous of these great structures is Mr. Clinton's Mutual Life Insurance building on Nassau street. It is built of a light-colored limestone, which gives it a certain elegance, and suggests, by the way, the streets of Paris. Its rather elaborate detail is sufficiently well distributed, and its mass has some excellence (though not striking excellence) of composition. Mr. Clinton has given us a work which is attractive in many ways, and is neither vulgar nor commonplace. And yet it does not interest us as much as does the Post building, because it is the result of richer opportunities, and because, moreover, it does not look so simply natural and indigenous. We feel that its architect has had a foreign model in mind, while before Mr. Post's work we feel that he has merely been trying to make the best of his problem in the frankest and easiest way.

A work that does not exactly rank with the foregoing, since its scale is so much less, we see in No. 55 Broadway, which is due to Messrs. Babb, Cook & Willard. Its modest extent did not, however, lessen difficulty, but increased it rather, since the height remained so lofty. Here there was absolutely no chance to use the truest sort of structural composition; but there *is* composition, nevertheless, in the arrangement of the string-courses, of the openings, and of the ornamentation. A treatment so detailed would be out of place in a broader building, but here it was the only thing possible, and has been most successfully carried out. Unity is not lost in variety, and yet the variety is great enough almost to hide from the eye the preposterous proportions of the wall. If such a front can be agreeably treated, there must be hope for all things—more hope than, upon theoretical grounds, we might be inclined to cherish.

A new building on the east side of Broadway below Cortlandt street, designed by Mr. Hunt, offered a less difficult problem. It is rich, dignified, and pleasantly effective. Yet we cannot give it quite unqualified praise since it is hardly a piece of true architectural composition. Its beauty comes from the polished columns which flank every window and is *applied* beauty, though honest and elegant in its own way.

A very charming work is Messrs. McKim, Mead & White's Columbia Bank, on the corner of Forty-second street and Fifth Avenue. Its masses are modeled by the strong projection of two bays on its longer side, the narrow Fifth Avenue front being analogous to these bays in the treatment of its upper portions. The lower story throughout is of stone beautifully worked, and is finished with a delicate cornice. The brick wall above is set back a little, producing a fortunate effect of variety and increased apparent stability. The windows are grouped in large square openings, and a delicate ornamentation of terra-cotta enforces the architectural lines and adds an element of quiet richness and elegance. The small *loggias* which surmount the bays are welcome features, lightening the structure in the place where lightness is appropriate. There is perhaps some confusion in the use of the terra-cotta, its *role* sometimes being constructive and sometimes decorative. Inside the bank we see the same refined treatment that always characterizes the interior work of these architects, though properly subdued into accordance with utilitarian purposes.

On the south-east corner of Broadway and Broome street is a building which can hardly be called a successful work of art. But beneath the infelicities of its execution we perceive a general idea which seems deserving of much praise. This is the idea of treating the central portion of the long wall in a somewhat screen-like fashion, subordinating it to bays which project at its extremities. These bays correspond in width to the narrower façade, and the corner, of course, is treated as a whole. I should like to see what the architects of the Columbia Bank would make of this arrangement, which is well suggested, but not well developed, in the Broome street work. With a front as narrow and a height as great as those of their bank, a rather tower-like treatment of the corner might be an interesting experiment.

I may note, in passing, an accessory detail which we find in this Broome street store. This is the attempt (and it is not unsuccessful) to bring the sign-boards which so disfigure our business structures into harmony among themselves, and to render them as little hurtful as possible to their architectural background.

But the most conspicuous of all the new commercial buildings of New York still remains for notice. This is the Produce Exchange of Mr. Post. There is no recent work of which it is so difficult to speak with fairness,—so great are its defects, and yet so great in some respects its excellence. I may as well confess at once that its ornamental details are as bad as bad can be. Also,—and this is a more important point,—that it is an extremely untruthful structure, so far as expressiveness is concerned, its exterior being quite unrelated to the disposition of its interior parts. The problem was not an easy one, I know—to build an immense hall for public use, and to put small offices beneath and around and above it in every inch of space it left unfilled. But a better solution, if not a perfectly true one, might well have been secured; and knowing Mr. Post's ability, we may believe he would have found it but for the feverish haste with which the work was pushed—a haste that is likely to do us ill service very often in the future, as it has done in the past in more instances than this. But, after all possible deficiencies are noted, it remains true that the Produce Exchange, superficially considered for beauty only, is one of the most imposing monuments we have. I have often spoken of the sort of composition which results from the harmonious disposition of diverse masses and features; but there is another sort which comes through the emphatic repetition of a few well-chosen motives. This is the kind Mr. Post has used in a broad, powerful, and singularly effective fashion. Take away in imagination the story above the cornice, which was, I believe, an addition to the original design; suppress the utterly superfluous and disturbing tower; forget the unfortunate porches and the crude ornamentation, and we have a structure which is very fine in general proportion, and in the shape, sequence, and contrast of strong and even noble features. The good qualities of the Produce Exchange must be good indeed, since they so easily persuade us to shut our eyes to so many and so grave defects.

I might, of course, very much extend this list of our commercial buildings. Without going further afield,—where I doubt not there is much of value and of interest to be found,—I might note other good works in Boston, and certain bank buildings in Philadelphia which are rich and ambitious without being vulgar or inadequate. But no good purpose would be gained. This is not, as I have said before, a *catalogue raisonné* of everything we have lately done. It is merely an attempt—how imperfect and unduly brief no one knows so well as I—to indicate the direction in which our architects are turning their steps and the degree of progress they are making. I cannot really *record* this progress. I can only *illustrate* it by a few examples, and try to explain it so that some hitherto indifferent eyes may be interested in its true nature and its best possibilities. If I have not done this—if I have not explained the excellence of certain works in a clear enough way to enable my readers to appreciate the kindred excellence of such others as may fall beneath their notice, and to see wherein lie the faults of less successful essays—if I have not done this, I say, I have lamentably failed in my chief intention. I have rendered of no avail the only excuse that could justify a layman in passing criticism upon the work of a profession which, more than any other in our day, is surrounded by limitations, fettered by difficulties, and discouraged and hampered by a lack of true popular understanding.

If I may still be granted a little space, I will utilize it to dwell upon an important point, to which thus far I have only incidentally referred. I have said that what, for want of a better term, may be called *structural finish* is an influential factor in architectural beauty, and one which cannot at all be appreciated in illustrations. By structural finish I do not mean the arrangement of features nor the execution of ornamental details. I mean an architect's treatment of his materials in the main portions of his work.

Structural finish may be imperfect in two different ways—mechanically or artistically. It may sin through mere carelessness, stupidity or dishonesty of workmanship. A structure may be badly built through being

Fig. 12.   Forty-Second Street Entrance, Columbia Bank Building. [McKim, Mead and White, 1882–84.]

weakly or clumsily put together; but the best built structure, mechanically considered, may sin artistically through the unwise selection and arrangement of its units. Most of our work *did* sin conspicuously in just this way until a very few years ago. Either there was no attempt at beauty and variety in the shaping and disposition of the units of construction, or that attempt was made in wofully mistaken fashions. I do not know which is the worse,—an average brown-stone dwelling, built of uniformly proportioned blocks, often sadly out of scale with the size of the structure, and always smoothed to the dreariest monotony of surface, or such a basement as that of the Sherman building, with its brutal masses of rock and its various other vagaries of treatment. Look now at the lower story of the Columbia Bank, and you will see what I mean by *good* structural finish. The stones are neither too small nor too large, too rough nor too smooth, for their position and for appropriate contrast with the brick wall above; and they are disposed in a way which gives them a truly decorative beauty of their own. We are improving rapidly in this point, I rejoice to say. We are beginning to feel how greatly beauty depends upon the proper size, surface finish, and arrangement of our building-stones, and to divine how under given circumstances it may best be gained.

With bricks, even more depends upon judicious treatment, since they have less individual excellence to redeem bad disposition. Awhile ago there was but one way in which we cared to use them. We built all our visible brick walls as smooth as possible, painting them bright red as soon as they showed signs of "weathering," and "pointing" them into conspicuous individual life with strong white lines. Certainly, we could have hit upon no worse device; for when our units of structure are hopelessly ignoble, their individual effect should not be insisted upon. It should be allowed to sink unperceived into the effect of *mass,* or to produce mere vague diversities of tone. This is the way in which the Lexington Avenue storage warehouse has been built. If it is left intact, its present crudeness of color and hard smoothness of texture will after a while be subdued into softer beauty. But suppose that as soon as it begins to show traces of dust and weather, it is spruced up after our time-honored fashion with bright paint, and its million little units "pointed" into exasperating prominence! I do not care to dwell upon the thought.

I may add, moreover, that judging from the beauty of the old brick-work of Spain and Italy, a rougher, so-called "commoner," surface than that of our pressed brick would often tell to better advantage; and also, that the introduction of more varied sizes and shapes is a great desideratum. The bricks the Romans used, for instance, were more like what we call tiles in form, and were set with very much thicker and rougher mortar seams between them. The result is, that the impression of tiny units is lost in an impression of mass, and that this mass has a less mechanical surface and a pleasanter variety of tone than are attained in our regular and neatly laid constructions.

I am glad to note, therefore, one instance in which a bold innovation has been made upon our current practice, and with the distinctest success. Messrs. McKim, Mead & White are building a large house on the corner of Madison Avenue and Seventy-second street, and the bricks used in its upper stories have been made under their directions. They are, if I remember, some sixteen inches long by hardly more than three in width, and are less close and hard in texture than our "best pressed brick." And they are not monotonously alike, but considerably varied in tint, the resulting tone being a soft light brown or very dull yellow. The effect of the wall is most delightful, both on account of the less mechanically regular shape of its units and of the broken and vital quality of its color. When we remember that it is as easy to make bricks of one shape as of another, and easier to make them varied than strictly uniform in tint, there seems, indeed, no reason why we should restrict ourselves to such monotony as has hitherto prevailed in this direction.

15

Churches

It is still too general an idea that his ecclesiastical work must be the easiest part of a modern architect's activity. It is still too commonly supposed that the mediæval styles offer him a multitude of models which, exactly copied or but slightly modified, will answer all his purposes,— that he must be able to imitate discreetly and skillfully, but need give no thought to the fundamental problems of his art, since these were fully worked out in ages past and settled once for all. Such belief in the present adequacy of mediæval precedents—a belief which awhile ago was almost superstitious in its protests against the use of any other style or the desirability of modern innovation—is, I need hardly say, of but recent origin. Gothic art died with the dying supremacy of the Catholic church, and till our own day no one wished for its reanimation. As the various classic fashions succeeded one another, each in its turn was used for all ecclesiastical as well as for all secular constructions. In the seventeenth century the genius of Wren brought practical fitness, and often structural though not decorative beauty, out of the elements then in favor. Later on, when the pseudo-Greek temple was in vogue, no good end was attained. And then came the "Gothic Revival," bringing change where change was sorely needed. Its results, however, were not of unmixed good, for reason and common sense were ostracized from

The Century Magazine (29) 7 (January 1885): 323–338.

its early counsels. The newly recognized beauty of mediæval work so intoxicated a generation that had been fed on the dry pabulum of classic nullities, that its eyes were blinded to the change which had come over practical requirements, or else persuaded that this change was a misfortune to be deplored and disregarded. Nor, in its new-found desire for the "ecclesiastical feeling" so evident in Gothic art, did it reflect upon the necessity of *truth* in architectural expression—a necessity which robs "ecclesiastical feeling" of all but a dilettante, archæologic, superficially æsthetic value, unless it is the unforced voice of the actual devotional mood of those who build. Many of Wren's churches were far more appropriate to current needs than those of earlier days; but his inventions were despised and a distinct backward step was taken—the pernicious doctrine being taught that architectural "art" need not concern itself with matters of fitness and veracity.

For a while we in America accepted this view of church-building almost as implicitly as did our English brethren. And with less excuse than they; for where the Anglican church is preëminent, far less change has come in practical or expressional necessities than where, as is the case with us, a majority of the people belong to the extremer Protestant communions. For a while we believed in the entire adequacy of an imitated mediæval art to meet needs which in truth are modern in the full sense of the word. But of late this belief, though still, as I have said, both wide-spread and strong, is neither so universal nor so implicit as it was; and we may rejoice to note the fact. Not that Gothic art is of necessity to be abandoned for some other; and not that we need wish for that "new style" for which the lovers of mere novelty are longing. "Style" is not the question at all— only the rational or irrational use of whatever style may be selected. The thing that is most important, and that will best justify a hopeful looking toward the future, is—here, no less than in any other branch of architecture—that we should *reason* about our work, should accept nothing on the mere authority of ancient precedent, or for the mere sake of artistic charm. If we do thus accept a style, we shall never work with it in a really vigorous way. We shall be copyists only, and, to judge by the average of modern work, not such successful copyists that even superficial beauty will result. But if our art is founded on reason and intelligent common sense, we shall learn to do *good* work at least. Whether it will eventually grow to be very beautiful work or not will depend upon the gifts with which nature sees fit to endow us. But neither fundamental excellence nor satisfying, vital beauty can grow from any other basis.

But perhaps I should stop a moment now to prove that our needs are indeed quite different from those of Gothic-building generations.

It will hardly be questioned that the mediæval architect was inspired not by the *fond,* the basis, the essentials of Christianity, not by those things which the simplest of Protestant sects may claim to hold in common with the church of Hildebrand, but by the specialized demands of this church. If we know the plan and features of a mediæval structure, we know how accurately they were fitted to the performance of the Catholic ritual. If we follow the course of architectural history, we know how they grew up and grouped themselves as that ritual expanded and crystallized into shape, absorbing a thousand beliefs, traditions, rites, and ceremonies with which fundamental Christianity had little enough to do and which Protestantism has cast aside.

It is true that such a church may be used for Protestant forms of worship. But we can say as much of any spacious interior; and the plea of partial appropriateness, which is valid with regard to existent and venerable structures, strikes below the mark when new creations are in question.

With those sects—dominant, as I have said, with us—that have abandoned ritual altogether, the whole character and whole intention of the service have been changed. It is no longer a sacrifice offered for the people by its priests, no longer a gorgeous ceremonial to be but vaguely seen, no longer an elaborate musical rite in a stranger tongue, but a common act in which the laity take a far more direct and personal share, and of which every word must be caught by all. It needs no chapels for a populous pantheon of saints; no spacious chancel for a numerous clergy; no broad aisles for processional pomp and show; and even the altar must change in place as well as purport when it is called a communion table. Moreover,—and this is no unimportant point,— that love of physical comfort which is a peculiarly modern characteristic asks for stationary cushioned seats, for unobstructed sight and sound, for warmth and ventilation, and for thorough lighting both by day and night. Do such needs get rational satisfaction from the old cathedral type, or even from that of the English parish church of other days?

And it is the same with regard to our expressional necessities. The mediæval architect expressed not some fundamental sentiment common to Christianity as a whole, but the special sentiments of its mediæval phase, the peculiar mental mood and social state to which those sentiments owed their birth. The church was then the one great social fact and influence that ruled mankind with undisputed sway. It inspired, demanded, and absorbed all the activity of man's more peaceful moods; took the entire tribute not only of his heart, but of his mind and hand and purse. And it absorbed nothing more wholly than art. In its cathedrals was expressed all that we now express in our public buildings, our charitable institutions, our civic adornments, and our sumptuous private homes. Into its treasuries went all those minor works which are now dispersed to a myriad secular ends. Hence the size and richness, the pomp and splendor, the magnificence in effect and the lavish care in detail of a mediæval sanctuary.

But to-day we have no "church" in the same sense of the word. We have a number of different communions, banded together for the simple purposes of common worship and moral teaching, which are without direct secular influence or importance, and absorb but a part of our mental activity, our artistic energy, or our superabundant wealth. Consider, too, the devotional temper of mediæval men. Consider their blind unreasoning faith in a thousand things we have long since questioned and denied; consider their mysticism, their love of symbolism and allegory, their passion for the gloomy, the obscure, the terrible, the grotesque, the vague, intangible, vast, and supersensual. Is this the devotional attitude of our time? Can their huge interiors, their vanishing perspectives, their soaring vaults, their dim religious light, their wealth of symbolic detail, their throngs of forgotten saints, their expression of the insignificance of the individual and the supremacy of the priesthood, their testimony that man should approach his Maker through the medium of a sumptuous allegoric ceremonial—can these things be in harmony with the mood a Protestant brings to the house of God to-day?

I do not forget the profound emotion that an ancient church must still excite in any susceptible breast. We need not try to analyze it at the moment; but when our future building is in question, then we must. Then we must ask ourselves how much of this emotion is really religious, how much artistic or historic in its promptings; and further, how much of its really religious portion is genuine and personal; how much sympathetic and imaginative. We must ask whether such a structure would be the natural results if our own needs and minds and hearts were given full and true expression.

We are gradually groping our way, I think, to a perception of these facts and a belief that we should respect them in our practice. Already we have acknowledged that in practical ways the ancient ecclesiastical type is not so entirely adequate as we once supposed. And if we do not so definitely question its expressional fitness, at least we no longer strictly limit the architect thereto in his search for "ecclesiastical feeling." Very rightly we demand that such feeling should exist, and neither unnaturally nor irrationally we believe that it may be wrought through the adaptation of some mediæval mode more easily than in any other way. Perhaps it would be too much to expect that as free an adaptation as is necessary should as yet be within the power of our artists to accomplish, or of our public to desire. Perhaps we should be unduly impatient did we feel surprise at the illogical attempts which are so often made by the architect, so often prescribed, and not merely tolerated, by those from whom he holds commission—attempts to secure a quite new type of interior, and at the same time to preserve the general exterior effect and all the decorative detail of the ancient type. Perhaps only repeated unsuccessful efforts will suffice to prove how illogical they are—how illogical it is to disassociate the practical from the expressional, artistic side of any art; how foolish to forget that the charm of Gothic was not abstract and superficial, but resulted naturally from convenient structural dispositions, and the true expressional impulse of its own day and land.

The problem our architects here have before them is as novel as it is difficult and important. Nothing just like it was ever proposed before, since other generations built naïvely, and we must build self-consciously, and distracted by the very richness of the legacy they have left us. It would be idle to hope that any one man or any one generation of men could fully master such a task. But it will be treacherous if any shirks his quota of the work. Each must do his little part, for it is only thus that architecture ever grows. Each must study his problem from the center outward, and not from the outside in, settling first the bones and sinews of his structure and then trying to fit them with a true integument of beauty. This may well draw its inspiration from mediæval precedents; but, even so, it will be something very different from what we most often find to-day—a mere patchwork of attractive but mendacious shreds stripped from the trunk and limbs of an ancient body quite unlike the new.

And now let us pass at last to a little definite description.

The first of our churches that were more than mere barn-like conventicles were built in the days of "good Queen Anne," and for more than a century the modern-classic styles were the only ones we knew. Mr. Grant White showed some of our earlier examples to my readers not many months ago, and did full justice to the finest of them all—St.

Paul's in New York. But upon one important point, it seemed to me that
he hardly laid sufficient stress—upon the interesting variety that resulted when wood was the chosen material, and the colonial architect
intelligently modified the English model to suit its new requirements.
This was a time when simple convenience was the architect's chief aim
in his interior, when the public seems to have had no conscious craving
for "ecclesiastical feeling." Yet, nevertheless, some of these interiors—
Trinity in Newport, for example, and King's Chapel in Boston—have a
certain grave dignity, simple sobriety, and homely, cheerful stateliness,
which are, perhaps, more truthfully expressive of the temper of modern
Protestantism than is a dim and shadowy, elaborate and sumptuous
Gothic church. But of course when I speak thus I leave all purely *artistic* considerations out of sight. These sensible and attractive if not eminently beautiful structures were succeeded by pseudo-Greek temples,
and then we, too, came in for our share of the Gothic revival.

Its first eminent apostle was the elder Upjohn, an Englishman by
birth, but American in his artistic life. Trinity in New York was his mas-
terpiece, and is still the most beautiful church in the city. When I add
that it is an orthodox, scholarly reproduction of a simple type common
among English parish churches, the admission must not be made to
prove too much. The conclusion need not follow that it would be best
for us to cleave faithfully to the same kind of work; for what we have
not yet been able to do is hardly a conclusive argument to decide for
what we ought to strive. Trinity proves that our inventive efforts have
not yet produced anything in all New York as satisfactory, from an
artistic point of view, as Mr. Upjohn's imitative skill could build. But the
artistic point of view is not the only one that should be regarded. In
spite of Trinity's beauty, it is far from impressing us with the belief that
here is the ideal modern church with which we should rest content. It
answers fairly well the needs of its own congregation—an Episcopal
congregation with High Church leanings and a choral service. But turn
to one of Mr. Upjohn's less conspicuous structures, and see how badly
even his hands succeeded in fitting the same type to the needs of other
communions. Take, for instance, the Presbyterian church on the corner
of Tenth street and University Place. Look at the long nave divided into
three by rows of massive columns, that inconvenience materially the occupants of the outer pews; look at the deep galleries which cut the long
windows in twain, and the support of which is unprovided for in the
structure of the walls from which they project; look at the lofty vaulted
ceiling, which absorbed so much light that it had to be spoiled by a coat

of pale-hued paint; look at the high-paneled wooden screen which fills
the east end, but so palpably does not belong there, and at the way the
pulpit clings to it without constructive rhyme or reason. Is this a good
way to build such a church—this way which results in something that is
neither a copy nor an adaptation, but merely a mutilation of the ancient
type, unsuccessful alike in the way of practical fitness and of architectural coherence?

Mr. Upjohn's exteriors, though not always in strict accord with his interiors, are sure to have much beauty of the best because most architectural kind. They all exhibit in a less degree the peculiar excellence of
Trinity—an excellence which springs from harmony of proportion,
strength and grace of outline, well-regulated size of feature, and discreet
employment of very simple decoration. They point a lesson which might
well have been regarded by our later Gothicists, who have too often
quite ignored the claims of these prime elements in architectural success.

For many years after Mr. Upjohn led the way, the style of our ecclesiastical work was almost always Gothic, though there were occasional
reversions to a classic type, such as we see in the Arlington Street
Church in Boston and the "Brick Church" at the corner of Fifth Avenue
and Thirty-seventh street. But the Gothic was of every imaginable and
unimaginable variety,—"natural, unnatural, and preternatural." Sometimes it was carefully and dryly "correct"; sometimes it aimed at cor-
rectness in a stupid and blundering way; sometimes it was plain to mea-
gerness, sometimes lavishly but inartistically elaborate. In our villages
we had poverty-stricken and ludicrous specimens, which were only
"Gothic" because their windows were pointed and their eaves were
bordered with a jig-saw ornament that looked like paper fringing for a
pantry-shelf. Sad contrasts must such things have seemed, even in the
eyes of the most devoted mediævalist, to our wooden relics of a former
century—so simple, so straightforward, so unpretentious, and yet so far
from bald or inartistic. And we had (and still continue to produce, alas!)
Gothic in stone which is less immediately funny, but far more distressing to the eye and contaminating to the taste: Gothic like that shown in
some of our most conspicuous up-town churches—a mere accumulation of features which are false to the interior they purport to explain,
which have no force or grace of outline and no proportion or harmony
among themselves, and which are not helped by a profusion of showy
ornament as monotonous in design and as hard in execution as though
its substance were cast-iron instead of stone. Simple, conventional, almost undecorated Gothic work is better than such work as this, as is

proved by Mr. Upjohn's two churches on Fifth Avenue below Fourteenth street, and by Mr. Renwick's Catholic cathedral, which is faulty
in many points, but still dignified, intelligent, and attractive. And "classical" work may, I think, be better, too, even if it is not so good as that
of the last century, even if it is only discreet and commonplace like the
"Brick Church" already mentioned. We cannot call this a beautiful ecclesiastical monument, but it has at least the excellence of repose, honesty, and dignity. It looks at least as though its author knew what he
wanted to do, and knew how to use his chosen style to reach his ends.
And this is more than we can say for the riotous yet mechanical effect
of our most glaring Gothic failures. And its expression, too, is it not
more in keeping with the simple, severe, non-mystical rites of the Presbyterian faith, than the bastard, pretentious mediævalism of many a
fabric which houses sister congregations?

But if we search we can find much good Gothic work, as well as bad.
Especially in our smaller towns there are many churches that are sensible and charming. It is natural that success should have come more frequently here than in our crowded cities, since site and surroundings are
usually more felicitous, and since enforced economy often acts as a
wholesome check on that vaulting ambition which is so apt to o'erleap
itself when unrestrained by the drawing of the purse-string. Listen to
what so good a judge as Mr. Edward Freeman has written:

> I found the modern churches of various denominations certainly better than
> I had expected. They may quite stand beside the average of modern work in
> England, setting aside a few of the very best. All persuasions have a great
> love of spires, and if the details are not always what one could wish, the gen-
> eral effect of the spires is very stately, and they help largely toward the gen-
> eral effect of the cities in a distant view. But I thought the churches, whose
> style is most commonly Gothic of one kind or another, decidedly less suc-
> cessful than some of the civil buildings.

And we learn from Mr. Freeman's context what we might have
guessed on general principles—that the better results of secular work
have come because here the effort has not so often been made to say one
thing while in reality we are meaning quite another.

But of late years many of our architects, breaking away from the
trammels of convention, and unseduced by the cheap charms of willful
novelty, have built churches where the desire to secure *fitness* shows in
a marked and interesting way. This is true, however, of their interiors
rather than of such structures as a whole.

Our new needs, let me premise, are not of a single sort. No one type of church will now answer every want as it might if one communion ruled our land. There must be varying solutions of a varying problem. Each will require the adaptation as distinct from the imitation of former fashions, and some will necessitate a process of thought as distinctly creative as can be any which concerns itself with architecture in this late age of the world.

Let us speak first of one or two of our new Episcopal churches, since here, of course, there has been a less radical divergence from ancient precedents than when other Protestant sects have housed themselves. But even here we are not surprised to mark a growing impulse toward innovation, a growing tendency, for example, to abandon the old elongated proportions of the nave and to do away with obstructive rows of columns.

Mr. Richardson's is, I am very sure, the first name I should cite in this connection. Several churches for different communions—among them the sensible "North Church" in Springfield, Mass., and the interesting, if not wholly admirable, Brattle Street Church in Boston, with its finely effective tower—were among his earlier efforts. But none of them predicted what he was to do when he should come to build Trinity in Boston. It is hard to approach this work in a mood of sober criticism, for it is very unlike any of our previous efforts, as well as very striking, imposing, and beautiful. Certainly we have no church that from an artistic point of view we can admire so heartily. Only Trinity in New York is worthy to be named beside it, and the two are so entirely different that actual comparison is impossible. I must try to describe it before we can ask whether it is as right as it is delightful.

Looking first at its interior, we find a Latin cross, the arms of which are very broad in proportion to their length, thus affording far better accommodation to modern worshipers than the old type gave. There are no rows of columns, and the four great piers which support the tower over the intersection of nave and transepts are placed close to the angles of the structure, so that they offer no obstruction to the sight. The so-called aisles are mere passageways beyond the seats, and above them is a gallery so shallow that it also is scarcely more than a passageway connecting the galleries proper, which fill the ends of either transept and of the nave above the vestibule. The eastern arm, which forms the chancel, is prolonged by a semicircular apse of equal breadth. The ceiling of the nave is sixty-three feet in height, but in the center, under the tower, it rises to a height of one hundred and three feet. That

Fig. 13.   Tower of Trinity Church, Boston. [Henry H. Richardson, 1873–77.]

a flat finish was adopted, instead of the more beautiful and architecturally appropriate vaulted form, may probably be attributed to those
acoustical considerations which are so important now. Great round
arches, forty-six feet in span, connect the piers and give dignity and
structural expression to the whole. The chancel and apse of this church
are certainly in harmony with the other proportions of the interior, but
are much too large for the Low Church service performed therein. This
fact is clearly proclaimed by their bareness and emptiness, wanting as

they do the choir-seats and screens, the splendid altar and elaborate desks which the eye demands. We hardly know whether we blame the architect for not building with more rigorous fitness, or the congregation for not utilizing their architectural opportunities, for not furnishing their chancel properly, and inaugurating a sumptuous High Church service. Theoretically considered, it seems as though Mr. Richardson's interior must have been less harmonious and less beautiful had he built more appropriately in this particular. And yet fitness is the fundamental law, and when Mr. Richardson seriously tries he can usually compel it to a finely artistic result.

It would be interesting, were space not so limited, to describe the decoration of Trinity. But it has often been described and discussed before; so I will only say that a complete color-treatment was planned for from the outset. All surfaces are plastered and painted; the great piers, now temporarily encased in wood, are some day to be covered with rich mosaic, while the wood-work throughout will be touched with color.

The site selected for Trinity was advantageous in being open on all sides and bounded by three broad streets of almost equal importance. Its triangular shape would have been ill-adapted to a structure of our usual ecclesiastical type; but in the form which Mr. Richardson selected—inspired by those early churches of central France which are less familiar to our eyes than the products of northern Gothic—Trinity looks as though its site had been planned for its sole sake. A great central tower dominates a composition which is pyramidal in effect, and includes, besides the church itself, a chapel with open outside stairway and connecting cloisters. Each point of view offers a different perspective of much vigor, beauty, and picturesqueness, and from each the tower retains its due preëminence and composes well with the lower masses, excepting from the front, whose flanking towers are brought by the short nave so close to the central tower that the effect is somewhat confused at this point. However, the present effect will be much improved by the addition of the proposed porch.

The central tower is not only the most important, but the most beautiful feature of the whole. It seems to have been prompted by the tower of the old cathedral of Salamanca, which is built in the Romanesque fashion which came to Spain from France, and is essentially the same as that from which the main inspiration of the church was drawn. But it is a free treatment of its original, not a literal copy. To me it gives an impression such as one constantly receives from actual mediæval work, but which I have never felt so forcibly in the presence of any other modern essay. It looks, that is to say, entirely spontaneous and living, distinctly non-mechanical or labored. It looks like the result of a genuine, powerful impulse, not like a lesson learned and then repeated. We accept it on its own evidence, and care little to ask whether it had a definite prototype, or to judge it by any standard of comparison. In the arrangement and proportioning of its features it has that felicity which we instinctively call artistic rightness, and that mystery which is one of the chief charms of ancient work, and the one we most rarely find in the cut-and-dried rigidity or the willful yet labored license of modern art. It does not become tame and commonplace on long acquaintance, but has the perennial novelty and freshness which always mark results that are artistic in the highest sense. The detail of Trinity's exterior is rich, and, for modern work, unusually artistic in design and in execution. We are promised that the sculptures planned for the western porch shall owe their chief features to Mr. St. Gaudens—a happy augury that in the future architectural sculpture may come to be regarded (as it always was in the great artistic ages) as the very noblest work to which the artist can devote his chisel. Nor must I forget to note the important rôle that color plays outside as well as within this church. Much of Trinity's beauty is due to the happy selection and arrangement of the yellowish granite (which looks, in truth, more like a sandstone) used in the walls, and the warm, red-brown Longmeadow stone lavishly employed for the trimmings and decorative features. And the red tiles add greatly to the general effect.

And now we must inquire into the *rightness* of Trinity, ungracious as the task appears in presence of such indisputable beauty. Is it throughout a good *type*—is it a good model for the inspiration of our future work, as well as a thing to be admired on purely æsthetic grounds? In many points I think it is. The ground plan is a very excellent one for an Episcopal church—convenient, "ecclesiastical," and architecturally fine. The arrangement of the galleries is a vast improvement on our past practice when galleries have been a sad necessity. And the color-treatment—the entire dependence upon the brush to the exclusion of the chisel—seems to me as sensible as in this country it was novel. The brush is with us a better-understood instrument of decoration than the chisel. Its results are well in keeping with the nature of our climate, and in their greater warmth, cheerfulness, and definiteness give, I think, a more appropriate expression to the home of a modern congregation than would such results as the chisel wrought in northern Gothic work.

Outside, now, we find that the notable picturesqueness of Trinity is not willful and mendacious, but truthfully expressive of its interior. The place and size of the great tower, for instance, and the way in which the other masses depend upon it, mark the position and the shape of the body of the nave and the lesser importance of its wings. Only in the tower itself do we find a slight violation of truthfulness. Its extreme solidity and the strengthening turrets at its angles might lead us to expect a vault within; and this, as I have said, does not exist, though possibly it was contemplated in the original design. But how is it with the artistic voice of this exterior? Beautiful though it is, does it correspond to the distinctly modern voice of the interior? Is it thoroughly appropriate to a Protestant church in the New England of to-day? Does it affect us as being not only beautiful, but, so to say, inevitable in its accent? When we stand in front of the Lexington Avenue warehouse in New York, for example, our wonder is that the same thing had not been done long before; we marvel how any one could ever have considered such a problem without finding just such a solution. Of course thoughts like these are instinctive, not really rational; but they are the thoughts which always come in presence of a perfectly appropriate architectural creation. What is really the discovery of a peculiarly gifted intelligence always looks like the mere course of nature, like a logical, unescapable deduction from the given premises. But do such thoughts come when we look at Trinity? Of course I am not trying to compare these two buildings, with which comparison would be utterly impossible. I am only trying to contrast, not the strength nor the delightfulness, but merely the *character* of the impression they produce. Do we feel that Trinity is the sort of thing other men ought to have done before? Do we wonder how such a solution could so long have escaped the ecclesiastical builders of to-day, and decide that here they now may turn for valuable hints and lessons? Or do we not wonder, rather, that any man should have attempted to build such a church in just this time and place, and, attempting, should have triumphed in the task? Does not Trinity strike us as a splendid anachronism, bewilder us with an exotic charm? Do we not feel that though all men must admire, none should try to rival it? And if a work of architecture, no matter what its beauty, so affects us that the last advice it prompts is, "Go thou and do likewise," are we justified in calling it the most helpful or most promising we might have had? For, be it remembered, architecture is not, like some of the sister arts, a means toward mere *personal* expression. Whenever its average results have been fine, they have represented not an individual, but a national mind and taste and temper. When it has developed, it has been by the assistance of a thousand, often unnamed, hands, all working with a common impulse and a common aim. I know that in this age of the world individuality everywhere plays a larger part than it did in ages past. But it is most probable that it will be *in spite* of this fact, not because of it, that our architectural progress will be made—if, indeed, Fate holds such progress in her hand for us. In building Trinity Mr. Richardson gave us the most beautiful structure that yet stands on our side of the ocean, and far be it from me to wish that he had built it otherwise in any of its parts. And yet we cannot but consider it (I speak now of its exterior only) an intensely individual, not a broadly characteristic, piece of work; a fascinating example, but one which stands apart and aside from the most hopeful current of our art. It is a splendid *tour de force,* rather than a natural, helpful, onward effort; a seductive glimpse opened for us toward the past, not a prophetic outlook toward a possible future of general success.

We find many other recent Episcopal churches with plans more or less akin to that of Trinity, and in every case at least the practical result seems good. As an example where the artistic result is also fine, I may cite St. Stephen's at Lynn, Mass., built by Messrs. Ware and Van Brunt. Here the pointed style is used throughout. We have again a central square marked off by great corner columns, which are connected by powerful arches and support a ceiling that rises high above that of the subordinated parts. The nave is prolonged to the west, but is short in comparison to its width. Beyond the eastern arch is the large chancel, this time appropriate in itself, and appropriately furnished, as the service is High Church; and out of the chancel, under a smaller arch, opens a semicircular apse, where the altar stands in proper state. There are no true transepts, but the wall to north and south of the central square is lightly recessed and treated like a transept end. Not only is dignity thus attained, but space is given for two great windows, which, with the one at the west end, amply light the church. The plan seems to me very good, and the execution is unusually rich, with a richness well subdued to artistic harmony. The two eastern arches, similar in outline and different in size, offer a beautiful perspective, closed by a rich arcade with marble columns that divides the apse itself from the ambulatory which encircles it. The elaborate wooden ceiling is another fine feature, and its lofty central portion is not only very effective and beautiful, but, so far as I know, novel in design as well. Adjoining the church is a chapel, and the two are connected by a small cloister surrounding the burial-plot of him to whose munificence the structure owes its birth.

The exterior of St. Stephen's does not seem to be so wholly admirable. Some of its features are beautiful, but it is broken and unquiet in effect. And yet, if we examine, we find that this result has not come from a superficial striving after picturesqueness, but, on the contrary, from an effort to express the interior with more definiteness than are often the objects of desire.

In many of our other recent churches—Baptist, Methodist, Congregational, and Presbyterian—we find a much greater degree of novelty than any Episcopal interior shows. We find the "long-drawn aisle" and the cruciform plan alike abandoned, and a simple rectangle frankly utilized. In Mr. Cady's Methodist Church, on the corner of Park Avenue and Eighty-sixth street, for example, we see a square interior with deep galleries running around three sides. At each corner of the inner square marked out by their face stands a column. Round arches connect these columns, and are thrown from them to the outer walls. Above the inner rectangle thus formed, the ceiling rises higher than it does above the galleries. At the east side (one can no longer say east *end*) is the large pulpit platform, behind it are the seats for the choir, and behind these, again, the tall organ pipes. Unfortunately the columns and arches, which are painted throughout, appear to be of iron, and the spandrels above are filled in with an open net-work of turned wood. The effect is therefore too fragile to be architecturally fine. It is not a very beautiful interior, but it is very convenient, and I do not think its purpose could be mistaken. It looks certainly not like an ancient church, but still not unlike a place for religious use.

But we have other churches which are still more unlike all past examples of ecclesiastical architecture—which, in truth, have been inspired by the secular lecture-room or concert-hall. One of the first among them was Dr. Hall's church on Fifth Avenue. We can hardly be surprised if the architect who essayed to treat so immense an interior on so novel a scheme has failed to satisfy the eye. Convenience he has secured, but no particle of beauty can be found in his vast, bare galleried room—no expression of structure, and no more ecclesiastical effect than Steinway Hall exhibits, unless, indeed, we are to find this last in the Gothic detail of his woodwork. Others coming after him, and working on a smaller and therefore less difficult scale, have done a good deal better. Much more successful, for example, is Mr. J. R. Thomas's Calvary Baptist Church, on Fifty-seventh street near Seventh Avenue. The interior is about one hundred feet square, but an amphitheatrical effect has been given by slanting the floor somewhat steeply, curving the rows of seats, and also giving a curvilinear form to the face of the shallow gallery which runs around three sides and even along a portion of the

fourth. A great rose-window opens above the gallery opposite the pulpit, and there is another large window group on one of the sides. The
other side unfortunately shows no opening, as subordinate rooms here
adjoin the church. The choir seats are again behind the pulpit platform,
but the organ pipes are disposed in two groups to right and left, and a
window is pierced between. Light is also admitted in the center of the
ceiling, where rises what I may call a little clear-story of metal. Decoration in color is alone possible in such an interior, and here it is deep-
toned and sufficiently harmonious, though not artistically remarkable.
In spite of its analogy in plan to a secular interior for public use, this
church, too, looks not unlike a place of worship, for the difference is
marked by the sober decoration, the low ceiling, and the ecclesiastical-
looking windows with their colored glass.

Such churches as this (showing, of course, many variations of the
same general idea) have rapidly grown in numbers during the last few
years—so rapidly, indeed, that the type which is based on the secular
concert-hall bids fair to be the most prominent of all in a future near at
hand. There may be other examples better than any I have seen, but I
doubt whether a thoroughly good solution has yet been found. I doubt
it not only upon the evidence of my own experience and the testimony
of others, but upon theoretic grounds. It is almost impossible that so
difficult a problem should have been mastered so very quickly. It is
much more probable that we shall have to wait yet many a year before
we see an amphitheatrical church-interior that will be architecturally
faultless, unmistakably ecclesiastical in its expression, and beautiful in
all its features.

But it need not be thought impossible that such a church should some
day be developed—no, not though its parent be something as alien as a
concert-hall. Was not the mediæval church itself derived from the secular basilica of pagan Rome? Architectural origins seem strange enough
when we try to trace them out. Their history teaches that we may borrow where and what we will—even a plan in one place, features in another, and details in a third. Only—and this is the vital fact that justifies
or condemns—we must blend them, so to say, *chemically* and not mechanically; we must make of them a new body, and not merely a patchwork.

I have already hinted at the fact that the interiors of our new churches
exhibit, if not always more beauty than their exteriors, at least more
palpable signs of the thought and intelligence and desire for truth which
are the foundation-stones of excellence. Their exteriors sometimes

show "originality," but this seldom has veracity and common sense for its inspiration. For example, such churches as I have last described consist of the great rectangular auditorium, together, almost always, with a number of subordinate but still large apartments used for mildly festal congregational purposes—lecture, Sunday-school, and class-rooms, "church-parlors," and sometimes even kitchens too. Truthful external expression is often aimed at in individual features, but the composition as a whole is commonly most untruthful. We find it difficult to decipher, and when we think we have deciphered it, our imaginings have led us quite astray. I have yet to see or hear of any such exterior which frankly exhibits the size and shape of the church itself, and makes it evidently supreme above its dependencies. And a really good exterior we shall never have until this is done.

At Fifty-ninth street and Ninth Avenue is a new church which, built by the Paulist Fathers for Catholic use, naturally follows the ancient plan, and yet is one of the most sensible and non-mediæval structures we have produced. When I last saw it, it was still incomplete both within and without, and its exterior was not remarkable except for size and solid simplicity. Inside it showed a huge-aisled nave, with a chancel of equal width, but without transepts. The aisles were divided from the nave by an arcade with very plain columns and lofty arches of slightly pointed shape. Above this rose a deep belt of unbroken wall, and then the clear-story with single windows of large size. The ceiling was a barrel vault of wood, slightly pointed in section. The walls still showed the same undressed, irregular stones inside as out, and the effect, though rugged enough, was so massive and imposing that one would almost have been content to know that no further finish would be given. But they are to be plastered throughout and decorated with color. If, as has been prophesied, Mr. La Farge receives the commission for the work, he will have in these vast fields a chance such as seldom comes in an artist's way. And the success he has hitherto achieved—in Trinity in Boston, and in the beautiful mosaic work that almost redeems the architectural nothingness of the interior of the "Brick Church" on Fifth Avenue—leads us to believe that he may make it one of the most beautiful interiors of our day. It is already one of the very *best*. There could hardly be a more convincing proof than it afforded in its unfinished state that good architecture is a matter of *construction,* not of ornamentation; that from fine proportions and the artistically regulated size and shape and disposition of very few and simple features, may come the most impressive beauty, without the aid of a single decorative chisel-stroke or a single touch of brush. It proved, too, how unnecessary it is for us to aim at the literal imitation of ancient fashions; how much more important it is to build rationally than to build conventionally. I can hardly say with what "style" one should rank this church. We may call it Gothic, if we will, since its openings are pointed; but it shows no window-tracery and no Gothic decoration, and its broad wall-spaces remind us of very different fashions of construction. Whatever its "style," its effect will certainly not be that of an imitated mediævalism.*

It would be almost impossible, in this day and land, to build a cathedral that should be such in more than name, that should have the actual, not to speak of the relative, importance of the cathedrals of old— almost as impossible as undesirable. Look at an ancient example—at Durham imperious on its rock, or at Antwerp soaring from the human habitations that cluster like swallow-nests around its base, and dwarfing even the huge municipal palaces of a later century. Why should we wish to build the like? On our soil, would not such a cathedral be an anachronism of as palpable a sort as would be a Lanfranc or a Becket among the upper shepherds of our flocks? Even in old days such structures were raised only partly to the glory of God and partly to the glory of a dominant hierarchy. To-day we have no such hierarchy, and we have learned to glorify God in other ways. So, even when we pretend to build a cathedral, it is not such in the ancient sense. The Catholic cathedral on Fifth Avenue, for example, is only a parish church of not excessive size; and the Protestant cathedral at Garden City on Long Island is of very moderate dimensions indeed. It is a pity, by the way, that it is not more accessible to the public, so striking a lesson is it in the art of how not to build. Its plan is that of a true cathedral, but reduced to a size which robs it of all convenience and of all effect. Its exterior features are so large as to be out of keeping with the proportions of the composition. And the same may be said of the decorative detail, which, moreover, is not only out of scale, but applied with so indiscreet a hand that the general effect is hopelessly confused and overdone. Nor does the elaborate richness of the interior atone for the want of artistic feeling and of good taste it shows.

---

*I hardly know to whom the credit for this church should be given. I believe it is the result of the good sense of the Paulist Fathers themselves, aided with regard to certain points, such as the shape of the openings and of the ceiling, by the advice of one of our younger architects.

Fig. 14.   St. Sylvia's Church, Mt. Desert, Maine. [William Ralph Emerson, 1880.]

But it was not long ago determined to build at Albany another Protestant cathedral, and to make it more consonant with its name. It is to be erected by Mr. Gibson in a florid, pointed style, and, of course, after an ancient type. It promises to be larger and more sumptuous than one might deem appropriate to its time and place and actual practical purpose. But had Mr. Richardson's design for it been carried out, we should have had a cathedral indeed. So beautiful is this design that one is tempted to believe it must have been chosen if the millions it demanded had been forthcoming—if, that is to say, our people had really desired a real cathedral. It was a learned, grammatical study in a sterner type of that southern Romanesque which Trinity in Boston exhibits. No effort after novelty could be traced in any part, and yet it was not imitated from any one original. It was a splendidly logical *résumé* of ancient precedents, hints, and intentions, all amalgamated into perfect harmony. On simply artistic grounds one could not but have rejoiced to see it taking shape. But for the reasons I have already mentioned, and

Fig. 15.   Episcopal Church, Rockland, Maine. [William Ralph Emerson, 1880.]

also because we are sure that Mr. Richardson can do better with his life
than to devote many years of it to what would have been an anchronism
from end to end,—and most of all in the desire which gave it birth,—we
are content that it should remain on paper.

Much good practical sense, and no little artistic skill as well, have of
late been shown in our simplest country churches. Take, for example,
Mr. Emerson's church of St. Sylvia at Mt. Desert. It is thoroughly suited
to its locality,—plain, unassuming, and rustic,—yet has sufficient dignity to be in keeping with its purpose. We do not ask what "style" such
a work belongs to, and should care not at all if it exhibited even less
affinity with any we could name. The satisfaction it gives is evidence
enough of its rightness. Only to one point must we take objection. To
shingle the entire outside was a natural and pleasing expedient; but to
shingle the *inside* too—walls and pulpit and all—savors more perhaps
of willful eccentricity than of artistic discretion.

At Andover, Mass., there is a little church built by Messrs. Rotch and
Tilden, which may serve as an example of how easy it is (presupposing
intelligence) to build at once durably, prettily, and cheaply. The walls
are of rough stone, which, at least in New England, need cost little more
than the taking. The east and the transept ends take a circular form, and
avoid all angles, since the careful trimming and shaping of stone is the
chief expense connected with its use. The low superstructure, where are

the small but numerous and sufficient windows, is of wood; and there is, not a little porch for ornament, but a sensible deep shed across the whole width of the front. Is not either of these churches, or Mr. Emerson's other example at Rockland, Maine, a vast improvement on the clap-boarded barn with jig-saw ornamentation we should have had in its place only a few years ago?

I shall be pardoned, I trust, if I conclude this article with a word of personal explanation. It is with regret that I note so few of our recent churches, and am forced to omit definite mention of some which I know very positively would have interested my readers. Among these are Mr. Russell Sturgis's college chapel at New Haven, and Messrs. McKim, Mead and White's church at Stockbridge, Mass. [. . .] and also one built by Mr. Cady after our most novel type at Morristown, New Jersey, which, I hear, is a much more satisfactory example than his Park Avenue church. But it has been my misfortune to be obliged to leave the United States before I had collected all the material I desired, and to finish my work far from the influences which inspired it.

16

City Dwellings (1)

The days are long since past when the temple or cathedral, the royal palace, the feudal castle, or the civic hall overshadowed the homes of men as the oak-tree overshadows the grasses of the field. The progress of modern civilization has meant the growing importance of the average individual, and this can nowhere more clearly be traced than in the history of architecture. It is true that even in our republican land the average does not mean the noblest, either among men or buildings. But it means that which is *collectively* most prominent. The general effect of a modern town depends less upon its monumental structures than upon the aggregate of its dwellings, humble in comparison though these individually may be. So there is no architectural branch in which success is more desirable than in the domestic branch. And there is none, perhaps, where it is so difficult of attainment. For here success can mean only a very *general* success—must mean that a hundred artists are working together without discord, and a thousand patrons are harmoniously minded.

It may seem at first sight an earnest of success that this branch should be more universally interesting than any other; that while the majority of men feel no responsibility for monumental undertakings, and care so little for art as to be indifferent even in face of their results, every man has a

The Century Magazine (31) 9 (February 1886): 548–558.

home or hopes to have one; and that—if not for the love of art, then for some other equally potent though less admirable reason—he will wish his home to present a beautiful appearance. But, we must remember, almost all men think that here at least they are entitled to suggest how beauty should be wrought; and amateur ideas are apt to be all the more obstinate when very vague, all the more decided when very ignorant. And this will lead us to suspect that popular interest may, in fact, have tended to retard, not hasten, progress. And it will convince us, too, that in this branch especially we must be careful not to identify the architect too closely with his architecture, lest we should impute to him alone transgressions for which his patron has been in great part responsible.

It is not necessary for me to speak of the older domestic building of New York—Mr. White has described it so sympathetically in these same pages. I will but pick up the story's thread where he let it drop,—in the neighborhood of Washington Square, and of the year 1840,—premising that I cannot hope in the strict sense to complete the tale of so delightful an historian.

More than fifty years ago the old Dutch influence had ceased to reign alone. English examples had been widely followed, though never so as to subordinate those of New York's true mother-country. For example, prototypes of the "Colonnade" on Lafayette Place are to be found in London squares and "crescents," and English inspiration shows in those houses on the lower part of Fifth Avenue which by courtesy we call Gothic. But the most conspicuous importation from Britain was the house New Yorkers call the "English basement"—the house which has its entrance at the level of the street and its drawing-rooms upstairs, as distinguished from the Dutch type with its "high stoop" giving immediate access to the chief apartments. We have since built basement-houses in not inconsiderable numbers, but they have never been really popular in New York, and the demand for them seems to be waning now. Nor are they nearly as frequent in our newer Western towns as is the high-stoop pattern.

In the neighborhood of Fourteenth street we come upon work of a later day, of that which as yet must be called our most characteristic epoch—work which was soon to give our city an individual aspect that it has not wholly lost even in its newest portions. The "brown-stone front" was as barren of true architectural ideas as the older brick box, but it sought stateliness by the aid of pedimented windows, of columned porticoes, and of heavy overhanging cornices of—zinc. It is "a poor thing, but mine own," a style— or, much more properly, a

pattern—that we did not borrow ready-made, but formed by retaining
the Dutch high-stoop, joining it to a provincial translation of Italian Renaissance ornament, and executing the result in a local material. The
type has spread far and wide—is visible even at the Golden Gate. But
we are responsible for its every appearance, and he is no true-souled
New Yorker who does not feel a homesick thrill whenever in his Western travels he meets its ugly, stupid, but familiar face. Even if the pattern
had been better, we could hardly have made a beautiful street with the
material we chose. We once admired our brown-stone very heartily; it
became, indeed, an almost proverbial synonym for all that is desirable
and elegant. But it is nevertheless one of the most unfortunate sub-
stances that ever went by the honorable name of stone—cold and unat-
tractive in color, and too poor in substance to receive carving well, or to
stand well though not carved at all. It does not take time and get de-
cently weather-worn; it simply cracks and splits and scales to pieces.

Mr. Griffith Thomas was the most conspicuous among those who established this "New York vernacular." The brown-stone fronts he built
are innumerable, and one scarcely differs from the other. But in spite of
their pretentious nullity they have often the merit of a comfortable spaciousness;—not until the real-estate speculator began to raven in our
midst, not until his ally, the cheap-building contractor, began to follow
Mr. Thomas's lead, did we see the worst to which the type could be reduced. It is impossible to exaggerate the faults of our speculative building, or the degree to which they have contaminated building that is not,
or that ought not to be, speculative in character;—the poverty of its materials, the flimsiness of its construction, the passive stupidity of its
planning, the hideous vulgarity of its details; its neglect of architectural
essentials and distortion of architectural desirabilities. There is only one
civilized habitation worse than these narrow New York dwellings, and
that is the house we often find in fashionable London districts which
has but one room on a floor, and out of that room a great corner cut to
make place for the stairway. And there is, I may add, at least one material worse than our poorest brick or stone—the wretched kind of stucco
that has been so generally used in London.

The old domestic architecture of Boston and its neighborhood naturally followed English models. Very attractive are its relics—even more
worthy, I think, of such a commentator as Mr. White than the old
homes of New York. A good local feature was the bowed front, which
gave a pleasant room within and supplied variety to the unornamented
façade. A good example of such a Boston exterior is to be seen in [. . .]

the Appleton house on Beacon street; a still better one in [. . .] the Somerset Club near by. This is finer, not only because a beautiful light-colored granite has been used, but because the proportions are more agreeable, and dignity is increased by its elevation above the street level. There is no better house than this in Boston, and it is peculiarly instructive as showing how beauty may result from almost unornamented construction. It is not an old house, either, but an exceptional example, dating from only some thirty years ago. It was built for a private residence, and, I believe, by a Frenchman, who must have been liberally minded, since he was inspired to work with variations after the good old local type rather than to import the manner of his own land.

In our dark ages Boston never did quite such dreadful things as New York. Or, at least, it never did so many of them—doubtless because it was not the scene of so much speculative work. Yet the Bostonians were pretty stupid too at times, as when they degraded their bowed front into a cramped angular bay, and repeated it along rows of narrow houses, thus producing an effect as of corrugated iron on a large scale.

English parentage is, of course, apparent in Philadelphia too. The basement house is again the rule, though when small it is differently disposed inside. The New York high-stoop has been generally preferred in Washington, where, except in the suburbs, we find no houses that can be called old even in the limited American sense. Nothing could be more comfortable-looking than a few of the larger homes near Lafayette Square, nothing more ugly or mean than many streets where the ubiquity of the boarding-house seems only too well expressed.

Let us now look at some of our most recent dwellings, giving the first word to New York.

When our conventional pattern was broken in upon some fifteen years ago,—when we first began to look about for more varied materials, to try sometimes for at least partial isolation, and to remember that there were other available fashions besides the "vernacular,"—what was the immediate result? It was an increase of display, but not always an improvement in art. Indeed, we felt very often that art must have been left entirely out of the calculation. We felt inclined to apply a quotation from the genial old chronicle of "Tom Jones," which speaks of the buildings "with which some unknown hand hath adorned the rich clothing town, *where heaps of brick are piled up to show that heaps of money have been piled up before.*" The sin is, we see, no novel one; but it is a sin to blush for all the same. That is, unless its iniquity be purged by *art* in the result. In every land and in every age the love of display—

the delight in spending money and in *proving* its expenditure—has been perhaps the mightiest motive force toward architectural creation. But the fact is masked, condoned, forgotten,—nay, approved,—when it is artistically expressed. Fortunately we too may already count dwellings not a few where evident costliness is amply justified by beauty.

The great marble house on the north-west corner of Fifth Avenue and Thirty-fourth street was one of our earliest attempts at novelty, and in ambition it has certainly not since been surpassed. But it was not really a new departure—it was merely an effort to glorify the "vernacular" by increase of size, by isolation, and by change of material. In the last-named respect the effort was commendable. Under our bright sky and with our sootless atmosphere, white stone is very well in place and might much more often be employed. But not in just this fashion. For here we have no good proportioning and no skillful composition either with masses or with features. Beauty has been sought only in the applied columnar decoration, and this is not architecturally valuable because it has been used without moderation, without care for contrast or relief or structural subordination, and without artistic knowledge in design or artistic grace in execution. We can only call it a very showy house, and add that to some eyes it may seem imposing—may seem to deserve the epithet "palatial," which epithet, I imagine, it was the first New York home to suggest to the reportorial pen.

But a little later we really did begin to build in more unfamiliar ways. "Queen Anne," for instance, became very popular. It has wrought some not unpleasing results, but has often been conspicuously misconceived and misapplied—as, for example, in the Union League Club-house, on the corner of Fifth Avenue and Fortieth street. Picturesqueness seems to have been the chief desire, and picturesqueness was an unworthy aim in a building of this size, in this position, and devoted to this purpose. If it had really been secured, however, we should not grumble greatly. But we find instead a restlessness, a want of unity, an unmotived variety, which strike us as irrational, and which are peculiarly unfortunate with features so large in scale. The great roof is simple and imposing, but the rest of the work cannot be said—either in general effect or in detail—to satisfy the mind or to please the eye. Is it a better building than, for instance, the Union Club at the corner of Twenty-first street, which is a good example of the "vernacular"? Hardly, I think, except as a sign of effort, a sign of commendable discontent with the old *régime*.

Pass now a little father up the avenue, and we shall see the famous twin Vanderbilt houses, where we have brown-stone again, though not of the old poor quality, and used in a very different manner. They are not ostentatious or vulgar or distressingly ugly houses, but neither are they really good or beautiful. In their quieter way they are great architectural sinners too. Stripped of their carving, they would be, as I have heard it expressed, merely "brown-stone packing-boxes." And their carving does not help them save to a superficial eye. We know that decoration is not *architectural* decoration unless it emphasizes construction. I may add that it is not architectural decoration unless it is *itself constructed*. Here neither requirement is fulfilled. The carving— one must not call it by any nobler name—is applied in just those places where it does not belong, and where it hurts, not helps, the structural expression. And it is not itself in any sense constructed. It consists simply of broad bands (of naturalistic foliage for the most part) which have no beginnings or endings, no moldings or framings, nothing to prove that they were designed for the rôle which they attempt, much less for the places that they fill. Their relief, moreover, is so low and uniform that they suffer doubly from want of proper setting, and utterly fail to perform not only the first purpose of ornament, structural emphasis, but the second also, the creation of effects of light and shadow. Abstractly considered, the carving is pretty enough in design and quite charming in execution; but in both respects it is carving such as a cabinet-maker might use in wood, not such as an architect should use in stone. And, I repeat, it is displayed for its own sake only. It is an interesting testimony to the fact that these dwellings were built, in truth, not by an architect, but by a clever decorator of interiors.

On the corner above we see another Vanderbilt house, built of light gray limestone, which *is* a house and not a carven chest. I think, too, that it is the most beautiful house in New York. Mr. Hunt has long stood at the head of his profession in America, his preëminence acknowledged not only by ourselves, but by the Frenchmen who elected him one of the seven foreign members of their Academy. So long had we known his learning, his taste, and his ability, that it was an oft-mentioned subject of regret that he should have found no favorable opportunity to show what his idea of a city home would be. So we are all the more thankful that it should have come to him at last. We may pick little faults in his building if we will. We may say—and the more we admire it the more apt we are to say, I think— that it would be better as a country than as a city house. We may think, too, that it has an overabundance of features; yet unity of effect has not been sacrificed to them—unless, perhaps, in the treatment of the roof. We may feel, again, that since it *is* a city house its ornamentation is rather too

Fig. 16.   Mr. W. K. Vanderbilt's House, Fifty-Second Street and Fifth Avenue.
[Richard Morris Hunt, 1879–82.]

profuse and delicate. But it is so skillfully applied and so charmingly executed; is so *architectural* in spite of its delicacy, that we have not the heart
to wish it altered. Indeed, I think we may greatly rejoice in this sumptuous accumulation of beauty; for, while it is necessary that the virtues and
possibilities of simplicity should be preached, it is well to be reminded occasionally that they are not the only virtues or the finest possibilities. It is
well that we should see that the richest elaboration need not be ostentatious, much less vulgar; that lavish art may be as refined as modest art;
that excess means *wrong* work, not always *much* work. I am sure the

most captious critic cannot deny that Mr. Hunt has carried out a very ambitious and elaborate design in a very successful way—in a way that is
marvelously successful considering what the level of our art has been. If
we examine his decoration closely, moreover, we shall see how great an
improvement we have made in manual skill. What would have been the
use had Mr. Hunt designed such work even a dozen years ago? Can we
think with tolerance of how it would then have been translated into
stone?

There are many large houses a little farther up the avenue which have
the advantage of comparative isolation, or at least of a corner site.
Where all are very ambitious, it is much to say that some—not all—are
good; as, for instance, the one that Mr. Harney has built on the south-
west corner of Fifty-seventh street. The old brown-stone front is prominent still in less conspicuous residences, but "Queen Anne" and French
Renaissance fashions crowd it close.

Two houses of brick and stone on the lower corner of Fifth Avenue and
Sixty-third street seem to me to merit mention, as does also Messrs.
McKim, Mead and White's light-brick house near Seventy-fifth street,
which, with its doubly bowed front, recalls the old Boston type. And then,
if we turn into Madison Avenue, we shall see on the corner of Seventy-
second street another and a very different work by the same hands.

It is a huge house extending a hundred feet on either street and holding three homes, which are disposed neither in flats nor in vertical sections, but which (being intended for members of the same family) share
the various floors between them in a more irregular way. Below, the
structure is of rock-faced blue-stone, and is pierced with a broad, low
archway leading to an interior court; above, we find the beautiful and
novel brick-work to which I have already referred in an earlier chapter,
harmonizing well with the ruggedly treated basement; and the great
steep roof is of very dark-toned tiles. There is scarcely anything that can
be called detail, the windows being simply framed in molded brick, and
the stone being quite innocent of the chisel. I need not enumerate the
various features upon which the effect wholly depends, for they are at
least suggested in the illustration. I will only call attention to the design
of the upper portion of the main front, where one side balances the
other sufficiently well to secure harmony and avoid restlessness, but
where, nevertheless, there is enough variation to obviate monotony and
produce an allowable, desirable, moderate degree of picturesqueness;
and add that if we examine the different features with the key afforded
by interior necessity, we find them dictated by common sense, and not

Fig. 17.   Mr. Tiffany's House, Madison Avenue and Seventy-Second Street.
[McKim, Mead and White, 1882–85.]

by fantasy. For example, the whole upper floor immediately beneath the
roof is an enormous studio; and this explains not only the prominence
of the roof itself, but also the great dormer with its many lights, which
might seem "willful" did they illuminate an attic merely. In color I think
the building very successful—alike in the blue and brown tones of its
stone, in the yellow and brown gradations of its brick-work, in the rich
duskiness of its tiling, and in the harmonious way these all work in together. Nor must we fail to mark how very quiet the color is, for it is
well to know that architectural color worthy of the name may be attained without vivid tints or pronounced oppositions.

To me this is a very beautiful house as well as a very good one. But I know there are many eyes which, while acknowledging its excellence as a piece of construction and an architectural design (as to this there can hardly be serious question), find it too uncompromisingly massive, too grave and somber, too forbidding, almost, to fit in with the idea of what is beautiful in domestic building. I can but reiterate that I myself do not feel thus about it, and then explain why, whether it be very beautiful or not, it seems to me the most interesting and most promising house we have yet constructed—more interesting even and much more promising than Mr. Hunt's indisputably beautiful French château. This is because when we come into its presence we do not for a moment think of asking what "style" it follows, or care a whit whether it follows none or draws inspirations from a dozen. Style it has—that style which means harmony of proportions, accord of features, unity of effect; which means that the artist has had a definite, homogeneous conception to express, and has expressed it clearly, coherently, and in each and every proportion, form, and detail. But it is a style of its own— one which must be judged by intrinsic standards, and not by reference to bygone fashions and antiquarian dogmas. For this reason I believe it must have a good influence upon our art; not as inciting to direct imitation,—that would perhaps be a dangerous essay,—but as showing that it is possible to be "original" without being fantastic or unscholarly (no work is unscholarly which is perfectly coherent and harmonious), and to build admirably without a particle of ornamentation. Nothing could be more instructive than to compare (or, rather, to *contrast*) the two finest houses New York has yet to show—this house and Mr. Hunt's. They prove how wide are the limits that bound architectural excellence even in the one branch of city domestic work; how foolish it is to try and fetter effort with narrow artistic creeds, with rigid dogmas as to style and treatment and amount of decoration. Each is an admirable house in its own way—I am almost afraid to say how admirable in my eyes when judged by the standard of current performance even in its better phases, and even in Europe as well as here. Yet no two houses could well be more unlike in idea, in material, in treatment, or in degree of ornamentation.

Continue down Madison Avenue now, and at the corner of Sixty-seventh street we shall find three houses built by Mr. Hunt—again in a rich and charming French transitional style. Here, too, we see the *artist*, and in work that has much beauty. Yet certain parts of it are, I think, inferior to the rest. The Madison Avenue side contents us thoroughly as a piece of composition, the Sixty-seventh street side less entirely; and the corner, which should have been the strongest, is the weakest portion of the whole.

Farther on, just back of the cathedral, we find Messrs. McKim, Mead and White once more. The whole block is occupied by four houses treated as a single composition. In happy variation on our usual arrangement, the central ones are thrown far back, giving space for a turfed court with a fountain in the middle, while the others form projecting wings on either hand. The southerly wing contains Mr. Villard's house, so justly famed for its interior beauty. The external treatment is throughout very simple, after an Italian Renaissance fashion which wins a local flavor from the use of "brown-stone,"—better, however, than the average, both in quality and in color. The broad plain walls and regularly spaced and delicately ornamented windows are enlivened by the introduction of a *loggia* in the central portion, and are *composed,* moreover, by intelligent proportioning. The effect is very quiet, a little cold, perhaps a little tame; but it is extremely refined, and affords an interesting contrast to the effect of those "vernacular" examples whose inspiration was drawn from similar sources. Perhaps a careless eye will not see at first all the difference between the two; but it is there, both in structure and in decoration,—all the difference that marks off art from no art. As in their great house just described, so here as well, though in a very different language, these artists seem to be protesting against frivolity, tawdriness, unrest, and ostentation.

These have all been exceptional houses as to situation, or, at least, as to size. Individually they are, of course, more interesting than their humbler neighbors. But collectively considered, our average homes are the most important and should be most carefully studied. If *they* cannot be made good, then our city will never really be redeemed from the reproach of its ugly monotony.

The old average house is an unsuccessful thing indeed. In fact, it is not a *thing* at all, for a thing, at least in architecture, means an organism, and this house is merely a mechanical accumulation of spaces and openings, unbeautiful in themselves and uncombined with one another. For too long a time we apathetically excused it as the result of unalterable and unfortunate conditions. What could we do with a façade that was sixty feet or more in height and but twenty-five feet—as often, indeed, but twenty or even less—in width? We might have answered *much* if we had cared to use, not even our imagination, but our memory merely. For the same problem had been at least agreeably treated in almost every foreign town. The "obelisque style" of house, as Balzac calls it, was characteristic of the old Paris that he loved. It was very lofty, often only three windows in width, and commonly built of but humble materials. Yet it was an organic structure and a picturesque. It was not a lifeless screen like ours. And similar houses in countless European streets have such charming fronts that they find illustration in every architectural hand-book.

Nor was another familiar plaint any more reasonable than this. It was very untrue that we could not light our houses better and yet give sufficient solidity of effect. I think the open, late-gothic façades of Venice look strong enough; and I know of many an old German house-front which is almost all windows, yet which looks delightfully secure,—as, for instance, the beautiful Leibnitz house in Hanover, pictured in Lübke's "History of Architecture."

It has often been said, again, that New York building was bad chiefly because it showed no roofs. Surely there has often enough been good street architecture without visible roofs, and surely there is no possible reason why we might not have had as many roofs and gables and dormers and chimneys as heart could wish. They already exist today on most of the large houses I have named. [. . .]

I have heard Mr. Haight's basement house on East Fifty-fifth street described as "Queen Anne." If the reader cares to see how widely things may differ that are called by this one name, he has only to contrast it with a group of four houses—*not* by Mr. Haight—at Fifth Avenue and Sixty-seventh street. These were built at the same time and by the same hands, yet each is as different as possible from its neighbors, and each is as distressingly fantastic as a house well could be.

Messrs. McKim, Mead and White's two houses on Fifth Avenue show varying adaptations of a delicate early Renaissance style that has refinement as its very essence. These three dwellings, together with others not a few, prove that composition *is* possible even with our average proportions. They prove, too, that composition does not mean a multitude of features—an idea that has too often found expression since we began to have ideas at all. There are scores and scores of houses in our up-town streets which have tried to be more "architectural" than the brown-stone front, but which show almost less of definite conception on their designers' part and visibly less of unity in their results—which are mere medleys of as many alien "things" as could be crowded into the given surface. There are but few "things" in our illustrated examples, but these few express structure and are combined with one another. Neither of them, perhaps, can we call quite perfect; yet we should be glad enough if all our houses were as good. And we should hardly complain if none of them were less attractive than a still simpler work of Messrs. McKim, Mead and White's—the Mercantile Library office on Fifth Avenue near Thirty-eighth street.

17

City Dwellings (2)

In my last chapter, after referring to a few of the most conspicuous among the new homes of New York, I had but brief space left in which to say that even our average homes are also beginning to show marked improvement.

In nothing is this improvement more apparent than in the effort that is being made to use good and varied materials, and to treat each of them so as to reveal and to accentuate its best possibilities. We are at last trying to shake ourselves free from the monotonous tyranny of mechanically "pointed" red brick and mechanically smoothed and devitalized brown-stone. We handle our surfaces more vivaciously, and we proportion our units more artistically. It is not wonderful that in the first reaction against lifeless nullity we should have run a little to the opposite extreme of over-ruggedness and over-emphasis, not only, as I have already said, in our monumental work, but also in our domestic. Spirit and vigor exist, for instance, in the basement of the house on Fifth Avenue near Thirty-fifth street; but they have been achieved in a rather too impetuous fashion. The stones are perhaps too large to be "in scale" with the general proportions; and they are certainly too rudely wrought to be in keeping with the quiet refinement secured in other parts, or with the delicate nature of the decoration. Compare this basement with

The Century Magazine (31) 9 (March 1886): 677–687.

that of the Columbia Bank, already once cited as a model, and we see a distinct progress in work that has come at short intervals from the same office.

Our newest houses prove, no less, that we are beginning to do something better with our beloved high stoop than send it up straight and steep and narrow to the door. Some of the entrances on Fifty-seventh street are interesting examples; there is a good one on Madison Avenue not far below the railway station; and there are others in certain recently remodeled façades in the lower portion of Fifth Avenue.

Again, we find cheering promise in our decoration. Look at the ornament of No. 724 Fifth Avenue, and see how artistic it is. If anything, it is too delicate, too quiet, too refined. But these are the best of faults; and they would be even if their opposites had not so long been our crying sins.

Boston too has grown ambitious of late years, and now shows many varieties of conspicuous good and bad. The bad need not detain us, yet even thus we shall have but little space to note the good. The New York high stoop is becoming almost as frequent as the local type, and is often combined, more or less successfully, with the bowed front. Boston architects are fortunate in their beautiful red Longmeadow stone, and diligent in their efforts to make the most of it, both by itself and in combination with brick. Here as well as in New York the first revolt against mechanical smoothness led to the use of units too large in size and too unrefined in finish. There is a certain brutality of effect about many houses in the new "Back Bay" streets that springs from no defect but this. But here too there has been great improvement very lately—as, for example, in some houses on Commonwealth Avenue built by Messrs. Rotch & Tilden, where we see units which are suitable in size, and which in their finish hold the proper middle-ground between insignificance and rudeness.

Messrs. Sturgis & Brigham and Messrs. Peabody & Stearns should be cited for their numerous attractive façades in which successful efforts after a sensible novelty in design reveal themselves. A type, for example, which we already see quite often has a bowed front running up through two or three stories and surmounted then by a deeply recessed *loggia*, agreeable to use and most effective in its powerful shadow.

In other new dwellings we find a return to last century models—colonial or English—which savors almost too strongly of direct imitation. The colonial type is excellent as a point of departure rather than as a pattern to be copied literally. Our ideas, our tastes, our habits of living, *our-*

selves—all have changed very greatly in the hundred years. And something of our wider views of life and art, of our more conscious desire for beauty and brightness, of our gayer, livelier—and more sophisticated— way of living, needs to be expressed in our domestic architecture.

If we wish to see perhaps the very simplest good houses that have been built in Boston, we may look at a group in red brick erected by Mr. Emerson on Huntington Avenue, near Trinity Church and the Art Museum. And then, to take a very wide step and reach the other extreme, we may turn to the two great houses on Beacon street . . . the one to our left being Mr. Richardson's, the other Messrs. McKim, Mead & White's. They differ greatly in style and treatment, but each has considered the other in its own growth, and consequently is helped, not hurt, by the presence of its neighbor. Mr. Richardson's is the more striking of the two, and there is always a fervor about his work that seduces the would-be critic. But it has been called a trifle too "mediæval" in its massiveness and in the element of grotesqueness introduced into its ornamentation. Perhaps it is true that the expression of the other is better suited to a modern home—to the voicing of that modern life whose ideal is elegance rather than physical force. So charming a house is it, indeed, that one longs to give it unstinted praise. And one might if only the porch worked in better with the general design—looked more as though it had taken its place and shape by virtue of an unmistakable impulse of artistic *growth*.

In Washington a very large amount of domestic building has been done during the last ten years. The land is cheap, and the streets are so laid out as to offer an unwonted variety of sites. But one can hardly say that the very best use has yet been made of these advantages. Many houses are generously and agreeably planned, but all their charm must be sought inside. Part of their exterior unattractiveness is often attributed to the fact that Washington is a poor and economical town as compared with its rivals north and west. But such an excuse is quite invalid. Even though brick has been the main material, even though there has not often been much money to spend on decoration—even so, there is no reason why Washington houses should vary almost exclusively between barren nakedness and rather frantic essays in "Queen Anne." Yet we may note a few exceptions, and note that they are increasing in numbers from year to year. Certain very simple brick structures are assuming not unpleasing shapes, as, for instance, Mr. Hornblower's little apartment-house, the "Everett," on H street. And Mr. Richardson has built a great brick house which is impressive because very simple and very strong, but looks a trifle eccentric—perhaps because the latter good quality is somewhat over-emphasized. Mr. Richardson's manner is, in truth, almost too monumental to lend itself gracefully to domestic work. Yet he is always much more than well worthy of attention, and we are interested to see what he will do with two other houses he is building now among the respectable old homes on Lafayette Square.

It would be an endless task did I try to go through our Western towns, noting all the variety of their efforts and all the tokens of progress they reveal. Many influences are striving in the West for mastery. English and German Gothic, French and German Renaissance, "Queen Anne," the Boston "swell front," the New York and also the rural "vernacular,"—all these dwell side by side, if not in harmony, at least in mutual toleration. The speculator and contractor have not set the fashions here; the Western spirit is peculiarly prone to investigation, and Western towns offer a very wide field for experiment, since closely built blocks are hardly more common than spacious avenues lined by detached houses of great size and cost. In the general effect of these latter streets there is often much stateliness; and many individual houses are stately too, even when their details do not bear examination. As might be expected, we seldom find a slavish adherence to precedent, but very often a wildly eccentric "individuality" or an ignorantly audacious eclecticism. Yet I think the present tendency is toward the middle course of scholarly adaptation. I think each year shows more simplicity of conception, more reticence of manner, more artistic feeling in matters of detail. I may note especially that the great roofs which have always been beloved "out West" are getting to assume quieter, more organic, and more reasonable shapes. I have no space to cite examples of success, but I cannot pass without a word Messrs. Cobb & Frost's new Union Club House in Chicago. It is not faultless as a composition, but it is massive, simple, quiet, dignified,—a structure we would gladly take in exchange, I am very sure, for any New York club-house, whether "vernacular" or "Queen Anne" in style.

And now to speak of our domestic interiors. If anything could be stupider than our old average exterior, it was certainly our old average interior. Yet it has been improving of late years with even swifter strides, and has now attained to a completer excellence. Here, again, we long excused our laziness with complaints as to the difficulty of a problem which certainly was not easy, yet was by no means so unmanageable as we said. Surely we ought sooner to have done something more than we did even with a plan twenty-five feet by seventy—something more than to make the narrowest possible dark hall with the narrowest impossible staircase, and to put three equal-sized rooms one behind another. Nor need we so have forgotten all rules of proportion as to believe that a very high ceiling was intrinsically "elegant," and must be secured no matter what our other dimensions. We might more properly have decided that if there is one thing a ceiling ought *not* to have, it is excessive height; better far that it should be too low, especially as with this decision would have come an amelioration of the chicken-ladders we were pleased to call our stairs. Nor would it have been difficult to improve these stairs still further, even though the rest of the plan had remained unaltered. Look at [the] hall at No. 16 East Forty-first street, and we shall see how an ordinary house has been altered by Messrs. McKim, Mead & White. The stairs have simply been torn down, started again from the back, and turned on a landing half-way up. And the result is— an entrance space of decent width; a pretty effect of carved screen and balustrade and archway instead of the ugly old perspective; complete privacy for those who in using the stairs are no longer obliged to pass the entrance and the drawing-room door; and, consequent upon this last, a possible omission of that servants' stairway which was so often a most harassing necessity.

Our plans will show how very much more than this has been accomplished in building new from the beginning. No. 724 Fifth Avenue is only a twenty-five foot house, but it looks a great deal larger when one is in it, and offers infinitely more of comfort and of beauty than we might think possible. The entrance-hall is a mere passage the width of the doorway. The front room, which thus gains greatly in breadth, is reached by a door at the end of this passage, where we step from it into the true hall, which fills the center of the house and has a great fireplace on one side and on the other a broad stairway with comfortable landings. But I will not describe what a drawing of the plan alone could tell with clearness, noting only the novel treatment of the back stairway, which is entirely built in and concealed from all save those who use it. The whole interior is transformed, and the wonder is that it took us so very long to see how such a transformation might be wrought.

A house by the same architects at No. 10 East Fifty-fifth street shows a similar arrangement of central hall and staircase. But as the lot is wider, the entrance-passage is broader, is no longer merely decorated but furnished too, and gives immediate access to the drawing-room. Such halls are sufficiently lighted by day through a skylight over the well, and at night are the most charming rooms of all. Many other houses of average size have been built upon the same general idea both by these architects (Messrs. McKim, Mead & White) and by others, and for a good result even twenty-five feet of width are not essential. For none of all their many innovations are we more grateful than for the honor they pay the staircase. It may be, it always should be, and now it *is,* the very backbone of the house, not only as to use but as to beauty too. Yet for years we suppressed and compressed it into a shabby hideous instrument of torture.

In a physician's home domestic life and professional life should be separately accommodated, and the apartments devoted to the one should be isolated from those devoted to the other. Is it possible to do this within ordinary city limits? Or, if possible, will not space be too largely sacrificed? We might answer doubtfully did not Messrs. Rotch & Tilden show us, in a house on Commonwealth Avenue in Boston, a quite ideal resolution of the problem.

It is a twenty-five-foot English-basement house, with an entrance-passage in the middle that admits to a waiting-room on the one hand and to a consulting-room on the other. At the end of the passage is the true house-door beyond which no patient comes. This opens into a central hall with its fire-place and broad stairway well lighted from above. Beyond is the dining-room, the drawing-room being as usual upstairs. The back stairway is in an inclosed space reserved at one side of the hall—a doubly advantageous arrangement here, since by its means the physician can pass from his consulting-room to a library above, and above this once more to a bed-chamber. When he desires—at night, for instance, or with infected clothing—he is thus able to live and move and have his professional being not merely without disturbing his family but without passing through those parts of the house that are used by them. When we realize all this, and that there is not a corner lacking ample light, can we say that *nothing* is to be made even of an average house in the middle of a block?

The planning of a larger house may seem a less vital and a less diffi-cult matter. It is certainly true that unintelligence will not here produce results intrinsically so bad. But its results will be just as bad when com-pared with the possibilities which offered—will sacrifice just as large a relative proportion of possible comfort, light, and beauty. More inge-nuity and variety were sadly lacking in the arrangement of even our largest houses, but are conspicuously displayed in most of them to-day. We shall see this more clearly when our country homes are considered.

There is another important subject upon which too I need not dwell just now—the subject of interior decoration. Certain articles are ere long to follow these in which such decoration will be treated specially and fully, and in which, I may add, a particularly complete description will be given of Mr. Villard's house on Madison Avenue—undoubtedly the finest interior we have to show, and one that would do us infinite credit if shown beside the best of any land. There are, nevertheless, certain remarks which must here be made. It is in itself a fortunate sign that I can say they *must;* for it is a sign that our interior decoration is a part of our *architecture* strictly so considered. A necessary state of things, it may be thought, and one which in itself is not much to boast of. Yet it was not so necessary but that we entirely escaped from it during very many years. The architect was utterly banished from our interiors during all the time that divided our old houses from those of the very recent renaissance we are now reviewing. When he had built his walls he seems to have been quite satisfied. And we were quite satisfied when we had called in the carpenter to insert flimsy pine doors and meager machine-made moldings, the marble-cutter to set a clumsy stolid white mantel, and the plasterer to affix a ghastly cornice and to sweep a flourish of absurdity in the middle of the ceiling. We did not even remember the word decoration. We built our houses and we furnished them—that was all; and inside, *building* never meant anything accessory to the mere rude fabric. Even when we began to long a little after beauty, even when we first made our furniture more attractive, the same ignorance prevailed. We did not try to beautify our *house,* we only tried to fill it with beautiful things; and our subsequent attempts at real decoration were for a while superficial only—were demanded of the painter and the paper-hanger, not of the architect. It is only within years so few that we can almost count them on the fingers of one hand that we have tried to *build* interior beauty, to make it part and parcel of the house itself. But in our best work to-day it is the architect who has imagined the general effect and has planned for it in every detail—in the richly screened or balustraded staircase, in the wood-work everywhere, in the mantels which are a portion of the wall and not a mere excrescence, in the colors and patterns and materials for wall and ceiling, often in the shapes and colors and materials of the furniture itself. The good impulse has already descended, indeed, even to our speculative building—though, of course, it is not apt to reveal itself here in the most delightful manner. We have space for but one or two illustrations, and

Fig. 18.   Dresser in Mr. Horace White's House, 51 East Fifty-Fifth Street.
[McKim, Mead and White, 1880–83.]

for no commentary whatsoever. I will only explain that the "extension room" of the house No. 50 West Thirty-seventh street is shown, not because of any great excellence, still less because it is at all characteristic of the work that Messrs. McKim, Mead & White enchant us with today, but simply because of its interest as one of our very first tentative essays in the right direction. The hall of No. 10 East Fifty-fifth street is a better example of their work. The Boston hall is theirs also—rather inadequately pictured, I am sorry to say; and the mantel is from Mr. Richardson's house in Washington. Let me only add, lest I should be grievously misunderstood, that I do not in the least undervalue the work that has been done by our decorators who are *not* architects. Certainly it is only by the aid of such that the architect is likely to succeed in his higher decorative efforts. No architect—in these days when artists are not Michael Angelos for versatility—can himself supply what a painter like Mr. La Farge will give him, or a sculptor like Mr. St. Gaudens. But, on the other hand, neither Mr. La Farge with his beautiful color in paint and glass, nor Mr. St. Gaudens with his beautiful form in bronze and stone, can do his best if the architect has not prepared the way for him. Such art as theirs, moreover, is a luxury for the very few, while architectural decoration is within the reach of every man who builds himself a home. For to be sufficient it need not imply the introduction of any unavoidable feature or any unnecessary detail. It need only mean that each obligatory detail and feature, no matter how small or simple, has been included by the architect in his conception of the structure.

Many sins of omission rise before me as I try to bring these long pages to a close. For example, I have not even mentioned our hotels and our huge apartment-houses. Perhaps, however, the less said of them the better. They vary, writes an epigrammatic critic, "between the Scylla of monotony and the Charybdis of miscellany." Scylla is, without doubt, the better haven. The Astor House and the Fifth Avenue Hotel seem at least more peaceful than those enormous up-town structures that are enwrapped in miscellanies at once riotous and puerile and vulgar. I know that the problem offered by huge buildings of the kind—with their twelve stories sometimes, and their innumerable small rooms within—is supremely discouraging. I know, too, that a large expenditure of pains and skill has often produced very good results in the interior. Nor do I presume to say that there may not be good exteriors among the multitude that have been built in these latter years. I would only testify that, so far as I have seen in New York and elsewhere, there is but *one* which merits praise. This is Mr. Hardenberg's "Dakota," on the west side of Central Park.

And now I will give a final word to a very simple, plebeian little house lately built in New York on Greene street, just before it ends at Clinton Place. For I want to enforce once more the virtue—nay, the charm—that lies in mere solidity. Why is it that even when our walls are really quite thick and strong enough, they so often look like flimsy screens? It is partly because they are not well composed, but largely, also, because their strength is not shown outside, because we put the sash-frames close up to their outer surface, leaving no visible depth of wall and preventing all play of light and shadow. The deep "reveals"— excellent technical name, since they show so much we want to see— of our iron façades may be cited as a virtue to set against their many sins. But it is a virtue often wanting to work that should in every way be better. We find it, though, in this Greene street house, and all the more conspicuously since there is no decoration to assist it. The windows— square and round-headed—are nicely proportioned, the wall-spaces are broad and quiet, and the string-courses are structurally expressive. But the effect would be far less satisfactory were it not for the unusual depth of the reveals and the consequent bold marking of the shadows. If something better could take the place of the present sordid little steps, this would, in its own modest way, be a very satisfactory little house indeed.

18

American Country Dwellings (1)

Passing from one branch of our architecture to another, we realize how many are the dangers which beset its path. Much of our ecclesiastical work, as we have seen, has been fettered by the wish to follow inappropriate precedents; very many of our buildings for commercial use have been pauperized by complete indifference; and for long our city dwellings were stereotyped and stunted in dull reiteration of some unintelligent design. And now, in considering the domestic architecture of our smaller towns and our country places, we shall see still another tendency at work for evil—the tendency toward ignorant, reckless "originality." But the same fundamental sin has underlaid all these various superficial sins, and the reformation which now begins to show in each and every branch is due in each and all to the fact that we are repenting of this fundamental sin—are beginning to feel the necessity for basing all our work on *rational* foundations, for taking as our guide intelligent, cultivated thought, not apathy or impulse, not mere vague artistic aspirations nor a merely formal adherence to the examples of some other age.

It is not strange that in building our country homes we should have shown ourselves more original, more "American" than elsewhere. Here most of all have we been forced to meet— or at least to deal with—new and diverse requirements. Our climate and the habits of life it engen-

---

The Century Magazine (31) 10 (May 1886): 3–20.

Fig. 19.   Lodge of Charles J. Osborne, Esq., Mamaroneck, New York.
[McKim, Mead and White, 1883–85.]

ders, our social conditions and the variety of needs they create, our sites
and surroundings, as well as our main material, wood—all have been
most unlike those of other nations. In no other architectural branch
have we been thrown so largely upon our own resources; therefore in
none was the development of some kind of originality so probable. And
thus that native character which gives more general signs of its existence

than are commonly perceived—which somewhat tinges all our work, however featureless or however imitative—nowhere else reveals itself so clearly as in our country homes. Nowhere has its accent been so pronounced, and nowhere has its voice been broken by so few wholly alien notes. An inquiry into its various manifestations must begin with our very earliest products.

Every one knows what were the first of all our country dwellings—those old farm-houses, built by Dutch or English settlers, which still survive in many a quiet spot. Nothing could be more simple, more utilitarian, more without thought of architectural effectiveness. And yet such a farm-house is often extremely good in its own humble way—good in its general proportions, and especially in the agreeable and sometimes picturesque, yet simple and sensible, outlines of its roof.

More decided in character, of course, are those colonial dwellings which soon were built for a higher than the farming class. Whether of Dutch or of English origin, a family likeness marks them all, for the English model itself had been influenced by Dutch ideas. Everywhere the details are "classic," but in their choice and application many variations showed themselves as the years went on. Sometimes a very plain pattern has been followed, sometimes columns and pilasters give a more ambitious air. The openings are now rectangular and now round-arched, with fan-lights in their heads. The porches, and especially the doorways, are often charmingly designed and delicately carved. But here again, as with the farm-house, the roof is apt to be the best and most attractive feature. Truly good and very charming is the "gambrel roof" with its quaint and useful dormers, and the hipped roof, which does not run to a peak but is stopped at a broad balustraded central platform—as, for example, in the oft-illustrated Longfellow house at Cambridge.

Hundreds of these colonial dwellings still stand all through New England and New York State and all along the Atlantic seaboard; and even when they are built of wood their charm is incontestable. Of course we know that many of their features are not intrinsically appropriate to this material. Yet how much of the original excellence survives the unlawful translation from one material into another—how much solidity and simplicity of effect, how much of the truly architectural merit of good outlines and beautiful proportions, how much of that expression of mingled dignity and refinement, which is surely a pleasant expression for any dwelling to put on. In his sparse but intelligently applied detail, moreover, the colonial architect showed a truly artistic perception of the way in which the ornamentation appropriate to stone should be altered when it came to be wrought in wood. And inside his structures he built such spacious, well-proportioned rooms, such comfortable or such stately stairways, and, once more, such simple yet pure and artistic decoration, that we cannot but respect his memory, cannot but rejoice in the legacy he has left us.

Greek temples copied in wood and put to domestic uses (an innovation which Thomas Jefferson did very much to foster) were of course much less defensible—were wholly indefensible, in fact, since they showed not merely a translation from one material into another, but a radical and foolish transformation of the structure's very purpose. Yet even for these houses one is tempted to say a good word or two—such a word as I have already tried to say for our public buildings and churches of like fashion. At least they are not vulgar, wild, and frivolous in effect, as have been our products so often since their day.

But there came a time when the traditions of classicizing art died out, when our early forms and ideals were abandoned even by the most conservative, the most provincial. Imitative experiments of various kinds were tried at this time, as they have been tried at all subsequent times; but in general we renounced all outside help, all attempts at "style" of any sort, and fell back upon such native intelligence as we possessed. The resultant product was a mere plain, bald, clapboarded box, surrounded with a wide piazza and arranged inside in the simplest and most obvious fashion, and, inside and out, wholly lacking decoration. The presence of the piazza, however, and of the "Venetian blinds," and the total absence of anything else that possibly could be called a feature, of themselves sufficed to make these houses distinctively American, thoroughly original in effect.*

Beautiful they certainly were not; and yet when they were built the New England village put on the aspect which made its name proverbial

---

*The illegitimate employment of the word *piazza* instead of *veranda* hardly deserves to be called, as it so often is called, an Americanism. According to an English glossary, *piazza* is "very frequently and very ignorantly used to denote a walk under an arcade." But not only the ignorant have thus used it even in England; for I know of treatises on architecture, written nearly a century ago, wherein the cloisters of a convent are called *piazzas*. Be its illegitimacy as it may, however, the term has in its present American sense all the warrant any term need have—that of long, consistent, and exclusive use. The common term in the South is "veranda," which is absolutely correct; and in the West, "porch," which, again, is incorrect. But in the Northern and Eastern States one invariably *says* "piazza," and therefore I should feel it to be sheer pedantry did I oblige myself to *write* a different word.

for a neat, cheerful, pretty domesticity. This aspect, in truth, was not primarily architectural, but resulted chiefly from the lack of all poverty, squalor, and unthrift, and from the wide spacing of the houses, which turned the village into a succession of green lawns, gay garden-plots, and broad grassy streets, over which the thick-set elms and maples arched their vaults of verdure. And yet the houses themselves did contribute something to the pleasant picture. Their universal white paint, unbroken save by green blinds and gray shingled roofs, increased the air of cheerfulness and purity, and was not discordant with the omnipresent foliage and with the bright blue of our sky. Then, although they had no architecture properly to be so called, though they were bald and bare and unsubstantial-looking when winter stripped off nature's beauty, and were marred by the close, rigid lines of their clapboard covering, they gave a negative sort of satisfaction by their utter modesty and frank simplicity. They looked like the work of a people who could not do anything in the way of art, but who had at least the good sense to recognize the fact and to make no abortive efforts. And finally, the one real feature they did possess—the long and wide piazza—was a most excellent invention, though an invention in a quite rudimentary stage as regarded artistic treatment.

But it was not very long ere we began to be dissatisfied with such negative qualities as these—to ask for something more positive, which, we hoped of course, would be something beautiful to the eye and satisfactory to the mind. And then our "rural vernacular" entered upon its would-be artistic stage.

There have been critics of late years (not only in this country but in England also) to lay all the shortcomings of modern architecture upon the very existence of the "professional architect." They find the root of all evil in his undisputed supremacy, as having disinherited the "naïf artisan"; in his antiquarian study, as having led to a soulless eclecticism or a dogged attachment to some bygone style; in his self-conscious cultivation, as having killed all native impulse. In the great architectural ages, they say, architecture was a popular art, of which there were no theorizing, dogmatizing, controlling professors, but to which few men were wholly strange. It was merely a part and parcel of the world's general work, practiced spontaneously and developed unconsciously with the general development of the people. And, as the future must always repeat the past—again an assumption which I quote—never, unless the same state of things can be brought about with us, need we hope to see a living, characteristic, national, and therefore worthy architectural movement.

In view of such theories, it may be instructive to call attention to the fact that our country is the only one which in this age has known a development such as they approve. Our "rural vernacular" developed in ignorance, not in knowledge; instinctively, not self-consciously; and it was wrought by the hand of artisans, and not of an educated architectural profession.

It took nothing from the earlier colonial work; it was based wholly on the wooden box, and sprang from a truly popular desire to give this a beauty it too plainly lacked. There is plenty of literature relating to its development, but literature only of a certain kind, in the shape of curiously illiterate hand-books for the use of client and mechanic, filled with ready-made designs which are prolifically varied, and yet are alike from first to last in their general spirit and effect. The great number of such books—"Every Man his Own Architect" may be given as their generic title—goes far to prove the unprofessional, spontaneously popular nature of the movement; and the entire absence of all other contemporary literature, theoretic or critical, is sufficient to complete the evidence. These copy-books, assisted by the witness of our memory, show how we went to work to give our box "more architecture." Intelligent thought was not the wind that filled our sails, nor was trained skill at the helm. A vague, ignorant wish for something agreeable to the eye, a bold ignorant use of superficial, rapid, showy means toward getting it—these were the moving, guiding powers. Client and mechanic worked harmoniously together, undisturbed by the professional architect with his inherited styles and methods and ideals, and his conscious, definite aims. The "simple artisan," whose advent we are told is so desirable, actually had for a time full sway. Nor ought our theorists to cavil at the fact that he was not the master mason but the "boss carpenter"; for should the artisan have been any other than a carpenter when wood was the material we chiefly used?

This carpenter, then, worked as spontaneously, as untheoretically, as entirely after his own native lights, as carelessly of school traditions, rules, and precedents, as is possible to a modern man. He did not invent all his features, but no man has done this since the very dawning of the art. He invented some, however, and he borrowed just as his untutored taste saw fit, and adapted just as his untutored hand found most convenient. He twisted his square box into odd card-house shapes in a determined desire for "picturesqueness"; or he left it square and, with a peculiarly bold and naïf movement of appropriation, crowned it with that form of covering which Mansard had applied to the palaces of France.

None too pleasing, it seems to me, even in its proper size and station, this so-called "French roof" was ludicrous indeed when set on top of our flimsy little wooden walls in a greatly diminished but still all-too-massive form. It was supremely ludicrous and supremely ugly, yet no feature we have ever made our own has been more universally beloved.

Then our customary white paint was deemed too simple or too "unæsthetic," and all the tints of the diligent but tasteless modern manufacturer were essayed, either one by one or a dozen at a time. Scarlet and canary-yellow were not too bright, malarial greens were not too depressing for the experimental energy of the moment. One house would almost imitate a circus-tent, and the next would look like an emanation from the Dismal Swamp. Nor do I exaggerate when I say "a dozen tints at a time." I have counted often, and once, for example, I counted nine colors in the body of a house, with several more in the "Scotch-plaid" pattern of its roof.

And then we borrowed features here and there and everywhere to give them queer, abortive shapes in our soft pine wood. Cornices, brackets, balustrades, and pediments of Renaissance lineage; turrets, pinnacles, finials, and gables which had once been Gothic—all were now Americanized together, and were adorned with decoration that was chiefly, I should say, American in its first estate. And all the decoration took flat, shallow, mechanical, outline shapes, fitted for execution with the jig-saw and for application with the glue-pot. With these delightful helpers, with the eccentric paint-brush, and with a clumsy turning-lathe and molding-plane—all their colonial skill and grace forgotten— our builder wrought both his borrowed and his invented motives into structures unlike all else on earth besides, but with such a consistent, persistent family likeness among themselves, and such an identity of feeling and effect running through all their varied items, that they reveal indeed a "national style," all the more national since it was accepted with such national satisfaction. The "rural vernacular" was neither local in its birth nor local in the degree of unanimity with which it was adopted. It seems to have developed everywhere almost at once, and for a generation its authority was everywhere supreme. From the tiniest cottage to the most ambitious residence, from the suburban villa to the huge "summer-resort" hotel, from the village street to the Newport avenue, everything for a time spoke the same dialect, though, of course, with diversities in emphasis and elaboration. I do not say there was no dissent. The plain wooden box still survived; occasionally we had a would-be Gothic cottage or a pseudo-Swiss chalet; and when

brick or stone was used a simple utilitarian respectability was sometimes preserved, though perhaps the more common tendency was to
overlay even these materials with showy decoration wrought in wood.
Nor were instances wholly wanting when a much more positive, a distinctly artistic, excellence revealed itself. One such example we see in
[. . .] Mr. Fearing's house at Newport, which was built before the recent
rise of our "new school" of domestic architecture, yet is still one of the
most attractive among all its varied neighbors. But I am sorry to say
that a Swiss and not a native artist must be credited with its virtues. If
we count up, however, all the dissentient voices of every kind and value,
we still find that they hardly weaken to a perceptible extent the unanimity of the vernacular chorus.

Evidently we failed in this attempt to produce architectural art, but
not because we lacked for aspiration. The very extravagance of our mis-
deeds shows the eagerness of the effort we had been making. Why was
it so fruitless an effort? Must we conclude that its outcome proves us
wholly and hopelessly, then, now, and forever, without artistic aptitude?
Or should we lay the whole blame on mere immaturity? Should we
argue that failure in this early stage counts for little as proof or
prophecy of any kind, having been but a youthful, temporary stumble
on what was none the less the right path to follow? Or ought we to decide, on the other hand, that we failed because the path we followed
was *not* the right one—because the ignorant, naïf, popular way of attempting architecture is intrinsically mistaken, is a way that will kill,
not foster, such gifts as we may possess, that will prevent and not insure
such progress as we may be capable of making? I think, in spite of the
critics I have quoted, that the last explanation is the true one.

Of course there was a period with many nations in the past when
their builders were not learned, cultivated, theorizing—when instinctive, untrained effort did such work as was done and conquered such
steps as were gained. But these were *primitive* periods, when work of no
kind was "professional," when no knowledge was codified, and no effort was theorizing or self-conscious. Art in its earlier stages was then
certainly brought out of ignorance, as were all the other treasures of civilized humanity. But we are not in a time or a condition when such
births are in order. We are not a primitive people, but the heirs of all the
ages; for surely the mere fact that we have crossed an ocean does not
disinherit us. It is as utterly foolish to talk of throwing away our legacy
of art, and of beginning afresh with the intent to develop "something
American," as it would be to hold the same language with regard to sci-

ence, industry, morals, manners, feelings, tastes—with regard to any other of those civilized necessities or sentiments or requirements which are ours as much as Europe's. All history proves this fact, if proof is needed. Every page and line of that long record which certain critics have so misread (for the mere delight, it would seem, of championing a paradox) proves, when rightly read, that no people ever deliberately threw away its artistic inheritance; and proves also and as a natural consequence, be it noted, that never, save in really primitive periods, was architecture pursued in a thoughtless, untrained, "popular" way. There is no presence more clearly and constantly to be recognized all through the varied story, which begins in the gray Egyptian centuries and carries us over so many lands and ages, than the presence of him whom in the strictest sense of the word we must call the "professional architect." Especially often has it been said that in the middle ages there were "no architects"—nothing but a multitude of artisans who were consummately skilled in practical things, but who applied their skill un-reflectingly, instinctively; who labored much as bees labor at their hon-eycomb; who "builded better than they knew"; who built well, in fact, just because they did not know *how* well, did not see distinctly what they were aiming at, but were guided in some occult way by the "spirit of the age." "Inspired masons" is the queer term that has been invented for them, and that is used as a counter-term to the "professional archi-tects" of modern days.

How absurd such ideas seem when one knows what the mediæval styles really were—perhaps the very last styles of all that could possibly have been wrought untheoretically by even the most "inspired" of arti-sans, could possibly have been developed without definite, conscious aim, were a people never so "artistic"; how absurd when one knows that their fundamental power and excellence lie, not in that decorative richness which strikes and holds the popular eye (and which was in truth largely the work of the subordinate artisan), but in their incorpo-ration of the profoundest scientific knowledge, their logical following out of the strictest mathematical formulæ, their realization of the high-est and the subtilest artistic theories. And how foolish must seem the at-tempted elimination of the "professional architect" to those who have even a slight acquaintance with contemporary records. Scanty, muti-lated, casual, confused, and superficial though those records are, there has been compiled from them an astonishingly long and unbroken list of men who were widely famous just for their theoretic knowledge of their art, men who were recognized as professional architects, and were never called aught else. And if in other cases the architect *was* something else as well—was prince or monk, bishop, sculptor, master mason—what does it matter? The educated, deliberating, theorizing mind—this is the thing in question. This always directed in all ages, though, of course, with varying degrees of knowledge and of skill, according as the general intellectual standard of one age varied from the general intellectual standard of another. This should have the credit of mediæval no less than of classic triumphs—this, and not that mere blind, passive, multiple human tool, wielded by the "spirit of the age," which certain critics have imagined as a fetich for their worship. Perhaps it may seem, as we look back where all things are blurred in a dim far perspective, as though the spirit of the age had done it all; and in truth it is a potent spirit, one upon which the architect is greatly dependent for help or hindrance, nay, for his own birth and nature and impulsions; and it is often a naïf, unconscious spirit. But all history shows—and nowhere more plainly than in the very chapter which tells of mediæval architecture—that it can never do great and lasting work save through the hands of specially qualified instruments, can never fully express its impulses save through the mouth of accredited high priests. And these instruments, these priests, can never themselves individually be blind, naïf, and ignorant in their efforts. They must know very well what they want to do, and must have learned very thoroughly all that their age can teach them with regard to the best way of doing it.

Believe me, to manage rightly our inheritance of art, we must have as our executives those who really know and understand it. And we *must* manage it rightly, for we could not get rid of it if we would. It would not only be a folly to throw it away—it would be an actual impossibility. If it does not remain to help, it will remain to hinder; if not for inspiration, then for contamination. For look once more at our own unfortunate essay in independence. I have said that the artisan who developed our "vernacular" wrought as spontaneously, as instinctively, *as is possible to a modern man.* But this is just the point: no civilized modern man, however ignorant, however self-reliant, however far removed from the sources of transmitted knowledge and the springs of transmitted influence, can ever hold himself quite outside the current, can ever be in a state even approaching to primitive ignorance, absolute simplicity, aboriginal independence, unsophisticated freshness of memory and thought and eye. Untutored effort meant with our artisan what it must always mean with modern men—merely a crude and insufficient, instead of a wise and successful method of inventing; and a haphazard, stupid, tasteless, instead of a skillful, law-abiding, artistic method of adaptation. Dim and fragmentary as was our builder's knowledge of precedent and architectural theory, it was still great enough to preclude the possibility of his beginning at a really independent starting-point and working out a new salvation for himself. Nor could we, his clients, have suppressed our complex, imperious, practical necessities, our vague but strong and sophisticated expressional and artistic aspirations, and have waited while a slow, century-long development from some primitive starting-point went on. He knew too much, we knew and desired too much, for this. But for the other method—for the sensible, scientific, and artistic use of the inherited materials which forced themselves upon us—both he and we knew far too little. This is the truth—the truth that mere common sense might teach, and that all history but illustrates: our *contented ignorance* is the scapegoat which should bear the burden of our failures. All history teaches this, I repeat once more; for if we are to judge the present by the past at all, we surely must be careful that the terms of the comparison correspond. And then it is not with the primitive communities of old, but with the most highly complex and sophisticated communities that have ever been, that we shall compare our own. For what is the superficial fact that we are a new nation on a new soil to the fundamental fact that we are an old *people* with all the characteristics this term implies? And the history of our prototypes proclaims, I say, that instead of blaming our architecture for being "too professional," we should blame it for being not by a thousand degrees professional *enough*—should blame it in that its executives, whatever they have called themselves, have too commonly lacked the knowledge, the training, the cultivated taste, and the educated, refined common sense which in every great building age have been the corner-stones of effort and the inspiration of success.*

It is possible that, even though we long follow the best path and strive in the best way, we may never have a really great building age in America; for its advent will depend in great part, of course, upon whether or no we are gifted with artistic aptitude. I wish only to insist that our results need not be taken as decisive upon this last point until we *do* follow

---

*The architecture of the rural Swiss is sometimes cited as an example of an appropriate and artistic product which must have been developed "unprofessionally," and, therefore, as an example for our following. But there is no real analogy between the two cases—nothing more than the very shadowy analogy which lies in the use of the same materials under totally different social and temporal conditions.

the best path and strive in the best way; until we go to work, and long persist in working, as we confess we ought to work in every other department of human effort—building intelligently on a wide knowledge of what has been done before, not thinking a bastard modern primitiveness a desirable foundation; systematizing our efforts, not wasting ourselves in crude experiments; keeping definite aims and ideals in view, not waiting lazily for "the spirit of the age" to speak through empty minds and untrained hands. If hitherto we have seemed to show little enough of artistic aptitude, let us take comfort from the confession that we have been very ignorant, and that we have had a very childish trust in the capabilities of ignorance. For, be it noted, not only in the branch which I have dwelt upon as the most conspicuous example, but in every other branch as well, the name of American architecture has been disgraced by a multitude of works in which no architect ever had a hand. What should have been *his* task was confided too often to those who claimed his name without sufficient warrant, and as often to those who did not even dream of claiming it at all. Have we not seen how the "builder" wrought in our city homes when the speculator was his partner? Are we not well aware that he was often joined in a similar partnership with a very different client from the speculator—with the most lavish and ambitious of owners? Do we not all know in our own home neighborhoods the builder's factories and warehouses, his town halls and his public schools, his railway stations, even his churches? And can we say that their species is not still prolific? Now at last it has come into active competition with another and a better species. But that the "fittest" shall survive in this one special struggle for existence, depends almost entirely on you to whom I speak— on the wide general public of future clients, on the patrons who in this art are so immensely potent a power. Certainly, as compared with even a very recent period, this public has to-day a better appreciation of the importance of trained professional skill in building. But such appreciation is still not distinct or strong enough; and it is by no means *thorough* enough. That is looked upon as a luxury for great occasions which is, in truth, a necessity for all occasions great and small, and which, under the right conditions, is an economy instead of an indulgence. I do not say that we could always have acted up to this belief, even had we held it very firmly. When the local builder bore undisputed sway there certainly was not a trained and skillful architect languishing for want of patronage in every little village. Nor even when, in village or in city, one who believed himself to be such was given the helm, was he always able to steer a triumphant or so much as a safe and sensible

Fig. 20.   Mrs. Mary Hemenway's House, Manchester, Mass. [William Ralph Emerson, 1884.]

course. Nor would I insinuate that builder and architect were always themselves to blame for not better deserving the higher title—except in so far as they were contented with the lower. But I *do* say that their condition and ours was a great misfortune, a hopelessly hampering misfortune; not a necessary stage in progress, nor, still less, a fortunate chance which, had we only been a "more artistic" nation, we should have utilized toward the best possible results. And I do insist that it is the duty of our public as well as of our architects themselves to try to make our art ever more and more "professional."

But enough and more than enough of generalities. It is quite time that I should prove my own arguments by the evidence of our most recent work in the branch with which at the moment we are specially concerned. For such proof can, I think, here be found.

It is certainly not open to question that our best country homes and our average country homes of to-day are infinitely better than the best and the average of twenty or even of ten years ago. But it is just as little open to question that the "professional architect" now plays a much more important part in their construction; or, again, that this architect is becoming year by year more professional himself—that is, more widely differentiated from the mere artisan in quantity of knowledge, in thoroughness and quality of training, in refinement of intelligence, in width of artistic horizon, in processes and theories and ideals.

One name, I think, deserves to be mentioned here with especial honor. It would be difficult to overestimate the good influence Mr. Richard Hunt has had both upon the profession itself and upon its status with the public. When he began to practice such an education and equipment as his were almost anomalous with us, while to-day (of course not by any means solely, but yet, I think, partly through his example) they are getting to be thought essential and getting to *be* not quite exceptional. He was so industrious a worker, moreover, that the sum of his results formed a very large lump of leaven—a remarkably large lump, seeing that they were not all, like the results of too many others, patterned upon one shallow, monotonous scheme. He was so full of ideas that he experimented very widely and diversely. Not all of his experiments, we may grant, were successful. But as they were based on knowledge, not ignorance, all were useful as systematizing future efforts and marking out future paths, and most especially those which dealt with the new necessities of iron. He was so enthusiastic and versatile that every branch of the art appealed to him—even the then despised branch which includes country homes. All this did good, I repeat, not only as influencing other workers, but as raising the generally received opinion with regard to the utility of an architect in architecture. But in this last respect we are most of all indebted, perhaps, to the force of character and witchingness of tongue that enabled Mr. Hunt to lay hold of the stolid, indifferent, obstinate, or timid client, and lead him whither he would have him go. I do not feel that in saying this I overstep the line which divides legitimate impersonal from illegitimate personal commentary; for, let it be in the other arts as it may, in the architect's art personal force and persuasiveness are essentially part and parcel of the required endowment. As I have said so often, this art depends upon direct, special, reiterated acts of patronage to a degree quite peculiar to itself; and as every new commission differs from every other, an artist's past record is not always taken—indeed, cannot always be taken—as a guarantee of future success. Therefore he who has not a modicum of personal persuasive power runs a great risk of being obliged to follow those whom he ought to lead. I do not say how it might be in an ideally artistic community; *there,* perhaps, all excellence would be self-evident to all in anticipation as in fact, and no discussion or persuasion necessary. But as communities stand to-day, that architect will be most serviceable to his clients, as well as to his art and to himself, who (other things being equal, I mean, of course) can persuade them most convincingly *that he knows best*. When Mr. Hunt began to practice this seemed a very strange proposition to the ears of the free and independent American citizen—especially when he was intent upon the structure of his own home. The fact that it now carries with it a sound much less of novelty and offense is largely due just to this one champion.*

Of course Mr. Hunt was not the first to try to improve upon the "vernacular" type of country dwelling—to try to put architectural coherence and something which might truthfully be called design in the place of the fantastic and yet mechanical medley which prevailed. Doubtless he was not even the first to do this with real ability and radically right ideas to back the effort. But so far as I know he *was* the first who perceptibly stemmed the popular current, who started any conspicuous and permanent stream of improvement. His work differs in many ways from that which is most characteristic of to-day. And yet he should be ranked as the forerunner—as what the Germans call the "road-breaker"— of the younger band who are doing such good service now. In the matter of interior treatment—both as regards the nice provision for complicated practical needs, and as regards variety and beauty of architectural effect as well—his innovations were especially remarkable and salutary. When speaking in a former chapter of the gradual growth in beauty our domestic interiors have undergone, I remarked that it showed at first in the shape of mere extrinsic charm— of upholsterer's decoration, so to say—and that we were satisfied for a time with this ere we bethought ourselves that intrinsic architectural charm might be still better worth the having. But Mr. Hunt's houses should be noted as exceptions. His efforts after architectural beauty began long before the decorative movement declared itself. For a long time the homes he built were much better in their main constructive features than in their deco-

---

*How often do we still hear some "house-father" of the elder generation proclaim with child-like pride: "I had no architect; the builder and I did it all"— or, more likely, "*I* and the builder." And how invariably does the fact reveal itself in a very different way from that which he supposes! Perhaps this is as good a time as any to acknowledge the personal debt of gratitude I feel to Mr. Howells for having set before my readers so delicately trenchant a dramatic picture of the difference between the old *régime* and the new in matters architectural. Silas Lapham and his new house and his architect will, I am very sure, advocate my conclusions far more persuasively than all my own theoretic preachments.

ration or their furniture, though at a much later day the rule was the reverse of this.

Coming now to speak of our current work in this department, I find the task extremely difficult. In no other branch do controlling needs, desires, and opportunities vary so widely and perpetually; nowhere else are possibilities of excellence or failure so manifold in themselves or so dependent upon the differing characters of different sites. And this makes it peculiarly hard, of course, to select examples—these being necessarily few in number—so that they shall be in any sense *typical* examples. That is to say, a town hall which is successful in one small town might have been just as successful in a hundred others; the plan and façade which are good for a narrow city lot might be just as good in Chicago or St. Louis as in New York or Boston; but a country home that is admirable at Newport, for example, could hardly be repeated at Mt. Desert or in the Catskills, not even to meet the same owner's needs— often could not be repeated on any other Newport site. It is peculiarly difficult, moreover, to describe even the individual excellence of any country home, for this excellence is not only individual to so exceptional a degree, but in this country is also, in the majority of cases, of a comparatively modest, unaccented kind; lies in the harmony of minor, detailed virtues; is not to be explained by the citation of conspicuous features, or characterized by reference to anything very pronounced in the way of "style." The architectural virtues of a palace or a mansion are emphatic and describable, but the architectural virtues of a cottage are retiring and elusive—are very apt to evaporate entirely from the words in which one tries to write them down. I must therefore make it my chief aim to point out certain factors which, in spite of the endless diversity of our problems, nevertheless enter into almost all of them; and to note certain tendencies which, in spite of the varied character of our efforts, nevertheless may be said to characterize those efforts as a whole. The examples I shall briefly note in illustration must not be accepted as being better than all others, but merely as being most familiar to my eyes. Indeed, their illustrative value depends to no small degree just upon the fact that I can say they are *not* better than all others.

I have already hinted that when the American architect labors in this branch he can get an unusually small amount of help from his foreign brethren. Continental excellence cannot be very useful to him, for the fundamental ideas which prevail in continental lands with regard to what country homes should be are radically different from those which prevail with us. The fundamental ideas which prevail in England, on the other hand, do strongly resemble ours. But our social conditions are so peculiar to ourselves, and our climate also, and our consequent habits of life, that even English teachings must be vastly modified in the application. Of course I do not mean to contradict everything I have written above—to say that we do not need to use all possible learning, to incorporate many transmitted ideas and many borrowed motives, here as elsewhere in our art. I merely mean that here even more than elsewhere we should not, cannot *copy*—should study the results of other lands and ages "only as one studies literature, not as one studies grammar."

This fact has clearly proved itself within the last few years. An effort has been made to copy the domestic style which now rules in England,—that so-called "Queen Anne," which our grandchildren will call "Queen Victoria,"—and it has proved the impossibility of direct imitation as distinctly as the "vernacular" had already proved the futility of thoughtless, ignorant originality. Fortunately we have not been as long in learning the second lesson as we were in learning the first. It is true that we cannot just yet say that it is thoroughly learned—cannot say that our imitative Queen Anne is yet extinct. But it is dying fast, I think, and to-day it does not include those which we deem our most characteristic, much less those which we deem our most successful efforts.

But why is not the Queen Anne cottage, which in its best state at home has charmed the eye of many an American and thoroughly fulfilled his conception of what a country home should be—why is it not able, if transplanted to our own soil, to meet at least a certain class of needs? Try to live in one, and you will see. In the winter season you will have snow where the Englishman has rain, and will find his picturesquely complex roof a snow-trap, not a snow-shed. You will have far greater cold than he, and will need a plan that does not put too many difficulties in the way of warming from a common center. Winter and summer you will have sunshine of a strength he knows only in his dreams, and his house will very likely give you more windows than you want. And in summer you will have heat of a potency he would hate to know even in his dreams, and his house will most certainly *not* give you the thing you want most of all—a piazza. And, again, you will very often wish to make a much more extensive use of wood than he ever makes in these modern days. Of course you may use your wood in place of his brick; you may modify his roofs, change his plan, alter his openings, and add your own piazza. If, however, you do this with the intent to copy the effect of his house as nearly as you can, you will utterly spoil his creation and produce a bastard thing which will neither satisfy your eye nor wholly meet your needs. And this is just what has been done in a very great many cases. If, on the other hand, you make the necessary changes with intelligent thought and artistic feeling as your helpers, instead of with imitative effort as your fetter, the result will not be the Englishman's house at all, but something essentially different, essentially your own. And this too, let us rejoice to note, is done more often and more successfully year by year.

From current English fashions we have certainly learned a great deal besides the mere fact that we cannot copy them; and we should be peculiarly grateful that our interest in them has led us to take an interest in genuine Queen Anne and Georgian work—that is, in the work so many examples of which are to be found upon our own soil. Our colonial homes have of late been the objects of much earnest attention, and the fact is very fortunate.

It would have been unfortunate, however, had not our architects approached them in a more sensible spirit than that which has swayed some of the critics already quoted. For, after saying much in a vague way with regard to what ought *not* to be done in America, these advisers have given at least one bit of decided counsel with regard to what *ought* to be done—have declared that we ought to look back at our colonial examples and to "reproduce" them as faithfully as we can. These examples, they assert, are the only examples at once "American" and good; and they are so very good—so charming, so characteristic, and so appropriate to our wants—that we need not try to improve on them. If, however, we throw aside a very natural sentimentality which clings about the subject, and if we then compare our colonial homes not merely with their later rivals, the clapboarded box and the "vernacular" villa, but with a sensible ideal of what the homes of to-day might be and should be—if we do this, we find that our critics' assertions hardly sustain themselves.

We need not quarrel over the question whether the colonial house is "American" or not. In any strict sense, of course, it does not deserve the name; nothing does save the wigwam of the North and the pueblo of the South. Of course its patterns were all imported, and sometimes their treatment was very strictly imitative—more strictly imitative, I should say, than the treatment of any of our later products whatsoever. But certain frequent features—as, for instance, one or two sensible and charming modes of roofing—may fairly be called original; and when the translation into wood occurred, that was certainly American enough. Then our colonial work has stood longer than any other, and is identified with whatever historic associations we can call our own; and it is all so analogous as to offer an instance of the flourishing on our soil of something that may be called a coherent, comprehensible, all-pervading "style." All these facts, together with its undeniable charm, certainly give it a strong hold upon our affections, and a priority of claim among the proper objects of our study. But the main question is not as to its Americanism, and is not as to its charm; the main question is, does it indeed wholly meet the needs of to-day, practically, expressionally, and artistically?

Practically it does not. Its air is indeed as of a delightfully complete domesticity, but it by no means fulfills to the modern American mind the promise it holds out to the eye. In relation to the habits we have acquired during more than a century of rapidly changing existence, it is not one-half so "livable" as it looks. It provides only for the simplest, most unvaried and homogeneous domestic and social customs, and only for housekeeping of what now seems a very primitive pattern. Whatever the *paterfamilias* might feel about it, neither the *mater* nor her executives could live at their ease to-day or work at their best in an unmodified colonial interior. If they happen to dwell in an old one, there are sentimental compensations which perhaps suffice. But when a new home is in question the case seems wholly different. And the alterations in plan and arrangement which are necessary to meet the change in main requirements, and to provide for a hundred subordinate new requirements, must be of such a character that the old exterior pattern cannot often be retained. For this pattern is certainly not flexible, elastic, given to indefinite extension and the indefinite multiplication of minor constructive features. The effect of quiet dignity which is its greatest charm depends very largely just upon its simple, unbroken outlines, and its broad, unbroken masses.

And in thus deciding with regard to its practical sufficiency, have we not also decided with regard to the expressional and artistic sufficiency of the colonial home? Our more freely social, more lavish, more varied and complex ways of living cannot find full and truthful expression in any colonial pattern, nor our growing love of art full and lawful satisfaction. We still want to be dignified in our architectural voice, still to be refined, still to be quiet; but the dignity, the refinement, and the repose must be of a different character from those which appropriately marked the dwellings of our ancestors. The simpler types among these are extremely puritanical; and I do not think the adjective fits ourselves. And the ornater types, even if they had not also much of the same accent, are the least well fitted for reproduction in our most usual material; for, excusable though the practice was a hundred years ago, it would be inexcusable to-day to build Doric porticoes or to frame Ionic pilasters out of pine boards painted.

In short, we may say of our colonial homes what we may say of the contemporary homes of England: our architects should study them, but cannot copy them. When to a certain degree their features and their general effect have been reproduced, the result seems peculiarly pleasing and most appropriately "American." (At least this is true of the Eastern States. It would not be so true, I think, of the Western—which may be taken as proof in passing of how desirabilities vary in this department of our art.) But many extraneous features and many variations of old features and old modes of working must be introduced if the result is to be sensible and satisfactory. And for some of these the point of departure must be found in the "vernacular." Incapable of self-development into anything good, it yet cannot be cut down root and branch; it must yield us certain buds of excellence for development along with other grafts. Its piazza, for example, absolutely imposes itself upon the conscience of every American architect. To develop it into a beautiful and constructive instead of an ugly, make-shift, superadded feature, and to bring it into perfect harmony with all his other features, many of which will have come from very different sources—this is one of the most vital problems with which he has to deal; and also one of the most difficult, and the one of all others which most emphatically forbids him to imitate any previous product, most emphatically prescribes that if he builds good country houses for the Americans of to-day, they will be essentially unlike all others.

But I have come to the utmost limits of a long chapter, and must postpone all further comment to another. The illustrations herewith given reveal something in the mean while with regard to our current efforts. I would only say once more that the revelation is of necessity imperfect; that no such illustrations can tell the whole truth as to form and proportion, much truth as to detail, or any truth as to color; and, especially, cannot speak distinctly as to that perfect adaptation of a house to its surroundings which is one of the most vital of all virtues. As our conditions run, it is sometimes a virtue very difficult of attainment. Nevertheless it is one which we are earnestly striving to attain, and already with a degree of success that goes far to prove there lie within us some latent sparks of true artistic aptitude.

19

American Country Dwellings (2)

In a former chapter I tried to point out some of the special difficulties and dangers which have always met us in this department of our architecture—to show some of the reasons why here even more than elsewhere it has been impossible to depend on formula and precedent for direct guidance, or to take current foreign practice as lawful text and binding rule. I tried to explain why our rural domestic work was forced to be peculiarly "American," and also why it happened to be peculiarly bad. I ventured to say that the two qualities had not yet been proved of necessity identical; to believe that we failed in our novel task simply because we went about it in the wrong way, because when cast loose from our anchorage we had no compass and no pilot and no well-trained crew, but drifted on the wind of lawless impulse—let thoughtless minds and unskilled hands and crude artistic aspirations sway us.

To-day, as I have also said, our results are very different—not because difficulty has decreased, and not because we ourselves have suddenly grown "more artistic," but because we have grown more intelligent in applying whatever natural faculties we possess to the meeting of all difficulties and the avoiding of all dangers. Our best new country homes are still the most "American" of any of our products; good or bad, I say, they hardly could be otherwise. But their individuality is now

The Century Magazine (32) 10 (June 1886): 206–220.

a thing we can contemplate with satisfaction, and in which we can read
the signs of a greater satisfaction yet to come.

We must not look to them for examples of that almost palatial dignity and richness which we conceive, for instance, when we speak of the
best country homes of England. We are not essentially a country-loving
but a city-loving people; and our country homes are thus allotted, in the
great majority of cases, but a secondary station. Our most frequent,
most characteristic, most typical product is not the country residence in
the old world acceptation of the term, but the mere *summer residence*
built for those whose longer days are passed in a city home. Moreover,
our gregarious tendencies are so strong that most (of course not by any
means all) of our summer homes are more or less closely grouped together in colonies which have no exact parallel abroad. There is nothing abroad which really represents such a place as Newport, for example, or as Mt. Desert or Lenox, or any of those resorts which line the
northern Massachusetts shore. The most "select" of English watering-
places is a mere congeries of lodging-houses, intermixed with villas
whose in-dwellers' thought is but for repose or recuperation. In the
most modest of American watering-places, on the other hand, social
ends have largely been considered.

The fact may seem unimportant, but it is vital enough to decree a
wholly different architectural problem. Though in the majority of cases
the owner's chief home is not his summer "cottage" (the term has survived its literal truth), yet this is none the less a *true* home, wherein he
wishes not only to gain new life but to *live*—wishes to have his most private and personal needs as completely provided for as in town, and
often to have his social needs quite as completely met. And this last
point is not unapt to mean that his "cottage" must be big enough to
house many guests as well as to provide for those transient demands
which occur in cities.

Does not all this indeed imply that for other reasons, as well as for
those which lie in difference of climate, our most frequent and most
characteristic summer homes cannot be patterned on any foreign
scheme? And does it not also imply that the task of building them is extremely difficult? In truth, it is not easy to build on a restricted site, and
amid clearly visible rivals, a house which shall be but a warm-weather
home (and look like one), and yet in size and beauty, in comfort and in
elegance, shall keep pace with the city home itself—nay, in size, at least,
shall often far surpass it. Much that is elaborate, much that is ambitious
and costly, must often be wrought within the house and expressed with-

out; yet neither within nor without, neither in plan nor in form nor in decoration, must its merely summer purpose ever be denied, nor, of course, its non-independent station. It must not have a "citified" look, and neither may it have just such a look as is appropriate to a country home of the same pretensions when it stands in dignified solitude. Nor, once more, may it be too modest, too simple, too rustic of aspect, for thus it would sin against expressional truth and fitness in another way.

And even when these summer colonies are less ambitious, more modest and rural in their character, even when their units are small and simple and inexpensive, the difficulties are hardly less. The personality, so to say, of each house must be preserved; no common pattern can serve for all, as we are not building lodging-houses, but individual homes. And in each a certain amount of dignity, of refinement, even of elegance must be expressed; although the cottage in name is now a cottage in size, still it must not look like a cottager's cottage. It must look like a gentleman's home if it is meant to be one.

The problem, I say, is always difficult, and its difficulty constantly changes character. But it varies sensibly in degree as well according as one colony differs from another in the closeness of its grouping and the natural felicity of its site.

At Lenox, for example, in the beautiful Berkshire country, there are many summer homes which are practically isolated—which have wide lands about them and are screened into privacy by the rise of the hills and the sweep of the forests. Deluded by these facts, some of them have taken upon themselves far too self-asserting, far too independently dignified an air; forgetting that though their relation to their neighbors is more a matter of imaginative than of ocular concern, it should nevertheless not have been ignored, not have remained unexpressed. They are not content to look just what they are—mere units, though outlying ones, in a summer colony of many such; and the discrepancy between look and fact is, I think, distressing to many an eye which perhaps does not clearly feel the cause of its distress.

For an example of a different kind, an example of a large and luxurious home in which the general expression is of just the proper sort,—neither so rural as to be affected and untruthful nor so ambitious as to be pretentious and, again, untruthful,—I may point to the house which Messrs. McKim, Mead & White have built for Mr. Ward. It is set on the side of a hill, so that the front, which looks out on the steep wooded slopes above, has but two stories, while the rear, which looks down over the broad and beautiful valley, has a basement story in addition. The de-

Fig. 21.   Hall and Stairway in House of Samuel Gray Ward, Esq., Lenox, Mass. [McKim and Bigelow, 1877–78.]

sign is not only one of extent as opposed to height, but also one of breadth as opposed to depth or to our former rectangular pattern. The nature of the site almost prescribed this; but an unintelligent designer either would not have ventured to choose such a site or would not have made a virtue of its necessities. (That is to say, an architectural necessity becomes a virtue when, as here, it is hidden from the eye by charm in the result and patent only to the analyzing thought.) The long hall has its length skillfully masked by diversities of trend, and by diversities of level too. Nor is there any monotony in the long succession of rooms which open out of it all on the same side; we merely think how fortunate it is that they all are placed so as to command the lovely valley landscape.

No interior could be better fitted for comfortable, refined, hospitable country living; and the exterior is perfectly in keeping. It tells plainly of the inside, and its quaint rusticity—suggested doubtless by a certain type of English farm-house—is not a thought too rustic. The model has been altered into greater refinement and dignity of expression, and has also been adapted in all its features to our new climatic needs.

All about Boston, and all along the beautiful rocky forest-fringed shore to the northward (near those early towns where so many of our

Fig. 22.   Gen. Loring's House, Beverly, Mass. [William Ralph Emerson, 1881.]

best colonial relics may be seen), lie summer colonies in thick succession;—some of them rich in the revelation of architectural eccentricity, but others yearly growing rich in better wealth. Here Mr. Emerson is at home, and here are many of his most successful essays in the branch of work to which he has almost exclusively devoted himself. One—a house for Mrs. Hemenway, near Manchester—was pictured in a former chapter. And herewith is given a quite insufficient sketch of another, which from the nature of its site could not be more adequately portrayed.

It stands near Pride's Crossing, on one of the narrowest and ruggedest of those high wooded promontories which, alternating with little valleys (also filled with forest to the very beach-edge), make the Beverly shore so uniquely lovely— on such a rocky and broken and limited site, indeed, that many thought it folly to talk of building there at all. It is hard to explain the charm of this house, for it is impossible to explain either the beauty or the difficulty of the site, or the way in which the structure adapts itself to the difficulty and harmonizes with the beauty. It was wisely felt that the natural features which made the spot so seductive in spite of all practical obstacles, should be preserved in their general effect and as far as possible in their details too. Not a rock or a tree or a shrub was injured save when no ingenuity could save it; and this, to Mr. Emerson's skill, meant singularly little alteration. In part the house seems a vital growth from the rocks themselves; in part it rests on the connecting brickwork which alone made the rocks an available foundation. Quaint irregularities of arrangement and diversities of level therefore show within, and the exterior outline is quite unsymmetrical and broken. The result charms by its picturesqueness rather than by architectural virtue of a stricter sort; yet the picturesqueness not only attracts but satisfies us because practical needs compelled it, because the aspect of the site makes it thoroughly appropriate, and because unity and harmony are preserved in its despite; and each of the varied interior features is delightful because each was dictated either by a material necessity or by the laudable desire to make the most of all contrasted points of outlook. Of course much of the picturesqueness had been wrought by Nature, and wrought in one of her most rarely artistic moods. But her gifts were hedged about with hindrances that from a practical point of view seemed all but prohibitory, or seemed to necessitate for their overcoming a great mutilation of her charm. Yet the house has been built and well built, and her charm is but increased by it. The spot could never have seemed so lovely while it lacked this house, which nestles on the one hand in the very heart of the woods and on the other sees the sky and the close-lying ocean over a foreground of rugged rocks and through a crowding tracery of pine-branches—its wide, low windows framing pictures such as we had only known before in some drawing from Japan. Even had the practical conditions been less difficult, it would still be great praise to say that while Mr. Emerson's house is thoroughly good *as* a house,—as a dwelling-place for its own especial owner,—it also seems almost as much a part of nature's first intentions as do the rocks and trees themselves; to say that while it has material fitness it has also such artistic fitness that its site and its surroundings seem to have been designed for its sole sake and service.

In these two cases (which I cite as types of many more) nature gave rich gifts, but the designer had to mold them carefully to his purpose. But even when her aid is still more freely given, even when it is hampered by no patent difficulties, even then there is no smallest cause to underrate the designer's share in any ultimate success. For if a good chance always meant a good result, then Nature only would deserve the name of architect. When eyes are unintelligent and hands unskillful, a good chance merely means a chance for doubly sinful failure.

But, on the other hand, there are many times when even the intelligent, even the skillful and artistic designer is thrown back wholly on his own resources. Sometimes nature works directly against him. For example, in those summer colonies which fringe the northern New Jersey shore the sea has been the sole attraction; and this natural fact has brought with it, as a necessary consequence, an excessive contraction of site, such as is not compelled where the land as well as the water offers beauty to the eye.

And even were there no excessive crowding towards the water's edge, how difficult still would be the designer's task! For how shall he bring his work into harmony with nature's; how make it look as though it were an unforced growth, and not a forced bit of manufacture; how let it bear witness to man's community with all terrestrial things, and not merely to his casual presence on the earth—how, when nature herself is but sea and flat land, with no suggestive, helpful irregularities of surface, with no leafy backgrounds, with no "features" whatsoever that can be worked into an artist's scheme?

If we look at the cottages in and about Long Branch, we are only too glad to remember that their builders' task was difficult; for I doubt whether there is anywhere else on earth a panorama of such ugliness produced at such an outlay of inventive effort. Of course there are better units among the very bad; but their comparative excellence lies almost smothered in the mass of fantastic sin. We grow from astonishment to laughter and from laughter to despair. Is it possible that the thing can ever be well done when it has been tried so many times already, hopefully, eagerly, persistently, inventively, yet always with some degree of failure and most often with ludicrous defeat?

But that it is not an impossible thing to do well, that we cannot lay the whole burden of Long Branch on nature's shoulders, we may convince ourselves by a glance at one of the newer colonies near by—at Elberon, for instance, where the conditions are the same but the effect is very different. The hotel is neither a great bald barrack nor a flimsy gingerbread agglomerate, but a long, low, rural-looking inn,—a little too scattered and restless in design, perhaps, but yet refined, not vulgar, homelike, not barnlike, sensible, not stupid or fantastic. And its interior shows even more plainly than its exterior how great an architectural revolution is in progress—how we have improved both in the nature of our intentions and in the expedients with which we try to work them out. Almost all the private houses at Elberon are at least respectably good, too good to excite the scorn and laughter which move us at Long Branch. And some of them are quite as good as we have any right to ask, seeing that we cannot ask for that complete beauty which comes when Nature and the artist labor hand in hand.

Fig. 23.   Exterior of Mr. Victor H. Newcomb's Cottage. Elberon, N.J.
[McKim, Mead and White, 1880.]

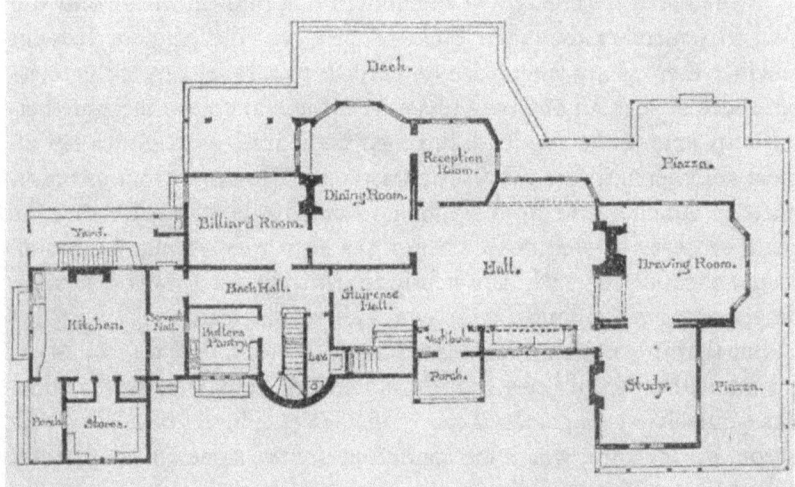

Fig. 24.   Plan of Mr. Newcomb's Cottage. Elberon, N.J. [McKim, Mead and
White, 1880.]

Especially successful are some of those built by Messrs. McKim, Mead
& White—the "Francklyn Cottage" (known by name at least to all the nation since the day when General Garfield died there), Mr. Horace White's
house, and Mr. Victor Newcomb's. The last is perhaps the best of all,
though as it is the largest and most ambitious it was doubtless the most embarrassing to design. A very just medium has been struck, I think, between
that dignity which would have been too dignified for the environment and
that utter simplicity which would have been out of character with the inte-

rior. And the house looks, moreover, as thoroughly as any house can which lies between a broadly magnificent ocean on the one side and a broadly monotonous stretch of flat land on the other, as though it belonged on the site it holds. It looks as though it stood firmly on its feet, as though it were rooted and grounded, as though it had *grown*, while too many of our seaside houses look as though they had not even been built in place, rather, as though they had been dropped down ready-made by accident, and might move off somewhere else with the first breath of a stormy wind.

But to the student of domestic architecture Newport is the most interesting of all our summer colonies. Its history is the longest, and the problems which it sets are the most widely varied among themselves. Colonial houses are abundant, both on outlying estates and farms and in the old closely built portions of the town itself. Its newer portions show a characteristic instance of that way of village-planning which I have already spoken of as peculiarly American—wide streets of detached houses, each with its own small lawn and garden, and all overshadowed by thickset and lofty trees. Here the architecture includes every post-colonial type: the plain, square, piazzaed box; the "vernacular" villa with "French roof" and jig-saw fringing and abnormal hues of paint; the pseudo "Queen Anne" cottage; and that still later product which is again thoroughly American, but in a new and better way.

Then, as we leave the town proper, and seek Bellevue Avenue and the adjacent roads which skirt or lead towards the sea, we find a long succession of more purely summer homes, standing now well screened by trees and well isolated in grounds that are sometimes of considerable extent, but now on treeless sites and in far closer contiguity. And here the architectural types are again of many kinds, while each kind shows more conspicuously and speaks with a more emphatic accent. Certain houses are built of substantial materials, and are very simple in form and finish; are unbeautiful, inartistic, if you will, but quiet, sensible, respectable, and occasionally even dignified in a prosaic sort of way. Certain others show the "vernacular" in its most riotous mood—as, for instance, a large wooden house well out on the west side of Bellevue Avenue, which may be identified by its curiously ugly gateways—the lich-gates of the burying-grounds of Wales translated into our local dialect and put to singular no-service. Here, too, the "Queen Anne" fashion shows its most emphatic, its most erratic face. In short, no place reveals so clearly as does Newport the extreme of each direction that our would-be art has taken; except, perhaps, the very best extreme of the most recent kind of effort.

In its summer garments it is a pretty place indeed. But its prettiness is due chiefly to nature, to nature and her ministrant, the gardener. Newport with bare trees and leafless vines and withered lawns and flower-beds, Newport when its architectural lines and colors stand simply on their own merits and show clearly in their every detail,—Newport in winter,—is by no means a source of unmixed pride and joy. Of course, winter is not the time to see it, is not the time when it was meant to be seen and *is* seen. And of course the architect must think of nature when he builds, and may reckon largely on her charms when he is building summer homes; but he should depend on them only to assist the general beauty of his work, not to hide its shortcomings or overshroud its sins.

In many parts of the town and of its outskirts we have failed to build well simply and solely because we have been stupid; there were no hindrances to the easy conquering of excellence. But in other parts there have been great difficulties to contend with. Far out on Bellevue Avenue, for instance, and all along the border of the Cliff, where there are no trees, and where the sites are comparatively small or are actually cramped and crowded, it is no easy thing even to imagine just what sort of work would be both appropriate and beautiful. The task is harder here, indeed, than in any other spot I know.

Compare the Newport Cliff with Elberon, for instance, and we find that as a rule the house must be still larger and more ambitious, and must have a still more strongly accented dignity of expression, if it is to interpret local life and its own interior. And we find, too, that while nature again offers the artist no help in the way of details or backgrounds, she does not efface herself so completely. Instead of a mere wide monotony of sandy ground, she now supplies a line of broken cliff, lovely alike in form and color. But its loveliness being of a quiet, subtile, gentle sort, is easily marred by the touch of man. There are some cliffs where man might do his worst and not do much to injure nature; but here anything that is not entirely harmonious is a striking and distressing discord. Nowhere does nature tempt man more irresistibly to build; nowhere does she leave his result more conspicuous, and nowhere does she so imperatively demand that it shall have an impeccable artistic title to exist. Thus it is that when houses in this part of Newport are not very good they seem so very bad; thus it is that a degree of excellence, which would almost satisfy us elsewhere, here seems scarcely excellent at all.

It is instructive to compare two recent and very ambitious houses which stand near together on Ochre Point. One design would not be very good under any conditions; but its multitude of diverse features, its effect as of unmotived variety, its evident effort after superficial picturesqueness, and the flimsy look of certain of its features, are doubly distressing, since they are executed on so large a scale and set on such a site as this. The other house is in many ways a very good one, or might be if transported somewhere else. Dignity, stateliness has now been the aim, and has been clearly expressed in its stone-built solidity and its monumental-looking features. But this aim— of course a good one, abstractly considered—has been followed too blindly, in too uncompromising a way, for the result to be "in character" as a mere summer home closely set about with alien neighbors. The house, in short, looks so out of place that its good qualities hardly please us more than do those which are less good. Both these houses transgress, we may say, by lack of discretion, of modesty, though the sinning of the one has been done in a wholly different fashion from the sinning of the other.

As we might expect, the best among the recent Newport houses do not stand on quite such exacting sites or deal with problems quite so ambitious. Some of the smaller homes built by Mr. Luce, by Mr. Emerson, by Messrs. Rotch & Tilden, and by Messrs. McKim, Mead & White are extremely sensible, attractive, and appropriate in design. The one which the last-named artists have built for Mr. Samuel Coleman, on Red Cross Lane, seems to me particularly happy in expression—dignified yet rural, simple yet refined, almost picturesque yet quiet, and wholly devoid of that affectation, that attitudinizing (so to say) which too often accompanies picturesqueness. The colonial roof has been cleverly adapted on the one hand and the "vernacular" piazza on the other. These points may be guessed from our illustration; but I am sorry to say it does not reveal the best qualities of the design, its pleasing outlines, its harmonious general effect, or the way in which a commonplace situation has been given individuality and dignity by a terrace which unites the house with the lawn below. It fails to show that it is a *good house,* and not merely a house with certain good features. But it is, I think, one of the very best in Newport, in spite of the fact that we can take exception to a few minor features here and there—as to the details of the piazza in the foreground of our print; and it is also one of those which are most distinctly "American" in effect.

It is time, however, that I should speak a little of the interior of our country homes. As a rule they are more entirely satisfactory than the exterior. Even some of those houses which most painfully affect the eye as features in the Newport landscape, are models within of intelligent de-

sign and artistic decoration. In truth, the interiors of our country homes
are getting to be so good, not only in exceptional but also in average examples, that I think I should point to them first of all, were I asked by
the "intelligent foreigner" of fiction to show what art can do in the New
World to-day.

It is impossible for me to dwell at length upon the great, the vitally
important matter of planning. I should have to use far too many words
and far too many large-scale plans in illustration. Be it only said that
that peculiar kind of ingenuity which in directions other than artistic
has long been recognized as a distinctively American gift, now at last
shows very clearly in our architectural planning too—that ingenuity
which combines practical good sense with quick imagination, and is
heedless of conventions while not in love with needless novelty.

I said in my last chapter that our general ideas with regard to what a
country home should be are similar to those which prevail in England,
dissimilar to those which rule in continental countries. But by *similar* I
did not mean *identical*. I merely meant that we believe domestic comfort
should be first considered and first expressed; that, therefore, a flexible
variety in plan and in exterior form is preferred by us to that internal
and external symmetry to which the French, for example, adhere in
their love for the harmonious, the monumental, and the "grammatical"
in art. When it comes to putting this general belief into practice, our
specialized demands are apt to have a very un-English character of their
own. In fact, it is with our planning as with our exterior design: we may
learn much from English precedents, but we cannot copy them.

For a long time the most usual pattern followed in our country
homes was symmetrical enough—not because we really cared for symmetry or even knew it by that name, but simply because we were too
unintelligent to do more than build a rectangular box with a straight
"entry" through the middle and two square rooms on each hand. If
greater size was desirable, we added other rooms and "entries" on this
side and on that, but gave the plan no center, no coherence, and no
nicety of convenience or charm of architectural effect. Now, however,
we go very differently to work. Our smallest cottages show an ever-
varying irregularity of plan which might seem "unarchitectural" to a
classically-minded, symmetry-loving French architect, unaccustomed to
our different ideals, but which has, in truth, the great architectual virtue
of perfect fitness to definite, highly specialized needs, and offers at least
the beauty of evident comfort and a pretty pictorial effectiveness; and
our larger homes are planned in a way which secures these qualities in

higher potency, and adds to them a dignity, a stateliness amply expressive of our most luxurious and hospitable modes of living.

The chief point to be noted is the great importance now given to the hall. Colonial architects made it very important and very charming, though not often in just the way which would be most desirable now. But in our transition period it fell into a condition which was not more deplorable than it was utterly inexcusable outside of city limitations. Even in the country, as I have just remarked, it was most often nothing more than a narrow "entry," an ugly, contracted passageway, which occupied valuable space and gave us nothing in return but the mere means of access to the various apartments. Mr. Hunt, so far as I know, was the first to make this innovation. But now in homes of every size the tendency is to make the hall at once beautiful and useful, the most conspicuous feature in the architectural effect and the most delightful living-room of all; not a living-room like the others, but one with a distinct purpose and therefore a distinct expression of its own. In our climate and with our social ways of summer-living, we absolutely require just what it can give us—a room which in its uses shall stand midway between the piazzas on the one hand and the drawing-rooms and libraries on the other; perfectly comfortable to live in when the hour means idleness, easy of access from all points outside and in, largely open to breeze and view, yet with a generous hearth-stone where we may find a rallying-point in days of cold and rain; in short, a spacious yet cozy and informal lounging-place for times when we cannot lounge on our beloved piazzas. Try living in a house with a hall of the new yet already customary kind, and then remember how you used to live in a house which had nothing but an "entry," and do not forget that the space once wasted on that "entry" is now utilized in every inch; and you will see that the change in our methods of planning has not been prompted by caprice or even by the desire for beauty. Yet, as we might feel sure, a great gain in beauty has come hand in hand with the great gain in practical fitness. Not only the hall itself but the whole house profits by its alteration. It supplies what was lacking before, a logical center to the most extended and complicated design. It makes grouping possible; it divides and yet connects the various apartments; it unifies the plan while permitting it a far greater degree of variety than was possible with the old box-like scheme.

And with the rehabilitation of the hall has come the rehabilitation of that staircase which also our forefathers once treated so charmingly, and which also we long maltreated so abominably and inexcusably.

Even in the tiniest cottage the staircase must now be seductive to the foot and pleasing to the eye; and in some of our larger homes it is a very splendid feature.

Of course the possibilities of treatment offered by hall and staircase are infinite in variety. In a hundred different ways the staircase may be made the chief feature, or a more subordinate feature, of the hall itself; in a hundred different ways it may be set a little apart from this and yet be sufficiently connected with it for architectural coherence and for perfect comfort. And the expression secured may be merely snug and cheerful, or be of any degree of stateliness leading up to the very highest, and yet the effect as of a true hall and not a mere room still be preserved. If I could describe, for instance, those halls which may be seen in the houses which Messrs. McKim, Mead & White have built for Mr. Tilton and for Mr. Bell at Newport; in their Francklyn cottage and their Newcomb house at Elberon; in General Loring's smaller home, built by Mr. Emerson, at Pride's Crossing; and in a larger one built for Mrs. Bowler at Mt. Desert by Messrs. Rotch & Tilden (I cite but a few examples out of many just as worthy of citation), I should describe designs utterly different each from the other in conception and effect, each perfectly in keeping with the general character of the structure, each a delightful and most comfortable living-room, yet each very plainly to the eye a hall and *not* a room, its own due and proper purpose well preserved in plan, in features, and in decoration.

One of the finest halls we have yet to show is in the large house Messrs. McKim, Mead & White have built for Mr. Robert Goelet on the Cliff at Newport. It runs the whole depth of the house, with the entrance door at one end and wide windows looking on the ocean at the other, yet is wide in due proportion; and it runs up to the roof as well, and the beautiful curved staircase near the entrance leads to encircling galleries. Above the great fire-place rises a carved chimney-piece of oak which once held its place in a French château. But its origin is not unduly apparent; it has not been left as an isolated, alien trophy, but is used as the key-note for the whole decorative scheme, the entire hall being paneled with oak to match and roofed with oaken beams. When I say *to match*, moreover, I am quite conscious of the force of the term; for the new carving strikes no note of discord with the old either in motive or in execution.

The decoration all through this house is very charming; and it is all conceived architecturally and carried out in harmony of design. And something similar may be said (although, of course, with very different degrees of emphasis and very different grades of praise) with regard to our new houses as a rule. The architect is now called upon to finish his task of house-building, not merely to begin it; to complete his interior, not merely to block it out. There is a change, indeed, since the days when we tried for no interior beauty whatsoever; as great a change since the days when we left the carpenter to work his will in machine-cut black-walnut monstrosities; and almost as great since those when we tried very hard for something better, but tried in the wrong way; when instead of a beautiful room we got merely a room full of pretty furnishings and ornaments and hangings. Then our one thought was to cover up the interior of our home as completely as we could; then all its charm would vanish with the exit of its owner. Now this charm *is built in*, is integrally part and parcel of the fabric. It is the architect's hand which has fashioned the richly screened or balustraded staircase; which has placed the cozy window-seats with an artist's eye for every item of loveliness the landscape offers; which has built the great hospitable fireplaces and the graceful mantels—now part of the wall itself and not mere excrescences; which has designed every portion of the wood-work from kitchen up to attic; which has colored the walls and ceilings, and often has prescribed the colors and the forms and the materials of the furnishings which are to complete his scheme.

Nor when our new interiors are most simple are they by any means least interesting, least excellent. Indeed, there is no task more imperative, and none which some of our architects have taken up more intelligently and enthusiastically, than the task of showing that almost utter simplicity need not mean barrenness, that economy need not be synonymous with poverty of effect or artistic dearth. Some of our new country homes (I cannot mention their creators' names; I should have to cite too many) are very admirable in the way they give just this valuable sort of evidence. They are chiefly dependent for their charm on good arrangement and good proportions, and the good placing and shaping of their necessary features. Yet they have been skillfully perfected by simple yet harmonious coloring, by a little delicate molding of inexpensive wood, a little graceful decoration—usually in adaptation of colonial motives—applied to chimney-piece and staircase. Such rooms demand no covering-up to make them livable, no mass of *bric-à-brac*, no crowd of furnishings and shroud of hangings to make them lovely. In truth, one of their greatest virtues is that, to the eye of any intelligent owner, they absolutely prescribe that their contents shall be simple—so distinct and so distinctly simple is their own architectural expression.

Nor is this merely a negative virtue, saving the owner's pocket. It is a
very positive virtue, preserving to his summer home that effect of air
and space and unencumbered lightness which is the artistic voicing of
the very purpose of its existence. Unfortunately it must be noted that
not every owner *is* intelligent; not every one who is given a simply
charming home to live in is wise enough to let it retain the accent a wise
architect's hand has given. Too often its modest architectural charm is
covered up with the upholsterer's devices, or with the motley trophies of
foreign travel, or the plunderings of some antiquary-shop at home; with
things beautiful in themselves, perhaps, but inartistic in effect, as any
beauty must be which is out of place—and, especially, which hides and
kills some other beauty that has a better right to show itself.

There seems even a wish, sometimes, to protest against the architectural completion of a home's interior; to say that architectural decoration means the adopting of some one definite "style," and that this
means the proscribing of that variety, that contrast, that unlikeness of
one room to another which the uneducated eye delights in almost as
much as it delights in the accumulation of heterogeneous stores of artistic (and very inartistic) trifles. Not always, however, in these eclectic,
catholic days of art need any one style be strictly adhered to in each and
every apartment of a house. Yet when no pronounced variety is attempted, when the same style, the same spirit, the same motives, the
same fundamental ideas prevail throughout, when there is architectural
and decorative unity, with only that harmonious amount of variation
which *any* style admits of, then the result is certainly best from an artistic point of view. And surely the degree of variety then permitted will
seem quite sufficient to any eye which cares for beauty and appropriateness, and not for mere diversity as such; which cares to be charmed
and satisfied, and not merely to be surprised and tickled. Look, for example, at the great oak-lined hall in Mr. Goelet's house which has already been referred to, and then at the exquisite drawing-room in ivory
and gold. The same beautiful Renaissance style prevails throughout, but
the contrast in color and material and in application of forms and details, and consequently in general effect, is as entire as it is harmonious.
Nor need we fear to place in such an interior any *good* object of any period. All we need fear is so to crowd it with many objects—good or
bad—that its own expression will be lost, or to intrude into its beauty
things that are not things of art at all, but are merely showy, fashionable, costly, new. Shall I be believed when I say that in another white-
and-gold drawing-room of a modified colonial pattern I once saw a

chandelier formed of a hanging basket—gilded straw and artificial roses? For *such* things there is certainly no home nor haven in our new architectural creations. Blessed be the fact, and soon may it impress itself more clearly than it does to-day upon that somewhat ungrateful beneficiary whom we call the client. Soon may he learn more thoroughly than he yet has learned that when a work of art is given into his keeping he has no right to ruin it—no, not even when it is the interior of his own home.

I have not half said all I wished to say and began to say about the exteriors of our newest houses, but the rest must now stand over to a final chapter.

20

American Country Dwellings (3)

The exteriors of our new country homes are so various that it is easier to characterize their general virtues by negative than by positive description. We may most clearly note their divergence from "vernacular" results by noting what "vernacular" expedients and features have been abandoned or greatly modified in their creating. The "French roof," for example, has disappeared. I do not mean altogether: there is still no quarter of the land where it does not often recur in work produced by the rural builder. But this builder and his devices are no longer typical of our best temper, and doubtless will gradually die out before the spreading of that new influence which naturally shows as yet most strongly in the neighborhood of our larger towns. When an *architect,* as we may fairly interpret the name to-day, has been set to work, then it is certain the French roof will not show itself. Truly it is, as the children say, a very "good riddance."

We may rejoice almost as heartily that our adherence to the clapboard is no longer so single-minded as it was. The old-time shingle, long despised as the humble expedient of unskilled, primitive hands, has very generally been adopted in its stead, and is a better thing, its small size and irregular shape being far more helpful as regards possibilities of good tone and color. In place of a succession of straight, close-drawn,

The Century Magazine (32), 10 (July 1886): 421–434.

mathematically parallel long lines, it supplies an infinitude of short, broken, varied lines, which of themselves give tone to the surface. And this surface is no longer mechanically smoothed, but is pleasantly roughish to the eye, and may be stained instead of painted, or left to the "weathering" of its natural hue. Thus its color may have gradation and vitality, and the resultant tone may be as soft and broken as we will. We have already experimented widely in this direction; indeed, a little too widely. We have sometimes tried for too much variety of color, and have lost simplicity, even temperance and unity, in the result. We have sometimes tried for too much mellowness, and ended by being weak and vague and over-subtile in our tone. And we have often shown a desire, which cannot but savor of affectation, to antedate those effects which only the hand of time can legitimately give. But all this has been, perhaps, a not unnatural reaction from the old hardness and monotony of our clapboard days. Doubtless we shall soon see and respect the limits of the really good possibilities in the way of tone and color which the shingle offers.

Except in very small houses, we ought not, I think, to use it quite alone; for it is palpably a mere sheath and covering, expresses nothing of the true structure, and if used by itself in a large building can hardly give sufficient evidence of solidity. But we do not very often thus employ it. Much more often there is at least a visible foundation of more solid aspect—another improvement on our "vernacular" practices; and the best effect results, solidity is still more apparent, and the design gains in both coherence and variety, when the stone or brick is not strictly confined to the foundations or to a low basement-story, but is carried up in certain places, as in outside chimneys or possibly in the staircase wall. A very good example of such treatment may be seen in the illustration, given with my last chapter, of Messrs. McKim, Mead & White's house for Mr. Newcomb at Elberon, and in a Newport house built by Messrs. Rotch & Tilden for Mr. Augustus Jay. Here bricks were the most natural and therefore the best resource; but in many places, especially in those New England regions where half the surface of mother-earth is not soil but rocks, a stone substructure, not too carefully "finished," commends itself alike to common sense and to the eye. And in a cottage for Mrs. F. R. Jones built at Mt. Desert by the architects last named, the lower story is of smoothed logs,—a simple enough expedient, but pretty, and appropriate to the thickly wooded site and the modesty of the structure, while expressive of much greater solidity than would have been the unmixed use of shingles.

But there are certainly cases when, however it may be blent with other factors, the shingle seems a mistake—displeases both eye and mind by being out of keeping either with the character of the exterior design itself or with the size and character of the rooms within. For example, I think it is out of keeping both with the design and with the interior in Mr. Goelet's house on the Newport Cliff, the interior of which has already been referred to. Such an interior, so large, so dignified, so sumptuous and refined in decoration, is not fittingly to be sheathed in shingles. And while the design, already too heavy, too massive in effect for the place it holds, would have looked still heavier had it been executed in sterner materials, yet nevertheless as a design judged in the abstract (judged intrinsically, without reference to site and purpose and surroundings) it would, I think, have greatly been the gainer. It is an idle speculation, of course, but I should be glad to know just how the same artists would do the same piece of work if they might do it over now. There is so much that is good about the house, and the aim which it expresses seems to have been so nearly right, that we feel a second and somewhat different expression might be something wholly admirable. For even now it is very dignified while very simple; it shows great feeling for breadth and mass, for the beauty of repose, and is a valuable protest against that heterogeneous accumulation of "features" for which we have too great a fondness still. As it stands it is not a beautiful house outside, though within it has that high kind of beauty we call architectural *style*. But even outside it seems to me, despite its patent faults, an interesting and a promising conception.

Neither clapboard nor shingle is always, I repeat, a very good resource. Yet it is not true to say—as so often has been said—that wood is in itself a poor resource, is essentially but a primitive, makeshift material; that our work must suffer, must be condemned to pettiness in treatment and to poverty or at least rusticity in effect, just in so far as we insist upon its use. We should rather rejoice that we have it to use, since it gives us one more factor than is possessed by any other civilized land toward the production of variety in effect, which means toward the true expression of varied needs and purposes. If we look at current work abroad, we shall see how hard it is to build small and pretty country houses when it is wholly denied the builder. Even if it gave us nothing but the shingle, it would be richly worth the having. But the shingle by no means exhausts its possibilities of excellence. There is a solid way of using it in logs for which we may find happy hints in the architecture of the Scandinavian lands. And, best of all, there is the "half-timbered" method of construction,—with great interlacing beams and a filling-in of brick or of rougher units plastered over,—which may be studied almost anywhere in Europe.

If we have been at Warwick, for instance, and Stratford-on-Avon, and the neighboring Shottery, we have seen it used in a variety of ways that are simple and more or less humble, yet charming in expression; and we had not to go far afield to find it, in some old manor-house, expressing with equal felicity a more dignified estate. In Chester we may learn that it is just as well adapted to the street as to the country; and in many a French and German town, that it may take on a truly rich and stately aspect. It is a method which looks delightfully stable, and which, if rightly used and not superficially imitated, is just as stable as it looks. The beams may be smoothed and painted, or may be carved (as they are in the continental street-fronts I have cited) with any degree of richness up to the most lace-like elaboration; and in color, too, one may do pretty much as he wills with it.

Truly it is a sensible, flexible, and attractive way of building; and it is one which to a non-professional eye seems as though it ought not to be expensive. Not nearly so often as we might guess has it yet been used in this country, but we find occasional examples, as, for instance, in Messrs. Rotch & Tilden's large house built at Mt. Desert for Mrs. Bowler. Good use has here been made of its possibilities in the way of color. The high substructure is of gray trimmed with red granite; the tower, and the terrace, and the piazza walls are of red; and the same tones are repeated in the wood-and-plaster work above: the wood is painted of the darkest possible red, and the gray slap-dash is filled with red granite pebbles. Surely so effective and variable a process ought to prove popular, especially in houses of just this kind—houses which are so large and dignified that the shingle is too naïf and rustic-looking a device, yet which by reason of their placing and their merely summer purpose would appear too massive and ambitious if wholly built of brick or stone. Moreover, while the conspicuous use of stone was here very sensible, since both the red and the gray granite were obtained from ledges on the place, yet it is by no means always necessary, for, as I have said, half-timbering is in itself satisfactorily sturdy-looking; and many a large and charming country home in older countries was built with it alone in those older days when they too had free command of wood.

I cannot but pause a little over the virtues of this method as regards the good use it allows us to make, not only of wood, but of plaster too.

Unaccustomed as we are to the thought, plaster is yet a very admirable material for many of our purposes. Not in the shape of thin coats of stucco, painted in futile imitation of some other substance, but solid and straightforward, frankly confessing itself for what it is, plaster may be given qualities unattainable in any other material; a surface, for example, that is neither too rough nor too smooth, but exactly suited to the production of those effects of *tone* which we have learned to recognize as most desirable. And for color, especially for color at once light and strong,—which is to say, for color peculiarly well in keeping with our atmospheric conditions,—there is nothing like it. What pinks and yellows, what golden browns and lovely grays and tender greens one sees in the plastered walls of Italy and South Germany, and even of the southern English counties; and what dullards we shall show ourselves if we fail to take the hints they offer! Moreover, there is nothing but plaster (save only that marble which is all but out of the question as concerns summer houses) with which we can well get *white*.

The way in which we used white in our clapboard days—in unbroken stretches of oil-paint applied to a hard, smooth, mechanically ruled-off surface, and contrasted with grass-green blinds—was certainly not an artistic way. But when we became convinced of this fact, we were rather stupid to fall into the opposite extreme—to condemn white as such, *in toto*, without appeal. Surely it is not a bad color for our use. Who can say so if he knows its effect in those southern lands abroad the physical condition of which resembles ours, and where the use of white has been constant in every age? Who can say so if with an unprejudiced eye he judges its effect even from one of our old-fashioned home-examples, when this is seen at such a distance that only the white and not its quality is perceptible? As yet, I think, we use our eyes too little in such matters—depend too much upon theories and sentiments drawn from that north of Europe whence we came, which from an intellectual point of view may be our proper teacher, but which from an artistic point of view has much less than we have fancied in common with ourselves and our environment. When we *do* learn to use our eyes, then I believe we shall often ask for white again, and for other light and bright and cheerful hues; and perhaps decide that in wood and plaster we have one of the very best ways—if not *the* very best way—of getting them.

A word now as to the development of that piazza which was the one good feature of the "vernacular" period. Two tasks were laid upon us with regard to it. On the one hand, we had to make it more architectural in itself—less fragile and shed-like and trumpery-looking; and on the other, we had to bring it into more vital architectural relation with the main body of the structure. From the illustrations in this and the two foregoing chapters some idea may be gained of a few of the fashions in which we have tried to deal with it; but it would take a far longer list of pictures to typify our general advance or to suggest all our best experiments.

Fortunate is it, indeed, that we *have* advanced in our efforts to bring it within the domain of art; for, as I said long ago, it is the one thing which no one who builds a country house in America can escape from,—the one thing more essential than all others to the comfort, dearer than all others to the affection, of every American client. Better do without even that "livable" hall which we now enjoy so greatly than without that piazza which went far to compensate us for the lack of so much else in our "vernacular" homes. It is more necessary to our well-being than is his *loggia* to the Italian, or his paved terrace to the Frenchman, or his vine-clad arbor to the German. As far as comfort and variety of service go, it is a better thing than any of them; and it remains for us to prove that it may be made, from the point of view of art, as good a thing as even the first named of the three.

In "vernacular" days it was so beloved (perhaps because there was so little else about a house that could be loved) that we thought we could not have too much of it. Now we are a little more chary of its use, as indeed could not but be the case with the different ground-plans we have adopted. Yet niggardly in using it we are not; or if we have thought good so to be upon occasion, our mistake is forced upon us very quickly. I know one or two houses (but only one or two), built with English models in mind, which try to make shift with a mere upper bay or so, and an abundance of broad windows and bays to the main apartments below. It was supposed that they could do without piazzas, as they would be "all piazzas" themselves. But the analogy is not very vital, and I think even their builders and owners only try to believe in it.

Many, I repeat, are the variations in our treatment of the real thing itself, and many are the outside hints which have been utilized in its improvement. Not always is it now covered along its whole length, though always, of course, it ought to be to a very considerable extent. Sometimes it is combined with an open terrace, whose flights of steps unite it pleasantly with the lawn below—the influence of French fashions being clearly manifest. Sometimes, in addition to the main projecting piazza, there are others of a recessed sort, prettily adapted from the *loggias* of Italy. As for the roof, it is now flat and balustraded, forming an uncovered piazza to the upper story, now steeply sloping, and now a prolongation of the slope of the house-roof itself. Stone or brick is often used for the foundations, and even for the parapets and roof-supports; while if these last are of wood, they are given forms of a more sturdy kind than those they took in our old jig-saw days. It is interesting to see here and there wooden pillars with corbeled-out capitals, such as are common in the far East and the oriental South, and to see how well—being sensible straightforward shapes, truly characteristic of the nature of the material—they fit in with elements drawn from very different sources. But it would take much more space than is here at command really to describe our piazzas in their present state, I will not say of perfection, but of steady and varied approach toward excellence and beauty. I can only add that it is a distinct disappointment nowadays to find one which looks as they all looked but a few years ago—like an excrescence, an afterthought, a mere disconnected shed, and not a vital portion of the house-fabric proper.

If it is difficult to describe our piazzas, it would be still more hopeless to try to describe the houses of which they form a part. Sometimes they are adapted from current English types, and have a modified flavor of "Queen Anne" about them; sometimes they are glorifications of the humble, early, shingled New England farm-house with its gambrel-roof and dormers; sometimes they are intelligent modifications of the later, more stately, "classic" colonial type; and sometimes they can be called by no other name than late-nineteenth-century-rural-American only. For modest dwellings in really rural situations, the farm-house pattern is peculiarly well suited; while the colonial is better fitted for use in less distinctly rustic localities. Two of the most charming small colonial designs I have seen show houses built at Mt. Desert by Messrs. Rotch & Tilden; but I doubt whether they look quite so well on this rocky coast as they would, for instance, at Newport or in the neighborhood of Boston. Here, of course, colonial reproductions are perfectly at home, alike to the eye and to the memory when it seeks their genesis; and here they are very frequent and very charming. In feature and detail they are now more modest than they sometimes were of old—a true sense being preserved of the nature of wood, and its unfitness to a "monumental" classic design. Yet the classic flavor is preserved, and gives a charming air of dignity and refinement. The irregularly shaped and applied shingle would strike a note of discord in such a design, and we accordingly find it giving way either to the clapboard itself or to shingles cut square and arranged in parallel lines. Nor would broken tones and irregularly

Fig. 25.   House at Braintree, Mass. [Chamberlin and Whidder, c. 1885.]

varied colors be appropriate, symmetry and regularity being essentially part and parcel of the idea. The usual device is to paint the body of the house a red that is not too dark and is not too strong, or a yellow that is pale and clear, and the trimmings white. If the tints are well chosen, the effect is not crude or staring, while cheerful and bright enough to be thoroughly in keeping with the strong blue of our skies and the clearness which our atmosphere gives to all the hues of nature.

Among our illustrations are a few which typify our recent endeavors to bring the colonial type into accord with those interior arrangements which do not readily submit themselves to the old rectangular outline. The house at Braintree was built by Messrs. Chamberlin & Whidder, and the Newport houses for Mr. Taylor and Mr. Edgar by Messrs. McKim, Mead & White. Of the three, the last named seems to me the most successful, the old idea being developed with at once the most of freedom and the most of unity. In smaller structures with less exacting interiors, the old-time shape may often be preserved without detriment to comfort. The piazza, as will be noted, is likely to bear a discreet and far-away resemblance to the classic portico.

Fig. 26. Millwood—House of R. Percy Alden, Esq., Cornwall, Penn.
[McKim, Mead and White, 1880–84.]

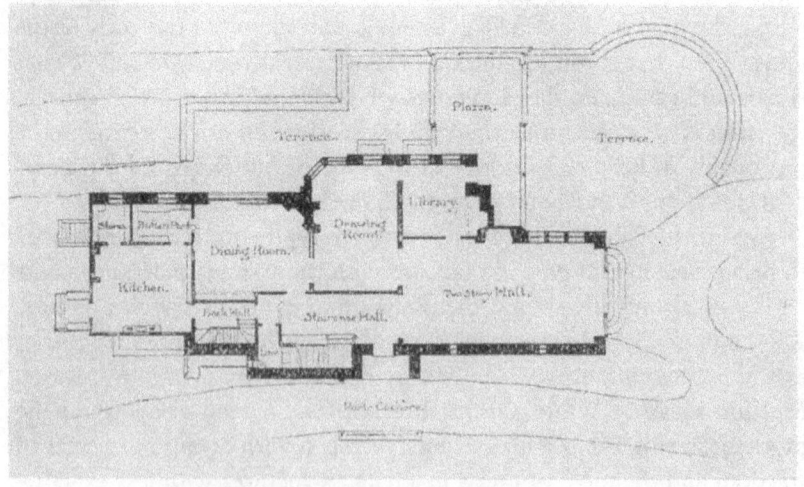

Fig. 27. Plan of Millwood. [McKim, Mead and White, 1880–84.]

Fig. 28.   Archway and Seat, at Dr. R. H. Derby's House, Lloyd's Neck, Long Island. [McKim, Mead and Bigelow, 1879.] The house was originally built for Mrs. Derby's mother, Mrs. A. C. Alden.

Mr. Alden's house at Cornwall, Pennsylvania, is pictured here chiefly for the sake of its great window. As a house it does not seem to me very successful, bearing too close a resemblance to a studio or something of that kind. But the window, I think, is very interesting, showing how it is possible to build such a one—whether for the lighting of a studio or, as is here the case, of a large three-storied hall—in a truly *constructive* way, so that it will look solid and architectural, and not like a mere screen of glass suggesting a photographer's atelier within.

Many more things occur to me which might be said with reference to our domestic architecture, and many more names which might be cited with reference to its good results. To omit to speak of the country homes built by Mr. Bruce Price, for instance, by Messrs. Rossiter & Wright, by Messrs. Cabot & Chandler, Messrs. Andrews & Jacques, and more than a few other artists, is to omit many things that would be pleasant in the saying. But I dare not suppose either an editor's or a reader's patience indefinitely elastic.

And, in truth, I have said quite enough if only I have said it rightly. For I did not set out to give a complete summary of the state, the needs, and the possibilities of American architecture, or a *catalogue raisonné* of the best among its products. I merely meant to show in a general way, and to illustrate by a few examples, that there has been a recent movement in our art which may fairly be called revolutionary; to indicate the main ideas and impulses which have prompted it; and to explain why and how these seem to be prophetic of further excellence to come. I ought to have said enough for this, I repeat; yet there are still a few words I must add in order that the last-named point may be made as clear as possible.

I know the danger of letting one's self be tempted into prophecy about a matter one has near at heart, but it is a danger I cannot quite escape from here. In fact, if from the first I had not meant to incur it,—if from the first I had not meant to express the strong hope I feel in the future of our art,—these pages would not have been written at all. For, good and interesting as are, intrinsically considered, many of our new results, I hardly think I should have been justified in speaking of them at such length and to so large and so mixed an audience if they had seemed to me to have intrinsic worth and interest *only;* if I had looked upon them as casual, sporadic, merely individual examples of success—uncharacteristic of any growing, widening, spreading stream of effort, unprophetic of any broad and common excellence to follow. No; the chief importance of our best results seems to me to lie in the fact that they are but the most successful outcome of aims which have much more often been followed; their chief value to consist in their hopefully prophetic character.

This character I identify with the fact—I think it *is* a fact—that in them all, beneath their manifold degrees of excellence and diversities of aspect, we can discern as a common foundation *the desire to do rational work and to prepare for it in a rational way.* We can discern that their creators have felt that the main question was the manner in which their own particular problems might best be resolved, not the manner in which some other problem had been resolved by some other hand; and that, while feeling this, they have felt none the less that they could not approach the main question intelligently or answer it artistically unless they had made a preparatory study of the history which tells and the monuments which show how an infinite number of other problems had been resolved by a long line of other hands. In short, I think we are getting to desire, not that we should be independent merely, and not that we should be scholarly and nothing else, but that we should be *independent in a scholarly way,*—unconventional, yet law-abiding; spontaneous, yet cultivated; free to do new things, yet bound not to do them in crude and blundering and illiterate fashions. I am sure this is the right, the only right, ideal. But I know, of course, how lofty an ideal it is—so lofty that no modern people can dare to boast of its full realiza-

tion. Far be it from me to boast thus of ourselves, even in remote anticipation! I only think that we are beginning to *perceive* the right ideal,
and to strive toward its realization in a vigorous and not unintelligent
or inartistic manner. Yet this belief is surely enough to warrant the cher-
ishing of a hope that there may be a future in store for American architecture,—not a future of immediate general excellence, certainly not a
future of quick-coming perfection, very likely not of perfection at all as
we use the word when thinking of the great old times of art; but still a
future of growing, spreading, developing excellence, and perchance
even of an ultimate degree of accomplishment which will be an expression of national characteristics through a truly national and artistic
form of speech.

If a foreign critic should read these words and test them only by the
evidence of the illustrations it has been possible to print with nine brief
chapters, he might perhaps think them too confident. Even if he should
come here and look about for himself, he might still not see the full
grounds of my faith. He would view as an undecipherable, undated
mass the whole of the work we have so rapidly built during our century
of national life, and would see the bad results outnumbering the good,
the senseless results the sensible, the ugly results the beautiful, in the
proportion of hundreds to one. But I can see what he could not—the
date when each was built, the circumstances under which each arose. I
can see, as in a panorama by themselves, the products of the last ten or
fifteen years, and can contrast them with the aggregate of those of earlier days. I can see how young our art is in its best estate, and how
young are many of the artists who have wrought it; and thus can speak
with confidence of advance and promise.

Moreover, I could cite for his convincing many items of evidence besides those which stand revealed in our new work itself. For example,
there has lately been an immense improvement in the equipment, the
standards, and the frequentation of our architectural schools. There is a
strong and waxing belief in the desirableness of foreign study, the
necessity of foreign travel. We have recently seen established such stu-
dent-clubs as the "Architectural League" of New York, which prove the
serious and enthusiastic way in which the young profession now approaches its life's work. And such facts encourage us to believe that the
days are fairly over when a man could open an office and call himself an
architect, pretty much as he might open a shop and call himself a gro-
cer,—indeed, with far less sense of responsibility, and with far less time
and thought and money spent in the laying-in of a stock-in-trade.

We have more than one architectural journal, unborn ten years ago, which is now well established and well entitled to respect. And another good sign, another good influence, deserves citation,—and, be it said, should excite to imitation on a generous scale. Those who founded the "Rotch Traveling Scholarship" for architectural students of the State of Massachusetts have done much more than the mere good work of promising to send every year for a two-years' stay in Europe a properly prepared and capable young artist. They have offered an incentive to earnest study which will yearly profit many more than the one who wins the prize; and they have proclaimed, distinctly enough to impress the most indifferent ear, that our architecture should be fostered, and that private generosity must play the part which our governments are not yet in a mental condition to assume.

And now, in conclusion, there are certain interesting questions we may ask ourselves. If there is indeed a possible future for our art, what is likely to be the character of its development? Will it have a very marked or only a very slight degree of originality? Shall we have a new style, an "American style"? If so, what is it likely to be? If not, what historic style are we likely to embrace? Or shall we embrace no one more closely than another, but always have, as we have had thus far, many men of many minds, only each one touched to a finer issue? Or these questionings may take a different turn: instead of asking what we are likely to have, we may ask what we *ought* to have. Indeed, we not only may but must ask ourselves all these questions in both these ways, if we really take an interest in the matter. But to answer them—even to think of answering them—is quite another thing!

As regards, for instance, what we *ought* to have, certain of our architects are convinced in theory and pretty consistent in practice. But they are not in agreement among themselves, while many of their brethren seem to have no very marked convictions—try one road with one kind of problem and another road with another kind; often, indeed, now one road and now a different, although the problems are analogous. When the doctors thus not only disagree but fail to arrive at individual conclusions, how shall a layman hold even the shyest theory?

Yet there is just one oft-propounded query which I think even a layman is justified in answering with decision. If our art is to be good—practically, expressionally, and æsthetically—must it be radically *novel*? Must we pray, as for our sole salvation, for the dawning of an "American style"? Its advent, its perfectioning would be agreeable, of course: it is always pleasant to create, to originate, to found, and not to follow. But a *necessary* advent it is not. We want an American architecture which shall be perfectly fitted to our needs, perfectly expressive of ourselves, and perfectly satisfying to our eyes. But we might have it, I am sure, with but few new forms or features or details of decoration. The general effect would at times be new—as we see in our country homes which are as "American" in their late and good as they were in their old and evil state. But this is not all that is meant by those who have raised the foolish clamor for an "American style"; and it is no more imperative that we should have such a novel architectural language as they desire, than that we should write something else than English ere we can have a literature essentially our own.

And it is idle even to discuss the question; for even if both the possibility and the desirability of a "new style" could be clearly proved, such proof would not help us toward it. It could not be formulated in advance. It ought never to be held up as a definite goal. The mere effort to foretell it and work up to it would be a negation of the true principles of progress. For that intimate coherence of forms and features and details which constitutes a *style* has never been, can never be, the starting-point even in idea. It always has been and always must be the final flowering of a long and gradual development. If an "American style" is to come, it will come step by step and inevitably—not suddenly and by an effort of will.

But we have no more need, I say, to pin our hopes upon its advent than has any other people. In truth, we have less need than any other, for we are peculiarly entitled to make free with all earlier inventions of every age and clime. We are more at liberty than is any other civilized nation to choose what and how and where we will from the world's great museum of precedents and ideas. No style, no scheme, no motive, feature, or manner of expression has with us an ancient local root. No venerable monuments excite a fear lest what is erected now shall strike a clashing discord. No existing or once existing form of architectural speech can show a really valid title to our allegiance. The little parallel I just drew with regard to literature was not quite correctly drawn, for in architecture we have a score of languages to choose among for the expression of our ideas, and are not bound to the artistic tongue of England only. Not the north more than the south, not the west of Europe more than farthest Asia, need be accepted as our magazine of forms and details; and not any one alone, but all together, may be drawn upon for the notes of a possible future harmony. To some this limitless freedom of choice seems but an added difficulty in our path. To my mind, on the contrary, it seems a vast advantage, of which the good results may already be traced with much distinctness, while the current efforts of most European countries do not seem to force an envy of the conditions amid which *they* work. But from either point of view that logic is equally at fault which would deduce from *our* condition an especial need for some absolute novelty of our own invention.

I might easily let myself be tempted quite beyond the bounds of discretion, and try a little definite prophesying with regard to what the future holds in store for us. But the attempt would be as profitless as indiscreet unless I could put my readers actually in face of all the evidence which has worked on my own mind.

So I will only say that it seems as though the architecture of the South (broadly speaking), and not the architecture of the North, would furnish us with our main devices. Theoretical examination—based not on mere facts of descent in blood, but on climate and atmosphere, and on our actual tastes and habits and minds and tempers—would lead us to such a belief, and the aspect of the majority of our best results seems to confirm it. I think that of all the constructive and decorative schemes which have been born in elder times, and are now struggling together for readoption in the Europe of to-day, the ones least likely to be acclimatized in America are those Gothic schemes which are most characteristic of the spirit of the North. But to say this is not to say much in the way of prophecy. How wide is still the range of possibilities with the round arch and the lintel of the South as our resources!

The round arch, we know, has been very conspicuously used of late. Alike in its Romanesque and in its Renaissance phases (both essentially creations of the South) it has many devoted adherents and many skillful adapters. Mr. Richardson has been perhaps its most energetic champion, and has preferred not only its Romanesque development, but the most pronouncedly Southern type of this. His work is always seductive and impressive; and if sometimes it seems exotic in its charm,—individual, willful, rather than purely natural and exactly *right*,—very often it has an accent which could hardly be imagined more appropriate, truthful, sensible. In marking this difference I do not mean that he sometimes seeks charm at the expense of usefulness; that his wish to reproduce the beauty of ancient examples sometimes works to the detriment of practical fitness. I only mean that sometimes, in the features and the decorations of those buildings which he plans so wisely, he reproduces the almost barbaric strength and exuberance of Romanesque days without

due remembrance that those days were unlike our own, and that the unlikeness springs from our greater intellectual refinement, and from the
greater feeling this gives us for *artistic* refinement as distinguished from
artistic vigor and luxuriance. We, who know so well the art as well as
the thought of classic Greece, cannot but exact from modern art a fuller
measure of repose and reticence and balance and grace and purity than
satisfied the mediæval nations.

It is not to be wondered at that many of those who recognize this fact
should have but small faith in the wisdom of attempting to draw at all
from mediæval precedents; should say that a better quarry is to be
found in that Renaissance art wherein mediæval ideas have already
been modified by the reborn influence of Greece; wherein we have the
language of a time whose civilization is the true parent of our own. Yet
there are arguments which plead the other way, or, at least, which plead
that we need not base our efforts wholly on Renaissance suggestions.

All the various Renaissance schemes save one or two of the very earliest came, alike in construction and in decoration, to be pretty definitely and completely worked out. It is hard, therefore, to treat them
now with freedom without incurring the reproach of unscholarliness.
Nay, it is hard to treat them with freedom even if we are content to
incur such reproach; for there seems to be a singular analogy between
architectural and human life. When a style has really run its course, has
developed gradually and naturally up to the highest imaginable perfection, and then gradually and naturally fallen into decay, it seems impossible that it should be resuscitated and made the basis of new developments. For example, we have seen the experiment tried in England with
that Pointed art which there lived a long life of many phases and died at
last of inanition. We have seen it tried very faithfully and earnestly and
cleverly, but are growing every year more conscious that the trial has
been a failure.

Of course the styles we call by the general name of Later Renaissance
have not died out in the same hopeless way. They are certainly vital still
in France, which is the only modern land that can boast of a living and
national form of architectural speech. But it would be useless for us to
try to take them up as employed by France to-day. For they are *fully developed,* and French wants, French tastes, French ideas, are so singularly unlike our own that French expedients would but poorly serve our
turn even if we could make ourselves content to copy them.

What we need is some scheme or schemes able to meet all demands,
however lofty, however modest; fitted for use with many different ma-

terials; possible of modification into new expressions; and (should we ever work these out) capable of receiving new decorative motives. That is to say, we want some scheme or schemes more susceptible of *fresh development* than is any which has already once run a complete and perfect course. Those are undoubtedly right who think that such a scheme is offered to us by the earlier Renaissance fashions of the northern parts of Italy—by those which used the round arch and the lintel very straightforwardly without much reliance upon the column; for in the first place they are very sensible and very flexible, and in the second place they never lived out their life and came to a death of natural exhaustion: they were replaced, while they seem to us to have been still instinct with latent capabilities, by those columnar fashions known as "Roman" or "Later Renaissance."

But these early Renaissance styles are close akin in spirit, though not always in superficial effect, to the Romanesque fashions of a still earlier day. Both sprang from the same primal root; both incorporated the same general ideas and used the same main features. See, for example, how hard it is for an unskilled eye to tell in Venice which are the true "Byzantine" house-fronts, and which are those that were built in the first flush of the classic revival—although the long interval that lay between included all the Pointed work that Venice ever wrought. And the Romanesque of the South is another scheme which never lived out its life to natural expiration. The true Byzantine style of the East flowered very early into the most splendid blossoms, but then ceased from effort and neither developed nor declined. And its foster-children in the West—alike in Auvergne, in Tuscany, in Lombardy, and in the upper Rhine lands—were superseded, while still very vital, by Pointed fashions imported bodily from those more northern countries where they had had their birth. It is important to note that their typical ecclesiastical structures offer us, in the rectangular ground-plan, something far more appropriate to our modern needs than do the Gothic churches of the North; and quite as important to remember that in every other class of buildings we may take up their somewhat primitive elements and develop them as we will without any very stringent fetters in the way of precedents which it would be "unscholarly" to ignore. Their decoration, as I have said, if literally reproduced from western prototypes, seems too emphatic, too luxuriant, too barbaric for the expression of modern sentiment; yet it offers us—and especially in its eastern, Byzantine examples—types and motives and manifold lovely suggestions capable of development into a most appropriate form of artistic speech.

Nothing, for example, could be fresher, more unhackneyed, newer to modern western eyes, than the decoration based on Byzantine motives which Mr. Richardson has wrought in many of his interiors—as, for instance, in the exquisite wood carvings which line the Quincy Library; yet nothing could be more refined, more modern in feeling, more entirely appropriate and satisfactory.

Of course it will be understood that I have not said all this with the foolish idea of "giving advice," with the least wish to point out any road which our art "ought" to follow. I have only been trying to explain that the impulses which already have so strongly led our artists in these two directions are both sensible, both promising; and that they are *kindred* impulses, and therefore perhaps prophetic of some still closer accord to follow in the future.

Mr. Richardson's example seems already to have had a very strong influence upon the younger rank of the profession. But if it proves to be a *lasting* influence, the reason will be found, not in his mere personal force and accomplishment, but in the fact that through these he gave the first outspoken voice to tastes and sympathies latent in his countrymen at large. If our architecture ever really develops upon the basis of the round arch into anything that may be called a *style* proper to ourselves, it will be because such a style is really what would suit us best, and because our artists will have felt the fact in their own souls and not believed it upon the mere evidence of one single man among them.

But (I must remind myself, I see, as well as you) speculation is quite idle. We cannot even pretend to guess whether we shall grow into architectural concord of any sort whatever. But here, you may protest, we can surely say what *ought* to be our course. Yes, surely, if this is a point where the course of past developments must be accepted as illustrating a natural, unescapable law. Success in the past has certainly meant concord in style. But can we be sure that success in the future *must* come in the same manner? Can we be quite sure that individuality, personality, which today in so many directions is so much more potent a force than it ever was in days gone by, may not be destined to play a greater rôle in architecture than it has ever played before? Of course I am not desirous of predicting that such will be the case; I only think that no one should too dogmatically say that the case is in itself impossible.

Time alone can give the answer to this as to all questions of the sort. Our task is not to theorize or prophesy, certainly not to guide, dictate, or dogmatize; but first *to help in the education of the artist and then to give him liberty to work in his own way and opportunity to work his best.*

And if almost always we yet find something in our architects' results to criticise, and sometimes much to condemn, much to deplore, let us remember how difficult are many of their tasks, and how often we make their difficulty greater. Let us remember how ignorant we are ourselves, and how our ignorance reacts on them. Let us remember what our condition was but a few short years ago—how young, as I have said, is our good work, how young are most of our good workers. Let us remember all this, and then, not their sins and stumbles, but their virtues and successes will seem to us remarkable. We shall then pause from condemnation, hesitate to criticise, and cultivate a grateful mood;—at the same time frankly confessing with the French philosopher that the liveliest source of gratitude is the expectation of greater benefits to come.

PART 3

Landscape Architecture and the Environment

21

Landscape Gardening: A Definition

Some of the Fine Arts appeal to the ear, others to the eye. The latter are the Arts of Design, and they are usually named as three—Architecture, Sculpture and Painting. A man who practices one of these in any of its branches is an artist; other men who work with forms and colors are at the best but artisans. This is the popular belief. But in fact there is a fourth art which has a right to be rated with the others, which is as fine as the finest, and which demands as much of its professors in the way of creative power and executive skill as the most difficult. This is the art whose purpose it is to create beautiful compositions upon the surface of the ground.

The mere statement of its purpose is sufficient to establish its rank. It is the effort to produce organic beauty—to compose a beautiful whole with a number of related parts—which makes a man an artist; neither the production of a merely useful organism nor of a single beautiful detail suffices. A clearly told story or a single beautiful word is not a work of art— only a story told in beautifully connected words. A solidly and conveniently built house, if it is nothing more, is not a work of architecture, nor is an isolated stone, however lovely in shape and surface. A delightful tint, a graceful line, does not make a picture; and though the painter may reproduce ugly models he must put some kind of beauty into the reproduction if it is to be esteemed above any other manufactured article—if not beauty of form, then beauty of color or of meaning or at least of execution. Similarly, when a man disposes the surface of the soil with an eye to crops alone he is an agriculturist; when he grows plants for their beauty as isolated objects he is a horticulturist; but when he disposes ground and plants together to produce organic beauty of effect, he is an artist with the best.

Yet though all the fine arts are thus akin in general purpose they differ each from each in many ways. And in the radical differences which exist between the landscape-gardener's and all the others we find some reasons why its affinity with them is so commonly ignored. One difference is that it uses the same materials as nature herself. In what is called "natural" gardening it uses them to produce effects which under fortunate conditions nature might produce without man's aid. Then, the better the result, the less likely it is to be recognized as an artificial—artistic—result. The more perfectly the artist attains his aim, the more likely we are to forget that he has been at work. In "formal" gardening, on the other hand, nature's materials are disposed and treated in frankly unnatural ways; and then—as a more or less intelligent love for natural beauty is very common to-day, and an intelligent eye for art is rare—the artist's work is apt to be resented as an impertinence, denied its right to its name, called a mere contorting and disfiguring of his materials.

Again, the landscape-gardener's art differs from all others in the unstable character of its productions. When surfaces are modeled and plants arranged, nature and the artist must work a long time together before the true result appears; and when once it has revealed itself, day to day attention will be forever needed to preserve it from the deforming effects of time. It is easy to see how often neglect or interference must work havoc with the best intentions, how often the passage of years must travesty or destroy the best results, how rare must be the cases in which a work of landscape art really does justice to its creator.

Still another thing which affects popular recognition of the art as such is our lack of clearly understood terms by which to speak of it and of those who practice it. "Gardens" once meant pleasure-grounds of every kind and "gardener" then had an adequately artistic sound. But as the significance of the one term has been gradually specialized, so the other has gradually come to denote a mere grower of plants. "Landscape gardener" was a title first used by the artists of the eighteenth century to mark the new tendency which they represented—the search for "natural" as opposed to "form" beauty; and it seemed to them to need an apology as savoring, perhaps, of grandiloquence or conceit. But as taste declined in England it was assumed by men who had not the slightest right, judged either by their aims or by their results, to be considered artists; and to-day it is fallen into such disesteem that it is often replaced by "landscape architect." This title has French usage to support it and is in many respects a good one. But its correlative—"landscape architecture"—is unsatisfactory; and so, on the other hand, is "landscape artist," though "landscape art" is an excellent generic term. Perhaps the best we can do is to keep to "landscape gardener," and try to remember that it ought always to mean an artist and an artist only.

Frederick Law Olmsted

In answer to a question asked not long ago, Mr. Olmsted said: "The most interesting general fact of my life seems to me to be that it was not as a gardener, a florist, a botanist, or one in any way specially interested in plants and flowers, or specially susceptible to their beauty, that I was drawn to my work. The root of all my work has been an early respect for and enjoyment of scenery, and extraordinary opportunities for cultivating susceptibility to its power. I mean not so much grand or sensational scenery as scenery of a more domestic order—scenery which is to be looked upon contemplatively, and is productive of musing moods." It will be well to keep these words in mind in following the thread of a life which has been so rich in the ability to create landscape beauty and so useful in the devotion of this ability to the service of our people.

Frederick Law Olmsted was born in Hartford, Connecticut, on April 27, 1822. He came of the best possible stock— of an English middle-class family, first settled at Plymouth, which had been among those to cross the wilderness and establish a new colony by the Connecticut River. There were deacons, of course, and other quiet home-keeping citizens in all its generations; but an adventurous strain was not lacking in the Olmsted blood. Our artist's great uncles were seamen, one dying on

The Century Magazine (45) 24 (October 1893): 860–867.

a British prison-ship, another living through strange privateering expe-riences, and another, a very successful shipmaster in the China trade, ending his life as a rich and cultivated citizen of Hartford. His grandfa-ther was likewise a shipmaster, but a less successful one. His father, after receiving little more than a common-school education, was in early life a "dry-goods" merchant in Hartford. A shy and reserved man, we are told, and not a scholar, he was yet a great reader, and a man of distinc-tively rural tastes, having a small farm near the town, in which he took constant interest, riding and driving a great deal, and often taking his little boy with him on a pillow on his saddle-bow.

Mr. Olmsted's mother—Charlotte Hull, a relative of Commodore Hull—had died when he was three years old; but his father soon mar-ried again, and a woman with tastes similar to his own. Their chief recreations were long summer journeys to the sea-shore or through the inland country. When the boy was six years old he was taken to Nia-gara, and another year to the Wadsworth homestead in the beautiful, park-like Genesee Valley. After his eighth year he lived in the country in clergymen's families; but his vacations coincided with his parent's sum-mer journeys. In a two-horse wagon the whole family would drive slowly through various parts of New England, stopping to lunch in some pretty spot, sleeping at convenient rural inns—living with Nature, contemplating, absorbing, and appreciating her as people seldom can in these rushing railroad days. Often appropriate books, drawn from the Hartford library, would be read aloud at the noon resting-hour—Dwight's or Silliman's travels, for example. Thus (and Mr. Olmsted himself cannot now lay too much explanatory stress upon the fact) from his very earliest youth the future landscape-gardener was brought up amid rural influences, and all unconsciously was imbibing a love for natural beauty from people who did not speak of it by such a term—who, indeed, rarely spoke of it at all, but felt it, and indulged it as sim-ply and constantly as their desire to breathe.

And the boy's own impulses led to a deepening of the impressions thus received. He was instinctively, persistently a rambler, spending all the time he could in long, solitary walks, when he forgot why he carried rod or gun, and was never tempted into any scientific study, but gave himself up to the silent influence of wood and field, hillside, brook, and cloud. Zimmerman "On Solitude," he says, was the first book which led him to any conscious thinking about natural beauty, although, when he read Gilpin and Price in later years, they vaguely came back to him as chance acquaintances of his childhood.

When he was about fourteen a severe case of ivy-poisoning injured his eyesight. The physician forbade him to attend school or to read, and here was a fine excuse for the still wider indulgence of his rambling, contemplating propensities. While still forbidden to use his eyes much, he was sent as a pupil to a clergyman who had formerly been a civil engineer, and with him remained two years, at Andover and in Collinsville, Connecticut. He now studied a very little engineering, amused himself much with a sort of "play-practice" in laying out imaginary towns, but spent most of his time, as before, in wandering afield, strengthening his love for natural beauty, unconsciously storing his memory with countless impressions of characteristic New England scenes. He boated, of course, on the Connecticut, and he now believes that this river-meadow scenery influenced his mature taste more forcibly than anything else. The family practice of summer journeyings was still kept up, and now the lad gradually learned to notice (still half unconsciously) why towns are founded in certain spots, how villages develop, and other facts pregnant with the seeds of future usefulness.

The idea of an engineer's life for him was soon abandoned. Placed at sixteen in a large importing-house in New York, he could not compel himself to commercial life for more than two years. Then the adventurous drop in his blood asserted itself; like his forefathers he went to sea, and a year was spent before the mast in great hardship and repeated illnesses. He came home with his health impaired, but bringing memories of many hours when he had indulged his dreaming, contemplative spirit, and of scant, exciting glimpses of tropical scenery caught in Chinese ports.

A farmer's life was then decided upon; and after two years' training on the lands of others, two winters' partial experience of college life as a special student in the scientific classes at Yale, and a year spent on a farm of his own near New Haven, he purchased a larger farm on the southern side of Staten Island; and this for a number of years was his home. Interested and capable as a farmer, and active in all local public enterprises, his life was further enlarged by the frequent visits of his younger brother, John, then a medical student in New York, and of his brother's friends. Chief among these was Charles Loring Brace, already a budding philanthropist. The friendship of Andrew J. Downing, the well-known landscape-gardener, was also gained at this time, and, while visiting him at his home in Newburg, Mr. Olmsted made the acquaintance of a young English architect, Mr. Calvert Vaux, who was then Downing's partner, and afterward was long and closely associated with himself.

In 1851 the two brothers and Mr. Brace made a pedestrian tour through England, and a short Continental trip. The record of this summer we have in Mr. Olmsted's "Walks and Talks of an American Farmer in England." No more instructive or charming book on rural England has been written, and it throws valuable light upon the writer's personality, proving the genuineness of his love for Nature and simple forms of life, and the keenness of his perceptive faculties. Here and there is a passage of double interest in the light of later facts: a description of the new Birkenhead parks, for instance, which shows that such things were appraised from an intelligent point of view, not carelessly enjoyed as they are by most non-professional tourists; and again, this little preface to the account of Eaton Park:

> What artist so noble, has often been my thought, as he who, with far-reaching conception of beauty and with designing power, sketches the outline, writes the colors, and directs the shadows of a picture so great that Nature shall be employed upon it for generations before the work he has arranged for her shall realize his intentions?

After this journey, life on the farm was resumed and the book was written. A year or two later came the Fillmore election, with its fierce slavery discussions. Mr. Brace was something of an abolitionist; Mr. Olmsted was not, and he felt that the condition of things in the slaveholding States had never been painted impartially. From their conversations resulted Mr. Olmsted's decision to spend the winter traveling through the South, and to report his observations in the pages of "The New-York Times." The following year his brother married Miss Mary Perkins, whose grandfather, a prominent New York physician, was a neighbor on Staten Island and a close friend; and some time later Mr. John Olmsted's failing health brought him and his family to live at the farm; and then, in the belief that change of air and outdoor life would profit the invalid, the brothers determined to spend the winter on horseback, starting from Texas and making their way to California. Indian outbreaks changed their plans, however, and a southward course through Texas was taken, with an excursion over the Mexican border. When Mississippi was reached again in the spring, the younger brother returned to the farm, while Mr. Olmsted, desiring to make a book of his "Times" letters, and believing that he should first know the slave States better, took to his saddle once more, and, accompanied only by a plucky dog, made his way slowly northward to Richmond, Virginia.

Three books resulted from these journeys*—two written by Mr. Olmsted's own hand, the one on Texas put into shape by his brother from his notes. Their picture of the rural communities of the South just before the war has great historical value; but their incidental autobiographical value should not be overlooked. They show that, despite the daydreaming of his boyhood, Mr. Olmsted was an eminently practical person; and no one needs to be practical more than the landscape-gardener. They prove great breadth and strength of human sympathy, and this trait must afterward have inspired him to work enthusiastically and lovingly upon his pleasure-grounds for the poor of our great cities. They are marked by a simplicity, a lack of self-consciousness, which, although the Philistine may not think so, almost always characterizes a true artist. Even more than the "Walks and Talks" they reveal a power of perception keen and catholic enough to excite the envy of a professional reporter; and this faculty is, of course, a needful part of an artist's equipment.

Except from the strictly agricultural standpoint, very little is said about natural scenes in these three books. Yet one hardly needs to hear Mr. Olmsted talk about his Southern journeys to feel that, like his boyish wanderings, like his saunters among English parks and meadows, they helped his artistic development. Camping out of doors daily for many months, always at noontime and in Texas at night as well, he not only made intimate acquaintance with many new phases of natural beauty, but gained practical experience with regard to sites, soils, exposures, prospects—with regard to problems which must always be studied when human habitations are to be founded, or pleasure-grounds or estates laid out.

After his return to the North, Mr. Olmsted gave up his farm to his brother, connected himself as editor with "Putnam's Magazine," and gradually engaged in an allied publishing business. Obliged by this business to go to London, he remained there for half a year, after taking a leisurely little journey through Italy with his sisters, seeing and learning, once more, much that was of future use to him. Difficulties in the New York publishing-house then called him home; and in the year 1856, through no fault of his own, he found himself out of occupation. It was a chance meeting at a little watering-place near New Haven, whither he had gone for quiet with a pile of proof-sheets, that then brought about

---

*"A Journey in the Seaboard Slave States," "A Journey Through Texas," and "A Journey Through the Back Country."

his connection with the newly begun Central Park, and led eventually to a landscape-gardener's career.

A member of the Board of Park Commissioners happened to be Mr. Olmsted's neighbor at table, and told him that they were looking for a superintendent to take practical direction of the work then being done in accordance with a plan prepared by Captain (afterward General) Vielé, who, as engineer, was in chief control of the park. When asked what kind of man was needed, the commissioner replied, "A man like you—one with your agricultural knowledge and your other experience"—referring to Mr. Olmsted's long-cultivated love for nature and to that acquaintance with European parks which was then very rare among Americans. Assured that he spoke in earnest, Mr. Olmsted returned that night to New York, obtained the requisite letters of introduction, and, after some disagreeable experiences, was appointed superintendent.

If these experiences, and others of a like character which persisted and, indeed, grew worse during the whole of Mr. Olmsted's connection with the Central Park, could be recounted, they would make a picturesque bit of biography, and a very instructive one to students of our New York methods of conducting municipal affairs. But I can only explain that while as an artist he was not seriously troubled, and managed to carry out his designs in his own way, practically his path was always filled with rocks and thorns, and at times was almost blocked. In doing public work of any sort no man was ever more grievously hampered by political jealousies, great and small, and the pulling of overhead and underground political wires. In his dealings with certain high-placed officials, as in his management of his humblest workmen, there was never a moment when his hands were unfettered, his mind at leisure for its artistic tasks, his spirit untried by a myriad illegitimate vexations. Nevertheless, by hard personal work, beginning at dawn, after a journey on horseback from his home in Grand street, the new superintendent very quickly made his energy, honesty, and capability felt.

After a few months, work in accordance with General Vielé's plan was stopped, and Mr. Olmsted was given absolute control of the laborers, who, in accordance with his advice, were employed in such preparatory tasks as breaking up stone for roads, and building a low wall around the park borders. Then it was decided to abandon the old plan and to advertise for new ones. At first Mr. Olmsted had no idea of entering the competition; but he was asked by Mr. Vaux to collaborate with him in the preparation of a plan; and being urged by some of the commissioners, and personally ascertaining that his former chief would not resent such action, he accepted the proposal.

The main ideas for the scheme then worked out by the two young men were Mr. Olmsted's, including the one which probably did more than anything else to determine its success—the idea of conducting traffic across the park by means of sunken transverse roads. But Mr. Vaux's part in the task was equally essential. His architectural training fitted him not only to do the actual work of draftsmanship, and to design all structural features, but also to veto, correct, modify, or elaborate the expedients and features proposed by his companion. Together they had all the knowledge and ability required; but alone, Mr. Olmsted is always anxious to explain, he could at that time have done nothing to good purpose. Working almost altogether at night, but reviewing their result on the ground by day, the collaborators barely got their drawings done in time. Thirty-two other sets were presented; all were publicly exhibited and excited much interest; and— of course in the face of some opposition—the plan of Messrs. Olmsted and Vaux was accepted, and they were put in control of its execution, Mr. Olmsted with the title of architect-in-chief and Mr. Vaux as his associate.

The trials and veritable persecutions, more than the normal labors, which then followed, so worked upon Mr. Olmsted in body and mind that in the spring of 1859 he was prostrated by typhoid fever, and, recovering, was ordered to go abroad. He spent the summer chiefly in England, making a very useful tour, completed by a visit to Paris, where Alphand, who was then altering the Bois de Boulogne and creating the new boulevards, showed his young American *confrère* much professional kindness.

On his return to America, Mr. Olmsted married his brother's widow, who, with her three children, had been under his care since his brother's death at Nice eighteen months before; and the new household was soon established in a brick house near the old Convent of the Sacred Heart within the park, while Mr. Vaux lived close at hand in the priest's former dwelling.

Persistently recasting and retouching their design, consolidating their corps of young engineers and gardeners, managing the thousands of workmen who were often rendered insubordinate by the consciousness of political "pulls," and fighting the politicians themselves, the two artists led a life that was no easier than before. It was a perpetual struggle to obtain the money legally at their disposal, while their steps were incessantly dogged by men in search of employment—men often wholly unfit for service, but armed with insistent letters from one "boss" or another. The extent of this latter annoyance may be read in the fact that it was only in moonlight hours that they could walk about the park, to consider what had just been done, and to decide what should next be undertaken. Moreover, a runaway horse, a heavy fall, and a badly broken thigh soon put Mr. Olmsted on his back again. For months he directed the park work from his bed; then he was carried about to superintend it on a litter; for a long time afterward he walked on crutches, and ever since he has been slightly lame.

Yet, in spite of everything, his force of workmen, numbering at last nearly four thousand, practically completed in about four years the great work of making a park of some 800 acres on a singularly unfavorable site. To accomplish this meant not only high artistic power, but indefatigable energy and much organizing, executive ability. In every energetic man there is a fine leaven of combativeness, and the unrighteous obstacles perpetually piled in Mr. Olmsted's path aroused this spirit to righteous intensity. While fighting his own artistic battle he felt that he was fighting, too, the battle for better municipal conditions; and any one who knew him at the time will testify that he threw himself into his park work much as our young soldiers, just then, were throwing themselves into martial combats. Doubtless it was a general recognition of this power of absorbed devotion, as well as of his executive ability, which led Dr. Bellows, the president of the newly formed Sanitary Commission, to ask him to become its secretary—that is, its practical manager. Aware that there was little more work which could then be done on the park, and glad to escape from a life open to the persecutions of local politicians into the service of a nation in distress, Mr. Olmsted accepted the offer, and removed to Washington. He was still on crutches at the time. His work during the next two years was very laborious, the servants coming to set the breakfast-table often finding him still at his night-long tasks; and his health again broke down beneath the strain. But the results of these two years form a bright feature in the history of the war which our people will not forget. I think it may be told that, while his salary had been fixed at $4000, he felt that for doing patriotic service he should accept as little pay as possible, and drew only some $2000 a year.

After severing his connection with the Sanitary Commission, Mr. Olmsted was for two years in California, trying to bring order out of disorder in the affairs of the great Fremont estate at Mariposa, but spending much time in the Yosemite Valley, in an official capacity, and doing much to make the nation understand the national value of this wonderful region. Then he returned to New York,—making an adventurous journey with his family by way of the Nicaragua route,—and formed a partnership with Mr. Vaux; and since that time, during a period of more than twenty-five years, he has steadily devoted himself to the practice of his art.

In 1879 he made another journey to Europe, and, returning in poor health, settled himself at Cambridge, Massachusetts, for a summer of outdoor recreation. The Boston Park Commission had been organized six or eight years before, and had then tentatively consulted Mr. Olmsted. Now it appealed to him again, and he was soon engaged to undertake the redemption of those half-submerged lands in the Back Bay district which he has transformed into a pleasure-ground of uniquely interesting character. This engagement made his residence near Boston desirable; and the presence at Brookline of Richardson, the architect, who had been his neighbor on Staten Island, led him thither. He found Brookline, he says, "the most civilized community in America" as regarded the management of municipal affairs; and there he permanently established his home and his office.

The works to which Mr. Olmsted has set his hand during the past twenty-five years have been very many; and they have been very varied, not only because of diversities in purpose, but because natural conditions, determining artistic conceptions and expedients, differ widely between Massachusetts and California, Montreal and North Carolina, and between seashore, mountain, and lowland sites. Since 1875 an office record of his chief undertakings has been kept. It mentions thirty-seven public pleasure-grounds; twelve suburban districts which have been laid out in preparation for the building of villas; the grounds of eleven public buildings and hospitals, thirteen colleges, four large schools, four railroad stations, and twelve considerable private estates; and also the names of some two hundred clients, to whom, in addition, Mr. Olmsted has given actual service or advice.

Some of the undertakings mentioned in this list have, of course, been much more important than others; some were fully carried out under Mr. Olmsted's direction, while in others his plans were not faithfully executed, and in most of them he has not worked alone. At first, as we know, Mr. Vaux was his partner; since 1875 his son, Mr. John C. Olmsted, has held this place; it is now held also by Mr. Charles Eliot, son of the president of Harvard University, and was held by Mr. Henry Sargent Codman for some time previous to his untimely death in 1892. But these three young men studied their profession in Mr. Olmsted's office, and were trained upon work which he had designed; and whatever deductions we can possibly make from the sum total of his own work, there remains a remarkable amount as the achievement of twenty-five years, and by a man whose health has not been robust.

It is difficult to name the most interesting among Mr. Olmsted's creations. From the artistic point of view, the largest do not deserve this distinction merely because of their size, or the most beautiful merely because of their beauty. A comparatively small piece of work, less perfect in its beauty than some others, may best prove a landscape-gardener's power, as having been wrought amid unusually hampering conditions— as being a blossom of art plucked from the nettle difficulty. Prospect Park, Brooklyn, for instance, may easily be thought more beautiful than Central Park; but to an eye which remembers what its site originally was, Central Park will always seem Mr. Olmsted's greatest achievement of the kind.

Again, Beacon Parkway in Boston (more often called the Back Bay Fens), to which I have already referred, may be less immediately impressive than certain pleasure-grounds of a normal sort; but it fills us with peculiar admiration when we realize the cause of its singularity— the need that wide sunken marshy tracts, alternately overflowed and left partly bare by tidewaters, should be so redeemed and beautified that they might appropriately be bridged by streets and surrounded with rows of city dwellings. Riverside Drive in New York, and the adjacent Morningside Park, are other instances of peculiar problems very successfully treated—instances which would be still more impressive had Mr. Olmsted's plans been faithfully carried out. Again, I may name the Arnold Arboretum, where the aim was to accommodate a scientific collection of trees and yet make a beautiful public pleasure-ground; and if I were as familiar with Mr. Olmsted's Western as with his Eastern work, I might add other examples of equal individuality.

But of one great Western example I hardly need to speak. Every American knows how beautiful are the Chicago World's Fair Grounds, how wholly the chance to make them beautiful has sprung from Mr. Olmsted's preliminary treatment, and how singularly novel, how boldly imaginative, as well as practical and skilful, this treatment has been. Every one who honors a great and conscientious, a public-spirited and widely useful, artist must be glad that Mr. Olmsted had this conspicuous opportunity to win his fellow-countrymen's praise; and every one who loves the art he practises must rejoice that, in thus distinguishing himself, he has lifted landscape-gardening to a higher place than it ever held before in the interest and respect of our public.

But in doing this he has merely carried on a great educational work which began with the creation of Central Park.

Thirty-five years ago there were no large public pleasure-grounds in America. No city possessed more than a few small squares, with, perhaps, a tract of common-land inherited from primitive days of public pasturage, carpet-beating, and musket practice. These seldom had anything of the beauty which Downing had conferred upon Lafayette Square in Washington; collectively they were quite inadequate to the needs of the day, much more inadequate to the evident needs of the future; and there was nothing in the suburbs to supplement them except the cemetery, while the way in which this was frequented by pleasure-seekers showed that something else was indeed required.

Even in Europe large pleasure-grounds, public in the modern sense, were comparative novelties. They had been among the good results of that limiting of kingly prerogatives and that breaking down of aristocratic barriers with which our century opened, and which were repeated, more quietly but more effectually, in the revolutionary days of 1848. When city walls were destroyed, their sites were utilized for extensive boulevards and promenades, while royal and princely parks, gardens, hunting-preserves, and forests were thrown open to the people. Forty years ago some of these were still nearly in their old condition; others had been remodeled into greater efficiency, and new areas were being specially fitted for the public's use.

But when a few wise citizens determined to give New York a large park, few Americans realized the benefits of such places, and still fewer believed that they should be formed here after European patterns. Seeing the decorous, law-abiding, rule-respecting throngs which now fill Central Park of a Sunday afternoon in spring,—throngs much larger and of much more motley composition than were anticipated in the fifties,—it is amusing to know that, when the plan of Messrs. Olmsted and Vaux was accepted, some of our influential citizens cried: "Such a park is too aristocratic to be sanctioned in America, too artistic to be respected by the American populace. It would be an unrepublican waste of money to make it, for only the rich would use it; or, if the poor used it, they would quickly destroy its beauty." One well-known architect declared in a newspaper letter that our people should have a rustic pleasure-ground, not an elegant park; that the thing to do was to fence in the area, introduce cows and geese, let them make the paths, and let the public enjoy the result with perfect freedom. And another prominent person said that the place should be turned into a forest,—planted preferably with Ontario poplars alone, as they grow very quickly,—and then given over to the unaided ministrations of Nature. I fancy that these gentlemen now realize they were mistaken; but their mistakes excellently explain the great responsibility which rested upon Mr. Olmsted and Mr. Vaux. Had their park been a failure, artistically or practically, the making of public parks in America would have been retarded during many years—during years each of which would have rendered the acquisition of suitable lands more difficult and costly. But their success was quickly achieved, was as triumphantly apparent on the side of utility as on the side of beauty, and was welcomed with pride and respect by all the people of New York. Indeed, the whole country soon learned to feel a pride in Central Park, and a respect for the ideas upon which its formation had been based; and the result shows today in the scores of public parks possessed by American cities large and small.

Of course it is not yet a result with which we are satisfied. Hundreds of towns and villages still need to be impressed with the fact that they should secure public pleasure-grounds without another year's delay; and the people at large need to be awakened to the vital concern they have in the right management and quick enlargement of their magnificent possessions in the mountains of the East and the West. But who can compute how far behind even our present condition we might have been to-day had not an artist of Mr. Olmsted's force, intelligence, versatility, and public spirit been given us at just the most critical time? At no other time and in no other place, I think, could Mr. Olmsted have served the cause of art and the cause of humanity so well. And I may lay special stress upon his versatility—upon that originality in conception to which I have already referred. The works in which it most prominently appears have more than an intrinsic value. They have a widely instructive value as showing that there can hardly be a site upon which the hand of an artist may not confer serviceableness and charm; that, therefore, no city, whatever its natural resources, need despair of possessing a satisfactory pleasure-ground.

Serviceableness and charm—these are the two qualities which every work of landscape-art, like every work of architecture, should possess. But as problems vary, so too does the degree of attention which should be concentrated upon each of these qualities. When we wish to pass judgment upon any given piece of work, it is as needful to remember this fact as to remember the limiting, directing force of pre-existing natural conditions. And when we understand it clearly, we see that success in the art to-day proves higher ability than was demanded a hundred and fifty years ago. It is evident that it must be more difficult to create or preserve beauty in a park which is daily visited by many thousand people—passing on foot, on horseback, and in carriages, and demanding facilities for the sports of men and of children—than to do as much in a private estate of the same size. It is evident, too, that the greater the area, the greater the difficulty, if only because in a very large park a wise artist will strive for more distinctively rural effects than in a smaller one—for more of the broad charm of scenery as distinguished from the charm of successive landscape passages; and because character of this kind lends itself least readily to the incorporation of a multitude of useful artificial features. Mr. Olmsted's success in securing such character, even amid natural conditions as unfavorable as those offered by the site of Central Park, has been very remarkable, but not more remarkable than his ability to secure the utmost practical efficiency in combination with it. His uniting of these qualities—utility and broad, simple, impressive landscape beauty—in so many discreetly varied ways, gives him, I think, an unrivaled position among the dead and living masters of his craft. Nor should it be forgotten that he had to teach himself how to do such work as this. I do not think that there are any large parks in Europe which offer such varied facilities for the refreshment and recreation of the great mass of the people as do the best of ours; and moreover, most of the European parks which at all resemble ours are—at least in their present estate—younger than Central Park.

Catholicity is another distinguishing mark of Mr. Olmsted's art. Despite his preponderant love for the naturalistic style in its broadest, simplest developments, he is quick to see when the formal, architectural style puts in a valid claim; and he realizes that even the most naturalistic landscape-work should not strive to appear actually natural, and should even incorporate distinctly formal elements when they are required for use or for the right explanation of art as art.

But neither catholicity of taste nor versatility in conception has led Mr. Olmsted into the great mistake of confusing radically different ideals. Formal elements may enter into a naturalistic scheme, freely treated elements into a formal scheme; gardenesque features may be furnished somewhere in a park; park-like vistas may open from a garden; or, indeed, a pleasure-ground may have a clearly confessed composite character. But whatever its character, there must be a clear confession of it. We should be left in no doubt as to the broad ideal which guided the artist, the general impression he tried to produce. This great fact Mr. Olmsted always remembers, and the public has learned from him at least some vague knowledge of the truth that not all pleasure-grounds should be designed on the same principles or judged by the same artistic canons. The confusion which still, however, prevails with regard to this matter is revealed by the lax use of all the terms involved, and especially of the word *park,* which has been so misused that we seldom remember it has any distinctive meaning at all. Mr. Olmsted knows, of course, that any lax use of terms tends to deepen the confusion from which it sprang; and he has steadily tried to teach artists, clients, and the public better verbal habits. For this reason—but by no means for this alone—his articles in various cyclopedias, and the many reports upon his works and explanations of his ideas with regard to proposed works which he has written, should be sought out by all students of landscape-gardening. In short, he has not been merely a capable, diligent artist: he has been in all directions an apostle of his art, crying in a wilderness, truly, but not without finding some eager and intelligent disciples whose number, I am sure, will now rapidly increase. This fact, and not only his last pronounced triumph at Chicago, was fittingly recognized during the past summer when, on the same day, the universities of Harvard and Yale conferred upon him their highest honorary degrees.

I do not dare to dwell upon those more personal traits which have assisted Mr. Olmsted's high artistic gifts in establishing his influence. His friends understand and deeply appreciate them, and they must have impressed to some degree even the most casual client. But they could hardly be explained to strangers, and in making the attempt I fear I should give more pain than pleasure to a singularly gentle and modest spirit which does not yet realize why anything that concerns it must be interesting to the world at large.

It may seem almost as though mere chance had determined that Mr. Olmsted should be an artist. But the best chance can profit no man who is not well prepared to turn it into opportunity. If, at the age of thirty-four, Mr. Olmsted had not been fitted for a landscape-gardener's tasks, the chance which made him superintendent of the workmen in Central Park could not have led him on to the designing of parks; while, on the other hand, knowing how well fitted for such tasks he was, we feel that if just this opportunity had not offered, another would somehow have presented itself.

In the conduct of Mr. Olmsted's education up to the age of thirty-four, chance certainly played a preponderant rôle. But we should not therefore decide that a landscape-gardener's education may always be accidental, or even that it may be modeled consciously upon Mr. Olmsted's unconscious course. This course sufficed, with him, to develop that creative power which must always rest upon a reasoning, analyzing love for beauty, upon a sense for the harmonious, the fitting, the appropriate, as regards the application of special kinds of beauty to special purposes, and upon practical judgment as determining which among possible fitting schemes may most wisely be selected. But, while similar experiences could not fail to have much good effect upon any sensitive spirit, what sufficed with Mr. Olmsted would probably not have sufficed with another. It is safe to say that, as a rule, a landscape-gardener's creative power must indeed be nourished by long contemplation of nature, but also by systematic study of art; and I may add that a knowledge of art is often the influence which best develops an intelligent eye for nature.

Again, while Mr. Olmsted's equipment has proved itself extraordinarily fine in some directions, it has been deficient in others. His statement that without the collaboration of Mr. Vaux he could not have presented a plan for Central Park, shows how needful a thorough knowledge of architecture, engineering, and draftsmanship is to the landscape-gardener. Much knowledge of this sort Mr. Olmsted has since acquired, and his power of architectural conception is sufficiently proved by the single fact that it was he who perceived the necessity for those great marble terraces which have incalculably increased the architectural excellence of the Capitol in Washington.

But, as he would be quick to tell you, he has always been hampered by his lack of practical knowledge with regard to plants. This has forced him to depend upon others, in the execution of his works, even more than every busy landscape-gardener must; and it may also have limited his imagination somewhat, at least in relation to matters of detail. When defects exist in his work, they are sure to be defects in treatment, not in design—mistakes or shortcomings in the elaboration of his scheme, not in the scheme itself, not in the fundamental artistic conception. Here great intelligence and good taste always reveal themselves, and remarkable originality very often; and with a more thorough technical training the same qualities would undoubtedly always have marked all the minor features and details of his work.

In short, Mr. Olmsted's peculiar education, so deep and rich in some directions, so scanty in others, acting upon a singularly receptive yet naturally analytical temperament,—a temperament at once poetic and keenly, practically observant,—gave him an imaginative force which has probably not been equaled in the history of landscape-gardening in any land. But it did not perfect his executive skill, and this deficiency he has been unable to repair entirely during a long life of diligent application to the problems and resources of his art. Would-be landscape-gardeners should remember that they can hardly count upon offsetting blanks in their training by natural abilities as remarkable as his, and that most likely they do not possess temperaments as well adapted as his to profit by what I may call a passive course of education. They should remember that genius can learn much where talent or mere intelligence would gather sparse instruction, and may go very far with an equipment which would carry talent, stumbling, only a little way.

Proposed Plan for Madison Square, New York City

On another page are reproduced the plan of Madison Square, in this city, as it is to-day, and a plan for its rearrangement which was shown at the recent Architectural League Exhibition, by Messrs. Bell & Langton, landscape-architects.

Sixty years ago few buildings, except rural ones, stood north of Union Square, and the area now called Madison Square was an open tract some ten acres in extent, in the centre of which stood a House of Refuge for unruly boys—an altogether neglected and unsightly tract, of which the only useful feature was a little pond used for skating in the winter. When the House of Refuge burned in 1839, efforts were made to improve the place, but nothing substantial was accomplished until the mayoralty of James Harper, between the years 1844 and 1847. This was some ten years before Central Park was thought of, and although Downing had already done some of his best work, he had not yet laid out those urban squares in Washington which first showed American eyes what might be accomplished in this direction.

When studied on paper the plan of Madison Square shows the working of design, not of accident; yet its treatment is so petty and monotonous, so wanting alike in broad unity, in effective variety and in conspicuous points of interest, that, we believe, few New Yorkers realize

---

Garden and Forest 9 (April 8, 1896): 142–144.

that it has any plan at all. When seen from the encircling streets it has a pleasantly verdurous and shady look, and it contains some very good trees, an Elm which stands near its north-easterly corner, opposite the University Club, being the most symmetrical and beautiful tree which New York possesses south of Central Park. But its trees are not properly grouped—they are simply scattered about. Its lack of shrubs permits the surrounding houses to reveal themselves too clearly from all points of view, and deprives it of that charm of mystery, contrast and surprise which may be achieved even within very narrow limits if shrubberies are artistically employed. It affords no proper place for the display of flower-beds, and none for the proper placing of statues. The one virtue of the design is that those who wish to cross the park diagonally may do so with reasonable directness. And its chief defect is that its many minor paths cut up its lawns so pitilessly that the eye nowhere rests upon a quiet, reposeful stretch of green.

Truly naturalistic schemes of park design are, of course, more difficult to manage well on a small than on a large scale; and they are not as appropriate as others when the architectural surroundings of the pleasure-ground are of an obtrusively urban sort. Therefore, Messrs. Bell & Langton have sensibly conceived their rearrangement of Madison Square upon semi-formal lines. It may appear that in drawing their main paths anew they have made diagonal circulation less direct; but measurements show that, if anything, they have shortened the diagonal courses. By suppressing the minor paths they have won space for wide lawns. Yet the accommodation for strollers and for playing children, and for rows of seats as well, which is lost in this way, is more than made good by the broad mall which forms the central feature of their design, the two parallel paths which lie beyond its flanking flower-beds, and the large open circles which surround the basin that now exists, and the one which they indicate as balancing it toward the north. The formal flower-beds, thus properly conceived as important parts of a formal scheme, would be effective and delightful in themselves and would increase that beauty of general effect which they ruin when they are intruded into a purely naturalistic scheme. The Farragut Monument is left in its present place, while its back is screened by shrubs, as was intended when it was built. The statues of Seward and Conklin, which now look as though they had been dropped down by accident, are properly incorporated with the more formal part of the pleasure-ground. The kiosk, a necessary convenience, has rightly been removed to a less conspicuous station and discreetly screened by foliage on all sides.

In explaining their design Messrs. Bell & Langton say that the improvements they suggest would be accomplished with "no sacrifice worth mentioning of the existing trees," while those that would necessarily be removed would be compensated for by their new central avenue. They point out that "the careful planning of the shrub-planting has isolated the formal centre" of their design from the noisy streets on all sides, although particular care has been taken to avoid interference with the cooling breezes so grateful in summer. "It would probably prove advisable in execution," they add, "to follow the accepted rule of utilizing a number of species, though we propose so to concentrate these as to make effective masses of one or two kindred species which blossom or fruit at the same season, thus providing a constant succession of attractive blossoming throughout the year. But a more satisfactory and artistic proceeding in a city like New York would be to treat the entire park as a unit, filling it with trees and shrubs all of which reach their prime of beauty at the same season. Thus, if Madison Square were so planted as to blossom in May, it might be made an object of enjoyment and pilgrimage not only to New Yorkers, but to the residents of the entire neighborhood. When this blossoming season was over, the flowers in the formal garden, set in the green park, would take up the succession and carry it through the year. One of the other parks might be so planned as to bloom later in the summer, and yet another to be at its prime in the autumn."

This is an interesting suggestion, yet there are some reasons against its adoption in a large and busy city like New York. The pleasure of the majority should be chiefly considered. The majority of those who enjoy our small parks are the persons who have the habit of frequenting the same one day by day, or who pass it perforce in their daily round to and from their places of business, or whose windows look out upon it. And these people might—I do not say that they would—prefer to have their park display as many as possible of the beauties characteristic of each season in turn rather than to find it supremely attractive at any one season.

But, be this as it may, Madison Square would be improved for all seasons if it were rearranged according to Messrs. Bell & Langton's plan. This does not mean that the plan is faultless. In the first place, its authors were obliged to accept the trees as they stand instead of conceiving their plantations as an harmonious whole. Then, this fact puts difficulties in the way of shrub-planting; for, while many shrubs grow well under trees if they are planted when the trees are, and become well established before the ground is shaded, it is harder to induce them to thrive when set after the associated trees have attained their growth. And, finally, an actual mistake may be pointed out in the new plan: lawns which run to sharp points are undesirable in public pleasure-grounds because unruly feet are almost certain to trample upon these points, and also because the grass will dry out and the lawn-mower does not easily reach them. Nevertheless, considering the attendant difficulties, the plan is interesting. It is published here less with the idea that Madison Square may actually be renovated according to its indications than in the belief that a comparison of it with the existing state of the Square will be instructive to those charged with the arrangement of new small parks in this and other cities. Sometimes, even in small urban parks, conspicuous features may prescribe a naturalistic method of treatment. This was the case, for example, on Mount Morris Park, in Harlem, where the existence of a bold rocky hill, as tall as the surrounding houses, inspired the reservation of the tract around it. But such instances are very rare. As a rule, a formal or semi-formal manner of treatment, resulting in a pleasure-ground which is properly to be called a large garden rather than a park, must be most appropriate for restricted areas in the heart of a great city. And Messrs. Bell & Langton show that such a manner of treatment need not exclude variety in design, abundance of shade, the reposeful effect of wide green lawns, or even such seemingly unstudied, yet artistic, arrangements of trees, shrubs and grass as may produce pleasingly naturalistic impressions and illusions.

Japanese Gardening

One of the best accounts of the aims and results of Japanese landscape gardening that have ever been written in English was published in a periodical which seldom comes beneath the eyes of the general public— the *Transactions of the Asiatic Society of Japan.* Therefore, although it bears date as long ago as November, 1886, a brief summary of it may not be unacceptable. It is itself, however, so condensed, as well as so full of varied and interesting information, that I can do no more than select passages here and there, with the confession that almost all those omitted are of equal value.

"Landscape gardening as practiced in Europe," says the author—Mr. J. Conder, a Fellow of the Royal Institute of British Architects—"is subjected to greater formalities of design than in Japan, and in theory it harmonizes less closely with the features and disposition of real scenery. It is more of a science and less of a fine art." Even in our most naturally designed gardens a certain element of formality is prescribed by the canons of European taste. "Houses being objects exhibiting formal and geometrical lines, it is maintained that such lines should be repeated to a greater or less extent in the adjoining garden, in order to produce an approximate combination." And this feeling expresses itself in details as well as in the general scheme; "trees and shrubs are often selected for

Garden and Forest 2 (January 30, 1889): 51–52.

their uniformity in size and shape, and grouped in equidistant rows and phalanxes," while it is unnecessary to refer to our use of formal flower beds and minor features. The Japanese have attained to no such skill in the cultivation of exotic plants as has been attained in Europe, "but the absence of such artificial refinements is considerably to the advantage" of landscape gardening as a fine art. "Constructing only with the materials native to the country, the designer is able to follow consistently the arrangements suggested by nature, the landscapes he seeks to reproduce being in all cases identical with the natural types that are familiar to him." As regards scale, the gardens of Japan are far less imposing than those of Europe. "There is little here to compare in gardens to our spacious English parks. . . . The Japanese artist confines himself to narrower and humbler lines, but it must be recognized that within his limits he produces results unrivaled in natural beauty and loveliness. . . . Unnatural regularity is generally most studiously avoided, but the variety obtained is the result of well considered arrangement, and by no means that of hazard."

The theory of the art, like so many other intellectual things, was derived from China, but greater simplicity prevails in Japanese developments. "It is usual to divide garden compositions into three styles expressive of their general character, . . . the Finished, or labored style, Intermediate style, and Free, or bold style. In practice these styles are not sharply divided, but a garden, according to its rough or elaborated character, may generally be classed under one of the three heads, . . . and it is an important law that whatever character is decided upon should be consistently followed throughout." The Finished, or elaborate style, is the one least commonly employed. "There are other guiding principles, . . . such as suitability in character to the pursuits and rank of the proprietor . . . and the expression . . . of some predominating sentiment. The garden is regarded as a poem or picture intended to arouse particular associations and inspire some worthy sentiment. . . . If, for instance, a garden be designed for a poet or philosopher, its general disposition should express dignified seclusion, solitude, virtue, or self-abnegation." It is difficult for us, with our less strongly poetic temperament, to sympathize with such aims or even to see how they can be effectually carried out or clearly understood. But to the Japanese the thing seems clear and simple enough, and with the following paragraph even Europeans should be in heartiest accord: Gardens, it is said, should be undertaken from a genuine love of nature "and with a desire of enjoying the beauties of natural scenery, and should be so arranged that the four seasons may each contribute in turn to their artistic excellence. They should be pleasant retreats for hours of leisure and idleness; and as one writer has poetically expressed it, 'places to stroll in when aroused from sleep.' ... In western designs the idea of displaying wealth and luxury is paramount, and our gardens are principally regarded as resorts for the pleasures of society and fashion; whereas in Japanese gardens the prevailing intention is rather that of a place exempt from public haunts and fitted for unrestrained ease and meditation." Such ideas as The Happiness of Retirement, Modesty, Peace, Gentleness and Chastity, Connubial Felicity and Old Age, the Japanese strive to express in their arrangements. In part their success depends upon the emotions naturally excited by scenery of various kinds, but in part upon traditional historical or philosophical meanings which are associated with many of the arrangements adopted, and, of course, cannot be understood by foreigners.

Passing from theory to practice, Mr. Conder notes that the first step in the artist's education is to visit good scenery and make notes and sketches. These, of course, "cannot be closely followed in preparing designs, but will supply suggestions and lead to originality in composition. ... Before proceeding to execute a landscape-garden a careful survey of the site and its surroundings is necessary. If it be a bare and level area, the designer is free to arrange his composition in any way that he may please according to its size, bearing in mind the locality and surroundings, and the character of garden suited to the particular proprietor. But if it be a site possessing natural facilities, such as fine trees in prominent positions, hillocks, a stream, or even a natural cascade, the artist will consider how such natural features can be utilized and worked into his design. ... A neighboring view may be cleverly taken advantage of, and the garden so arranged as to harmonize with it, the distant landscape when seen from the rooms of the house actually appearing to form part of the whole composition. Aspect must be considered as well as prospect. ... Great care is recommended in considering the scale of a garden. If a small garden be arranged on the same plan as one of a larger model, it will look weak and unsatisfactory; and ... if a large garden be designed upon the lines of a smaller model, it will lose all its grandeur. ... For example, the arrangement of two or three large rocks in front of a clump of fine trees in a large garden will look more imposing than a greater number of smaller ones. Multiplicity of detail within small compass is, however, necessary in a little garden, in order to give it interest and add to its apparent scale. ... A garden is, above all, a place for summer enjoyment, . . . and must therefore, by all means, look cool and refreshing; but such coolness is not produced by planting trees too densely and crowding the area with many objects. A few masses of foliage, judiciously arranged in the background, may be made to impart a fresh and cool effect. The presence or suggestion of water is necessary; but it must be remembered that clean, shallow and running water looks much cooler than deep, stagnant or weed-covered pools. The total absence of litter and untidiness, added to the presence of water, produces the most refreshing effect. A garden, therefore, should have large, open spaces, cleanly kept, with stretches of white sand or gravel in the foreground and moss in the background. . . . In large compositions the distribution of areas and contours demands the first attention. In some cases advantage will be taken of natural elevations and depressions in the ground. Sometimes a site may possess a stream, cascade or natural inlet of water. Supposing no such facilities exist, the aspect and prospect which the plot possesses will be carefully studied, and the best positions for hill and dale, lake and waterfall, determined. It often happens that water cannot be obtained; and if the character of the scene to be represented requires it, it is not unusual to arrange the hills, rocks and plants in such a way that the idea of water may be suggested. Sometimes a stretch of bare, beaten, brown earth or of well-raked sand will indicate a lake or sea, and a meandering, pebbly bed a river, the surrounding rocks, plants and piles further assisting the delusion." No rules strictly direct such arrangements, yet several general guiding principles are respected, for a Japanese garden is "more than an artistic disposition of trees, flowers, shrubs and stones. It is a real picture composition, intended to represent some imaginary landscape. . . . The principle of suggesting to the imagination the idea of space by means of blanks and obliterations, so common in Japanese pictorial art, is followed also in horticultural compositions. A hill, it is said, should never be constructed touching an outer fence or boundary; a space behind it, however small, produces an idea of greater extension of the garden. By a similar theory the spaces immediately behind the nearer hills should be left open and not filled with detail. There are five principal hills specified for gardens . . . in the Finished style. Hill No. 1 forms the most central feature of the nearer distance. . . . As it represents a near mountain of considerable size, it should have broad and sweeping sides, and may have a pathway and a little house or pavilion upon it. Hill No. 2 should be placed adjacently to No. 1, a cascade and rocks often dividing the space between the two. It is secondary to No. 1, and should be somewhat smaller and of different character. Hill No. 3 is placed upon the other side of No. 1 near the base of its broad slope and more in the foreground; it suggests the idea of a lower hill divided from the main mountain by a depression. This depression may be supposed to be occupied by a hamlet, road or stream, in which case its sides should be clothed with a few thick-foliaged trees or shrubs to add to the impression of a sheltered and inhabited dale. No. 4 is a small hill generally introduced into the near foreground; it should have none of the characteristics of a large mountain, should be low, rounded and covered with much detail in the form of stones, shrubs and flowers. Hill No. 5 is in the remotest part of the garden, and, as it represents a distant mountain, it should be steep and mysterious without much detail."

This, then, in general terms, is the scheme upon which a Japanese constructs one type of garden, varying it, of course, in multitudinous ways to suit the suggestions of the site or the leanings of his individual taste. It may seem at first thought as though, while avoiding artificiality in one direction, the artist who works thus falls into it in another direction— our idea of a "natural" landscape arrangement is certainly not the wholesale creation of features which sometimes are not even suggested by the site, nor the simulating in miniature of large natural forms, nor the effort to make sand or gravel do duty for water or small shrubs produce the effect of trees. Could anything, we ask ourselves, be more unnatural than a small garden designed to imitate an expanse of mountain scenery, with bare earth instead of living water for its lakes and streams?

But it seems to me, after much reading upon the subject, that the Japanese aim is not more wholly different from ours than is the spirit in which this people looks at works of gardening art. It is often said that they have less imagination than Occidentals; but the statement refers merely to abstract imagination, so to say—to metaphysical, spiritual imagination. As regards material imagination—the picture-making power of the eye, the ability to recognize, appreciate and enjoy the beauty and sentiment of a thing which is not actually imitated or even portrayed in art, but merely suggested—the case is exactly the reverse. Here the Oriental imagination is much stronger than our own. Whether we try, in our garden arrangements, to be formal and architectural, or natural and free, we demand that the desired effect shall be actually, practically, materially obtained, that the things we see shall be literally themselves, and depend not at all for their significance upon the imaginative faculties of the observer. The Japanese, on the other hand, never desires anything but a strictly natural effect; but he is content that it shall be suggested rather than displayed. The elements before him are valued less for themselves than for their power to act upon his imagination and recall the forms of beauty which they typify rather than reproduce. We demand in a natural garden that it shall be a beautiful passage of scenery. The Japanese demands that it shall suggest a beautiful passage of scenery. His garden is to him less a landscape, properly so called, than a picture of a landscape; and he does not see anything more unnatural in a small picture composed of piles of earth, rocks and shrubs representing mountains, trees and lakes, than we see in a small painting on canvas when it represents similar objects. We know that an adequate statue of a man can be made within the compass of a few inches, and never think of questioning its truth or "naturalness" because of its size. It does not purport to be the man, but merely suggests the man, and our imagination accepts it without thought of its discrepancies in size and color. Thus the Japanese looks upon his little studies of mountain scenery, and finds them as thoroughly natural as works of art can be.

How soon an Occidental can learn to assume his standpoint, how thoroughly he can learn to appreciate the suggestive beauty of Japanese gardens—these are questions, of course, with regard to which only travelers can speak, and Mr. Conder does not touch upon them.

The Protection of Road-Sides

To the Editor of *Garden and Forest:*

Sir,—No service your paper can perform is more needed, I think, than the awakening of our rural communities to a sense of the beauty of properly treated road-sides, and a feeling that this beauty has its useful side in making their localities attractive to summer visitors. You have named and rightly found fault with road-side devastators of various kinds. But there is one whom, as yet, I do not think you have held up to public condemnation. This is the lineman, who is perpetually stretching or re-stretching his wires between even our remotest villages. If he works in other districts as barbarically as he worked near Buzzard's Bay last summer, he is not the least harmful of our rural vandals.

Last summer the telegraph lines were repaired between the village of Marion, where I live, and the towns of Wareham, four miles away in one direction, and of Mattapoisett, five miles away in another. And there was not an eighth of a mile in this nine-mile stretch where wreck and ruin had not been wrought. Of course, the big, new poles shone out a ghastly yellow against the background of foliage which largely borders these nine miles of highway. But one did not complain of that, for it was felt to be inevitable, and, moreover, one knew that under Nature's treatment during a single winter they would weather to a more peaceful

Garden and Forest 6 (March 8, 1893): 115–116.

gray. But the new poles were a good deal taller than the old ones, although to the non-professional eye there seemed no reason why they should be; and in planting them not the slightest care had been taken to do the work in even a rationally conservative spirit. Here, a big Pine-tree had been ruthlessly cut down to give place to a pole which, one felt, might just as well have been set on a neighboring spot where no tree chanced to stand. There, the splendid branches which partially shaded the road had been lopped off as roughly as though by stone hatchets, to admit the free passage of the lifted wires; and almost always more had been thus lopped than the position of the wires demanded. Moreover, shrubbery and smaller trees had been recklessly cleared for the greater convenience of the workmen, and all the debris of big boughs and withered foliage had been left to spoil the beauty of the road-side during the entire summer. Of course, the damage was greater in some spots than in others; but it was so great in many that the aspect of a stretch of road which, before, had been beautifully natural and bowery, was changed into a resemblance with the aspect of the edge of some rude settler's clearing.

We do not pride ourselves greatly on our trees near Marion, but we do pride ourselves on our shrubs and creepers and flowers. The luxuriance with which they grow is surprising, and the borders they make, not only along our wood-roads but along our high-roads too, are of wonderful and very varied beauty. Almost everywhere, on the high-roads, there is a wide strip of waste land between the road proper (or improper—for many of the road-beds are extremely bad) and the rough stone fences which enclose the fields. And this waste land is apt to be thickly overgrown with shrubs and young trees along the fences, and with lower flowering vegetation near the road-bed, forming natural hedges as beautiful as those in any English lane.

But it is not only the linemen who interfere with these, the most strikingly beautiful features of our landscape. The road commissioners or highway commissioners (I do not know their legal title in Plymouth County, but their proper title is road-agents or highwaymen) whet their scythes when their private acres have been mown, and go forth about the middle of August to dull them along the road-sides. There seems no science or art, no reason or plan in their work. Here, where the wild border actually encroaches upon the road, it is left in peace; there, where it discreetly keeps its distance, it is pitilessly cut down clean back to the stone wall. Occasionally one sees the taller, more distant growth left intact; but one feels it has been by accident, not by design, for at the next step some perfectly wanton act of vandalage is noted. Fortunately, road-side Nature is so bountiful and energetic with us that, when one returns the following summer, the signs of August depredation are not often painfully visible—that is, they are not to unaccustomed eyes; it is only the eyes of the old resident which remember that here, where there used to be lovely tall thickets of wild Roses and Viburnum and tangles of luxuriant vines, there is now only rough grass and the sprouts of bushes and vines to come.

Where road-side growth is so very luxuriant, some trimming and pruning, and even cutting down, must, of course, annually be done; but there is no excuse for doing it so recklessly, and in the middle of summer, when many weeks of rich beauty are still possible, and no excuse for leaving the mowed-down plants in dead brown heaps. It is dismal and exasperating to see, where yesterday there were long broad patches of Golden-rod just bursting into bloom, to-day long broad piles of brown rubbish, hideously ugly in themselves, and destructive to the effect of the hedge-rows or forest-edges which lie beyond them. But Golden-rod is not the only plant which is thus piled up along our drives. Young Maples and Pines and Tupelos, which, if thinned discreetly, or even if left to themselves, would eventually shade tracts of road which now are hot and sunny, are felled without mercy, and likewise left to rot slowly on the spot, often to its disfigurement during more than one subsequent season. It is, indeed, fortunate for us that our soil is exceptionally favorable to the growth of way-side vegetation; for, otherwise, it is impossible to say how soon the loveliest portions of our high-road borders might be rendered wholly barren by the road-agent's scythe.

Changes

To explain with any fulness how the arts that are the subject of this book have fared in America during the last thirty years one would need to view the country from Portland in Maine to Portland in Oregon and from the winter colony at Miami to the Great Lakes in one direction, to Los Angeles in another. But from one's own part of the country and from pictures, printed pages, and word of mouth one may learn enough to speak in brief of main facts and general tendencies.

Such evidence makes it plain that landscape-architecture is a much more widely practiced art and is more ambitious and more versatile than it was a generation ago. And I think it is also true that good taste has developed together with enterprise. Some of the strictures in the earlier chapters of this book should now be modified if not expunged, and some of the warnings are not so greatly needed. For example, the cutting of trees which are injuring others or marring the general beauty of the scene is not now so commonly regarded as an act of heartless vandalism. The unfit use of rough fieldstones or boulders in constructions large and small has no longer the vogue that it had for a time, although,

---

Art Out-of-Doors: Hints on Good Taste in Gardening (New York: Charles Scribner's Sons, 1925), 389–429. *Art Out-of-Doors* was originally published in 1893. At the suggestion of the publisher, Van Rensselaer republished the book in 1925 with the addition of three new chapters and two appendixes. The chapter reprinted here was one of the new chapters.

I confess, I recently saw a sad instance of it in a village memorial to soldiers killed in France. Hardy shrubs are more generally used instead of mere flower-beds to unite the foundations of a building with the ground. The weeping willow is no longer, I think, greatly beloved. The liking for trees and shrubs of peculiar color, whether one-toned, striped, or mottled, seems to have waned. And, very evidently, so has the love for brightly colored pattern-beds in inappropriate places or of kinds that in any place are indefensible. Such beds no longer deface the wide emerald lawns at Newport, in the Boston Public Garden they do not so greatly abound, and, so I am assured by a correspondent on the spot, even in the parks of Chicago, the parks which used to be in this respect the worst of all possible offenders, "they have gone out of fashion."

But there are sins to set against our new virtues. We have been invaded, in park and cemetery, in spacious pleasure-grounds and smallest dooryards, by the most afflicting shrub in cultivation, planted in great masses or spotted about in casual profusion. I mean the panicled hydrangea, *H. paniculata grandiflora,* whose huge, tight, white, oval floral heads are much too large and too numerous for the weak sprawling body that bears them, are out of scale with everything else in the way of flowers, and long persist after they have turned to an ugly pinkish brown. Fortunately, the misguided passion for it seems now to be waning. May it soon follow the coleus-bed into the discard! Not in the same way distressing to the eye but to the taste that values good sense and fitness are the veritable plantations of delicate little flowering plants now often set between the flags of our garden walks. It is fancied, I suppose, that they look as though they had spontaneously discovered the cracks. But even if they could thus deceive us they would still be out of place, forcing us to tread uncomfortably upon pretty things or to pick our way between them as though on stepping-stones over a brook. How did it become the fashion to think a paved path a good place for a rock garden?

The formal garden in which pattern-beds of tasteful kinds may find an appropriate and effective place has rightly grown in favor. But so far as I know it is not yet used on a large scale in public work. Certainly it is not in New York. Here one excellent chance to create a fine flower-garden was lost when, as had been long foreseen, the old reservoir on Fifth Avenue was torn down: not a garden but the new Public Library claimed the site. And another good chance vanished when the wide plaza opposite the Fifth Avenue entrance to Central Park was appropriated for an almost waterless monument, called a fountain, surrounded by a rather dreary arrangement of steps and walks and balustrades.

It is not very evident that in general our out-door sculpture has improved. As before, we get good things and bad. In New York we have gained Saint-Gaudens's Sherman and one or two other fine figures, but also the senile lions of the Public Library and the Civic Virtue who dwarfs by his size the small and beautiful City Hall behind him as he tramples on the poor ladies that represent, one must suppose, possible civic transgressions. In Central Park, I may note as a rare but promising occurrence, a particularly bad figure, the equestrian Bolivar, has been removed and replaced by a better one.

Boston has gained Saint-Gaudens's Shaw monument, an example not only of fine sculpture but also of a fine union of sculptural and architectural factors. On the other hand, in Newark, New Jersey, one may see the utmost limit of bad taste in the placing of a commemorative figure which in itself has merit. Here a bronze Lincoln sits, just as might a living man, on an actual park bench with his feet on the actual ground, with no sculptural or architectural accompaniments whatever, unless one may so call the bronze hat resting on the bench beside him. Living children, I am told, sit in his lap and enjoy themselves, but even Mme. Tussaud knew that this is not what statues are for.

It would be too great a digression to comment here upon the progress of American architecture, but I may say at least that, to judge from pictures, the finest of our new war memorials are likely to be architectural monuments, sometimes of great size, with sculpture playing a subordinate part in them.

In spite of all persisting sins there is clear proof of our growth in good taste in our widening appreciation of landscape-architecture and the corresponding increase in the number of its practitioners. We need not, indeed, put faith in the census of 1920 when it says that there were then in the United States 4,462 landscape-gardeners, for any man who wields a spade or sows a lawn or sells a tree may, if he will, so describe himself. Really significant, of course, is the existence of the American Society of Landscape-Architects, which, formed in 1899, now counts five chapters in different parts of the country, and about 160 members, 14 of whom are women. If these seem modest figures, nevertheless our landscape-architects can no longer be called "very few in number," as I was obliged to write thirty years ago. Nor can we any longer complain that "the art of design as applied to landscape is nowhere taught in America," for it is now taught, ostensibly at least, in half a hundred places—in universities and colleges of divers kinds, most of them State institutions, and in independent schools. I say ostensibly because, it appears, the instruction is not, in most cases, in landscape-design and construction or in the contributory arts and sciences, but merely in a knowledge of plants sometimes expanded to include the kind of planting that is content to decorate the existing features of a given piece of ground. To some eyes this limited programme seems a good beginning, promising more thorough work to come; to others it seems an unfortunate barrier to progress, supporting a shallow mistaken point of view likely to perpetuate itself to the detriment of the public as well as the practitioner. But, however this may be, we have also some real schools of landscape-architecture, excellent and thorough schools such as those at Harvard University and at Cornell University, where they stand on an equal footing with the schools of architecture and give special degrees. If I name no more than these two it is not because I think no more deserve to be named, but because it would be difficult to gather information enough to make sure of fair dealing. I may add, though, that there are two schools for women only which I have heard praised, one at Cambridge and one at Groton in Massachusetts.

Good, I think, must come from such activities as the National Conferences on Instruction in Landscape-Architecture, the first of which was held in 1920. At the one which met at Ann Arbor in 1924 there was read a committee report on Appreciation Courses in Landscape Architecture, based upon information supplied by twenty-seven institutions where such courses are given, and noting the existence of almost as many more. Here we have an effort not to educate artists but to cultivate an acquaintance with their art—an effort to foster a love for natural beauty and a desire for its preservation "with an understanding of such artistic problems as most frequently present themselves," and thus to instil, says the committee report, "a knowledge of home and city beautification that will help people to be more useful and contented citizens"—and also, I may add, more intelligent clients. If here too the same fault must be found as with many of the professional schools, if, to quote the report again, some courses lay too much stress "upon planting rather than planning" and too little upon landscape-design as a fine art intimately related to others, none the less the movement as a whole seems of good augury.

Our progress in landscape-art, it should be understood, is only one expression, one result, of that love for outdoor life which has recently developed in many parts of America. I do not mean that in any part we can see a real "back-to-the-land" tendency. I mean that although, unfortunately, our cities wax ever greater at the expense of our rural districts, more and more the worker in the city wants to live in its suburbs (and not only because of mounting city rents) or to own a country home farther afield, while increasing scores of thousands spend their leisure time in open-air activities and pleasures. The proofs are many. We have only to think of the attention now widely paid to the building of so-called "garden" cities and suburbs, of the multitude of villas and cottages and bungalows that in many places are supplanting the once-beloved "summer hotel" and boarding-house, of the increasing winter migrations from Northern cities to Southern health and pleasure resorts, the great vogue of summer camps for boys and girls and the tourist camps permitted in our public reservations, and the wish of everybody and his wife and child to go a-wheel, if possible on extended tours but at least on Sunday excursions. In some parts of California, we are told, half the population seems to live for months in motor-cars and the camping-grounds prepared for them, and lately some one who had just come from the northern Middle West told me that more than by anything else she had been astonished by the number of the country clubs near all the large towns.

The same spirit speaks also in the activity of our national and State governments, "reserving" for use as public parks great tracts in especially beautiful or remarkable wild regions. Thirty years ago there were only three National Parks—the Yosemite, the Yellowstone, and the Sequoia. Now there are nineteen, including one in Alaska and one in Hawaii, all administered by the National Park Service created in 1910.

As yet there is only one National Park east of the Rocky Mountains—Lafayette Park on the island of Mt. Desert in Maine. But the States have played their parts well and are growing more and more interested, ambitious, and generous with the needful money. New York, for example, which was early in the field with its Adirondack preserves, has recently created in concert with New Jersey the fine Palisades Interstate Park, which is especially useful because so near to Manhattan. In Illinois a large society, called the Friends of Native Landscape, is pressing upon the legislature two allied yet separate enterprises, a Forestry Policy and a State Park Policy which hopes to preserve and to prepare for public frequentation so many beautiful tracts, in general not fit for cultivation, in so many parts of the State that with their connecting roads they will eventually, says one of the spokesmen of the society, make of the State "one great park." In Texas, again, 30,000 acres were given to the public by their owners in 1924, and as many more were promised. And from time to time we read in the papers of other new reservations, or of the intent to create them—in North Carolina, I have noticed, in Georgia, in Florida, Alabama, Louisiana, Mississippi, Tennessee, and I forget how many other States. Only by filling a whole volume, indeed, could I list all such newborn enterprises and describe the varied character of the areas in question and the various ways in which their beauty is to be preserved and to be utilized.

Active also have been our greater and lesser cities. Every one has heard of the reclamation of the lake front at Chicago and far beyond, and of the way in which Boston has treated the districts that border on the Charles River, and has developed for purposes of recreation the seafront of its southern quarter. New York City, after finishing the Bronx Parkway in partnership with Westchester County and extending Riverside Drive far to the northward, is about to redeem the bank of the Hudson along the older part of the Drive from the dominion of railroad tracks and coal-yards. And long is the list of such civic improvements, actual or intended, that might be compiled.

Far too large and multiform and complicated for description here are those essays in city or "regional" planning which involve the reshaping of wide areas, urban, suburban, and rural, for the present and future benefit of communities which are rapidly growing larger and larger. Between four and five hundred of our cities, we are told, have such betterment plans more or less completely worked out. The most ambitious among them is a Regional Plan, elaborated with the utmost care by the Russell Sage Foundation for the city of New York and its environs, which embraces 5,500 square miles of territory. And the people of the State have already spoken in favor of a scheme for studying as an entity the whole State of New York with a view to its improvement in manifold yet harmonious ways, and in the interests of beauty as well as of good housing, easy transit, and industrial and commercial development. Thirty years ago what dreamer could have thought of enterprises like these as possible, even in words or on paper?

But that all the world is now concerned with such matters was shown of late (in April, 1925) by a great conference organized by the International Federation for Town and Country Planning and Garden Cities, and held in New York. Held for the third time in the history of the Federation, for the first time in America (in conjunction with a dozen American societies) this conference brought together experts from many foreign countries, and must have done much to open the eyes of our people to questions of the first importance and to the wisdom of considering them with trained intelligence—with the intelligence of many men trained in different yet allied branches of science and art.

Of quite as much importance as the condition and the prospects of our cities are those of our rural villages. Here also there is a hopeful tale to tell. I do not mean only that any one who journeys by automobile must have noticed, at all events in New England, the greater neatness and comeliness of the average village as compared with its aspect even ten years ago. Much more than this appears from a bird's-eye view of many States that we find in certain reports on Rural Planning recently issued by the United States Department of Agriculture in its series of Farmers' Bulletins. Interesting and sensible reports they are, meant not to direct but to stimulate local enterprise, not telling what ought to be done to improve the villages where almost 20,000,000 of our people live and some 30,000,000 farmers come for reasons of trade or pleasure, but showing by word and picture what has already been done in certain places, by what means, and at how small a cost. Thus far, says one of the reports, only "a start" has been made, yet it cites examples from many regions—from New England and southward to Virginia, from the States of the Middle West, from Arizona, Washington, and California. Moreover, the report explains, "the impetus has come in almost every case from local initiative"—not from official or philanthropic agencies but from the efforts of a few residents inciting the little community to effective corporate action; and there could be no better sign that a general and genuine movement is under way. Evidently it is a movement due in part to the advent of the automobile, making it worth while to please the passing tourist's eye and so attract his custom, and in part to that need for special recreation-grounds which has followed the cutting of the forests and the gradual shrinking of the public domain and of unremunerative private properties where every one was free to disport himself as he might choose; but also, beyond question, it has been inspired by a new love for outdoor orderliness and beauty as in and for themselves desirable.

It is another good sign that these village enterprises illustrate no cut-and-dried scheme of improvement, follow no set patterns, but have sprung from local needs, and in diverse ways have utilized local opportunities. Here a fine little public library, a church, a high school, or a community club-house figures as the centre of a pleasure-ground, there an harmoniously designed group of modest public buildings stands in an harmonious environment, or river-bank or roadside reclamation has made beautiful the approach to the village, or athletic fields, ball-grounds, picnic-grounds, children's playgrounds, swimming-pools, have been laid out with beauty again in mind, or even the business street of a village has been transformed by arcaded walks and attractive planting. Sometimes a striking natural feature or an historic site determines the location and the character of a park. Sometimes improvement has begun with better care of the village cemetery. In some places the rail-road has cooperated, in others the county, or people in other parts of the county. Public-spirited citizens have given land, or trees, or their own labor, as in one place where at one time 400 men and women, vil-lagers and farmers, were at work together. It is surprising at how small a cost great improvements have been made and afterward maintained, but surprising also what relatively large sums have been raised in very small communities where there are no wealthy persons. For the work in one village, we read, $8,000 were subscribed by 260 of the 3,000 in-habitants of five townships, and a village of only 500 souls paid for 14 acres $2,800 gathered from 400 contributors, half of them living on neighboring farms.

There is no end to the possible variety in such undertakings, and there is no limit to the good they may do, not only by attracting, to the increase of business, the tourist and the farmer whom the automobile may bring from a distance, and by providing wholesome recreation for old and young, but also by inciting the householder to make his own grounds tidy and beautiful, by stimulating public spirit and co-operative activity, and by awakening interest in other than material things. The new park in a certain village in Kansas, so one of its residents testified, "has encouraged higher ideals, enlisted the interest of the community in other enterprises, aroused civic pride, and, last but not least, has trans-formed the knockers into boosters." And so, one hopes, it may help to stem that cityward tide which is one of the great dangers in America to-day, for it is less by the lure of greater gains than by the promise of wider activities, interests, and pleasures that the city draws in the young people from village and farm. Truly, as the report itself declares, the set-ting aside of rural parks, playgrounds, and places of historic interest or especial beauty should everywhere "be part of the social programme" as laying foundation-stones "which will make the economic superstruc-ture worth while."

Of course the best time to do this is at the very first. The best results can be secured with the least expenditure of labor and money if town or village is well planned in advance. And here again we have made beginnings, as at Mariemont on the Miami River, about ten miles from Cincinnati, where with funds from a private source a landscape-architect is laying out and building a town, the beauty of which is already manifest, that shall at once accommodate 5,000 people and eventually twice as many.

In all phases of these diversified activities the landscape-architect has his part to play. No task can cry more loudly for his aid than the preservation of a vast and beautiful wild region to receive many thousands of tourists and campers, and its preservation from such "improvements" as too often appeal to the imagination of the artistically uninstructed. On the other hand, his knowledge and skill are needed in the smallest schemes lest the impossible be attempted, or the best that is possible be missed. And even in city planning, which is primarily engineers' work, if the engineer does not ask help of those who have been trained in the designing, the planting, and the care of pleasure-grounds of various kinds, the city and its environs are not likely to get the best—the best in extent, in location, and in character—that they might and ought to have. Happily these truths are now more and more generally recognized by public officials, by local societies and clubs, and even, as the reports I have cited show, by very small rural communities.

I have implied that the automobile, born only twenty-five years ago, has largely helped to alter for us the conditions of country life, and I do not need to explain the good that it has thereby accomplished. But, even apart from its homicidal appetite and its noisy manners, there are heavy charges against it. The good roads that it has given us are so commonly hard and black and shiny, so much more disturbing to the eye, especially in pleasure-grounds, than roads of the older kinds, that more than ever the landscape-architect must be careful how many roads he makes and where he runs them. In much-frequented places the fumes of the motor-cars obliterate all sweet natural odors. And, of course, it is their multiplication that induces advertisers to set big and gaudy signs and billboards along rural roads, and at the entrances to towns and villages which may be trying in other ways to improve their looks. Again, pleasant though it may be to travel rapidly without the aid of railways, so travelling he who drives sees, or ought to see, nothing but the road ahead of him, and his passengers see the country at large less well than from the higher level of the railway, while they have no time to observe or enjoy the roadside vegetation or, so swiftly do they change their point of view, to appreciate the skill of Nature or of man in the art of land-

scape composition. Moreover, the covered car now so generally preferred, and even the so-called open car which retains its top, blot out
most of the sky and cut all near and large objects in two, so that we see
not the things we are passing but only the lower half of them. A world
without tree-tops and a sky is a poor mutilated world to the lover of
beauty who cannot but long for the old days of leisurely driving in open
vehicles, of peaceful, sweet-smelling roads, and a world all visible under
its dome of sky.

In truth, it is only on foot now that one can make real acquaintance
with Nature. So it is well that we hear more and more, from East and
West and South, of walking clubs, "trail clubs," "hiking clubs," formed
to explore picturesque regions near at hand, to make them better
known to other pedestrians, and to thread them with permanent but
not disfiguring paths. Those who have walked in England will understand what a general movement of this kind may eventually do for the
lover of our own countrysides.

And there is still another demerit mark to set against the record of
the automobile. Especially in the neighborhood of our cities it too often
carries far afield hordes of devastators of woodland and meadow, scattering rubbish, trampling, picking, breaking, uprooting the wild vegetation, until in some places the most generous landowners have been
forced to protect by tall wire fences what they would gladly leave open
for public enjoyment if this did not mean damage to the point of de-
struction. If these onslaughts upon wild flowers and blossoming trees
and shrubs are not soon checked, we shall have none at all except in
spots so remote and secluded that few will ever enjoy them.

The "Nature study" now favored in so many schools can be turned
to no better use than in eradicating the impulse to such destructiveness.
But it would not be fair to lay the whole blame for it upon the purpose-
less folk whom the automobile carries about. Sinners also, deliberate
sinners, are many with money-making aims, and these, sad to say, are
greatly encouraged at Christmas and at Easter by some of our churches.
How can I forget, how could any one forgive, what I saw one Christmas
in a large Episcopal church—the whole flat end of the apse from floor
to roof, the long gallery fronts, and all the pillars entirely hidden under
a solid sheathing of mountain-laurel? Acres must have been devastated
to "decorate," in a most undecorative way, this one church. Surely we
ought to have outlived the belief that the Almighty is a Moloch to be
pleased by murderous offerings.

As for the big advertising signs, there is good hope of their disappearance. There is now a National Committee for the Restriction of Out-Door Advertising, with which like-minded local agencies co-operate. One of these, a special committee of the Municipal Art Society of New York, said in a recent bulletin that an ever-growing opposition to all disfigurements of rural scenery is making them unprofitable, and reported that the Standard Oil Company of New York has promised to remove all its country billboards as soon as its existing contracts expire. An act recently passed at Albany prohibits all disfiguring signs in the Adirondack State Park, and in 1924 2,000 of them were removed. And here is a message for the readers of this book: any person, says the Municipal Art Society, may help in its protective work by writing to an advertiser that his signs do not attract but antagonize the passer-by.

Still other agencies, likely to become the most potent of all, are helping in protective and creative work, but my catalogue is already so long that I cannot dwell upon them—upon our new multitude of garden clubs and horticultural societies. Lately born for the most part, and still being born, they foster flower shows, publish magazines and bulletins, organize lecture courses, spread a knowledge of ornamental plants and of methods of cultivation, and popularize canons of good taste, to the benefit not only of their own members but of the public at large. And directly also they serve the public. The Federated Garden Clubs of New York State (if I cite New York so often it is simply because I know most about it), which includes a city club with 2,000 members and 34 others, names among its accepted duties the preservation of sites of scenic and historic interest, the reclamation of roadsides, the planting of trees in public places, the restriction of billboards, the preservation of wild flowers, and the encouragement of small gardens.

Let us turn now to some other matters with which my earlier chapters concerned themselves.

Not many things that we saw so long ago live as vividly in the mind's eye as the World's Fair at Chicago. It was so unlike anything that, whether we had travelled or not, we had seen before and, whatever its defects of detail, it was so splendid a spectacle, that it can neither be forgotten nor confused in the memory with anything else. No one could foretell at the time what its effect upon the arts in America might be. And to-day no one can answer this question so as to convince us all. There are some who think that the influence of the Fair upon our architecture, leading us out of varied and uncertain and conflicting paths and determining a general preference for the traditional classic styles, was the best thing that could have happened. There are others who protest that the Fair, in thus "chanting a Roman litany above the Babel of conflicting styles," * checked natural development, stifling "the more creative modes of architecture which might have derived from our fine achievements in science, from our tentative experiments in democracy," and who explain furthermore that "the capital defect of an established and formalized mode" is that "it tends to make an architect think of a new problem in terms of an old solution for a different problem." Of course the complicated questions that I have thus baldly suggested cannot here be considered. I may only note that during this last decade that "complete rehabilitation of the Roman mode" which marked the twenty years after the year of the Fair has been conspicuously impaired.

The one point that I want to make is that, whatever its other results, the Chicago Fair implanted among us a belief in the beauty of concord, of harmony, in the need for organization, for co-operation in the arts. There were no signs of such a belief at Philadelphia in 1876, but it was apparent in every exhibition later than Chicago's—at Omaha, at Nashville, at Atlanta, Buffalo, San Francisco, San Diego—with, of course, more or less satisfactory results, with the most satisfactory, I am told, on the singularly picturesque site at San Diego. At the Pan-American Exhibition in Buffalo, where the site was flat and featureless and the exhibition unusually compact, the highly important matter of scale was carefully considered in every mass and every detail of form and color, and "each part of the landscape scheme," wrote one of the collaborators, was studied "not only as a setting for the building adjacent to it" but also as part of a continuous design "tying the whole composition together, enhancing the salient characteristics of the individual buildings . . . and maintaining the scale of the whole work."

To thousands of those who imbibed at Chicago this idea of the prime importance of harmony, of unity, in artistic enterprises, Olmsted's landscape work must have given their first inkling of the existence of the art he practiced and of its intimate connection with the art of building. And, as I have already indicated, the expression of this new knowledge has not been confined to exhibition grounds. Often, of course, it is still

*Lewis Mumford, "Sticks and Stones: A Study of American Architecture and Civilization." 1924.

tentative, crude, inept, but it is a great thing to have grasped the right idea, the only principle that opens the way to more excellent results in the future.

It is so long since I have seen the parks in Europe that I cannot speak of their present aspect. I do not know, for instance, whether those of Dijon and of Dresden are still such beautiful examples as they used to be of a happy union of formal and naturalistic features. I do not know whether in others the unfortunate practice of cutting away the lower branches of shrubberies to make place—to make an inappropriate and disturbing place—for bright masses of flowers still prevails, but I think that, at all events, it has not been imitated in this country. On the other hand, so far as I know we have not adopted the charming kind of floral planting called French parterres, and this is a pity.

Of one thing, however, I am sure: in the capital of war-worn and impoverished France there has been of late such a generous activity in the making of new pleasure-grounds that our rich and peaceful cities may well think of it with envy. And with shame some of them should think of the well-kept, tidy, flourishing aspect of Parisian parks and tree-planted streets.

One of our chief sins, indeed, and one of the reasons why new enterprises are not always supported by those to whom they are expected to appeal, is the slackness, the indifference, we often show in maintaining highroads and public places which we projected with enthusiasm and created at great cost. The interference of the politician in things which he should not control is a chief cause of this evil. If we could have in each of our cities an official such as Paris has in M. Forestier, a distinguished landscape-architect trained in his special kind of work, appointed for life, and given a free hand, we might hope to have pleasure-grounds as well tended and as beautifully flourishing as those of Paris. Excepting, perhaps, in New York. Here we can hardly hope for long-lived, healthy trees; on our narrow, crowded, rocky island with its thin soil a tree must fight for its life as its congeners elsewhere need not. But even in New York there is no excuse for the ugly untidiness, the look of neglect, that afflicts the eye in Central Park and our smaller open spaces.

Nor, I grieve to say, is untidiness the only misfortune that has befallen Central Park. The worst that might happen to it has, indeed, been averted by the unwearying vigilance of the public: the admirable design of the Park has not been mutilated, although year after year it has been variously threatened by politicians and money-seekers, by narrow-visioned enthusiasts for some special scheme, perhaps a good scheme in itself, and even by self-seeking or misguided architects and sculptors. A list of the assaults upon Central Park any one of which, if successful, would have meant disaster, would be instructive if it were not too long to recite or even to remember. But as a specimen I may mention one of the latest—a scheme to cut the Park in two by a broad, straight, east-and-west avenue which should "unite," for what purpose it is hard to guess, our museums of art and of natural history, and should be called the "Roosevelt Trail"!

But although the design of the Park is still intact, much of its beauty is gone, for the vegetation that once so admirably clothed it has in many parts been worn and torn to tatters. It is hard to apportion the blame between man and Nature. It is no one's fault that the Park, placed in the outskirts of a relatively small city, is now in the centre of a huge one, so that its soil, originally very poor, and its atmosphere have been sadly contaminated, even the winds that should freshen it often bringing the fumes of factories, abattoirs, and other utilities from the suburbs beyond the two rivers. But many existing nuisances should have been suppressed or mitigated—and not for the sake of the Park alone. Sufficient money should have been granted for the proper care of the vegetation and for the nourishing and renewal of the meager soil. Not always have the officials in charge of the Park been well chosen. And so negligently has it been policed that unchecked vandals have wrought incalculable damage. Probably no park in the world is frequented by so many people. Nevertheless, the heedless and the mischievous might have been kept from trampling the undergrowth and treading out paths where none should be, from mutilating trees by climbing them, and from breaking not merely flowers but whole branches from blossoming trees and shrubs.

As for Nature's attacks, I do not know whether such a calamity as a sickening of the beech-trees which a few years ago killed almost all of them might have been successfully resisted. But certainly irresistible were the two hard winters, 1917–1918 and 1919–1920, that repeatedly brought severe cold, high winds, and sleet storms heavily icing branch and twig. Not Central Park alone but all the regions around New York and many parts of New England suffered terribly during these exceptional years.

The total result of its various misfortunes is that Central Park is in many parts shorn of much of its beauty while in certain spots it looks like the pictures of bomb-shattered places in France. Many things of which, thirty years ago, this book delighted to speak have disappeared, like the tall poplars on a point in the lake and the splendid group of weeping beeches on the West Drive. Of the latter only one small individual remains. Many surviving trees are merely gaunt trunks robbed of all but a few feet of their main branches. I do not think that there is a handsome conifer left in the Park. The long wistaria arbors, once its chief boast in spring, have virtually nothing to cover them. But most calamitous of all is the condition of the elms. The Mall, as an avenue, is a thing of the past, flanked now by a few wrecks of large trees and rows of newly planted saplings; and just as bad is the state of the elms on Fifth Avenue along the eastern borders of the Park. It seems odd indeed to read on an earlier page that the thing most needed in the Park was the cutting of thousands of trees. The planting of thousands is needed now. Of course, with money and interest and skill enough, Central Park may be restored to a large measure of health and beauty. But at the best we must wait many years. And it is doubtful whether even at the best the Park will ever be as beautiful as once it was. Of some deleterious influences we can never get rid and, besides, we may doubt whether any one else will be able to fill in the outlines of Olmsted's great composition with such a variety of effective, harmonious, and charming scenes and details as his hand gave us.

It is worth while, I think, to say all this because the chief recreation-ground of a city to which people from all parts of the country come year by year in ever greater numbers is not a merely local but a national possession, and because any stranger seeing it now and chancing to read anything that was written about it years ago may well be confused as to the value of an art of which (taking the difficulties of soil and site into consideration) Central Park could be called the most interesting example in any country, the most nearly a beautiful *creation*. But I am glad that it was not possible to delete from my earlier pages the references, descriptions, and praises which are now largely inappropriate, for the beauty that once existed should not be forgotten or, upon the evidence of to-day, denied.

It is pleasant to be able to turn from a work of landscape-art that has deteriorated to one that, beautifully complete thirty years ago, has nevertheless improved with the passage of time. This is the first-named of the two which I cited in my second chapter as examples of different kinds of beauty achieved under differing conditions by different methods of treatment—the long-tended, artistically developed, large suburban country-place. In general effect this place remains virtually the same, but it has profited by an extension of its borders and by the addition of new features, notably large plantations of mountain-laurel along the edge of a stretch of woodland. Its owner and creator, I may say now that he has grown famous, is Professor Sargent, who has also created, only a mile away, the Arnold Arboretum.

The other country-place of which I spoke, the one on the shores of Buzzard's Bay, where Nature had been the chief artist, changed hands long ago after the death of its owner. Since then I have not seen it, but I have heard that the house has been rebuilt and the lands divided, and I can hardly believe that the description I once wrote of it would fit any part of it now, for it is a very rare kind of intelligence that knows when doing little to Nature's handiwork is better than doing much and when doing nothing is best of all, and yet knows how to do with an artist's hand such work as must be undertaken.

In a recent essay called "America After Fifteen Years" an Englishman, a former Minister of Education, mentions first of all the great vogue of three new inventions—the automobile, the moving picture, and the radio—and also dwells upon the wide development of athletic sports, because, he says, no graver question can confront a prosperous industrial community than "How is it to dispose of its leisure time?" Fifteen years ago he did not think this problem insistent, for there was then less wealth and less leisure; now he finds it of supreme importance. So in other words says an American observer: one of the chief defects of current education is that it "takes no account of leisure as a permanent factor in our life," for mistakenly we assume that leisure and happiness are practically synonymous and ignore the probable relationship between increased leisure and the growing lawlessness of American communities. And in the same spirit other writers comment upon the possibilities of good and evil in the progressive diminution of the working man's hours of labor.

This means that here and now there can be no more useful work than increasing contentment by improving the conditions of daily life and supplying for leisure hours occupations and amusements which will not be mere anodynes or stop-gaps, mere fruitless if not harmful ways of killing time, but will refresh and cultivate body and mind, the senses and the spirit. We have just seen how in this direction lovers of the arts that collaborate with Nature have begun to make use of their opportunities. But the task is immense, it has only been begun, and not all its implications are as yet well understood. Especially should it be felt that the most satisfactory ways, whether physical or mental, of utilizing leisure are not passive but active. A great lesson that we need to learn and to teach is that to *do* is the surest and most lasting way to enjoy, and that doing means the use of the mind, the acquirement of knowledge and taste, as well as the use of the hand. All such words and works as may cultivate an understanding of the beauty and variety of Nature, of the beauty and interest of works of art, and may induce the young especially to take a personal part in their conservation or their creation, are deeply needed in America to-day.

If this chapter thus closes upon a more serious note than was struck in the earlier ones, it is because to-day our manifold tasks of enlightenment and betterment press upon intelligent men and women more insistently than thirty years ago they did, more insistently than we then foresaw that eventually they must.

27

Early Autumn near Cape Cod

To the Editor of *Garden and Forest:*

Sir,—I should much rather write myself down as living on Cape Cod than near it, for there is a distinctiveness, not to say distinction, in its name, a share in which all its neighbors covet. Every one knows where Cape Cod is, and thinks he knows what it is, although accurate knowledge on this latter point is, as a fact, extremely rare, while to say that one lives on the western shore of Buzzard's Bay conveys a very vague idea to most persons of other than New England birth.

However, though we are only three miles to the westward of the Wareham River, on the eastern bank of which Cape Cod begins, no one worthy to speak to the readers of *Garden and Forest* could claim to belong to "the Cape." For its nominal beginning is a true geographical beginning, and this means a distinct botanical beginning, or, more exactly, a distinct botanical leaving off. Everything that grows on Cape Cod grows here, from Cranberries to Pitch Pines. But many things grow here which do not grow beyond the Wareham River—White Pines, for instance, in profusion. And many other things flourish here which just cling to existence there, so that the whole aspect of our woodlands and road-sides is different; and as one drives still further to the westward, the difference grows ever more strongly accentuated, so that even five

Garden and Forest 5 (September 28, 1892): 465–466.

or six miles from the shores of the bay one can hardly believe that the sandy, heathy, boggy, rough-and-tumble stretch of the Cape country is covered by the same sky which covers these verdant rolling meadows, the sturdy Oaks and Maples and White Pines of the woodland, and the great Poplars and Locusts by the cottage-doors.

So, we think, we are repaid for not belonging to the Cape by the variety which our daily excursions can compass. The Cape is delightful, but it is all of a piece, and those who live on it cannot easily go elsewhere. But we can go to the Cape after dinner and be back to tea, and the next day can go to our pastoral inland country in an equally brief space of time. Nor do we always think that we must go far in either direction, for even the roads nearest about us offer perpetual variety, now crossing salt-marshes and causeways over rippling arms of water; now threading tall Pine-groves, and now Oak-thickets, to bring us out on modest elevations, which we are pleased to call cliffs, where, suddenly, the wide azure expanse of the bay is seen beneath our feet; now taking us between hay-fields and small fruit-farms, where the houses are prettily gray or white and the barns are bigger than the houses; and, again, leading us through miles of narrow roads, where woods of some twenty years' growth come close to the carriage-wheels, the boughs meet overhead, and the grass grows tall between the three ruts worn by the never frequent, but never altogether failing passage of the typical vehicles of the country—the shackly, faded buggy and the black-hooded, four-seated carryall, each drawn by its single horse. Two-horse conveyances cannot comfortably penetrate these wood-roads, although for a one-horse vehicle they offer very good driving, the sandy soil of the Cape only appearing here and there in very brief stretches. No visitor should bring his own one-horse vehicle to this part of the world, but should depend upon those he will find awaiting him. Our axles are so wide that an imported carriage does not "track," and the difference between driving in such a one and in one which does track is the difference between entire comfort and an exasperating tilt and joggle.

Of course, it is in the mountain regions of central and northern New England that the colors of the American autumn show in the grandest and most amazing way. But our vegetation "turns" very beautifully; and it reveals its beauty, so to say, in a much more intimate fashion. The finest autumnal features of an inland scene are distant stretches of parti-colored hill-side, tall, broken masses of variegated forest in the middle distances, and, sprinkled about in the nearer meadows, superb single examples of flaming red or yellow or purple trees. But we have no hill-sides; when we see a mass of woods in the middle distance it is low and draws a nearly straight line across the horizon; and, in our most characteristic drives, the trees are small, and one sees them very close at hand, crowded beside us, and their boughs close above our heads. Here and there we get fine open views of meadows and marshes bounded by woodland or sea. But they are all flat views, and, as a rule, there are few isolated large trees. The colors in autumn lie in low far-extending level masses, or, when we thread the forest-roads, strike the eye as a perpetual succession of details, rather than as broad effects. Roads such as these are called, I believe, "green-ribbon roads" in some parts of New England. Ours are certainly ribbon-like, perpetually and gracefully meandering with never the smallest stretch of straightness, and in summer they have a green all their own, for no inland light brings out the keenest emerald tints possible to foliage as does the salt-spangled light of these sea-shore parts. But when we look along them in autumn we feel as though we had put an immense kaleidoscope to our eye, so many are the colors they assume, and so impossibly vivid each one seems.

Of course, it is not in the first half of September, not until October, that, in these mild regions, one sees autumn in a very brilliant guise. But the beginning of the red and yellow season has a special charm of its own. Autumn is setting her palette, trying her effects with little streaks and spots and splashes, indicating what she means to do, sketching in her color-scheme; and every one knows that a great artist's sketches have a peculiar value to the understanding eye. A tricksy and willful sprite is this particular great artist, in those youthful days when her Christian name has not been changed from "Early" to "Late." There seems no reason in her work, although everything she does rhymes delightfully with the next thing. I pity any scientific student who should come to our woods in mid-September, trying to unravel why our foliage "turns." Neither frost, nor sun, nor moisture, nor dryness can be credited with any distinct influence; little can be laid to the account of family traits when tree is compared with tree; nor does soil or situation seem to have a discernible effect upon the gay beginning of the masquerade.

We may say, in a rough sense, that the Tupelos turn first. But some of them turned in August, and some have not yet begun to turn, while some are russet and others are redder than scarlet. And a green one may stand close beside the brightest red one, or one bough may be scarlet while all the others are emerald still. But even the Tupelos are not so individually willful as the Maples. They are all Scarlet Maples by name (the Sugar Maple does not grow with us), but they are not all equally scarlet by nature; or, at least, they do not all reveal this nature at the same time or in the same way. This year they began to enliven themselves unusually early—a week or more ago many of the smaller ones were already vivid. But I have never noted a year when they enlivened themselves in so fragmentary and fantastic a fashion. It is hard, as yet, to find an example which is red all over. I passed a wide swamp the other day which was surrounded by hundreds of them and thickly beset with others, all hardly more than saplings, gracefully tall and slender. Every one of them, I think, showed some brilliant red; but not one of them, as far as I could see, had more than one or two red boughs. It was not as though each tree had assumed a new garment; it was as though each had flung out a bold banner of its own. Often, in the narrow woodland roads, one comes upon a Maple with not a whole bough, but merely the end of a bough flaming; or not the whole end, but just a couple of swinging leaves. In my drive to-day I came upon a good-sized symmetrical specimen, still perfectly fresh and green, with one single scarlet leaf hung out over the roadway; and immediately beyond it was another with only half a leaf tinted, the line between green and red being as neatly drawn as though by a painter's brush. And as the Maples are behaving, just so are the Scarlet Oaks, while their big brothers, the White Oaks, give no sign that they know the summer is past.

Where the roads skirt the salt-marshes splendid effects of color may already be seen, although these are less vivid than those which will soon follow. The marshes (we call them "ma'shes" here, and so, says an English friend, are they called in South Devon) are not orange-colored yet, but they are a fine dullish yellow, streaked with green and brown, and here and there accented by big patches and ribbons of a blood-like deep red. From a distance the plant which gives this remarkable color looks like some species of Salicornia, but I have never been able to get near enough on the yielding soil to see it distinctly. Around these marshes the woods are still chiefly green. No brown tones yet appear, and of yellow tones only the dull neutral tints of the little Birches. But a splash of scarlet shows occasionally where a Maple or Tupelo stands with its foot in the wet.

Where the roads go beneath tall Pine-groves not a sign or symbol of autumn appears. The sparse growths beneath are as freshly verdant as the soft swirling canopy of needles above. But the open roadsides are gay, for we pride ourselves on our variety in shrubs and vines, and these turn early; and, moreover, the Asters and Golden-rods are still at their finest. No withered grayish plumes stand for the Golden-rod yet, but along the shores the thick-leaved maritime species is in perfection, and on drier spots other tall or low paniculated kinds, and the softer, more poetic flat-topped masses of the corymbose species. The Vacciniums, which later will spread a carpet of glory along the roadsides and through the woodland glades, are already, some of them, bronzed and some of them red. Here and there a Clethra has turned bronze-like too. Once in a while we come upon a little Sassafras whose mitten-like leaves are yellow and red in spots like a particularly speckled apple. Now and then, like a flash of flame, a thin garland of Virginia Creeper encircles a Pine-tree trunk; near it flaunts a mass of Poison Ivy, and, further on, a streamer of Smilax tries to make us believe it is a Virginia Creeper too. Sometimes, lying low beside the road, beneath an arboreal canopy still entirely green, there is a mass of varied tangled color enchanting to behold; and, again, the undergrowth is as green as the trees, except for tiny spikes and spots of russet and scarlet.

The eye which can appreciate accents as well as broad effects, which loves details as well as masses, and which can be delighted by a little colored leaf as well as by a huge colored tree, finds infinite satisfaction in our country in these early autumn days. And what a sky covers this diversified panorama of simple beauties! People who live among the hills must do without real horizons. They never know what it is to see the edge of their world in every direction, and to know what the sun's rays are about in all quarters of the sky. They never see a sunset as we see it here all around the margin of the heavens. This is particularly the month for sunsets, and we usually have four of them every night. There will be a crimson one flaring in the west and a rosy one blushing in the east; one with masses of dark purple clouds lying over a purple sea to the southward, and a colder, purer, even more enchanting one in the north, pale green as to its sky, palest lavender as to its clouds. No mountain region can do this for you, and you must come to our individual little corner of the world, just under the heel of Cape Cod, to know exactly what you miss by living in the mountain.

28

Wood Roads on Cape Cod

To the Editor of *Garden and Forest:*

Sir,—The following words, which occur in Professor Shaler's article called "The Betterment of Our Highways," printed in the October *Atlantic,* are of special interest to us dwellers near Cape Cod. "Many of the worst roads in this country," he says, "are brought into their abject state by an unreasonable interference with natural processes—an interference which arises from an ignorant prepossession that all roads should have the same general aspect. Thus, in sandy regions, such as those in south-eastern Massachusetts, and in many other districts near the southern margin of the area occupied by the ice during the last glacial period, the first wagon-roads belonged to the class which we may call trackways, in which the path was just wide enough for a single vehicle, with occasional turn-outs to permit wagons to pass each other. On these trackways a single pair of parallel ruts were quickly formed, the growth of bushes and low forest-trees pressing so close to the roadway as to form a wall of foliage on either side. In many cases the crease made by the hubs of the wagons could be distinctly traced in the thickset vegetation. Roads of this description afforded excellent wheeling and were maintained almost without cost. The falling leaves and small branches were swept into the ruts, and there mingled with the sand,

Garden and Forest 5 (November 30, 1892): 574–575.

forming a compact and elastic foundation for the wheels. The sandy soil permitted the rain-water quickly to drain away, so that no gutters were required. Although an unreasoning desire for improvement has led to the widening of almost all these old-fashioned trackways, we may here and there find bits which have escaped the merciless hand of the uneducated road-master. The present writer is accustomed frequently to pass over a stretch of road which was originally all of this nature; but a part of it has been altered to the regulation width of forty feet, while another portion remains in its primitive state. On the improved road the constantly shifting sands are not readily to be passed over by a pair of swift horses drawing a light wagon at a greater rate than six miles an hour. On the more ancient and natural type of way it is easy to attain twice that speed."

If Professor Shaler will come to the shores of Buzzard's Bay next summer, I shall be delighted to show him miles upon miles of these old-fashioned wood-roads, untouched by improvement, and unprovided even with turning-out places, the rather wide spacing of the trees in most places permitting one's infrequent opponents (I do not know what other word to use) to turn out comfortably enough into the low growth of bushes. I put the matter in this way, as a deserved tribute to the chivalry of the farmers of this region, for I have very rarely found that, when they saw a lady driving toward them, they were willing to lay even half the task of turning-out upon her.

There are, I say, very many miles of these roads in this neighborhood, running in all sorts of criss-cross directions between the greater and the lesser highways. As each stretch usually serves only one or two retired farms, which produce little but poultry, market-produce, hay or firewood, there seems little danger of their immediate "improvement." But some are more important and therefore more in danger, and so I offer my little appeal for them as a postscript to Professor Shaler's more influential one. These roads with their three ruts, one worn by the horse and two by the wheels, often with tall grasses and flowers growing between them, afford far better "wheeling" than most parts of our highways. "The roads here are so poor that I don't care much about driving," says many a new-comer. "They seem so to you," we old-timers reply, "because you probably keep to the highways." "Of course," is the answer, "the less important roads must be even worse." In a city man this reasoning is natural; but it is greatly mistaken. Many of our woodland roads are quite delightful to drive upon; and taken altogether they are better than are our high-roads as a whole, although here and there, near the towns, we have some good solid bits of highway to show. Only, if Professor Shaler comes to try them, he must be content with my one-horse buggy. He must not bring his own pair of trotters. For—as I think I have already told the readers of *Garden and Forest*— our wood-roads have their three ruts very clearly defined by the passage of vehicles, mostly belonging to small farmers. A pair of horses can traverse them without great discomfort; but they are meant for a single steed; and the pair is apt to do much damage to the pretty alternating ribbons of grass, Golden-rod and Aster! And, as Professor Shaler knows, our axles are eight inches wider than the axles of Boston Town; so that, in his own carriage, he could profit by only one of our three comfortable shallow ruts.

29

The Good Work of an Improvement Association at Narragansett Pier

To the Editor of *Garden and Forest:*

Sir,—A few years ago Narragansett Pier presented the ragged, shiftless look which is only too common in American seaside resorts frequented by large numbers of people. Just beyond it to the southward ran a beautiful line of rocky coast, backed by the pastures rich in the sturdy shrubs and flowers characteristic of the south-eastern New England coast. But its hotels were built nearer to the fine bathing-beach, along a rough road, between which and the water lay neither beach nor real rocks— only a narrow stretch of stony shore, covered for the most part with rubbish and refuse; and back of them spread an unkempt little village. Now it shows few spots which are disagreeable to look upon; in many parts it has grown very pretty, and elsewhere it is neat, at least. Part of the improvement has been due to the building of the Casino between the hotels and the beach and to the excellent care bestowed from the first upon its grounds, and part to the macadamizing of streets and roads and to the increase in the number of private cottages and villas lying along the streets back from the sea. But even four or five years ago much raggedness and roughness were still apparent, and little care was taken to keep the highways in a tidy condition. The influential men among the hotel-owners and summer residents had tried to exert an influence toward the

Garden and Forest 8 (July 31, 1895): 308–309.

betterment of these conditions, but without much avail until they conceived the wise idea of asking the women also to exert themselves. A ladies' improvement association was formed, and, although it has existed only three or four years, the good it has accomplished is remarkable. Among its members are owners of summer cottages, constant frequenters of the hotels, and also native residents of the village. The annual fee has, for obvious reason, been kept at a low figure—two dollars; but voluntary contributions are welcome, and have more than once been generously made, and money-making entertainments have been organized from time to time. The largest outlay of the association has been a contribution of $500 toward the building of a fine sea-wall along the ugly stretch of coast in front of the hotels. This, the most conspicuous improvement which could possibly have been made at the Pier, is now completed for more than half its length. Each season a man is hired by the association, whose duty it is to patrol the streets and keep them clear of papers and rubbish; with this same end in view large strong baskets, painted green, have been attached to fences and posts at frequent intervals, and I have found these baskets constantly well filled with things which, but for their presence, would have littered up the roads and walks. But, say the members of the association, its greatest utility has been a moral one, as stimulating the individuals who belong to it, and, through their example, all the residents of the Pier to keep their private grounds more carefully and to adorn them with plantations. And certainly the combined results of its various efforts seem strikingly great to one who now revisits the Pier after an absence of several years.

Once there was scarcely a tree to be seen except a few Willows. Now very many have been planted, and the cottages are draped with Japanese Ivy, Wistaria, Rose-bushes and Honeysuckles, all of which grow luxuriantly in this climate. Japanese Roses are frequently seen, but it is a pleasure to notice that the common Wild Roses of the region are likewise profusely used for the decoration of the summer visitors' houses. Their grass, and that around the hotels also, is now beautifully kept; and, as a rule, a taste much more commendable than that generally revealed in such places has been shown in shunning so-called "ornamental beds," and trusting to trees, vines, climbers and shrubs for the beauty of small grounds. Privet-hedges are seen in numbers; no plant grows so quickly or does so well as Privet in situations of this sort; and just at this season, when even the most carefully clipped are bursting into profuse blossoming, it certainly supplies as charming a method of fencing villa grounds as could be found.

But the main thing to be noted in the change that has been so quickly worked in this summer resort is not the individual beauty of this plant or of that, or of these grounds or those, but the general improvement in the aspect of the village as a whole, and the fact that it results even more from the neatness newly achieved than from the plantations newly made. It should certainly encourage the formation of similar societies of women in all seashore places where they do not already exist.

30

A Glimpse of Nantucket

For many years the population of Nantucket has been steadily declin-
ing. Counting nearly 10,000 souls in 1840, it does not count 4,000 now.
And these may be held to represent a "selection of the unfittest," for
year by year the more energetic and intelligent youths of the community
have gone to seek their fortunes in the outer world. Meanwhile, until
quite lately, the island has been scarcely thought of in the outer world
save in connection with bygone whales, and has generally been described as a featureless expanse, interesting simply as a bit of sandy
wilderness isolated in a wilderness of waves.

Now, however, a change has come—not, indeed, over the numbers or
the spirit of the natives, but over the minds of those whom they call
"off-islanders." Summer tourists have discovered the cool, bracing equa-
nimity of the Nantucket climate, the homely picturesqueness of its quiet
town, and its rich facilities for bathing, boating and fishing; and they
flock to its shores in increasing thousands summer after summer. How
the islanders lived before this influx began, some twelve years ago, it is
hard to imagine, for I have never seen a place more destitute of signs of
an attempt to earn a living. There is now no whaling, which is largely
the fault of external circumstances; but there is scarcely any sheep-raising,
and this must be the fault of the islanders themselves. Great flocks once

Garden and Forest 1 (November 14, 1888): 447–448.

pastured over the island. Wool was then the main concern and was chiefly used at home. But now, with improved means of transport and the summer immigration, it seems as though a little energy might make the raising of mutton profitable. Agriculture is almost as non-existent as sheep-raising. Nearly the whole population lives in the town and a few distant villages. Farm-houses are few and widely scattered, and the cultivated fields which surround them are rough and very scanty. In the town and along the edges of the shore the summer colonists are likewise gathered, so that a mile away from this shore one can fancy one's self a hundred miles away from anything that approaches to human activity, wealth or progress.

More negatives must still be used before I can begin to tell what does exist in the central regions of Nantucket. In the first place, there are no stones. Knowing that the island was formed during and after the glacial epoch, and is a mere mass of "drift," one does not look for the bed-rock of the mainland to which, for a time, it was attached. But it seems more reasonable to expect those boulders which are strewn over the whole surface of New England, and nowhere more thickly than along the coasts nearest to Nantucket. Yet they do not exist. Broadly speaking, the island is divided into a higher eastern and a lower western portion of almost equal areas. The latter I had no time to visit during a brief two days' sojourn; but many hours of diligent driving showed me the whole of the eastern portion, and I could count on my fingers the stones I saw. Of course, this means that there were none of the picturesque walls which I had left behind in Plymouth County, and which are to be found again on Block Island a little to the westward. But, from a practical point of view at least, the lack of such walls does not greatly matter. Where there is so little to fence in, only the lover of beauty need regret the lack of good fencing material.

Finally, there are no trees on Nantucket, except those which have been planted in the streets of the town, and some scattering plantations of Pitch Pine which were made about forty years ago midway between the northern and the southern shores. The farm-houses stand naked and alone, and even along the many little lakes and ponds one sees neither groves of trees nor thickets of shrubs. The so-called Pine woods, moreover, are almost caricatures of the term. There is no more dauntless and long-suffering tree than the Pitch Pine, but it can seldom have struggled with greater difficulties than on Nantucket. No individual rises more than ten or twelve feet above the soil; all are grotesquely distorted by the fierce sea winds; many are scarred and embrowned by the touch of fire, which starts readily and runs persistently in the dry matted grass; and they look, in consequence, like a collection of ancient dwarfs, not like young woods with possibilities of further growth. Yet from even a little distance these woods actually seem to deserve their name, for everything vertical "tells" with extraordinary force in this landscape, where vertical things are very few, and where slight inequalities of surface, therefore, give the look of far horizons to spots quite near at hand. The eye is so entirely deprived of help in its calculations, that even experience does not soon teach it how to compute distances or dimensions. The first mistake I made was to exclaim at the presence of a great hotel in the middle of a moorland wilderness, the building being, in fact, but a farmhouse of moderate size. And after several such mistakes, with a full sense of the likelihood of error, I pronounced a pair of isolated objects to be tall chimneys about five miles off and found them merely tombstones not a mile away.

These groves of gaunt yet dwarfish Pines, then, are the only trees which meet us outside the town, although we are told that White Oaks once grew in certain places large enough to be used for building purposes. The earliest local records speak of "meadows, woods and uplands," and one district bore the name of the "Long Woods;" but a full century ago the island was represented as "wholly destitute of firewood," and dependent, as it is to-day, on Cape Cod for its supply. In the town a great deal of planting was done in former years. When we stand on one of the railed "roof walks" that are so characteristic of a community which perpetually went down to the sea in ships, the panorama of gray roofs is interspersed with an almost equal quantity of foliage. The Elms have stood their long battle with the sea wind fairly well, but more interesting are the Ailanthus trees, which quite as frequently appear. One-sided, as a rule, and often naked of foliage save towards the extremity of their branches, their gray bark and picturesque structure harmonize admirably with the gray picturesqueness of the old unpainted houses; and their foreign air seems appropriate in a place which once was filled with trophies of every kind from many a distant shore.

But the real interest of Nantucket lies in those wide tracts away from the high sandy cliffs where, as far as the eye can reach, no tree is in sight. The prospect is peculiar even to eyes familiar with Block Island and the eastern portions of Long Island. At Block Island the surface undulates perpetually and abruptly, is thickly bestrewn with boulders and shows scarcely any vegetable covering save a close, yellowish grass. At Montauk there are also wide, boldly rolling stretches of such grass; but others where white sand is spotted with great tufts of Hudsonia, and others again where moisture has produced beautiful thickets of shrubs and veritable little forests filled with many species of trees. But at Nantucket the surface is either quite flat for miles or gently rolling in long swells; the ponds are encircled merely by a border of sedges and tall grass, and seem to have no effect upon the soil beyond; there are no reaches of naked sand, and few where the grass is not thickly beset with flowering plants. Where it grew most abundantly it was filled in September with Asters and Golden Asters and Golden Rods and Everlastings—all stunted by the wind to a few inches in height, but vigorously blooming—and with purple Gerardias, showing larger and more deeply colored flowers than I had ever seen elsewhere. But the most characteristic and charming tracts were those which bore no grass, but were covered by a close growth of low undershrubs and trailers—Hudsonia of both species, Bearberry and the Broom Crowberry. Acres upon acres in one direction were covered with the last two alone, alternating in large patches and growing with splendid luxuriance, the Bearberry clothing even the sides of the road with a thick mat of glossy leaves and dark red fruit, and the Heath-like Crowberry rising in dense miniature evergreen thickets, and contrasting exquisitely with its neighbor. A prettier combination I have never seen, and it is hereby recommended to the owners of sandy sea-shore places as an excellent substitute for a turfed lawn. It is as delightful to walk upon as to look at, owing to the springy, Heath-like quality of the Crowberry stems. Hudsonia did not grow with as much luxuriance as at Montauk, yet it was often beautifully effective here and there. I was told that the true Heather (*Calluna vulgaris*) could be found in a few spots on the island, did one know where to look, and its name is included in the list of native plants printed in the local guidebook.

This list—compiled by Mrs. Owen, of Springfield, Massachusetts—reveals how rich the island flora is. From the botanist's point of view the abandonment of sheep-raising must be accounted fortunate. For, as another contributor to the guide-book writes, when sheep were allowed to roam at large over the commons, it was only by the most diligent seeking that the botanist obtained perfect specimens of any flowering plant. "One feeble specimen of the blossom of the *Hudsonia tomentosa* could be found in perfection where now, freed from the sheep, . . . its yellow flowers are to be had for the glancing. Even the varieties of the Golden Rod, . . . which furnish the rich covering to our commons at times, were not a familiar feature, though known and specified by the scientists of the island." Then it must have been true that Nantucket was a barren waste to the eye; but it is truer to say at this present time that it is a garden of flowers from summer's end to end.

And, according to the belief of many persons whom I met, it might be made a wealth-producing garden, too. The soil, it is said, would be well adapted to certain cereal crops, were it only manured a little; and, even now, the vegetables it produces are of excellent quality. It seems as though there must soon come a time when these vast tracts of now unprofitable land will be turned to some account, perhaps by a revival of energy on the part of the islanders, perhaps through the advent of "off-islanders" intelligent enough to seize the advantages of a spot where a house, with considerable land about it, may be bought for one or two hundred dollars, and where the rapid growth of a summer population must create an enormous demand for market-garden products. But the time to see Nantucket is before this day arrives. Already the aspect of the town and of many parts of the shore has been grievously altered by the tourist throng; and when the savage simplicity of the interior shall have been softened beneath the plow, Nantucket will look a good deal like the rest of the world. To-day, when one turns his back upon the shore, it seems unique; and to an eye which can appreciate a landscape where almost all the conventional attributes of "natural beauty" are wanting, it seems uniquely attractive— or perhaps a better word would be, impressive. A splendid sky and the breath of a tearing wind tell us of the splendid sea, even when it lies out of sight. Seldom in civilized regions are we swayed by such a sense of breadth, vastness, freedom and the spontaneous action of elemental forces. Seldom do we see such beauty of color created with factors of such simplicity. And everywhere under our feet is the wide carpet of flowers and herbage in endless variety, in perpetual harmony and loveliness. The mainland is more picturesque; Montauk is grander; Block Island is more singular in surface conformation. But nowhere else on our coast is there so broad an expanse of uncultivated land, so simple as regards large features, so varied as regards those of minor size, so impressive in a general view, so interesting to the eye of minute examination.

Newport (1)

I think the first thing that strikes a foreign visitor to Newport must be the singular way in which evidence of lavish expenditure mingles with signs of an almost pauper disregard for appearances. Such contrasts often reveal themselves in America, but seldom so forcibly as here. The town to which the great colony of costly and ambitious summer villas is attached, is much less neatly kept than is the rule in New England, and certain of its outlying streets—constantly traversed by pleasure-seekers in gorgeous equipages—are a veritable offense to the eye. At one step we pass from little palaces, surrounded by exquisitely kept grounds, almost into "Shantytown" itself. Nor are striking signs of carelessness absent, even though we keep strictly within the villa districts. Even on Bellevue Avenue the borders of the road are left untended to a degree which, in Lenox, for example, would not be tolerated for a week; and where a vacant lot occurs, its fence is a tumble-down, weed-grown affair, that a respectable farmer in a rough country village might blush to own. I have heard it said that Newport, despite its claims to art and taste, to elegance and fashion, is, as a whole, a vulgar-looking place. The term is too harsh, yet there is some excuse for its application. In many places we seem to read a regard for what is visibly one's own combined with a disregard for what is everybody's; a love of display united

Garden and Forest 1 (November 18, 1888): 470–471.

to a lack of public spirit, which should certainly not characterize a refined community.

The best part of Newport is the beautiful Cliff Walk, which runs for
more than three miles on the edge of the lifted rocky shore, passing villa
after villa set back beyond verdant lawns. An old public right of way
has most fortunately kept this walk open and free, although the land all
belongs to the villa-owners; and the appearance of brotherly concord
between neighbor and neighbor and generosity towards the public,
which it seems to reveal, added to its intrinsic charms, has made it a frequent theme for praise with foreign writers on landscape gardening and
the arrangement of country towns. Here, at least, no signs of carelessness appear. The soil along the cliffs is, by nature, thin and poor, so it requires an immense amount of care and money to make and keep these
lawns, although the damp climate favors the work. Well kept and fresh
they are, indeed. "And no wonder," I heard a lady exclaim, "for when
there are signs of a drought, the owners come forth and water them
with their tears." The statement that the particularly beautiful turf
which covers the two or three acres of a certain gentleman is annually
taken up and roiled away in his cellars over winter, is an equally amusing fiction; yet this I heard told more than once, with an accent which
almost implied belief in its truth.

Beautiful and appropriate as are these lawns on the landward side of
the Cliff Walk, a mistake has perhaps been made in continuing them on
its seaward side, where they skirt with a very narrow border the rough
rocky edge of the cliff, or are carried down the slope for a considerable
distance in places where the rocks lie lower. In such places as these they
have too much the look of earth-works for defense; and everywhere
they unite but poorly with their bold rocky finish. The pathway might
better, perhaps, have been taken as the boundary line for the lawns, and
the spaces beyond, whether wider or narrower, treated in a naturalistic
way—made to look as though the hand of man had not tampered with
their original covering.

The fierce sweep of the sea winds in winter is, of course, injurious to the
growth of trees in such exposed situations as those along the Cliff Walk;
but shrubs and flowers can be made to grow with great luxuriance. The
lapse of five or six years has surrounded many of the newer houses with
rich thickets of tall shrubs and even with trees of considerable size; and
year by year veritable carpets, in the shape of formal beds of bright flowers and foliage-plants, are spread out around them. These beds deserve admiration from the merely cultural point of view—nothing could be better,

as far as luxuriance and neatness are concerned. Nevertheless, I think they may be counted as another item to excuse the cynic who speaks of bad taste in connection with Newport. Bold effectiveness, rather than beauty, seems, as a rule, to have been sought for alike in their composition and in their disposition. As a rule, their colors are crude and inharmonious, and they are multiplied out of all reason and placed where they do the greatest possible harm to the effect of the grounds as a whole. The fact is doubly to be regretted, for Newport is the very place where formal bedding might often be used to the best advantage. Nowhere do we see so many houses of the most formal and dignified character standing close to a road or even a street, and surrounded by very small grounds. In such cases a formal disposition of the grounds might well suggest itself as the most appropriate. But to be good in effect the scheme should be consistent. Formality should reign and rule, not merely occur in certain features. But, instead of straight-lined roads and paths and regular arrangements of shrubberies, clipped hedges and formally shaped trees, with which pattern-beds and borders would be in true accord, informal schemes are seen where landscape effects are simulated in miniature—where winding drives and paths are flanked by "natural" groups of trees and shrubs and tall flowering plants—sadly interfered with, often, indeed, wholly ruined, by a profusion of flat beds and borders, rigid in outline and gaudy in color. No outlines can be too formal for such beds, if they are graceful in their own way and if the general scheme sanctions formality; and no colors too bright, if harmony in contrast has guided their selection. But I think we may look in vain at Newport for a place in which all these conditions are respected.

There are exceptions, however, to the general and excessive use of bright set beds and borders. Here and there—as in the pretty grounds of Mr. Sheldon, on Narragansett Avenue—a small expanse of lawn is made the most of by plantations which merely fringe its borders, and lies in refreshing peacefulness, undisturbed by notes of gaudy color. Mr. Goelet's large place, again, where this avenue meets the Cliff Walk, needs the removal of but one or two beds to make it perfect. There is no other house in Newport at once so beautiful and so appropriate in its beauty, and none so charmingly connected with its grounds. When I saw it the wide lawns were in perfect condition, rising into a low, grassy terrace all around its base; vines had grown upon it to just the right extent; a few formal plants in pots appropriately adorned its steps, and the masses of green which decorated the piazza towards the sea were undisturbed by over-prominent notes of color—a single yellow flower-pot giving just the one needed touch of brightness.

This, I think, is a type of what a Newport house should be when its grounds are comparatively large, and when a further air of spaciousness and country freedom is given them by an open seaward prospect. But it would be less appropriate on a more contracted site with no frontage save towards a street. Here villa-architecture, properly so-called, is more appropriate—houses which shall be neither city residences of the usual pattern nor true country houses, but midway between the two. No one can find fault if a Newport house, no matter how small its grounds may be, is itself large and costly. It must be this, in very many cases, or it will not fulfill its purpose. But it is a mistake to imitate in its fashioning either an English type of country house, which needs a stately park about it, or the boldly picturesque shape of some American country home which commands a wide prospect over picturesque acres of its own. Dignity is required, and, to a large extent, symmetry also; an air of sumptuousness and generous accommodation combined with a · certain reserve as of a building near its neighbors and near the public gaze. The "colonial" style, which of late has been so extensively revived in many parts of the country, seems to offer, perhaps, the best type for such a house. And it seems as though here of all places we might expect to find it used, as the old town of Newport was one of the chief centres of colonial art. Nevertheless, new "colonial" houses are conspicuous by their absence. The only one I noticed is apt to be overlooked by the transient visitor, lying, as it does, in one of the older streets, half hidden by trees. This is the beautiful brick house built not long ago by Messrs. McKim, Mead and White for Colonel Edgar. It is as entirely appropriate to its place as is Mr. Goelet's house, and the difference between them is all the more instructive since the same hands designed the two.

The back of Mr. Fiske's house on Ochre Point is charming in both form and color—a happy relief in its lowness and its quiet browns from the towering outlines and strong tones which too often meet the eye. But its best feature is the wall of beautiful pinkish stone which connects it with the stable and the street. It was a wholly fortunate idea to edge the base of this wall with a narrow border of bright-hued plants, as they enliven the prospect but do not disturb it, being thus closely connected with architectural forms. And this summer the vines had grown upon the wall, as upon the house itself, to exactly the right extent—softening and adorning but not wholly concealing the surface. The great trouble in some places is to make vines grow; the great trouble at Newport is to keep them within bounds. The recent introduction of the so-called Japanese Ivy has already meant in many places the entire concealment

of the forms beneath it. When these are bad the result is a happy one—
a seeming wall of verdure is certainly to be preferred to an ugly fence or
foundation story. But when the forms and colors are good, then their
concealment detracts from beauty, while the vines themselves look best
with a visible background. On Mr. Fiske's house, and on Mr. Goelet's as
well, it will be a pity if the vines are ever allowed to exceed their present
estate. On many other houses one might wish them to grow to the very
chimney tops.

Newport (2)

There is as much variety among the fences at Newport as among the houses, and the fact is very conspicuous, as properties are so small that one form of barrier is perpetually giving place to another. It can hardly be said that a fence which seems exactly right often appears; sometimes it is too pretentious, more often, perhaps, not dignified enough. In at least one case we find a massive stone wall, some eight feet in height, which would be admirable for the protection of a large park, but seems out of place encircling a few acres in a thickly built settlement, and sins against that neighborly freedom of prospect which is beauty's sole salvation in such a settlement, and is generally preserved at Newport. And in many cases we see, on the other hand, a cheap wooden paling, without dignity or beauty, surrounding expensively kept grounds and a house of the most costly kind. But here and there we find admirable devices. For one of the best we must look again to Mr. Goelet's place, which has a very low, but broad, stone wall, built of rather thin slabs of slate in a way which hits just the right medium between over-precision and carelessness. A rustic fence recently put up on Bellevue Avenue is very well designed and pretty, but perhaps a little too rural in effect for just this situation. Low brick walls are sometimes used, but I saw hardly any which had the beauty possible to this material. Hedges, and espe-

---

Garden and Forest 1 (December 5, 1888): 482–483.

cially those of Privet, grow luxuriantly at Newport, and are often employed. Without exception they are well tended, but sometimes they
have been allowed to grow so thin that the eye can penetrate them
everywhere. No matter how neat a hedge may be, it is certainly a failure
when this is the case.

With entrance-gates the case is the same; sometimes they are too
mean in effect, sometimes self-assertive and showy beyond all reason.
Perhaps the most satisfactory is the fine, tall gate, with wide, lateral
wings, of wrought iron, which admits to Mr. Van Alen's new house. It
is of Spanish workmanship, and, from the design, seems to date from
the middle of the last century; but fashions so often persisted in iron-
work after they had died out in architecture, that it is hard to feel sure
of its exact time. The pattern is at once strong and very light, and the
gate is just what it should be to stand at Newport—very elegant, yet
comparatively simple, and not at all suggestive of mere display or of excessive powers of protection. It is to be hoped that it may inspire others
to employ this beautiful material. Iron-work as good as this in design,
and better in execution, can easily be obtained to-day in America. Better in execution, I say, for last-century ironwork is a combination of
welded and riveted pieces, while our best, like that of still earlier centuries abroad, is welded throughout, and therefore more durable. Nothing better for a Newport wall could be imagined than a low plinth of
brick or stone, surmounted by a light iron trellis. The idea struck certain
owners some years ago; but that was the age of cast, not wrought, iron;
and the results are by no means what they would be if well executed according to our present lights.

The oftener one visits Newport, the more one is impressed with the
beauty of the Casino, built, like Mr. Goelet's and Colonel Edgar's
houses, by Messrs. McKim, Mead & White. Here, indeed, is something
we may be willing to show a foreigner as a measure of our good taste
and of our success in artistic independence. In its erection a wholly new
problem was triumphantly mastered. It has no prototype in this country or in any other, yet it is so perfect that we can hardly believe it was
not the final outcome of a long series of tentative efforts—so appropriate to place and purpose, so consistent from end to end yet so varied between part and part, so thoroughly artistic, so delightfully pretty. If
there is anything it needs, it is the more careful planting out of the
fences in the second court. These might easily be made to disappear behind vines and shrubberies, and the charming effect of seclusion which
reigns in the first court be thus reproduced, in a different way but with

the same completeness. Otherwise the planting is excellent. There are trees and shrubs enough, yet not too many, and no formal beds except in just the right spots. The wide lawn in the first court is free from their intrusion, but on either hand, as one enters the gateway, filling the angle between the front building and the wings, is a large, gracefully designed, and pleasingly-colored bed. Thus closely connected with architectural forms, and in a place palpably artificial (in the best sense of the word) from end to end, no features could be more appropriate; and they give just the needed amount of bright color to the softly verdurous general effect.

The most interesting work now in progress at Newport is the laying-out, under Mr. Olmsted's direction, of Mr. Frederick Vanderbilt's place, which occupies a point on the cliff at the turn of Bellevue Avenue. The Cliff Walk, just after bending from a southerly to a westerly direction, here swerved a considerable distance inward to skirt a rocky ravine with steep sides, which breaks the line of the cliff. To regain the space it occupied, and carry it to a more agreeable distance from the house, a bridge has been built over the ravine quite at the edge of the cliff. Lying, I should guess, about thirty feet above the water, which breaks in beneath it over a rock-strewn bed, this bridge is of the simplest possible construction, with small irregular voussoirs in a single round curve. But for this very reason it is both appropriate to its place and admirably picturesque; and the way in which passers will be relieved against the sea and sky, when seen from the house, will make their passing an advantage to the scene rather than an annoyance. I am told that the owners are considering whether it will not be well to adopt a scheme for treating their grounds which will be an entire novelty in this part of Newport. This scheme would confine the lawns and garden shrubberies to the entrance side of the house, and treat the entire seaward slope in the most natural possible way. This portion is largely composed of visible rocks in varied shapes of the most interesting and picturesque character, and it certainly seems as though to plant it with low native shrubs and creepers and wild flowers, simulating, as far as possible, a spot which has not been planted at all, would be the best device. If the house stood farther from its neighbors— on a portion of the shore where conventional, gardenesque treatment has not yet intruded—there could be no possible question about the matter. But it has been objected that just here, with conventional methods of treatment on either hand, harmony will be injured by any deviation from such methods. The place has, however, a comparatively wide reach of water front, and, lying on a point, is isolated from its neighbors to an unusual degree; the ravine, the bridge, and the beautiful rugged rocks seem to demand a picturesquely natural arrangement of its surface; and I think it is certainly to be desired, if one loves either the best kind of beauty or the truest kind of appropriateness, that the new idea may be carried out. But only if there is to be no attempt at compromise. The scheme should be natural throughout or gardenesque throughout. A striking witness to the futility of trying to combine the two results is already shown on that portion of Ochre Point where, on the seaward side of the Cliff Walk, the space is broadest and the rocks are most conspicuous; and it would be a thousand pities were this, perhaps the most beautiful spot on the whole Cliff Walk, to be mutilated in a similar way.

Mr. Olmsted's hand shows again in the drives which, within the past two or three years, have opened up the interior of the southern portion of the island beyond the districts thus far built upon and behind the Ocean Drive. Here the ground is hilly with bold and beautiful high rocks, offering building sites of a very desirable kind—with no sea fronts, it is true, but with the most superb distant views of land and water. The new roads are admirably disposed for convenience and beauty; but it is a matter of regret that the spaces, usually of triangular form, which are formed here and there by their intersections, should have been carefully turfed and planted in a conventional way with young trees and shrubs. Rough grass and Huckleberry bushes and Sumach would have been more in keeping with the character of the landscape as a whole. It is to be hoped that those who may hereafter build in this neighborhood will carefully and artistically preserve its character, and not strive to subdue its rugged and individual charm to that neat prettiness which prevails in the level districts nearer town.

Bibliography

PRINCIPAL WRITINGS OF VAN RENSSELAER
ON ARCHITECTURE, LANDSCAPE ARCHITECTURE,
AND THE ENVIRONMENT

Note: For a much more extensive bibliography of the published writings of Van Rensselaer, see Cynthia D. Kinnard, "The Life and Works of Mariana Griswold Van Rensselaer" (Ph.D. diss., Johns Hopkins University, 1977), and Lois Dinnerstein, "Opulence and Ocular Delight, Splendor and Squalor: Critical Writings in Art and Architecture of Mariana Griswold Van Rensselaer" (Ph.D. diss., The City University of New York, 1979).

Bibliographic entries are arranged chronologically. Numbered series are placed by date of the first title in the series. Entries for *The Century Magazine* give volume numbers for both numbering systems.

"Optical Illusions as Affecting Architecture." *American Architect and Building News* 1 (May 27, 1876): 174–175.

"The Portal of the Old Palace Chapel, Dresden." *American Architect and Building News* 2 (August 18, 1877): 263–265.

"The Restorations at Goslar." *American Architect and Building News* 3 (April 6, 1878): 120–121.

"Decorative Art and Its Dogmas." Parts 1 and 2. *Lippincott's Magazine* 25 (February 1880): 213–220; (March 1880): 342–351.

"Mr. Ruskin's Drawings." *American Architect and Building News* 7 (February 21, 1880): 72–73.

"Art and Architecture in Berlin." *American Architect and Building News* 8 (October 16, 1880): 184–185.

"Newport Villas: Mr. Fairman Rogers's House on Ochre Point and What It Contains . . ." *New York World* (August 21, 1881): 3.

"Newport Villas: How Mrs. Paran Steven's House on Bellevue Avenue is Furnished and Decorated." *New York World*. August 28, 1881. p. 3.

"The Competition in Wall-Paper Design." *American Architect and Building News* 10 (November 26, 1881): 251–253.

Review of *Sir Christopher Wren, His Family and His Times*, by Lucy Phillinere. *American Architect and Building News* 11 (February 18, 1882): 78–79.

"In the Heart of the Alleghenies." Parts 1 and 2. *Lippincott's Magazine* 30 (July 1882): 84–92; (August 1882): 163–172.

"The Metropolitan Opera-House, New York." Parts 1 and 2. *American Architect and Building News* 15 (February 16, 1884): 76–77; (February 23, 1884): 86–87.

"Recent Architecture in America. I. Public Buildings." *The Century Magazine* (27) 6 (May 1884): 48–67.

"Recent Architecture in America. II. Public Buildings." *The Century Magazine* (28) 6 (July 1884): 323–334.

"Recent Architecture in America. III. Commercial Buildings." *The Century Magazine* (28) 6 (August 1884): 511–523.

"Recent Architecture in America. IV. Churches." *The Century Magazine* (29) 7 (January 1885): 323–338.

"Berlin and New York." Parts 1 and 2. *American Architect and Building News* 18 (July 18, 1885): 27–29; (July 24, 1885): 40–42.

"Prague." Parts 1–3. *American Architect and Building News* 18 (September 12, 1885): 123–124; (September 19, 1885): 136–138; (September 26, 1885): 147–148.

"Notes From England. I. Peterborough, Gloucester, Durham." *American Architect and Building News* 18 (October 17, 1885): 183–184.

"Notes From England. II. Bournemouth, Christchurch." *American Architect and Building News* 18 (November 21, 1885): 243–244.

Review of *Tuscan Cities,* by William D. Howell. *American Architect and Building News* 18 (December 12, 1885): 279–280.

Review of *Paris in Old and Present Times,* by Philip Gilbert. *American Architect and Building News* 19 (January 2, 1886): 8–9.

"Recent Architecture in America. V. City Dwellings." *The Century Magazine* (31) 9 (February 1886): 548–558.

"Recent Architecture in America. VI. City Dwellings, II." *The Century Magazine* (31) 9 (March 1886): 677–687.

"Recent Architecture in America. VII. American Country Dwellings." *The Century Magazine* (31) 10 (May 1886): 3–20.

"Recent Architecture in America. VIII. American Country Dwellings, II." *The Century Magazine* (31) 10 (June 1886): 206–220.

"Recent Architecture in America. IX. American Country Dwellings, III." *The Century Magazine* (32) 10 (July 1886): 421–434.

"The Architectural League of New York." *The Century Magazine* (32) 11 (November 1886): 157–158.

"Wanted—A History of Architecture." *Art Review* 1, no. 1 (November, 1886): 15–19.

"The Cathedral Churches of England." *The Century Magazine* (33) 11 (March 1887): 724–735.

"Canterbury Cathedral." *The Century Magazine* (33) 11 (April 1887): 819–838.

"Architecture as a Profession." *The Chautauquan* 7 (May 1887): 451–454.

"Peterborough Cathedral." *The Century Magazine* (33) 12 (June 1887): 163–165.

"The Growth of Ecclesiastical Decorative Art in America." *American Architect and Building News* 21 (June 11, 1887): 279–280.

"Ely Cathedral." *The Century Magazine* (34) 12 (October 1887): 803–818.

"Landscape Gardening." Parts 1–3. *American Architect and Building News* 22 (October 1, 1887): 157–159; (December 3, 1887): 263–264; 23 (January 7, 1888): 3–5.

"Durham Cathedral." *The Century Magazine* (34) 13 (December 1887): 226–243.

Henry Hobson Richardson and His Works. Boston and New York: Houghton Mifflin Company, 1888.

"Landscape Gardening: A Definition." *Garden and Forest* 1 (February 29, 1888): 2.

"Salisbury Cathedral." *The Century Magazine* (34) 13 (March 1888): 693–707.

"Landscape Gardening." Parts 1–6. *Garden and Forest* 1 (March 7, 1888): 14–15; (March 14, 1888): 27; (March 21, 1888): 38–39; (March 28, 1888): 51–52; (April 4, 1888): 63–64; (April 11, 1888): 75–76.

"Lincoln Cathedral." *The Century Magazine* (36) 14 (August 1888): 583–599.

"The Proposed Cathedral for New York." *The Independent*. August 16, 1888: 1031–1032.

"A Woodland Tragedy." *Garden and Forest* 1 (September 19, 1888): 351.

"A Glimpse of Nantucket." *Garden and Forest* 1 (November 14, 1888): 447–448.

"Newport." Parts 1 and 2. *Garden and Forest* 1 (November 18, 1888): 470–471; (December 5, 1888): 482–483.

"Japanese Gardening." Parts 1 and 2. *Garden and Forest* 2 (January 30, 1889): 51–52; (February 6, 1889): 63–64.

"York Cathedral." *The Century Magazine* (37) 15 (March 1889): 718–736.

"The Art of Gardening, An Historical Sketch. I." *Garden and Forest* 2 (March 20, 1889): 134–135.

"The Art of Gardening, An Historical Sketch. II. Egypt." *Garden and Forest* 2 (March 27, 1889): 147.

"The Art of Gardening, An Historical Sketch. III. Egypt and Mesopotamia." *Garden and Forest* 2 (April 10, 1889): 170–171.

"The Art of Gardening, An Historical Sketch. IV. Mesopotamia and Judea." *Garden and Forest* 2 (May 1, 1889): 206–207.

"The Art of Gardening, An Historical Sketch. V. Judea and Phoenicia." *Garden and Forest* 2 (May 22, 1889): 242–243.

"The Art of Gardening, An Historical Sketch. VI. Persia." *Garden and Forest* 2 (June 19, 1889): 290–291.

"The Art of Gardening, An Historical Sketch. VII. Persia (continued)." *Garden and Forest* 2 (July 24, 1889): 350–351.

"The Art of Gardening, An Historical Sketch. VIII. The Love of Nature." *Garden and Forest* 2 (August 14, 1889): 387–388.

"The Art of Gardening, An Historical Sketch. IX. Greece." *Garden and Forest* 2 (September 4, 1889): 422.

"The Art of Gardening, An Historical Sketch. X. Greece (continued)." *Garden and Forest* 2 (September 18, 1889): 447.

"The Art of Gardening, An Historical Sketch. XI. Rome." *Garden and Forest* 2 (October 9, 1889): 482–483.

"The Art of Gardening, An Historical Sketch. XII. Roman Country Seats." *Garden and Forest* 2 (October 30, 1889): 519–520.

"The Art of Gardening, An Historical Sketch. XIII. Roman Country Seats (continued)." *Garden and Forest* 2 (November 13, 1889): 542.

"The Art of Gardening, An Historical Sketch. XIV. Suburban Rome." *Garden and Forest* 2 (December 4, 1889): 579–580.

"The Art of Gardening, An Historical Sketch. XV. Rome (concluded)." *Garden and Forest* 2 (December 18, 1889): 602–603.

"The Art of Gardening, An Historical Sketch. XVI. Medieval Europe." *Garden and Forest* 3 (January 1890): 2–3.

"The Art of Gardening, An Historical Sketch. XVII. Ancient India." *Garden and Forest* 3 (February 12, 1890): 74–75.

"The Art of Gardening, An Historical Sketch. XVIII. The Mahometans in Persia." *Garden and Forest* 3 (March 5, 1890): 110–111.

"The Art of Gardening, An Historical Sketch. XIX. The Arabs in Spain." *Garden and Forest* 3 (April 16, 1890): 186–187.

"The Art of Gardening, An Historical Sketch. XX. The Mahometans in Spain and India." *Garden and Forest* 3 (May 7, 1890): 223–224.

"The Art of Gardening, An Historical Sketch. XXI. The Mahometans in India." *Garden and Forest* 3 (June 11, 1890): 283–284.

"Winchester Cathedral." *The Century Magazine* (38) 16 (July 1889): 323–340.

"The Advance in Steamboat Decoration." *The Century Magazine* (38) 16 (July 1889): 372–374.

"Impressions of the International Exhibition of 1889." *The Century Magazine* (38) 17 (December 1889): 316–318.

"Down the Rhone." Parts 1 and 2. *Garden and Forest* 3 (January 8, 1890): 14–15; (January 15, 1890): 27–28.

"Gloucester Cathedral." *The Century Magazine* (39) 17 (March 1890): 680–697.

"Client and Architect." *North American Review* 151 (September 1890): 319–328.

"Wells Cathedral." *The Century Magazine* (40) 18 (September 1890): 724–743.

"The Grant Monument for Riverside Park." *Garden and Forest* 4 (January 21, 1891): 27–28.

"Ivy in an Old French Garden." *Garden and Forest* 4 (May 27, 1891): 242.

"Sir Christopher Wren as a Gardener." *Garden and Forest* 4 (June 3, 1891): 254–255.

"Dijon." Parts 1 and 2. *Garden and Forest* 4 (July 15, 1891): 326–327; (August 26, 1891): 400–401.

"Architectural Fitness," *Garden and Forest* 5 (August 19, 1891): 385–386.

"Great Hill: A New American Country Seat." Parts 1 and 2. *Garden and Forest* 4 (October 21, 1891): 494–495; (October 28, 1891):506–507.

English Cathedrals. New York: Century Company, 1892.

"The Development of American Homes." *The Forum* 12 (January 1892): 667–676.

"St. Paul's Cathedral, London." *The Century Magazine* (42) 21 (March 1892): 643–665.

"Color in Rural Buildings." *Garden and Forest* 5 (March 30, 1892): 146–147.

"New Monuments. New York's Washington Arch and Grant's Tomb ... " *Boston Evening Transcript.* April 18, 1892. Vol. 23: 6.

"Flowers in Town." *Garden and Forest* 5 (April 27, 1892): 195–196.

"Pine Bank." *Garden and Forest* 5 (September 21, 1892): 446–447.

"Early Autumn near Cape Cod." *Garden and Forest* 5 (September 28, 1892): 465–466.

"Wood Roads on Cape Cod." *Garden and Forest* 5 (November 30, 1892): 574–575.

"The Artistic Triumph of the Fair-Builders." *The Forum* 14 (December 1892): 527–540.

"Picturesque New York." *The Century Magazine* (43) 23 (December 1892): 164–175.

Art Out-of-Doors: Hints on Good Taste in Gardening. New York: Charles Scribner's Sons, 1893.

"The Fair Grounds." In *Rand, McNally & Co.'s Handbook of the World's Columbian Exposition.* Chicago: Rand McNally & Co., 1893.

Handbook of English Cathedrals. New York: The Century Company, 1893.

"The Protection of Road-Sides." *Garden and Forest* 6 (March 8, 1893): 115–116.

"At the Fair." *The Century Magazine* (44) 24 (May 1893): 2–13.

"Spring in Virginia." *Garden and Forest* 6 (May 10, 1893): 208–209.

"Frederick Law Olmsted." *The Century Magazine* (45) 24 (October 1893): 860–867.

"Fifth Avenue." *The Century Magazine* (45) 25 (November 1893): 5–18.

"The Madison Square Garden." *The Century Magazine* (45) 25 (March 1894): 732–747.

Review of *Greek Lines and Other Architectural Essays,* by Henry Van Brunt. *Atlantic Monthly* 73 (June 1894): 847–849.

"The Churches of Provence." *The Century Magazine* (47) 27 (November 1894): 117–135.

"People in New York." *The Century Magazine* (49) 27 (February 1895): 534–548.

"Inscriptions on Public Monuments." *Garden and Forest* 8 (February 27, 1895): 87–88.

"The New Public Library in Boston: Its Artistic Aspects." *The Century Magazine* (49) 28 (June 1895): 260–264.

"The Good Work of an Improvement Association at Narragansett Pier." *Garden and Forest* 8 (July 31, 1895): 308–309.

"Eleventh Annual Exhibition of the Architectural League of New York." *Garden and Forest* 9 (February 26, 1896): 88–89.

"The Churches of Perigueux and Angouleme." *The Century Magazine* (51) 29 (April 1896): 918–931.

"Proposed Plan for Madison Square, New York City." *Garden and Forest* 9 (April 8, 1896): 142–144.

"Places in New York City." *The Century Magazine* (53) 31 (February 1897): 501–516.

"A Suburban Country Place." *The Century Magazine* (53) 32 (May 1897): 3–17.

"The Churches of Poitiers and Caen," *The Century Magazine* (54) 32 (July 1897): 421–439.

"Native Plants for Ornamental Planting." *Garden and Forest* 10 (September 22, 1897): 376.

"The Mother City of Greater New York." *The Century Magazine* 34 (May 1898): 138–146.

"Niagara." *The Century Magazine* 36 (June 1899): 184–202.

"The Churches of Auvergne." *The Century Magazine* 36 (August 1899): 568–575.

"The Cathedral of LePuy." *The Century Magazine* 36 (September 1899): 722–735.

"From an Art Critic's Point of View." In *Art Handbook: Official Handbook of Architecture and Sculpture and Art Catalogue to the Pan-American Exposition,* 25–28. Buffalo: David Gray, 1901.

"How to Look At Pictures." In *Art Handbook: Official Handbook of Architecture and Sculpture and Art Catalogue to the Pan-American Exposition,* 83–85. Buffalo: David Gray, 1901.

Niagara: A Description. New York: Gilliss Brothers, 1901.

"Midsummer in New York City." *The Century Magazine* 40 (August 1901): 483–501.

"Who Wants Art Nowadays." *North American Review* 204 (August 1916): 235–244.

"The Art Museum and the Public." *North American Review* 205 (January 1917): 81–92.

"Nature's Debt to Art." *Scribner's Magazine* 63 (June 1918): 765–768.

"Of Flowers and Men." *Unpartisan Review* 11 (April 1919): 379–385.

"Appropriateness in War Memorials." *American Magazine of Art* 10, no. 7 (May 1919): 274–275.

"The Art of Gardening." In *Essays in Agriculture,* edited by Shirley Dare Babbitt and Lowry Charles Wimberly, 47–60. New York: Doubleday, Page and Company, 1921.

"Love of Nature." In *Essays in Agriculture,* edited by Shirley Dare Babbitt and Lowry Charles Wimberly, 26–35. New York: Doubleday, Page and Company, 1921.

"Taste and the Mind's Eye." *Unpartisan Review* 15 (January 1921): 132–142.

"Museums of Art." *North American Review* 216 (September 1922): 393–404.

"Painters' Architecture." *Scribner's Magazine* 73 (May 1923): 635–640.

"Ancient Egypt in America." *North American Review* 218 (July 1923): 117–128.

"American Art and the Public." *Scribner's Magazine* 74 (November 1923): 637–640.

"Changes." In *Art Out-of-Doors: Hints in Good Taste in Gardening,* 389–429. 2d ed. New York: Charles Scribner's Sons, 1925.

WRITINGS ABOUT
MARIANA GRISWOLD VAN RENSSELAER

Dinnerstein, Lois. "Opulence and Ocular Delight, Splendor and Squalor: Critical Writings in Art and Architecture by Mariana Griswold Van Rensselaer." Ph.D. diss., The City University of New York, 1979.

Early, James. *Notable American Women 1607–1950*. Vol. 3, 511–512. Cambridge: Harvard University Press, 1971.

Gifford, Don, ed. *The Literature of Architecture: The Evolution of Architectural Theory and Practice in Nineteenth Century America*, 438–441. New York: E. P. Dutton & Co., 1966.

Hamlin, Talbot F. "Van Rensselaer, Mariana Griswold." In *Dictionary of American Biography*, 207–208. New York: Charles Scribner's Sons, 1936.

Kidney, Walter. Review of *Henry Hobson Richardson and His Architecture* by Mariana Griswold Van Rensselaer (1888. Reprint, Park Forest, Illinois: Prairie School Press, 1968). *Progressive Architecture* 49 (June 1968): 168, 172, 182.

Kinnard, Cynthia D. "The Life and Works of Mariana Griswold Van Rensselaer, American Art Critic." Ph.D. diss., Johns Hopkins University, 1977.

———. "Mariana Griswold Van Rensselaer (1851–1934): America's First Professional Woman Art Critic." In *Women as Interpreters of the Visual Arts, 1820–1979*, edited by Claire Richter Sherman and Adele M. Holcomb, 181–205. Westport, Conn.; London: Greenwood Press, 1981.

Koenigsberg, Lisa. "'Lifewritings': First American Biographers of Architects and Their Works." In *The Architectural Historian in America*, edited by Elizabeth Blair McDougall, 41–58. Washington, D. C.: National Gallery of Art, 1990.

Morgan, William. Introduction to *Henry Hobson Richardson and His Works*, by Mariana Griswold Van Rensselaer. 1888. Reprint, New York: Dover Publications, Inc., 1969.

Mumford, Lewis. *Roots of Contemporary American Architecture*, 429. New York: Reinhold Publishing, 1952.

Placzek, Adolf K. Review of *Henry Hobson Richardson and His Works*, by Mariana Griswold Van Rensselaer. (1888. Reprint, Park Forest, Ill.: The Prairie School Press, 1968). *The Prairie School Review* 5 no. 3, (1968): 48.

Van Trump, James D. Introduction to *Henry Hobson Richardson and His Works*, by Mariana Griswold Van Rensselaer. 1888. Reprint, Park Forest, Illinois: The Prairie School Press, 1968.

Warshaver, Gerald Edward. "Psycho-Geographic Traditions of City Folk in the 1890's as Revealed in Writings by Mariana Van Rensselaer, H. C. Bunner, and Stephen Crane." Ph.D. diss., Indiana University, 1979.

Zaitzevsky, Cynthia. "The Olmsted Firm and the Structures of the Boston Park System." *Journal of the Society of Architectural Historians* 32, no. 2 (May 1973): 167–174.

Index

Text: 10/13 Sabon
Display: Sabon
Composition: Impressions Book and Journal Services, Inc.

CPSIA information can be obtained
at www.ICGtesting.com
Printed in the USA
BVHW071759200522
637653BV00003B/59